A HISTORY OF
Presidential Elections

A HISTORY OF
Presidential
Elections

FROM GEORGE WASHINGTON

TO JIMMY CARTER

Fourth Edition

EUGENE H. ROSEBOOM

ALFRED E. ECKES, JR.

Macmillan Publishing Co., Inc.

NEW YORK

Collier Macmillan Publishers

LONDON

Copyright © 1957, 1964, 1970 by Eugene H. Roseboom
and 1979 by Eugene H. Roseboom and Alfred E. Eckes, Jr.

Macmillan Publishing Co., Inc.
866 Third Avenue, New York, N.Y. 10022
Collier-Macmillan Canada Ltd.

Library of Congress Cataloging in Publication Data
Roseboom, Eugene Holloway, 1892-
A history of presidential elections, from George Washington to Jimmy Carter.
Bibliography: p.
1. Presidents—United States—Election. 2. United States—Politics and government.
I. Eckes, Alfred E., 1942-   joint author. II. Title.
E183.R69   1979   329'.023'73   79-14845
ISBN 0-02-604890-6

FOURTH EDITION 1979

10   9   8   7   6   5   4   3   2

Designed by Jack Meserole

Printed in the United States of America

CONTENTS

PREFACE

This is the fourth edition of a work that Eugene H. Roseboom designed to give a connected account of the history of national politics built around the quadrennial struggles for control of the office of president. It covers not only the elections themselves but the developments in each administration that influenced the work of party conventions and determined the character and outcome of campaigns.

There are several significant changes that distinguish this volume from earlier editions. First, because thirty-eight individuals have occupied the presidency and there have been forty-eight presidential elections, it has become necessary to shorten and revise some chapters. For the period before 1936 the authors have drawn liberally from *A Short History of Presidential Elections*, which Roseboom wrote in 1966. Additional material has been added to that account at the publisher's suggestion to ensure that the general reader may understand easily the politics of the period.

Second, the fourth edition contains two new chapters bringing the story of presidential campaigns through 1976 as well as a selective, revised bibliography.

Finally, this book has become a joint effort involving two members of the Ohio State University history department. While both authors share in the responsibility for all changes and additions, Alfred E. Eckes, Jr., assumed the heavier burden of writing chapters covering the elections of 1972 and 1976.

We have had the valuable assistance of Mrs. Thelma Matheny Roseboom in preparing the manuscript for publication. Also, Henry W. Griffin and his staff at Macmillan Company have made a number of important suggestions for revising and improving this book about national politics.

A HISTORY OF
Presidential Elections

I

Politics Without Parties

ON THE LAST DAY OF APRIL 1789–a watershed year in both Old and New World history–a great crowd converged on Wall, Nassau, and Broad streets in the city of New York to witness the inauguration of General George Washington as first president of the United States under the newly adopted Constitution. Around noon there appeared on the Broad Street balcony of the new Federal Hall a tall soldierly figure in a home-spun suit of deep brown set off with eagle buttons, white stockings, and a bagwig, a dress sword hanging at his side. With him was Chancellor Robert R. Livingston of the New York judiciary–the Supreme Court of the United States was not yet functioning–who formally administered the oath of office. The vice-president was John Adams, who had only recently returned from England.

In the crowded Senate chamber, the first president read his carefully prepared inaugural address; his voice was low and unsteady, and the pages shook in his nervous fingers, for he was never at ease before an audience. Well aware of the magnitude and difficulty of making the new federal government a success, and too conscious of his own limitations, he was responding to the call of duty, assured that "no local prejudices or attachments, no separate views or party animosities" would misdirect the legislators assembled before him. This was his only reference to parties, and it was uncomplimentary. No army of eager job-seekers thronged the taverns and boarding houses of the little city, and he gave no thought to politics.

A little more than seven years later, Washington wrote a famed Farewell Address, paying his respects to the dangers of political parties and the "baneful effects" of party spirit. This last will and testament of his public life warned the people against party strife: "It serves always to dis-tract the public councils and enfeeble the public administration. It agi-tates the community with ill-founded jealousies and false alarms; kindles the animosity of one part against another; foments occasionally riot and insurrection." It was a road to despotism, a spirit not to be encouraged. "A fire not to be quenched, it demands a uniform vigilance to prevent its

1

bursting into flame, lest, instead of warming, it should consume."

Having been scorched by the fire of partisan conflict, the first president saw in it little that was good. His high-minded selflessness could not understand, much less appreciate, the all-too-human proneness of less-exalted Americans to divide into rival camps, to wage bitter war for ideals and offices, to call names and throw mud, and in the process to make government function as the majority willed, whether for good or for ill. For behind the party strife that bedeviled President Washington lay a long period of political apprenticeship.

Let us go back a little way over the road that our colonial ancestors traveled in acquiring their political education. Then we may understand why the warnings of the first president would not and could not be heeded.

The Start of Self-Government

Political parties were the fruit of a tree that had been long in growing. British Americans had been learning the art of self-government and the tricks of politics from the days when Virginia planters first elected a House of Burgesses, and when New Englanders began to hold annual "courts of election" and town meetings to provide governments tailored along Puritan lines. In time, each new colony acquired a representative assembly; and the transplanted tree of English liberty grew amazingly in a frontier environment of economic opportunity and social fluidity. By the middle of the eighteenth century, the growing independence of these elected assemblies was a thorn in the flesh of royal and proprietary officials, appointed from England. Controversies were frequent, and the political pot boiled vigorously in each of the provincial capitals strung along the seaboard.

Yet, although these years produced politics, there were no permanent parties and no political professionals. Several reasons explain this strange and not unhappy situation. First of all, there was no central government with a hierarchy of offices to reward the victors in elections, and in the separate colonies the elected assemblies controlled the purse but not the patronage. Eleven of the thirteen colonies had governors commissioned from England for an indefinite term who handled appointments and dispensed favors with little regard for the ambitions and interests of local politicians, as the disgruntled fathers of Boston's James Otis and Sam Adams discovered. The sons repaid the rebuffs with interest, eventually; but, while the Adamses and Otises might win control of the provincial assembly and sabotage the executive, their spoils cupboard contained few bones for their supporters. The material inducement for holding a party together was absent.

But there were other obstacles. Chief among them was the simple fact that the voters were not numerous enough to require formal party organization for guidance and discipline. There were no mass armies to be trained and deployed. The customary requirement for voting, that a man must own fifty acres of land (or its substantial equivalent), limited political power to a minority of the adult males; and these voters, it must be remembered, lived in thirteen independent jurisdictions. Britain's colonies were like the spokes of a rimless wheel, held together only by the London hub. National parties were impossible, and local organizations largely unnecessary.

Physical and psychological obstacles also complicated the situation. Much of the population was scattered over vast areas with roads often impassable or, in the interior, nonexistent. Outside populous New England, where town meetings performed electoral functions, the county seat was the usual polling place. This was a serious handicap for residents on the fringes of the county, twenty or more miles away. Add that the ballot was not secret and that voice voting was practiced in the majority of colonies, and it is not surprising that timorous folk chose to abstain rather than to offend. The candidates for assembly seats were usually weighty local magnates, and the little man was sometimes in a tight spot when he walked up to the election judges and announced his preference.

Another factor, which time has not remedied, was the sheer indifference of many voters, who did not trouble to use their privilege. The hard, grinding labor of pioneering was not conducive to an active interest in government except when it directly touched some everyday problem.

In many colonies, infrequent elections also kept voter interest and political activity at a minimum. Assemblies were dissolved and renewed by governors without restriction, a period of several years might elapse between elections—unbroken in the southern colonies even by local elections, as county officials were appointed by the governor. By contrast, the annual elections of New England and Pennsylvania were forerunners of the democratic systems of the later American states.

But the ways and wiles of politics will be practiced wherever people are free to discuss and decide. George Washington as president inveighed against the spirit of party, but he may have forgotten that he himself in his younger days had not been above taking a hand in the political game. When he ran for the House of Burgesses in 1757, military duties kept him from electioneering at the polls; but he provided his friends with the following customary means for winning votes: 28 gallons of rum, 50 gallons of rum punch, 34 gallons of wine, 46 gallons of beer, and 2 gallons of cider royal. The voters, 391 in number, averaged a quart and a half per man. Washington wrote to his manager: "I hope no exceptions were taken to any that voted against me but that all were alike treated and all had enough." He was elected.

In Boston in the 1760s Sam Adams operated by somewhat different methods. The members of a long-established Caucus Club meeting secretly in a large garret, did their drinking as an accompaniment to the more serious business of drawing up a slate for town offices and assembly under Adams' direction. The Merchants' Club then was asked to approve the selections. Later these choices were duly nominated and elected at the town meeting of the voters, with Adams and his henchmen pulling the strings. Sometimes disputes were started and warm debates staged to entertain the assembled citizenry, but the machine was always in control when votes were counted. Harvard-educated Sam's range of friendship took in tavern politicians, preachers, lawyers, mechanics, and merchants —which explains his political prowess.

Pennsylvania, with a mixed population of English Quakers and Anglicans, Scotch-Irish Presbyterians, Germans, and other nationalities and religions, had its own brand of politics in mid-eighteenth century. The governor, representing the proprietary Penn family, was often at loggerheads with the Quaker Assembly; the frontier Scotch-Irish had grievances against both; and the Germans preferred to mind their own business. During tense election struggles for control of the Assembly, stolid Germans were naturalized in droves, and the expenses needed to get their votes were handled by local politicians. Bribery, repeater voting, and election affrays were not uncommon. Benjamin Franklin and his son were active leaders on the Assembly side.

In these same years New York, governed by Hudson Valley landlords and city merchants, witnessed the battles of two rival houses, the De Lanceys and the Livingstons. They could march their tenants to the polls and watch how they voted; but they needed also to corral the votes of the rising middle class of small merchants, professional men, artisans, and independent farmers. New York City held a large proportion of these, and so the feudal magnates courted the popular leaders and sometimes used bruisers at elections to protect or intimidate, if need arose. Public meetings were held to nominate candidates and pass resolutions. Issues were played up in newspapers and broadsides. Neither faction was at all democratic, but the Livingstons catered more to the common man, later supported the Revolution, and established a family tradition of aristocratic liberalism that had a marked influence on New York State and even on national politics.

Press and Pulpit Propaganda

Propaganda, especially of press and pulpit, came increasingly into the political picture in late colonial politics. Some forty-two newspapers were being printed just before the Revolution, and their columns were open to all manner of space-filling contributions because the printer-owners did not write editorials but concentrated on setting type. Letters, usually long and signed by Cato, Publius, or some other distinguished Roman, discussed constitutional, economic, and political matters and played an important part in guiding public opinion.

As the controversy between mother country and colonies approached its revolutionary climax, the friends of Britain were confronted with what was almost a one-party press. The local pressure of organized radical groups made subversives of the printers. Governor Thomas Hutchinson of Massachusetts, a victim of Sam Adams's diabolically clever propaganda, declared that seven-eighths of his people read only the Boston *Gazette*, "that infamous paper, and so are never undeceived." Ministers, usually New England Congregationalists or Scotch-Irish Presbyterians, frequently preached on political themes and were actively anti-British in the revolutionary controversy. Their own hostility to the Church of England, and the attitudes of their congregations, explain these political parsons of the northern colonies. In the southern colonies where the established church was the Anglican, the clergy steered clear of controversial questions.

While politics matured without benefit of permanent parties, there is much truth in the oft-quoted statement of John Adams that a "court" and a "country" party had contended for power in every colony from the beginning. He was referring to the fundamental line of division that gave vitality to colonial politics, not to parties in the modern sense of the word.

Two centers of power constantly worked at cross purposes. One was the appointed governor representing an authority beyond local control. Vested with broad executive powers and an absolute veto, and assisted by an appointed council, he was under instructions to promote England's interests and to safeguard royal or proprietary powers and privileges. At the opposite pole was the popularly elected assembly, concerned primarily with local matters and struggling to increase its power at the governor's expense. By various devices, but especially by omission of funds for gubernatorial salaries and other administrative expenses, it could pressure executive authority into submission; and in the decades before the Revolution it made itself a center of resistance against all forms of outside control.

Behind these contending authorities were ranged the various economic interests in colonial society. Supporting the governor was the "court party" of appointed officials and substantial citizens who profited from British measures or through privileges conferred by the crown or its agents. In the other camp were the "outs," who wanted more freedom and less discrimination from the top. This does not mean that the assemblies were centers of democracy. More often they were controlled by those merchants, lawyers, and landed aristocrats who were denied the blessings of special privilege.

Yet the leaders voiced local sentiment, as the governors usually did not, and thus were closer to the views of the small farmers, shopkeepers, and laborers who formed the bulk of the population. In the arguments with governors and British ministers the assemblies spoke the language of democracy and encouraged the development of ideals that were far from being realized in practice. In these local forums before the Revolution appeared such influential figures as Patrick Henry, James Otis, Samuel Adams, and Thomas Jefferson.

Within most of the colonies a sharp social cleavage complicated the chronic controversies between governors and assemblies. The seaboard, dominated by merchants, planters, landlords, and land speculators, was usually at odds with the back country of farmers and frontiersmen over representation in assemblies, land policies, taxes, money and credit, the administration of justice, and defense. When assemblies proved too blind to demands for reform, the interior yeomanry even resorted to arms against their exploiters, who were eager enough in such emergencies for the military backing of crown and governor. Pennsylvania and the Carolinas are prime illustrations of this bifocal vision of the seaboard gentry, who could stand in the assemblies for their rights as Englishmen against arbitrary power but who turned their backs on the clamors of the back country for democracy and equality. In colony after colony a long pent-up flood of local discontents transformed the secession of 1776 from the British Empire into a genuine revolution. The local battles of colonial politics had set the stage for such upheavals.

The Emergence of Whigs and Tories

From 1763 to 1776, the blunders of British ministers and the skillful leadership and propaganda of American Whigs created a national issue—the problem of parliamentary supremacy versus local autonomy—and divided the colonists into two opposing camps without regard to colonial boundaries. British control was no longer a matter of a particular governor versus a particular assembly; it had become a momentous national problem. The spokes of the wheel at last had a rim.

Two parties—in a loose sense—emerged, labeled with the familiar English terms of Whigs and Tories. In the former group were to be found those whose interests were injured or threatened by British policies or who might improve their lot by change; in the latter, the beneficiaries of the status quo. Between the opposing forces was a large body of indifferent or uncertain folk whose attitude was, "A plague o' both your houses." Fearful of the penalties that would be inflicted on the losers and hoping to be let alone, they followed a policy of nonparticipation.

The radical Whigs, like any revolutionary group, drew into their orbit the direct actionists, the more ambitious, the more discontented, the underprivileged. As in other revolutions these left-wingers soon developed an organization, dynamic leadership, and a program; the conservatives were lacking in all three. Through a system of committees of correspondence, initiated at Boston by the first great American politician, Samuel Adams, the party of resistance developed an intercolonial organization that enabled it not merely to win elections and control assemblies (or the conventions that took their place when royal governors dissolved the legal bodies and fled) but, by propaganda, pressure, and finally force, to destroy the opposition and carry the Revolution along the path to independence. The Tories, isolated and unorganized, could offer only ineffective resistance to this Whig machine. One of its victims described it as "the barbarian rule of frantic folly, and lawless ambition—freedom of speech suppressed, liberty of press destroyed, voice of truth silenced, a lawless power depriving men of their natural rights, property taken without law—America arming east and west and pushing with madness in the high road of Sedition and Rebellion."

Yet the Whigs were more nearly representative of American desire for home rule than of American democracy. While they appealed to and made use of town workers and small farmers, they included too many conservative elements to accept a completely radical program. The Virginia planters, burdened with debts to British merchants, angry at restrictions on their land speculations, jealous of their control over the Old Dominion, and pushed toward revolt by the backfire of radicalism among the small farmers led by Patrick Henry, supported the war with as much zeal as the New England farmer-labor radicals under the banner of Samuel Adams. But they were not democrats.

In the northern cities a considerable section of the merchants, under the pressure of British restriction on trade, joined the revolt, running the risks a propertied class takes when it plays with the fire of revolution. Planters and merchants began with the hope of forcing England to abandon its coercive policy through boycotts and then resistance, but the radical leaders were looking toward complete independence and popular rule.

The adoption of the Declaration of Independence by the Continental Congress was a victory for the radical Whigs of the Sam Adams and Richard Henry Lee type over the moderate group represented by John Dickinson, Edward Rutledge, and John Jay. The latter thought such a declaration premature and watched the rising revolutionary tide with forebodings. Rutledge, a South Carolina Whig aristocrat, feared a confederation ruled by New England radicals. "I dread their low cunning," he wrote, "and those levelling principles which men without character and without fortune in general possess, which are so captivating to the lower class of mankind." Yet the radicals had their way as to independence, though the preliminary struggles in the different states were far closer than the vote of their representatives in Congress indicated. The pressure of the voteless lower classes, who now took part in the revolutionary movement, weighed heavily on the radical side.

Independence represented only the severing of the cord of empire. But who would now rule at home? On the whole, the radicals had their way in the writing of the Articles of Confederation. The powers of Congress were so limited that it could do little beyond managing the war and conducting foreign relations.

The states determined the internal course of the Revolution. Here conservatives battled radicals over new constitutions and for control of the new state governments to decide questions of suffrage, machinery of state government, apportionment of representation, relationship of church and state, preservation of landed estates, the fate of ungranted crown and proprietary lands, and confiscation of loyalist property. The radical gains were considerable, and the doors were opened to further changes by the large powers granted to the new state legislatures, no longer checked by royal governors or British imperial authority. With a general widening of the suffrage, even though it was still restricted to landowners or taxpayers, the agrarian democratic forces were in a stronger position than ever before. The results of the struggle varied from state to state; Pennsylvania and North Carolina, for example, swung sharply to the left, while Massachusetts and South Carolina steered a decidedly conservative course.

Although those loyalists who gave open assistance to the King's forces went into exile and lost their property, that considerable body of the well-to-do who supported, or at least accepted, the Revolution suffered no inconveniences, and some even waxed fatter on war profits and speculations or through the virtual extinguishment of their debts to British merchants. The old seaboard ruling class was still a political force to be reckoned with, despite the exiling of its right wing. Fortunately, its democratic opponents respected private property and every man's right to get ahead in the world, and had no thought of liquidating patriotic aristocrats.

The Post-Revolutionary Period

The period following the Revolution was one of economic depression and social unrest, caused by the disruptions and the devastations of the war. Confronted with an acute shortage of gold and silver, the state governments were under strong pressure to issue paper money, as in the Revolution, and to suspend the collection of debts. Debt-burdened farmers, suffering from low prices and unable to find cash for interest and taxes, demanded such relief. The commercial and creditor class, in the coastal cities and on tidewater, opposed measures that would delay the foreclosure of mortgages or force them to accept cheap paper as payment. Thus the old antagonisms flamed afresh, but this time the large propertied interests were decidedly on the defensive, without the backing of the British government to curb agrarian radicalism. Congress under the Articles of Confederation lacked both the power and the army to deal with crisis situations, and was almost bankrupt financially.

The conservatives, alarmed at the success of the paper-money party in seven states and the outbreak of Shays's Rebellion in Massachusetts, where merchants, lawyers, and creditors still ruled, resorted to a double strategy. On the one hand, they fought a defensive battle to curb radicalism in the state legislatures; on the other, they skillfully inaugurated an offensive movement to set up a central government powerful enough to preserve order, protect property rights, place the public credit on a sound foundation and facilitate the conduct of interstate and foreign commerce.

In this movement were merchants, shipowners, holders of government securities, moneylenders, large planters, former officers of the Continental Army, lawyers and professional men generally, and a good many former Tories—the classes that had most to lose through social upheavals and civil strife. A few among them were whispering of monarchy; some were concerned chiefly over their speculations in depreciated government bonds; but more were level-headed men of means who wanted a reasonably strong government to provide security and stability against agrarian levelers and provincial-minded politicians. The masses had imbibed sufficiently of the heady wine of democracy; economic distress was not to be cured by paper money and weak government. If self-interest governed the framers of the Constitution, it was an enlightened self-interest, and they entrusted their handiwork to the verdict of the voters, not to the arbitrament of force.

The movement for a Constitutional Convention aroused surprisingly little opposition. The more radical elements, engrossed in state politics, paid slight attention to it. They assumed that such a convention would do no more than propose amendments to the existing Articles of Confederation, and that the state legislatures would pass on these. Consequently, conservatives in the legislatures chose men of their own kind to go to the Philadelphia convention. Since its proceedings were secret, the radicals were taken by surprise when the Constitution was submitted for ratification.

Not only was a complete instrument of government offered to the voters instead of a group of amendments to the Articles; but the state legislatures were by-passed, and the Constitution was submitted to popularly elected conventions for their approval. When nine states ratified, it was to go into effect for the nine. The others might come in later. The insuperable barrier to amendments to the Articles, acceptance by all thirteen legislatures, was thus hurdled in highly irregular fashion. Indeed, the whole procedure was unconstitutional—if one may use the term—for it discarded the old government by a revolutionary, though peaceful, process and substituted a new one in its place.

Federalists and Antifederalists

Though the issue of ratification, like the question of independence, was a national one, it had to be fought out in each state; and local considerations naturally influenced the outcome. The supporters of the Constitution, who called themselves Federalists, avoiding the more accurate but unpopular "nationalists," had certain distinct advantages over the opposition, whom they dubbed "Antifederalists." In leadership and political strategy the balance inclined decidedly toward the party that included Washington, Franklin, Madison, Hamilton, James Wilson, John Marshall, Rufus King, the Morrises, and the Pinckneys, to mention a few familiar names. In the other camp only Governor George Clinton of New York, Luther Martin of Maryland, and the Virginians, Patrick Henry, George Mason, and Richard Henry Lee, could rival the Federalist captains.

At every juncture the Antifederalists were outmaneuvered. Where the Federalists were sure of their control, as in Pennsylvania and most of the small states, they called the elections to choose delegates to the ratifying conventions so soon that the opposition had no opportunity to organize effectively. Where the result was doubtful, they delayed action in the conventions and encouraged debate while they influenced wavering delegates to vote favorably. Pressure, flattery, all the arts of persuasion, even political deals, were resorted to with great skill. Thus in Massachusetts the two key popular leaders, office-loving John Hancock and liberty-loving Samuel Adams, were drawn into the Federalist net, the former by promises of support for the Massachusetts governorship and possibly high office under the new Constitution, the latter by the influence of the Boston workingmen, who had been induced to hold a meeting in favor of ratification.

Another type of Federalist strategy was the promise of future amendments to the Constitution. Several ratifying conventions took the Federalist bait and proposed amendments; but these were offered as recommendations, not requirements to be met before ratification became effective. Eventually, ten were passed by the first Congress and duly ratified, but they constituted a bill of rights to protect individual liberties and did not alter the machinery or powers of the new government.

Not the least factor in the Federalists' victory was the concentration of their strength in the populous coastal area. Here their wealth and power helped create a favorable public opinion and made the election of Federalist delegates comparatively easy. The unfair apportionment of colonial days, which overweighted the seaboard in the assemblies, had not been entirely removed; and this aided the friends of the Constitution because the convention delegates were elected in the same manner as the representatives to the legislatures.

In the Antifederalist hinterland the opponents of the Constitution had their difficulties in getting the sometimes unruly rural democrats to come to the polls. Prosperity was returning, the paper-money craze had subsided, the farmers generally were displaying an indifference toward politics and political issues. Franchise restrictions,* which in most states kept the propertyless from voting, had been regarded as a Federalist asset; but this may be questioned. Certainly, the mechanics, sailors, and fishermen of the seaports, voteless or not, resolved and paraded in support of the new ship of state, following the lead of their employers and customers.

The Adoption of the Constitution

Nevertheless, with all their advantages, the Federalists barely squeezed the Constitution past a reluctant electorate. Direct popular vote might have defeated it. Of the eleven state conventions that ratified in 1787–88, four—Massachusetts, New Hampshire, Virginia, and New York— had hostile or doubting majorities when their sessions began; but persuasion and pressure and even sharp practices, such as holding up Antifederalist letters, tilted the balance, and ratification won out by the narrowest of margins. Democratic, individualistic North Carolina and farmer-ruled Rhode Island rejected the Constitution, and only later, when the new government was a going concern, did they yield. Rhode Island might have continued longer on an independent course but for proposals in Congress to slap a commercial boycott on it. Then its convention met and ratified.

With the Constitution in effect, the way was paved for genuine national parties. Americans, after a long apprenticeship, had acquired as much experience in self-government as any people in the world. Now, with the political center of gravity shifted from states to federal government, and elections for national offices made necessary, some form of organization had to be devised for representative government to function on a nationwide scale. The clashes of classes and sections that had characterized colonial and state politics needed the tempering effect of national parties to keep them under control. Concessions and compromises were essential in this broader field. Contending propertied interests had composed their differences in the Constitutional Convention and presented a united front for ratification. That they would continue to cooperate in

* New York alone changed its voting requirements to permit all adult males to vote at the election of delegates.

order to make the new system operate in their interests seemed reasonably certain. That the defeated agrarian democrats would rally their forces and presently continue the struggle on the new field seemed equally probable.

Thus two national parties, built on the old foundations, would naturally come into being. Yet the founding fathers had made no provision for this vital institution of democracy. Realistic James Madison, chief architect of the Constitution, foresaw temporary combinations of special interest groups to put through particular programs, but not permanent parties.

Parties were needed for another reason. In the Philadelphia convention the members had been intent on building a structure of government that would ensure the blessings of order and opportunity to men of property without being offensive to men of liberty. The result was a carefully balanced system with wide powers but divided authority. This would presumably prevent an excess of democracy and also make control by any special interest difficult. An aristocratic Senate, chosen by state legislatures for six-year terms, would balance a House of Representatives, elected every two years by those qualified to vote in each state, while an independent judiciary and an independent executive, neither subject to popular election, would checkmate Congress and each other. Such an arrangement, ideal in providing checks and balances, was also ideally unworkable. The executive in particular was set off against the legislative body in a manner almost designed to produce constant friction.

But the system worked in spite of itself. The president fortunately had complete executive powers and a veto over the measures of Congress that could be overridden only by two-thirds of each house. And the original complicated method of election to the presidency was soon found to be no barrier to popular choice. Thus a democratic tribune of the people evolved, responsible to the voters of the entire nation, as Congress was not, whose "administration" came to be judged not by how well he administered the laws but how successfully he administered the lawmakers. Two major parties appeared, with capture of the presidency as a prime motivating force. Success at the polls carried with it the prestige, power, and patronage of the nation's highest office and usually control of Congress and of the majority of the states as well.

Inevitably the independent, unbiased magistrate the framers of the Constitution had visualized faded into constitutional mythology, though each incumbent at his inaugural continues to give the vision lip service. The successful presidents have been those who accepted the responsibilities of party leadership and policy making and acted accordingly; the "Constitutional" presidents—and they have not been nonpartisan—have generally won but a limited fame, if they have not actually been found wanting. The truth of this statement will be amply verified in the chapters following.

II

The Electoral System and
the First Elections

☆

1789-1800

THE FRAMERS of the Constitution of the United States did not rely on precedents in setting up the electoral system for nominating and electing the
president. Theirs was an original contribution to American political pro-
cesses. The crystal ball failed them here, for it did not reveal the emergence of national political parties, which made their carefully wrought
piece of eighteenth-century machinery a nineteenth-century anachronism.
They had hammered out a method of nominating and electing the chief
executive which, they believed, would not let in too much democracy,
would sift out the less fit among the possible choices, would let Congress
have a restricted share in the final selection, and would satisfy the states
by giving them a good deal of leeway in the initial stages of the process.

Except for the changes in the Twelfth Amendment, the old machinery
is still with us. It is cranked up quadrennially for what is generally
regarded as a meaningless performance, for it has been made to fit, after
a fashion, the operations of a party system that had no place in the thinking of its creators. But its rusty gears are dangerously defective and
might, under certain circumstances, be manipulated to subvert the democratic process of electing a president long accepted by the descendants of
the framers. The old electoral machine needs a complete overhaul or a
relegation to the scrap heap.

The original system provided that each state should choose electors
equal in number to the state's senators and representatives in Congress.
The state legislature was free to set up the method of election. It could
elect them itself; it could use some form of popular vote; or it could
adopt a hybrid arrangement, as Massachusetts and New Hampshire did
in the first elections. These electors were to meet in their respective states
on the same day, and each elector was to vote for two persons for presi-

13

dent, one not a resident of the state. The two houses of Congress, in joint session, were to tabulate the votes.

If one person had a majority of the whole number of electors, he became president; the second high man became vice-president. A tie in majority votes would be settled by the House of Representatives, each state casting one vote. If no one had a majority, the House would decide from the five highest. The authors of the system seemed to have assumed that support for local favorites would mean a wide scattering of votes and that, normally, no one would have a majority.

The First Presidential Election

The first presidential election did conform in a way to the intent of the founding fathers. No primaries, no nominating conventions, no campaigning, no national balloting, and no prognosticating opinion polls—this was the happy state of the nation when George Washington was elected. But all the paraphernalia of present-day elections would not have affected the outcome when the electors, chosen a month earlier in a variety of ways, met to cast their votes on the first Wednesday of February 1789. Washington had no rival in the hearts of his countrymen, and every one of the sixty-nine electors voted for him. But this was an exceptional situation not likely to recur, although Monroe came within one vote of unanimity in 1820.

In registering their second choices the electors performed more nearly according to the norm expected of them. Rotund, snappish John Adams, respected for his scholarly writings on governments, ancient and modern, and for his contributions to the American cause as legislator and diplomat during and after the Revolution, was a logical choice for the second office. But he received only thirty-four electoral votes while thirty-five were divided among ten other worthies. He accepted the office but wrote afterward to a friend: "Is not my election to this office in the scurvy manner in which it was done, a curse rather than a blessing? Is there Gratitude? Is there Justice?" Only his fears of "great mischief" and "the final failure of the government from my refusal" prevented him from spurning it.

Adams did not know that Alexander Hamilton influenced some of the electors in order not to couple him with Washington. Hamilton did this to make certain that the New Englander's total did not pass Washington's vote and give the former the first office, an unnecessary stratagem to guard against an unlikely contingency. He regarded Adams as a potential malcontent who had to be mollified with some high office—and the vice-presidency would serve. The first vice-president called his position "the most insignificant . . . that ever invention of man contrived, or his imagination conceived."

National political parties under the Constitution started not in the grass roots but in cabinet and Congress and spread from the top downward. Alexander Hamilton, first secretary of the treasury, offered a financial program that quickly aroused strong opposition. He recommended to Congress the refunding of the depreciated Continental securities at par value, the assumption of state debts by the federal government, the creation of a United States Bank, the levying of an excise tax on distilled liquors, and a protective tariff. All but the last were enacted.

These measures were designed to put the government on a sound financial basis, and they won the approval of the seaboard's business and financial centers. But representatives of rural constituencies, angry at the activities of speculators in securities and fearing that the measures meant heavy taxes, debt increases, and the rule of the rich, drew together to oppose the treasury cohorts.

The Philosophy of Alexander Hamilton

Hamilton's philosophy of statecraft involved the use of the power of the new federal government to advance the interests of the business and financial classes, which would form a bulwark to protect the government against the turbulent and changing masses who "seldom judge or determine right." His following kept the name Federalist for themselves and gave their opponents the now unpopular designation of Antifederalist.

James Madison, who had worked with Hamilton in the struggle for ratification of the Constitution, fought the Hamilton measures in Congress and soon had the ear of Thomas Jefferson, secretary of state. Jefferson had helped Hamilton get the assumption proposal through the House in return for support for a future national capital on the Potomac. But he opposed the bill for a United States Bank as unconstitutional and urged Washington to veto it. The president gave the treasury the benefit of the doubt and signed it. Thereafter the two secretaries opposed each other on major issues.

The Philosophy of Thomas Jefferson

Thomas Jefferson's politico-economic philosophy was primarily agrarian. He saw the United States as still a nation of farmers and he would keep it so. Every man could be a landowner and every landowner a voter. He assailed Hamilton's policies as in the interest of "paper capitalists," and he opposed the extension of federal power, particularly in the executive branch, as a threat to states' rights and individual liberties. Later he was to use that power when it benefited his nation of farmers. The Jeffersonians called themselves Republicans as opposed to the monarchists, or "Monocrats," entrenched in the Treasury Department.

A newspaper war between Hamilton's paper, the *Gazette of the United States,* edited by John Fenno, which enjoyed the public-printing plums, and the *National Gazette* of Philip Freneau, who received a part-time clerkship in the State Department, worried the president, who wanted harmony in the national councils.

Washington and a Second Term

Upon one point the rivals were in complete agreement. This was that Washington should accept a second term. Jefferson was insistent. "Your being at the helm will be more than an answer to every argument that can be used to alarm and lead the people in any quarter, into violence and secession. North and South will hang together if they have you to hang on." Washington, now sixty and afflicted with deafness and bad dentures, as well as the cares of state, reluctantly accepted as a matter of duty, though he longed for the peace and freedom of neglected Mount Vernon. But the Republicans regarded the second office in the government as fair prey, and they set to work to get rid of John Adams.

The Federalists accepted Adams as their vice-presidential choice without any formal action. Hamilton, at heart more of a monarchist than Adams, nevertheless thought the latter too indiscreet; but he made no attempt to offer another candidate. His efforts were centered on defeating the original opposition choice, New York's Governor George Clinton, an old enemy. The governor's chances were dimmed, however, by a bitter state election in the spring of 1792. Although Chief Justice John Jay, the Federalist candidate for governor, actually had more votes, the state canvassing board threw out the returns from three counties on technical grounds and counted Clinton in. This aroused intense feeling in the state, and there was some doubt as to the wisdom of supporting the veteran governor for the vice-presidency.

In the fall an undercover project to make Senator Aaron Burr the Republican choice was launched from New York. He was stronger than Clinton in New York City but less well known elsewhere. A Philadelphia conference of middle-state politicians on October 16 endorsed Clinton, and Burr gracefully acquiesced, perhaps with the hope of future support. He was only thirty-six and could wait. Hamilton, alarmed at the possible candidacy of Burr, an "embryo Caesar," now discovered virtues in Clinton, "a man of property, and in private life, as far as I know, of probity"; but his opinion had no influence on the Republican decision.

This campaign, though only the vice-presidency was involved, at least proved the existence of two embryonic parties. Neither had a formal organization, but the degree of unity achieved by private correspondence and through the newspapers was surprising. The advantages lay with the Federalists, but the Virginia–New York alliance did yeoman work in creating a Republican opposition. In almost every state little groups of Jeffersonians were active in nominating congressional candidates and laying the foundations for a powerful party. Adams, sulking in Massachusetts when Congress met in November, bore the brunt of their assaults. He was anti-Republican, an aristocrat, a monarchist at heart, they charged, and the Federalists were corrupt speculators and a moneyed aristocracy. In retaliation the Adams men brought up Clinton's opposition to the Constitution and referred to their opponents as the "mobocracy."

Congress had changed the dates for elections to make the first Wednesday in December the day for the presidential electors to cast their votes, and the second Wednesday in February for Congress to tabulate the result. The electors were to be chosen in each state any time within thirty-four days preceding the first Wednesday in December.* This spread the election period over the first two weeks of November. As in the first election there was no uniform method. Legislatures chose the electors in ten states; the voters, in three; and the Massachusetts and New Hampshire legislatures selected the electors only when candidates lacked a majority of the popular vote.

Most of the excitement over the election seems to have been confined to a few newspapers, for the popular vote was light. The choice of a vice-president was not a matter to arouse widespread interest. Nevertheless, the electoral vote reflected sharply the growing party solidarity. Adams had all of New England, New Jersey, Delaware, Maryland, 14 of Pennsylvania's 15, and 7 of South Carolina's 8—a total of 77 electoral votes. Clinton had 50, carrying New York, Virginia, North Carolina, and Georgia, and receiving 1 vote from Pennsylvania. Newly admitted Kentucky gave 4 to Jefferson, while a South Carolina elector cast a vote for Burr. Every elector gave Washington one of his votes, making a total of 132.

The Republicans might have elected Clinton but for Pennsylvania. Below the Potomac they had all the states except South Carolina; in the North, only New York. The victorious Federalists had good reason to be alarmed at the rapid growth of the opposition. Adams had won; but Jefferson believed that his personal worth and past services were responsible, not his political creed. The House, where the popular will was better expressed, seemed to be almost under Republican control. The "Monocrats" had been checkmated there.

---

* This was changed in 1845 to the Tuesday after the first Monday in November. In 1887 the day for the electors to meet was changed to the second Monday in January. In 1934, as a result of the Twentieth Amendment, this was shifted to the Monday after the second Wednesday in December.

Foreign Relations and Party Issues

In Washington's second term the problems of foreign relations became party issues. The French Revolution, with which Americans generally were sympathetic, whirled off on a radical course culminating in the Reign of Terror, and in 1793 involving France in a great European war.

Washington's policy of neutrality was assented to by Jefferson, but pro-French Republicans enthusiastically welcomed the new French minister, Citizen Genêt, formed Jacobin clubs in imitation of the Parisian radicals, and protested against British infringement of neutral rights on the Atlantic.

The Federalists, alarmed at the excesses of the Revolution and fearing the spread of Jacobinism in this country, upheld Washington's neutral course. Close business relations with England made them overlook her one-sided rule of the waves, her retention of Canadian border posts on American soil in violation of the treaty of 1783, and some other old sores.

The indiscretions of Genêt and his insolence toward the president brought on his recall and hurt his and the Republican cause. On the other hand, British seizures of American merchant ships led to demands for retaliation that Washington held back by sending Chief Justice John Jay to England in an attempt to secure a peaceful solution of all problems between the two powers. Jay brought back a treaty that settled several old issues and did relieve tensions, but it was damned as a sellout to the British by the Republicans. Even Hamilton had difficulty defending its limited trade and neutrality concessions. It became a major issue in the national election of 1796.

The Election of 1796

The election of 1796, with Washington eliminating himself,* soon became a struggle between Adams and Jefferson. Members of Congress from both parties and some outsiders apparently discussed the problem of candidates informally and reached an agreement as to their choices for first place. But there was no formal meeting of the "caucus," as in later

---

* He did not consciously set a precedent against a third term. He would have retired after one term if circumstances had permitted it. Now, disgusted with party bitterness and eager to enjoy the peace of Mount Vernon, he refused to consider another term. At the time of the adoption of the Constitution he had written to Jefferson defending the reeligibility of the president and opposing any restriction on the number of terms.

elections, and there was nothing to bind the electors. Hamilton, doubtful about the wisdom of supporting Adams, had considered Patrick Henry; but that old Antifederalist, now a conservative, showed no interest.

The need for a southern running mate for Adams pointed toward South Carolina, and Thomas Pinckney, negotiator of a popular treaty with Spain, was selected. Since there was no separate vote for vice-president, Pinckney's southern friends chose to regard him as a presidential candidate. He was expected to take votes from Jefferson in the South and thus ensure a Federalist victory for both offices.

In this situation Hamilton took a hand. His plan was innocence itself. All he asked was that the northern electors should be loyal to their party and give an equal support to both Federalist candidates, ostensibly to keep Jefferson from finishing first or second. Behind this plausible appeal was the possibility that Pinckney might do better than Adams in the South. Thus the New Englander would end up in second place—an outcome that Hamilton admitted afterward "would not have been disagreeable to me." The Adams electors in New England, however, took care of the scheme, as the electoral vote reveals.

Burr's nomination for second place on the ticket with Jefferson seems to have been taken for granted, certainly in the North and West; but if the Virginia leaders favored him they failed to inform their electors. Perhaps the fact that the New York legislature, which would choose the state's electors, was Federalist made Burr's candidacy of little value to the Virginians, as he had proved unable to control his home state.

The campaign raged up to the day in December when the electors were to meet. Though they were elected on partisan tickets, there were no binding pledges to prevent the exercise of individual judgment by an elector. Consequently, the party newspapers continued the battle until the results were known. While Jefferson and Adams remained in bucolic retirement far from the seat of government, their ardent supporters used every weapon of propaganda, from poisoned arrows to mud.

Adams was traduced as a monarchist, a lover of titles, an enemy of liberty; Jefferson, as an atheist, a coward in the Revolution, a tool of France, and an enemy of the Constitution. The French Minister, Adet, meddled in the campaign by supplying the Republican *Aurora* with copies of his notes to Secretary of State Pickering for immediate publication. His praise of Jefferson and his hostile tone toward the administration were obviously intended for public consumption. His actions proved more embarrassing than helpful to the Republicans.

With legislatures choosing electors in ten of the sixteen states, it is difficult to estimate the influence of campaign propaganda. Federalist electors were chosen from New England, New York, New Jersey, and Delaware, and the majority of Maryland's districts. One Maryland elector judiciously voted for both Adams and Jefferson. The Republicans carried Georgia, Tennessee, Kentucky, North Carolina, Virginia, and Pennsylvania, though each of the last three had a solitary Adams elector. A second Pennsylvania elector, reputedly a Federalist, voted for Pinckney and Jefferson.

The South Carolina electors also coupled these men as their choices. A bipartisan deal in the legislature was responsible for this all-southern ticket. This might have made Pinckney president had the Adams electors supported him equally with Adams elsewhere, as Hamilton had hoped; but 18 votes were thrown to other Federalists, and Pinckney lost even the vice-presidency. Adams had 71 votes; Jefferson, 68; Pinckney, 59; and Burr, 30. Nine others received votes. Republican newspapers charged the Federalists with fraudulent voting in Pennsylvania, where the popular vote was very close, and in one Maryland district where four votes separated the two parties; but their protests were unheeded. John Adams, a Federalist, was president; Thomas Jefferson, a Republican, was vice-president.

On the Republican side, Burr's poor showing was a surprise. The southern Republican electors from Virginia, North Carolina, and Georgia had given Jefferson thirty-five votes to Burr's seven. The alliance of the Old Dominion (Virginia) and New York had been dissolved without notice to the junior partner. Burr said nothing but was to be more astute when the Virginians looked northward for support in 1800.

The Philosophy of John Adams

John Adams took the oath of office on March 4, 1797, before House and Senate members in a simple ceremony completely devoid of the pomp for which he had been reputed to have a true monarchist's love. The new president was off to an excellent start. This crusty New England lawyer, short, baldheaded, with a little too much belly—"His Rotundity," his critics called him—had as much learning stuffed in him as any man in America. He sometimes seemed overfond of displaying his knowledge of peoples and governments, ancient and modern, in a pedantic parade of illustrations; but his observations were often acute, and his conclusions were a challenge to the toughest intellects.

Though he had signed the Declaration of Independence, the wine of liberty and equality had not turned his head. He believed that men were governed by their interests and passions, and that neither the rich nor the masses could be trusted with unrestrained power. In this age-old class struggle, liberty could be preserved by a balanced government that represented both classes in its legislature and included three departments, each a check on the others. He lacked Jefferson's faith in the people and Hamilton's belief in the rule of the few. Adams distrusted human nature. In his economics he was nearer to Jefferson. Brought up on a farm, he viewed property in terms of land; and in middle age he had become the proud possessor of a substantial New England farm. Without investments in trade or securities, he was not a sympathetic representative of the class interest of his party. Neither was he pro-British in feeling, for he resented the selfishness and the snobbishness of the British ruling class, which he had experienced firsthand when minister to England; and he saw the dangers to the young nation in European involvements. Hamilton's distrust of him was well founded.

Adams was also unfitted by temperament for party leadership. He was proud, independent, suspicious, tactless, cursed with a sarcastic tongue and a quick temper. He even antagonized when he meant to conciliate. Franklin described him as "always an honest man, often a wise one, but sometimes, and in some things, wholly out of his senses." His wife, Abigail Smith, also of an old Puritan family, was his intellectual equal, cultured far above the feminine norm of the eighteenth century. Her published letters are a contribution to American literature. Yet this strong-willed first mistress of the White House—occupied in 1800—accepted and shared her husband's likes and dislikes, if she did not at times activate them. Her jealousy for his fame did not help to soften his asperities.

Jefferson's defeat had its compensations. In the vice-presidential chair he could see and hear much, keep in touch with his friends in Congress, and yet preserve a discreet silence in public. Votes and speeches were not required of vice-presidents.

The Issues of 1800

The story of John Adams's administration largely revolves around the difficulties with France, including the XYZ affair, an attempt by three go-betweens used by Talleyrand to demand $250,000 as part of a treaty. This led to the undeclared French War of 1798. Martial fever caused Congress to make preparations for war and to pass a series of repressive measures, the Alien and Sedition Acts. Hamilton, field commander of the army newly created at Washington's insistence, found his visions of military glory dispelled when Adams, unexpectedly, renewed negotiations with France, now under Napoleon Bonaparte, and arranged a peaceful solution of the issues at stake. The president also purged his cabinet of two of Hamilton's satellites.

Adams was nominated for a second term, with C. C. Pinckney of South Carolina for vice-president, by a caucus of Federalist members of

Congress. Hamilton, unable to uncover a suitable candidate, proceeded to attack Adams in a pamphlet intended for secret distribution among leading Federalists. It soon became public, damaging its author more than its subject.

Perhaps the most significant deed of the Adams administration was the appointment of Federalist John Marshall of Virginia as Chief Justice of the Supreme Court of the United States. During his term (1801–1835), Marshall established three principles: (1) The Supreme Court has the power to determine that an act of Congress is unconstitutional; (2) The Supreme Court has the power to set aside laws of state legislatures as unconstitutional; and (3) The Supreme Court has the power to reverse a decision of a state court.

As the war fever subsided and the Federalists fell to fighting among themselves, Republican hopes rose. Working quietly through conferences with small groups and through a wide range of correspondence, Jefferson, Madison, Albert Gallatin of Pennsylvania, Burr, and other key leaders welded together a powerful party. Newspapers were financed, pamphlets were printed and circulated, congressmen wrote letters to their constituents, and the propaganda mills ground steadily through the campaign. New York, Pennsylvania, and South Carolina were the key states that must be won, though the Jeffersonians refused to concede even New England to the enemy without a battle.

The Republicans Woo Aaron Burr

In New York the election of the legislature, which was to choose the presidential electors, was held in the spring of 1800. Colonel Aaron Burr, whom Jefferson had been courting since 1797, became the Republican man of the hour. His task was to make Federalist New York City Republican, swinging the balance of power in the legislature to the Jeffersonians.

The arrest and harsh treatment of Jedediah Peck for circulating petitions for the repeal of the Sedition Act helped upstate; but in the city the clever tactics of Burr accounted for the result. The Society of St. Tammany *proved to be a useful ally. Organized in 1789 by William Mooney on the foundations of earlier groups of the Revolutionary period, it was at first a fraternal order with a membership of mechanics, artisans, and laborers. Its democratic personnel caused it to evolve into a Republican club, which met in Martling's Tavern in a room the scoffing Federalists called the "Pig Pen." It was soon playing an important part in local elections, and Burr, though not a member, worked with it.

In order to draw the widest possible popular support, Burr drafted an

* Tammany was named after a Delaware Indian chief friendly toward whites. He was later facetiously referred to as the patron saint of the United States.

assembly ticket of big-name Republicans including Clinton, General Gates, and a Livingston, and offered it to the voters in opposition to a group of Federalist mediocrities whom Hamilton had named to ensure control of the city delegation. Burr also created some new voters by a clever legal device that made them landowners. The polls, open for four days, were scenes of great excitement as the two rivals electioneered in person, though Burr depended more upon his disciplined organization to get results. The county voted Republican, and its assemblymen furnished the margin by which the new legislature chose Jeffersonian electors. An average majority of 490 votes was the balance of power in the county, and indirectly in state and nation.

One last card remained for the stunned Federalists to play. After conferring with friends, Hamilton proposed to Governor Jay that he call the old assembly into special session at once to enact a law providing for the choice of presidential electors by popular vote under a district system. This would give the Federalists a second chance and would ensure them at least a part of the New York electors. "It is easy to sacrifice the substantial interests of society by a strict adherence to ordinary rules," he wrote, urging the governor not to be "over-scrupulous." But austere John Jay had none of the arts of the political manipulator. He filed away the letter after inscribing on it, "Proposing a measure for party purposes, which it would not become me to adopt."

The outcome of the spring election in New York made it certain that the vice-presidential candidate would come from that state. But would it be Clinton or Burr? Gallatin asked his father-in-law, Commodore James Nicholson, to sound out the New York Republicans and let him know their preference for the benefit of the Republican congressional caucus. The details of the negotiations were later a matter of controversy. At least Clinton seemed unenthusiastic toward the nomination while Burr's friends were quite insistent. Burr agreed to take the nomination provided assurances were given that the southern Republicans would act fairly toward him. He had not forgotten their treatment of his candidacy four years earlier. The party congressional caucus met on May 11 and unanimously agreed to support Burr for vice-president.

In Pennsylvania the Senate, containing a number of holdover members, was Federalist, but the House of Representatives, elected in October 1800, was strongly Republican. Had a statewide popular vote been permitted for presidential electors, as in past elections, all fifteen would have been Republican. But the Federalist Senate blocked all attempts in this direction, refused to vote by joint ballot, and forced a compromise that gave the Federalists seven electors, the Republicans eight. The outcome in no sense represented public opinion, for the state elected ten Republican congressmen to three Federalists.

In South Carolina, which also elected through its legislature, the

Republicans carried the assembly in October, though the city of Charleston, as usual, was Federalist. The energetic Charles Pinckney, breaking completely with his Federalist kinsmen,* had organized the Republican cause upcountry and stirred up planters and farmers against Federalist tax burdens on lands and slaves. He wrote to Jefferson that the "Federal interest" at Charleston voted "the lame, crippled, diseased, and blind," whether taxpayers or not, and used colored ballots as a check on how their underlings voted.

While only four states permitted a popular vote, even the indirect choice through the legislatures reflected the swing toward Jefferson. The Republicans had found plenty of fuel for their propaganda in the record of the Adams administration. Militarism, high taxes, debt increases, and unconstitutional measures were played up along with the old refrains of aristocratic rule, the dangers of monarchy, and the power of the "monied interest." Republican journals joyfully quoted from Hamilton's pamphlet on the defects of John Adams.

The Federalists, thrown on the defensive by the effectiveness of the Republican appeal, resorted to a campaign of fear and smear in a vain attempt to save the day. Jefferson, they thundered, was an infidel, a fanatic, a believer in French revolutionary doctrines, who would destroy religion, set up agriculture over commerce, repudiate the public debt, and lead the country into bloodshed and anarchy. "Tremble then in case of Jefferson's election, all ye holders of public funds, for your ruin is at hand," wrote "Decius" in a Federalist newspaper. "Old men who have retired to spend the evening of life upon the fruits of the industry of their youth. Widows and orphans with their scanty pittances. Public banks, insurance companies, literary and charitable institutions . . . will be involved in one common, certain, and not very distant ruin." A pamphlet addressed to "Religious Republicans" charged that Jefferson, looking at a church building in a ruined condition, had said, "It is good enough for Him that was born in a manger." A Connecticut Federalist wrote in his diary: "I do not believe that the Most High will permit a howling atheist to sit at the head of this nation."

The electoral count gave Jefferson and Burr 73 votes each, Adams 65, Pinckney 64, and Jay 1. At last party discipline had been made completely effective. Only one Rhode Island elector, fearful that Pinckney might lead Adams, refused to support both Federalist candidates. Adams had all the votes of New England, New Jersey, and Delaware, five of Maryland's ten, four of North Carolina's twelve, and seven of Pennsylvania's fifteen; Jefferson had all the rest.†

* Charles Cotesworth Pinckney, Federalist vice-presidential candidate, and Thomas Pinckney.

† Only Virginia, Rhode Island, Maryland, and North Carolina chose their electors by popular vote, the last two using a district system.

With Jefferson and Burr in a tie, the House of Representatives had to choose between them, though everyone understood that the latter was intended for second place. Burr, in a letter to General Samuel Smith before the final results were known, made it clear that he "would utterly disclaim all competition." A little later he was equally positive, in a letter to Jefferson, that his friends would not think of "diverting a single vote from you."

Nevertheless, Federalist leaders, bitterly disappointed over their defeat, turned hopeful eyes toward Burr. He might prove to be the lesser evil. He was a northerner, a lawyer and not a farmer, a practical politician rather than a Jacobin fanatic, and he was on friendly terms with many of his opponents. His election by the House would disorganize the Republicans and might destroy the leadership of the man the Federalists hated most, Thomas Jefferson. These opinions were well summed up by one Federalist: Burr's "ambition and interest will direct his conduct—and his own state is commercial and largely interested in the funded debt. If he will honorably support the government for which he has undoubted talents, he will have support of the Federalists and some of the Jacobins whom he may detach—and his election will disorganize and embarrass the party who have given him their votes."

But Hamilton, in the unhappy role of choosing between two men he thoroughly disliked, differed with his party colleagues. There was for him but one choice. Burr was the "Catiline of America," a man devoid of scruples and possessed of an inordinate ambition and the "boldness and daring necessary to give success to the Jacobin system." Jefferson at least had "pretensions to character," though he was unscrupulous, not very mindful of truth, and was a "contemptible hypocrite." "Nor is it true that Jefferson is zealot enough to do anything in pursuance of his principles that will contravene his popularity or his interest. He is as likely as any man I know to temporize—to calculate what will be likely to promote his own reputation and advantage; and the probable result of such a temper is the preservation of systems, though originally opposed, which, being once established, could not be overturned without danger to the person who did it."

To Representative James A. Bayard of Delaware and others, Hamilton wrote in the above strain. But his pleas fell on deaf ears. The Federalist members of the House held a caucus, and though some dissented, the majority voted to support Burr.

Voting as individuals the Federalists controlled the House, for this was a lame-duck Congress, elected when the war fever was mounting; but the Constitutional requirement that the members vote by states in choosing the president placed them at a disadvantage. Their strength was too heavily concentrated in New England, whereas the vote of the Republicans was better distributed and gave them control of more states.

In addition, there were enough Federalist defections to deprive Burr of two states, New Jersey and Georgia, and to divide Maryland. Vermont was also evenly divided. Burr had four New England states, Delaware, and South Carolina; Jefferson was supported by New York, Pennsylvania, New Jersey, Virginia, North Carolina, Georgia, Tennessee, and Kentucky, eight in all. In the case of the last three, four members cast three votes for Jefferson, while twenty-five Federalists in New England could give Burr but four votes, voting by states. The vote by individuals gave Jefferson 55, Burr 49.

From the eleventh through the seventeenth of February the House balloted, with the result always the same: eight states for Jefferson, six for Burr, and two divided. The New Yorker needed three changes of votes—in New Jersey, Maryland, and Vermont—to get nine states. Maryland would have been his if Joseph Nicholson had let illness and a raging fever keep him away. Through a heavy snowstorm he came to the House to cast his vote for Jefferson from a bed fixed up in a committee room. This kept Maryland evenly divided. Gallatin, the cool-headed, was the floor leader of the Jeffersonians, carefully holding his lines intact while he waited for a break in the Federalist ranks.

Jefferson and Burr Elected

The balloting started on Wednesday, but not until the weekend were there signs that the Federalists were weakening. Burr was apparently doing nothing to get the three Republican votes necessary to win, and some of his supporters were losing heart. Fears of what might happen if the fourth of March came with the deadlock unbroken had some effect on the sober-minded. The Republican governors of Pennsylvania and Virginia were reported as ready to call out their militia to prevent a Federalist usurpation of the presidency.

Bayard of Delaware, sole representative of that little state, was now prepared to shift it to Jefferson. Hamilton's importunities or Burr's failure to act or fears of a civil war or some other factors may have determined his course. In any case, he announced in the Federalist caucus that the deadlock must end. The die-hards from New England denounced him, but had to yield. On the thirty-sixth ballot a Vermont Federalist was purposely absent, Bayard and the Maryland and South Carolina Federalists voted blanks, and Jefferson had ten of the sixteen states. Four New England states still voted for Burr on this final trial. Burr was now vice-president.

The whole plot—for it was hardly more than that—to elect Burr and frustrate the popular will had finally broken down. The good sense of the moderates had at least prevented the supreme blunder, a prolongation of the struggle until Adams's term expired. Without a constitutionally elected president or vice-president, the nation might have found itself plunged into civil strife. Before the next election the Twelfth Amendment was added to the Constitution. This provided that the electors should vote separately for president and vice-president. The original purpose of the electoral college had been altered by the development of parties.

Rumors of an understanding or even a bargain between the Federalists and Jefferson were circulated at the time of the election; but not until Bayard of Delaware lifted the curtain several years later was the nature of the negotiations revealed. Denials promptly followed from Jefferson and his henchmen, and a sharp controversy ensued. Bayard insisted that he had received assurances about Jefferson's policies on such points as support of the public credit, maintenance of the navy, the protection and encouragement of commerce, and the retention of subordinate officials in office, including a particular Delaware officeholder.

General Samuel Smith, who lodged at Conrad's boardinghouse with Jefferson and was in his confidence, had acted as a self-appointed intermediary to confer with Bayard and other Federalists. Smith's explanation, made years later, was that he had sounded out Jefferson on these points to quiet Federalist fears "without his having the remotest idea of my object." Then the busy go-between had let Bayard believe that he was authorized to speak for the Republican candidate. Jefferson's emphatic denial of any understanding or bargain still leaves unanswered the question whether he knew that he was being pumped when he expounded his views to General Smith.

Poor Burr was roundly denounced by the Federalists for his failure to give them pledges and to render aid in securing his election. "The means existed of electing Burr," wrote Bayard to Hamilton, "but this required his cooperation. By deceiving one man (a great blockhead) and tempting two (not incorruptible), he might have secured a majority of the states. He will never have another chance of being president of the United States; and the little use he has made of the one that has occurred gives me but an humble opinion of the talents of an unprincipled man." This remarkable left-handed compliment to Burr certainly exonerates him from any charge of activity in his own interest. The Machiavelli of the Republicans had behaved like an honorable man! The arch-intriguer had refused to use his base talents, and the Federalists were confounded in their efforts to help him. The humor of the situation was utterly lost upon them, for Thomas Jefferson had been elected president. The leaders of the party of "the wise and the good" had dug themselves a pit of their own misdeeds and follies and had fallen into it, never to emerge.

III

The Virginia Presidents and
the Second Adams

1804-1828

JEFFERSON, although putting the ship "on her Republican tack," did nothing very revolutionary. Rigid economy and simplicity in government, drastic reductions in the military establishment, repeal of the excise tax, and reduction of the national debt constituted a popular program. He did not disturb Hamilton's financial structure, and business benefited from an expanding foreign trade. A brief period of peace in Europe disposed of the problems of neutral rights for the moment. It was in this breathing spell in the Napoleonic wars that fortune favored Jefferson with his purchase of Louisiana.

Nor did the Republican president let his theories stand in the way of accomplishing his aims. He exercised a control over Congress that few presidents have achieved. Strict construction of the Constitution went by the boards with the Louisiana Purchase.

As Jefferson's popularity zoomed, a few die-hard New England Federalists in Congress talked of the possibility of dismemberment of the Union. They tried to draw Aaron Burr into a secession plot that would set up a northern confederacy. The vice-president, disgruntled at his treatment by the administration, ran for governor of New York, without, however, committing himself to the scheme. He was defeated by an administration candidate. Angry at Hamilton for casting aspersions on his character, he challenged him to a pistol duel, and the founder of Federalism went to his death on the field at Weehawken in New Jersey. Burr's political career was blasted, and he soon embarked on his western schemes, whose purposes are still a matter of conjecture.

Jefferson was renominated at a formal caucus of Republican Senators and Representatives on February 25, 1804. George Clinton of New York received 67 of the 108 votes cast on the one ballot for vice-president. An informal understanding among Federalist leaders made Charles Cotesworth Pinckney and Rufus King their choices.

Republican national victory was conceded, but New England Federalists fought desperately to save their states from democratic defilement. The Massachusetts legislature enacted a law for popular election of presidential electors but required that all nineteen be chosen by a statewide vote. The Republicans had demanded a return to the old district system, used before 1800, which would ensure them a share of the electoral vote. To the chagrin of the Federalists, the state went Republican by more than four thousand votes, and Jefferson secured all nineteen electors.

In Connecticut, Abraham Bishop led a Republican assault against the ruling Federalist-Congregational oligarchy. He denied the validity of the old royal charter, which had been used as a state constitution, and demanded a reform constitution with a simple taxpaying requirement for voters and an end of high property qualifications. Denunciations from press and pulpit and the power of the ruling hierarchy were too much for the reformers, and Connecticut voted Federalist as usual.

Where the Federalists campaigned at all, they were hard put to find issues. Peace, prosperity, the repeal of internal taxes, economy, and the acquisition of Louisiana were too much for them. Old issues and old prejudices were dusted off but made little impression. The godless, pro-French president had disappointed his detractors. On the more solid grounds of his attack upon the judiciary, his reduction of the navy, and the expense of Louisiana, it was difficult to arouse the voters. Even the charge that Louisiana cost every person in Massachusetts four dollars fell flat. The benefits were too obvious.

Seven states chose electors through their legislatures; seven used statewide popular vote; and three had a district system. Jefferson had 162 votes; Pinckney, 14. Connecticut, Delaware, and 2 of Maryland's 9 went to the loser. Federalism was almost extinct.

Conflicts with England and France

Jefferson's second term was troubled by (1) insurgency in the party and (2) mounting difficulties with Europe's warring powers over paper blockades and impressment of American sailors.

John Randolph, a brilliant, caustic-tongued, erratic Virginia member of the House of Representatives, feuded with Secretary of State Madison and won the support of a small group of old-fashioned, strict construction Republicans in opposing administration policies. Jefferson was able, however, by skillful tactics to reduce their power for mischief except for Randolph's tongue.

The second problem came from the war between England and France.

Both countries resorted to economic pressures, ignoring the rights of neutrals. In June 1807, the British ship *Leopard* attacked the American *Chesapeake* in an attempt to recover British deserters supposedly on the American vessel. Several Americans were killed and wounded, and four seamen impressed.

Jefferson favored economic sanctions and in December secured the passage by Congress of an act laying an embargo on American shipping. This drastic measure was a severe blow to the commercial interests, proved difficult to enforce, brought no concessions from the European belligerents, and put new life into the Federalist party. Jefferson gave in to its repeal just before he went out of office.

James Madison had long been regarded as Jefferson's successor. Their harmony of views and Madison's services made him the logical choice. Accordingly, a caucus of Republican members of Congress in January 1808, named him for the presidency and renominated George Clinton for second place. The action was almost unanimous, for the friends of Randolph and some other dissenters were absent. A group of them denounced the caucus system of nominations as a violation of the Constitution. The arrogant, acid-tongued Randolph hoped to create a diversion for James Monroe in the Old Dominion and destroy Madison's prestige at home. Curiously enough, although Clinton was the administration candidate for vice-president, he was also the presidential candidate of certain northern Republicans who were opposed to the succession of another Virginian.

His ambitious and aggressive nephew De Witt Clinton was the real force behind the candidacy of the cheerful old gentleman of sixty-nine, who found even the duties of vice-president too arduous and was manifestly unfit for the office of chief executive. He told the diarist William Plumer that "sitting three hours in the chair at a time was extremely fatiguing to him." His chances depended on the amount of insurgency in Pennsylvania and New York and the possible support of the Federalists.

Monroe, despite Jefferson's efforts to reconcile him to Madison, lent himself to Randolph's schemes. He had acted as a kind of diplomatic errand boy for the administration to the courts of France, Spain, and England, with little to show for it. The Louisiana Purchase had been largely settled before he arrived in France, and his work elsewhere was unsatisfactory. He had faced difficult situations in both Spain and England, but the treaty he and William Pinkney had arranged with England went beyond his instructions and was not even sent to the Senate. As a result Monroe felt that Jefferson had repudiated him.

The Virginia legislature divided between the two native sons, 124 members holding a caucus in January to name Madison electors, while 57 endorsed Monroe. John Taylor, an old-fashioned agrarian Republican, favored Monroe but tried to induce him to withdraw so as not to disrupt the party. The antiadministration men—the "Quids"—used the embargo as an argument against Madison and expressed fears that war would soon result. Monroe's candidacy probably was not helped by the endorsement of a group of Virginia Federalists, while the possibility of victory for Clinton as a result of the Virginia split drew support to Madison. Before the election it was clear that Monroe had no chance.

Some twenty-five or thirty Federalist leaders from seven states north of the Potomac, plus South Carolina, taking heart from the unpopularity of the embargo, held a secret conference at New York in August. The chief question at issue was whether the conference should support Clinton as the best means of defeating Madison. The majority accepted Rufus King's view and decided in favor of separate Federalist candidates. C. C. Pinckney and King were then named.

Fortunately for Madison, a bad factional fight in Pennsylvania—where Simon Snyder, Michael Leib, and William Duane, editor of the powerful *Aurora*, a radical trio, and Governor Thomas McKean, a conservative, had been at swords' points—was compromised sufficiently to unite Republican support for him. In New York De Witt Clinton failed to control the legislature, and it chose six electors for his uncle to thirteen for Madison. Largely as a result of these developments in Virginia, Pennsylvania, and New York, the key states of the Republicans, Madison won with 122 electoral votes to 47 for Pinckney and 6 for George Clinton.* Clinton was reelected vice-president with 113 votes to 9 for John Langdon of New Hampshire and 3 each for Monroe and Madison.

Jefferson had passed his scepter to his closest friend, but his joy was far from complete. The embargo had failed and now had to be repealed. Federalism, apparently defunct in 1804, had revived and was in control of New England. Its powerful business leaders, quiescent in times of prosperity, were aroused against a president who, they believed, aimed at the destruction of commerce and the dominance of agriculture. They continued hostile to the Republicans for many years.

Yet Jefferson had laid the solid foundations on which American liberalism was to build. He had demonstrated the falsity of the Federalist dogma that the propertied few alone were fit to govern and that democracy meant mob rule. He had shown the possibilities in wise, patient, skillful political leadership and—surprisingly, in view of his earlier predilections—had established the pattern of presidential direction of the party majority in Congress, which came to be the mark of reformer chief executives. He had secured an empire for his country that would give future generations of farmers the room they needed and would strengthen and prolong frontier democracy's influence. He was the master political architect of his day, and few have equaled him.

* One Kentucky elector was absent. Pinckney added to all the New England electors, except those from Vermont, three each from Delaware and North Carolina, and two from Maryland.

The War of 1812

In his grasp of governmental problems and in his experience in public life, James Madison was excelled by none of his contemporaries. But Madison lacked Jefferson's skill in political manipulation and his ability to appraise and use men. Concessions to factional pressure affected his cabinet choices, and eventually he had to replace his first secretary of state with his old rival, James Monroe, with whom he made peace. It is interesting that one of Madison's assets was his wife, Dolley, seventeen years his junior. Dolley Madison's beauty and charm as First Lady were to make her a Washington legend.

Madison tried diplomacy and a weaker version of Jefferson's peaceable-coercion policy in attempting to protect neutral rights but made no headway with either belligerent. The congressional elections of 1810 took matters out of his hands. From the West and South came the War Hawks, young men such as Henry Clay of Kentucky and John C. Calhoun of South Carolina, who were eager to defend the national honor and who would solve the western Indian problem by seizing Canada as a hostage. The War Hawks blamed the British for encouraging Indian unrest and for the atrocities of Tecumseh, a Shawnee chief who united the tribes east of the Mississippi to halt the white man's advance.

Their first move was to take control of the House of Representatives. Henry Clay, thirty-four years old and just beginning his years of service in the House, was chosen Speaker—a surprising overturn of the old order. Yet Clay was not unknown in Washington. He had represented Kentucky in the Senate for parts of two unexpired terms, the first in 1806-07 when he was actually under the age requirement for membership. The ready pen of Senator William Plumer of New Hampshire furnished this picture:

> Henry Clay, the senator from Kentucky, is a man of pleasure—very fond of amusements—gambles much. He told me that one evening he won at cards $1500—that at another evening he lost $600—He is a great favorite with the ladies—is in all parties of pleasure—out almost every night—gambles much here—reads but little. Indeed he said he meant this session should be a tour of pleasure.
>
> He has talents—is eloquent but not nice or accurate in his distinctions— He declaims more than he reasons. He is genteel polite and pleasant companion. A man of honor and integrity.

To the end of his days the ultrapuritanical regarded Henry Clay as a dissolute gambler even when they voted for him; but his warm, engaging personality won him hosts of friends, while his talents in politics placed him in the front rank of great American politicians. He was always "a man of honor and integrity."

The affable young Speaker filled the important committee posts with colleagues as young, energetic, and warlike as himself and made his office the directing force of the House. When John Randolph railed at this new crowd and attempted his usual obstructionist speeches, the Speaker promptly applied the House rules to squelch the fiery Virginian. But all was not easy sailing for the War Hawks. The older Republicans opposed their preparedness measures; the Federalists, numbering fewer than two-score members in the House and half a dozen in the Senate, sowed dissension between the groups, while the president, hesitant and wavering, had to be prodded into action. The war party itself was divided along sectional lines, the northern group eager for Canada, the southerners looking toward badly governed Spanish Florida.

Fortunately for the majority group, a presidential election was at hand. Here was their opportunity, for the congressional caucus was under their control. The power to nominate lay in their hands. There has been no proof that Madison bargained with the war party; but no bargain was necessary. He knew that only an aggressive attitude toward Great Britain would win him War Hawk support. In the spring of 1812 his actions foreshadowed a war message; in May the congressional caucus renominated him; in June war was declared. The caucus met much later than had been the custom. Was the war party waiting to see what the president would do?

John Langdon, a New Hampshire Revolutionary War patriot and a successful businessman, who had served as United States senator and as governor of his state, was named for the vice-presidency. He declined, perhaps because he was past seventy, and a second meeting of the caucus named Elbridge Gerry, "Gentleman-Democrat," governor of Massachusetts and leader of his party in New England. Formerly an independent and a friend of Adams, he had been ostracized by the Federalists for his part in the XYZ affair. While he was governor, his party had used redistricting to deprive the Federalists of control of the Massachusetts Senate. The device was not new, but it had lacked a name. The governor's enemies called it gerrymandering, and the name has stuck.

The Virginia–New York alliance, which had monopolized Republican nominations for national office since 1796, was now at an end, killed by George Clinton's death and De Witt Clinton's insurgency. The younger Clinton's friends had not attended the caucus. With New York's backing he intended to try for the presidency as an antiadministration Republican, appealing especially to northern jealousy of Virginia domination and New England antiwar bitterness. He was too shrewd to carry the peace banner, as this would hurt him where the war was popular. In his calculations the Federalists might be won without definite pledges because of their eagerness to divide the Republicans and defeat Madison.

The elder statesmen of Federalism, after consultation and correspondence, held a conference in New York in September to which the dwindling remnant of the party in South Carolina sent delegates; otherwise the region south of the Potomac was unrepresented. Rufus King proved to be the stumbling block in the way of outright endorsement of De Witt Clinton. Accompanied by John Jay and Gouverneur Morris, he had conferred earlier with Clinton and found him ready to promise much in private but unwilling to make public commitments. Dissatisfied, King bluntly told the assembled Federalists that an alliance with the Clintonians might place a "Caesar Borgia" in the presidency, and he favored a separate Federalist ticket. The majority, however, influenced by Harrison Gray Otis of Massachusetts, turned down this proposal; and, without formally endorsing Clinton, the conference adjourned, understanding that the shrewd New Yorker would get Federalist support in each state.

Publicity was avoided, and this suited Clinton well enough as he had no desire to appear openly as the Federalist-Peace candidate and thus offend his war following. The Federalist-Clinton understanding included support of Jared Ingersoll, a moderate Pennsylvania Federalist, for the vice-presidency. Although the term "Federalist" was dropped in some places in favor of "Friends of Peace," Clinton was pictured as a war supporter wherever it meant votes.

Some dissatisfaction with Clinton developed in the Federalist ranks. A Virginia convention put forward King and William R. Davie of North Carolina, and Federalist members of the New York legislature refused to support the Clinton electors; but these defections were not serious. Far more important was Clinton's failure to draw Republican votes, notably in Pennsylvania. The factionalism characteristic of the Republicans of that state did not prevent united support for Madison, and this was fatal to the hopes of Clinton. He had 89 electoral votes to Madison's 128. The West and the South alone could not have elected Madison, but Pennsylvania's 25 saved the day. To all New England except Vermont, Clinton added New York, New Jersey, Delaware, and 5 of Maryland's 11. His coalition had come very near to success.

The election was a weak vote of confidence in the administration. Even this was hardly warranted by the course of the war. Failures on the battlefield and maladministration plagued the American effort, and only the successful defenses against invasion in 1814 created the military stalemate that the Treaty of Ghent fortunately recognized.

Antiwar discontents in Federalist New England produced a movement for a northern confederacy, which led to the Hartford Convention of late 1814. This body, not controlled by the extremists, offered a moderate report for certain constitutional changes to strengthen New England's minority position in the Union. But the news of peace, coupled with General Andrew Jackson's victory at New Orleans, produced a belated outburst of patriotism that lumped together all war critics as Federalist plotters and disunionists. Federalism sank under the leaden load of the discredited Hartford Convention, which became a symbol of treason in wartime. With the Treaty of Ghent, the United States was much more independent of Europe.

But Federalism was no longer needed. It had become too narrowly sectionalized, and its Hamiltonian principles were now attaining fruition under the Young Republican leadership of Clay, Calhoun, and their associates. Taught by the lessons of the war, Congress passed measures for a larger peacetime army and navy, for the creation of a second United States Bank, and for the continuance of high war-tariff rates with some increases, while John Marshall's Supreme Court gave the new nationalism its blessings in a series of notable decisions. Madison accepted this Hamiltonian victory because of the great change of circumstances.

Monroe and the Era of Good Feelings

Monroe received the Republican nomination for president in 1816 after a sharp contest. William H. Crawford of Georgia, who had worked with the Young Republicans in Congress, had 54 votes in the caucus to Monroe's 65—a very narrow margin for the Virginian, who had been regarded generally as the heir apparent to Madison from the time of his acceptance of the primacy of the cabinet. Daniel D. Tompkins, the energetic governor of New York, favored at first to head the ticket by that state, was named for the vice-presidency, thus restoring the old Virginia–New York alliance of earlier years. No Federalist nominations were made, but the electors of Massachusetts, Connecticut, and Delaware, chosen by the legislatures, cast 34 votes for Rufus King. Three Maryland Federalists and one from Delaware did not vote. Monroe had 183. The only spark of interest in the campaign was provided by critics of the caucus system, and they accepted its choices.

Fortunately the decline of Federalism and the sweep of nationalistic feeling eliminated party rancor and gave Monroe a political security that no other president except the "Father of His Country" has ever enjoyed. As a mark of his desire to appear as the head of a united nation, the new president set out on a triumphal tour of the North and West. The acclaim with which he was received caused his administration to be termed the Era of Good Feelings—a phrase first used by the *Boston Centinel* in describing his visit to that city. New England, which had never looked upon the faces of Presidents Jefferson and Madison, outdid itself to honor their successor.

When Monroe was reelected in 1820 without opposition, the venerable John Adams served as a Massachusetts elector, and only William Plumer of New Hampshire cast a dissenting vote (for John Quincy Adams).

Monroe had not been formally nominated. A poorly attended congressional caucus decided against any action. That he survived the disastrous financial Panic of 1819 and a bitter sectional struggle over the admission of Missouri as a slave state without apparent loss of popularity is one of the anomalies of American political history. Yet Monroe himself was in part responsible for this. In his desire to blot out party differences he followed a course entirely compatible with his temperament, accepting congressional solutions to perplexing problems.

Fortunately for the country, his immediate successors had more positive qualities, and the power of the president was not allowed to slip into the hands of congressional politicians. Monroe had achieved the miracle of a partyless administration, but it was an abnormality. American political life was too vigorous to long endure an Era of Good Feelings.

Monroe's terms are especially noted for two events. The first, a treaty with Spain in 1819, saw the United States assume control of all of Florida. The second, on December 2, 1823, was the Monroe Doctrine, in which the president declared that the Western Hemisphere was closed to colonization.

The Term of John Quincy Adams

The Missouri Compromise of 1820 removed the slavery question as a political issue in the 1820s, but a different kind of sectionalism, mostly involving protective tariff and internal improvements, was breaking down the one-party system and creating serious problems for ambitious political leaders.

New England, the Middle States, the Old South, and the Mississippi Valley West were pulling in different directions on these economic issues. Yankeedom was shifting its capital from foreign trade to manufacturing, but because the textile manufacturers were not yet dominant, the votes in Congress on the tariff were divided. New England opposed federal spending for roads and canals. The Middle States, Pennsylvania in particular, were protariff and pro-internal improvements, although New York, with its Erie Canal nearing completion, was less inclined to favor federal aid for such projects in other states.

The South was anti-tariff and anti-internal improvements. Both meant burdens on its cotton-slave economy, as its chief markets were across the Atlantic. The West, especially the Ohio Valley, opposed the South. It needed to develop a home market for its surplus food and raw materials and to obtain federal aid for transportation projects to end its isolation.

Five candidates, all Republicans, were in the presidential race soon after Monroe's second election. Robust, genial William H. Crawford of Georgia, secretary of the treasury, was the politician's candidate. He had the backing of old-line party leaders, New York's Albany Regency headed by Martin Van Buren, and a considerable federal officeholder support. He avoided commitments on the tariff, but his southern connections created the impression that he accepted that section's viewpoint.

Henry Clay, Speaker of the House, was the voice of the West, in arguing for protective tariff and internal improvements—his "American System." But this destroyed him in the Old South, and other obstacles appeared in his path in the East.

John Quincy Adams, in the State Department, confided his opinions of men and issues to his diary, but this lonely statesman drew the support of New England and the areas where transplanted Yankees lived, and where the slavery issue mattered, as he was the only northern candidate. His silence on tariff and internal improvements was used against him in the West. Secretary of War John C. Calhoun, with a past record of favoring both the controversial issues, had only his home state in the South but had high hopes of northern support, especially Pennsylvania, where he had cultivated party leaders.

Andrew Jackson, "Old Hickory," offered by the Tennessee legislature, was not taken seriously as a presidential candidate at first, even by himself. His early backers sought to use him to advance their own interests and weaken a rival faction, and were surprised to find they had on their hands a "people's candidate" who was winning widespread grass-roots support. Jackson held western views on tariff and internal improvements, as his Senate votes showed in 1823–24, but it was the man, not the issues, that mattered to his mushrooming following. In his West, he was soon a dangerous rival to Clay, and he took Pennsylvania from Calhoun when a state convention endorsed him, as Scotch-Irish and Germans were reported as "Jackson-mad." Calhoun then retired as a presidential candidate.

De Witt Clinton was out of power in New York, or he might have been a formidable contender, for "the Father of the Erie Canal" was highly regarded in states with canal projects.

In 1822 Crawford had seemed to be far in the lead. But two factors combined to wreck his candidacy before the electors were chosen. The first was a stroke of paralysis in September 1823. Despite efforts to conceal his condition, it became evident that his health was seriously impaired. For months he could not attend cabinet meetings and was unable to sign official papers. When he reappeared at Washington, he was but a shadow of his former self. "He walks slowly like a blind man," wrote an observer. "His feet were wrapped up with two or three thicknesses over his shoes, and he told me that they were cold and numb. His recollection seems to be good, and he conversed freely. But it is the general impression that a slight return of his disorder would prove fatal to him." This was in April 1824. He seemed to improve gradually, but Adams recorded in November that his articulation was still much affected and his eyesight impaired.

The second factor was not an unkind Providence but the blundering of Crawford's friends. In spite of every indication that the move would be unpopular, they called a congressional caucus to make him the official nominee. Of the 216 Republican members, only 66 attended, 2 others voting by proxy. New York, Virginia, Georgia, and North Carolina sent 48 members. Crawford was formally nominated, receiving 64 votes, while Albert Gallatin, close to him for many years and coming from the important state of Pennsylvania, was named for the vice-presidency.

The holding of the caucus was a strategic mistake. The friends of the other candidates stayed away, making it appear as a rump affair with no authority to voice the will of the old Republican Party. The chief effect was to direct against Crawford the guns of all his rivals, who eagerly presented the caucus as proof that he was an intriguer and a political manipulator who would achieve the presidency through the machinations of congressional politicians. Their charge was especially effective in the West, where the new democracy regarded party machinery as a means of perverting the popular will.

Jackson probably was the chief gainer, as he appeared to be most removed from party politics, and the Tennessee legislature had been the first to oppose the holding of a caucus. Clay, Jackson, Adams, and Calhoun had been nominated by state legislatures, though popular conventions had been held in some instances, as in Pennsylvania and Ohio.

Foreseeing that the election would go to the House unless the field could be further reduced, friends of the rival candidates tried to use the vice-presidency as a bait to eliminate an opponent. The Jackson and Calhoun men did arrange a joint ticket. Adams earlier had expressed approval of Jackson as his running mate, thinking that the second office would afford "an easy and dignified retirement to his old age."* The rapid growth of the Jackson movement ended such a scheme, and with no other possibility for second place, the Adams electors generally voted for Calhoun, thus giving him an easy victory. The Crawford men, seeing that Gallatin's name brought no strength to their ticket, induced him to withdraw in favor of Clay and intimated to the Kentuckian that Crawford might not live out his term, if elected. Clay thought too much of his own chances in the probable event of a House election to listen. In the end, Clay and Crawford electors scattered their votes for the second office.

Eighteen of the twenty-four states chose electors by popular vote; but among the six using the legislative method was vitally important New York. A clean sweep here would give the successful candidate a block of 36 electoral votes, ensure him at least second place in the national total,

* Adams was about four months younger than Jackson.

and add to his chances in the House of Representatives. The Albany Regency, refusing to permit a popular choice, expected to control the legislature for Crawford; but the popular uprising that elected Clinton governor weakened their hold and offered an opportunity for Clay and Adams. Thurlow Weed, a young Rochester newspaperman just winning his political spurs as an Adams strategist, outwitted the veteran politicians of the Regency and made a secret deal with some of the Clay men. When the vote was taken in the joint session of the two houses, in an atmosphere murky with duplicity and intrigue, Adams emerged with 26 electors; Crawford had 5, Clay had 4, while one preferred Jackson.

Weed had promised the Clay men enough electors to place their candidate among the three highest before the House but was unable to make good. Even so, Clay would have achieved that goal had he secured Louisiana. But a combination of Adams and Jackson men got control of the legislature of that state and divided the 5 electoral votes between them. The Kentuckian finished with only 37 electoral votes in all, four below Crawford, and was eliminated from consideration by the House.

The New York result was almost equally fatal to Crawford. Had he received the entire vote of that state, as Van Buren and the Regency expected, he would have finished well ahead of Adams and in a strong position to bargain for the support in the House of Representatives necessary to elect him. With but 41 electoral votes, the odds were very much against him. Adams with 84 and Jackson with 99 votes were the logical contenders for the House majority when the balloting began.*

Henry Clay had the hard choice of throwing his influence to one or the other of the two rivals he most cordially disliked, Adams and Jackson. (Crawford, because of the state of his health and his reputed hostility toward the economic policies favored by the West, was out of the question.) Clay had to choose either the cold, suspicious New Englander, with whom he had crossed swords in negotiating the Treaty of Ghent, or the frontier military idol, who had wrecked the Speaker's chances in the West with his own ambitions. While he delayed any public pronouncement, Clay actually had little difficulty in making up his mind. There was in reality but one possibility. That was Adams.

Clay had long regarded Jackson as utterly unfit for the presidency. How could a hot-tempered, dictatorial military chieftain with so little experience in civil office be seriously considered? He had seen Jackson's star rise with mingled anger and disgust and, it is possible, with no small amount of jealousy. What did Jackson know or care about tariff and inter-

* Throughout this edition we have used voting statistics from the Congressional Quarterly, *Presidential Elections Since 1789* (2nd ed.). The popular vote was as follows: Jackson, 151,271; Adams, 113,122; Crawford, 40,856; Clay, 47,531. But six states elected through legislatures, and in most of the others a light vote was cast. Not much significance can be given to the popular vote.

nal improvements and other western measures? Yet Clay's friends saw another problem in the elevation of Jackson: Would the country give the West a president soon again? He might have to wait many years for his turn.

Adams, the impulsive, warm-hearted Kentuckian respected, even though the strait-laced, aloof Puritan was as unlike him as any man could be. "Clay is essentially a gamester," Adams had confided to his diary on one occasion; and again, "His morals, public and private, are loose, but he has all the virtues indispensable to a popular man"; and more fairly, "Clay has large and liberal views of public affairs, and that sort of generosity that attaches individuals to his person." The "large and liberal views of public affairs" proved to be the bridge between the former rivals.

Yet Clay was not willing to walk into the Adams camp without pledges. He must inform himself as to the good intentions of his former rival and have at least some assurances as to the recognition he might receive from the new president. Intermediaries—Washington was full of busybodies trotting from one candidate to another—helped to arrange the preliminaries.

But, by chance, Clay and Adams were seated in adjacent chairs at the great Lafayette dinner given by the members of Congress on New Year's Day. When Adams showed unmistakable signs of thawing, the friendly Clay suggested a confidential conference "upon public affairs." Adams readily agreed, and a few days later—on Sunday evening—the two conferred. Denying any personal interest, Clay declared that he wished to be satisfied with regard to "some principles of great public importance." Adams's diary is cannily silent as to his own side of the conversation, but Clay made it clear that he was ready to support him in the coming House election. The die was cast. Thenceforth the two men were friends.

Yet Adams had other obstacles to overcome. Not all his visitors were as discreet as Clay. Missouri's lone congressman, with that state's vote in his hands, was concerned about his brother, an Arkansas territorial judge, who had killed a man in a duel. Adams avoided definite promises, but his general attitude assured the Missourian that the brother was safe from removal. Daniel Webster, worried lest Federalists be proscribed, conferred and was satisfied. This involved the vote of Maryland, where a Federalist held the balance of power.

One is surprised at the dexterity of Adams in playing the game. Possibly his diplomatic training stood him in good stead, or perhaps his conscience was being subjected to a process of liberal construction. Through his own efforts as well as Clay's, he seemed to be reasonably sure of the votes of the six New England states and of Maryland, Ohio, Kentucky, Illinois, Missouri, and Louisiana. He needed one more to win. Virginia and Delaware were possibilities on later ballots if Crawford were abandoned, but New York seemed to offer better prospects.

Seventeen of the thirty-four house members from New York were ready to vote for Adams; but the wily Van Buren, straining every effort to hold the Crawford lines intact, seemed to have the rest under his control. What his game was may only be conjectured. Did he plan to transfer his supporters to Adams on the second ballot and claim the honor of electing a president? Crawford's cause seemed hopeless, and Van Buren had as yet no liking for Jackson. His autobiography, written years later, is too disingenuous and is colored by his later relations with Jackson. Whatever his purpose, he seemed to be determined to prevent the election of Adams on the first ballot.

Van Buren's weak point in New York proved to be General Stephen Van Rensselaer, head of an aristocratic family. Elderly, religious, muddle-headed, and much disturbed at the crisis confronting him in the pressure of the Clintonians to support Jackson and of the Van Buren men to vote for Crawford, Van Rensselaer was taken into the Speaker's office by Clay and Webster on the morning of the election and told that the safety of the country depended on the choice of Adams on the first ballot. How an average human being, left alone with Henry Clay and Daniel Webster, could withstand their eloquent persuasiveness is past understanding; yet, according to Van Buren's account, written later, the general held out.

Then Providence—or the Adams's goddess of luck—intervened. As the vote was about to be taken, Van Rensselaer bowed his head in prayer, seeking divine guidance. It came at once. On the floor in front of him was a ticket someone had dropped with the name of John Quincy Adams written on it. His startled eyes rested on the bit of paper. A few moments later it was in the ballot box: New York had cast 18 of its 34 votes for Adams, and the New Englander was elected president by 13 of the 24 states. John C. Calhoun was the new vice president.

Crawford had Delaware, Virginia, North Carolina, and Georgia; Jackson, the remaining seven—New Jersey, Pennsylvania, South Carolina, Alabama, Mississippi, Tennessee, and Indiana. In five of the twelve Adams states a change of one vote would have cost him their support. Perhaps a prolonged deadlock would have been disastrous. Yet it is equally possible that much of the Crawford vote would have swung his way. Election on the first ballot without Crawford aid left that group under no compulsion to support the new administration. Van Buren had lost, but he was free to choose his future allies. The prospects for a clever staff officer in the swelling Jackson army soon decided his course.

The circumstances of the House election and Adams's appointment of Clay as his secretary of state seemed, to Jacksonians, to confirm the charge (which had already incited an angry controversy) that a corrupt bargain had made Adams president. Jackson wrote: "The Judas of the West has closed the contract and will receive the thirty pieces of silver." This and the fact that Jackson had received more popular votes than

Adams in the four-candidate race gave the Jacksonians their propaganda weapons for a campaign of vindication and vilification in 1828.

The overconscientious second Adams refused to play politics with the patronage, made only twelve removals, would not punish disloyalty, and kept in office a "neutral" postmaster general, John McLean, who was placed on the Supreme Court by Jackson in 1829. In his messages to Congress, Adams enunciated broad nationalistic policies, believing that the government should improve the condition of the governed, but his ideas as applied to internal improvements, education, and land policies affronted southern state-rights beliefs and western individualism.

The Days of Andrew Jackson

The heterogeneous opposition was held together only by the prospect of victory with Jackson. There was no unity on tariff and internal improvements; the ruling class in the older planting states did not like rubbing party shoulders with frontier farmers and urban workers; Crawford hated Calhoun but could not swallow Adams's nationalism. In New York, Martin Van Buren and the Albany Regency led the Crawford following into the Jackson camp; but De Witt Clinton had gotten there first. The factions battled at the polls as in the past, Clinton squeezing in as governor again and Van Buren returning to the Senate; but the embarrassing problem of Jacksonian leadership in the Empire State was solved by Clinton's death early in 1828.

In Congress every administration measure had to face a battery of political criticism. An Adams-Clay proposal to send delegates to a Panama congress of American republics was finally approved, but only after misrepresentation by critics of its purposes, with charges that the slave trade and recognition of the Negro Republic of Haiti would be discussed. With regard to internal improvements and the tariff, the Jacksonians, unable to offer a united front, voted the interests of their states and districts, and their candidate back in Tennessee was discreetly silent. In the case of the tariff, much maneuvering produced the political "Tariff of Abominations" of 1828, constructed by the Jacksonians to divide the Adams supporters sectionally. It was not intended to pass, but did by narrow margins. Its political effects were probably unimportant. The voters are not moved by economics when emotions are aroused.

As the election approached, personal abuse seemed to displace all other considerations. Adams men, angry at the vicious attacks upon the president for misuse of the patronage and the supposed bargain with Clay, retaliated by bringing up various acts of Jackson that showed a violent temper and a quarrelsome nature that unfitted him for the chief office. A Philadelphia editor, John Binns, printed the "Coffin Handbill"—a circular ornamented with coffins, which described purported acts of violence and brutality in Jackson's career.

But the *Cincinnati Gazette* and *Truth's Advocate*, a campaign paper—both edited by Charles Hammond, brilliant journalist and friend of Clay—capped the climax by reviving an old story that Jackson's marriage to Mrs. Jackson had occurred before her divorce from her first husband. Legally, the charge was justified; but both parties had been innocent of intentional wrongdoing, and a second ceremony had satisfied both the law and public opinion. Other papers copied the story, and it appeared in pamphlet form. Jackson was aroused to a white heat against Adams and Clay: Why had they not used their influence to suppress the slander? Social relations with the two were thereafter impossible.

Had Jackson followed his natural impulses, the printing of these stories might well have produced further acts of violence. Certainly his enemies hoped for some such result. But the Old Hero realized that he was no longer a private citizen, free to defend his own honor. A committee of friends at Nashville was set up to meet and refute all charges against him and to handle correspondence, while Duff Green, editor of the *Washington Telegraph*, Calhoun's organ, retaliated with counterslanders, even concocting a cruel canard that Adams, while minister to Russia, had been involved in bringing about the seduction of an American girl by the czar. A billiard table in the White House, privately purchased for the president's son, was said to have been paid for with public funds. Such a "gaming table," whether sinful or a mark of frivolity, was politically damaging.

The result of the election was foreordained. A new democracy, ignorant, impulsive, irrational, but rooted in the American soil, had its way in 1828. The protagonists of the old order fought not for John Quincy Adams, whom they could not love, but against the new monster, the common man, whom they feared. To a degree, the candidates were symbols of a renewal of the old conflict between popular rule and property rule. This intensified the bitterness and the mudslinging.

Adams had called himself a National-Republican, whereas Jackson had preferred Democratic-Republican to describe himself. By the 1830s, Jackson's supporters were calling themselves the Democratic Party; their opponents called themselves the Whig Party.

When the electoral votes were counted Andrew Jackson had 178; John Quincy Adams, 83. Adams had New England (except for one Maine elector), Delaware, New Jersey, 16 of New York's 36, and 6 of Maryland's 11. All the rest went to Jackson.* Only Delaware and South Carolina chose their electors through the legislature, and so the result was a genuine

* In this election Maine, New York, Maryland, and Tennessee used the district system; the other states (except South Carolina and Delaware) used a general ticket. Twenty-four states took part.

popular verdict. The total vote for Jackson was 642,553; for Adams, 500,897. Nearly half of Adams's total came from New England and New York. Clay's support brought to the ticket not a single western electoral vote; and only in 2 states in the West and South, Ohio and Louisiana, was the result even close. Calhoun won the vice-presidency over Richard Rush of Pennsylvania, but 7 of Georgia's 9 electors voted for William Smith of South Carolina, in a Crawford gesture of dislike for Calhoun.

IV

Democrats and Whigs

☆

1832-1852

JACKSON introduced the spoils system as a democratic reform, calling it "rotation in office." His removals of septuagenarian clerks with arthritic hands had some justification, but he introduced a new concept of service —that an officeholder's first loyalty was to his party. Thereafter, both major parties practiced the spoils system after each party change. Needy newspapermen fattened at the federal crib, and this helped to provide a loyal administration press.

Jackson's Second Term

As to policies, Jackson committed his party to opposition to federal aid for internal improvements, acceptance of a moderate protective tariff, removal to the West of the Indians of Georgia and its neighbors, and hostility toward the United States Bank.

More important than policies in its effects on the next presidential election was the break between Jackson and Vice-President Calhoun. This was a compound of several factors. One was Jackson's resentment at the snubbing of the bride of his good friend, Secretary of War John Eaton, by Mrs. Calhoun and wives of cabinet members because of rumors of premarital misconduct (the Peggy O'Neale affair). Another was Calhoun's pronouncement in favor of the idea of nullification as a constitutional method of dealing with protective tariff. A third was the belated revelation to Jackson that in 1818 Calhoun, then secretary of war, had been his critic, not his defender, when Jackson had invaded Spanish Florida. A fourth factor was the growing reliance of the president on Secretary of State Van Buren; and a final reason was the hostility of Jackson's inner circle (the "Kitchen Cabinet") to Calhoun. The Kitchen Cabinet was the

45

derogatory term given to Jackson's advisers—a group of friends to whom he turned for advice.

To get rid of the Calhounites, Jackson reconstructed his cabinet and sent Van Buren to England as American minister. He had been received in London when the Senate rejected the appointment by the casting vote of the vice-president. The break was now complete, and Van Buren moved into the role of heir apparent.

Three national conventions provided the candidates in 1832. A third party, the Antimasonic, held the first nominating convention, which met at Baltimore in September 1831. The Antimasons were the outgrowth of the mysterious disappearance of William Morgan of Batavia, New York, who was preparing a book to reveal the secrets of Masonry. Bitter opposition to the Masonic Order developed in western New York when the case remained unsolved. It affected local politics, and Antimasons were elected to the state legislature. The movement spread into New England, Pennsylvania, and northeastern Ohio, and national conventions of these opponents of secret orders were held in 1830 and 1831.

The second, guided by a coterie of anti-Jackson politicians headed by Thurlow Weed of New York and Thaddeus Stevens of Pennsylvania, nominated William Wirt, former attorney general, as its presidential candidate, after failing to get Justice John McLean to accept. Wirt, a former Mason, virtually repudiated the party's principles in his acceptance statement, but no other candidate was available. He would have withdrawn later if the National Republicans and Antimasons had been able to unite behind a single candidate to oppose Jackson, a Mason.

The old Adams-Clay party, assuming the name National Republican, held a convention in Baltimore in December 1831 and nominated Clay for president and John Sargent of Pennsylvania for vice-president. The delegates did not adopt a platform, but they favored the policies Clay had long been advocating, particularly protective tariff and internal improvements.

The Democratic-Republican (or Democratic) convention also met in Baltimore, in May 1832. Jackson had already been nominated by various state legislatures and conventions. The national convention was held to choose a candidate for vice-president. States were allotted their electoral votes regardless of the number of delegates present, and a two-thirds majority was required for a nomination.

One ballot made Van Buren the nominee with 208 of the 283 votes. This reflected the will of Jackson, for the "Little Magician" was none too popular in the South and West. The nickname referred to Van Buren's political ability and acumen.

By far the most stirring and significant event of the campaign was Jackson's veto of a bill to recharter the United States Bank. He had never been friendly toward the Bank, and his attitude should not have surprised anyone. Coming from a section that had had unfortunate experiences with banks and paper money, he hated "ragg, tagg banks" and inclined toward a hard-money currency. Ignorant of banking and often the victim of prejudices, he made little distinction between the "wildcat" banks of the West and the well-managed, highly centralized institution at Philadelphia under the efficient Nicholas Biddle. He disliked and feared the Bank, and it was easy for him to say, in bland disregard of John Marshall's decisions, that it was unconstitutional.

Jackson's first two annual messages raised the constitutional issue and questioned whether the Bank had established a uniform and sound currency. He suggested another type of institution "founded upon the credit of the Government and its revenues." Meanwhile, Biddle had established friendly relations with many politicians, was lending money to congressmen and editors, and had secured favorable reports from congressional investigating committees. In the new cabinet, Secretary of the Treasury Louis McLane was friendly, and only Attorney General Roger B. Taney was openly hostile.

The Bank's charter did not expire until 1836, and Biddle was not inclined to ask for a recharter before the election of 1832. Jackson's message of 1831 merely expressed a willingness to leave the matter to the investigation of an enlightened people and their representatives.

Henry Clay was not so willing. At first in favor of postponing the recharter question, he felt the need of a popular issue after his nomination —particularly one that would divide the Jacksonians. Biddle was wary, but after sounding out nearly everybody in Washington through a special agent, he accepted Clay's view that the omens were favorable. Congress would pass the bill, and Jackson would hardly dare veto it with the election so near. If he did, he would lose Pennsylvania, home of the Bank, and other eastern states, and Clay would win.

A recharter bill, in charge of a Calhounite in the House and a Jacksonian in the Senate, passed by safe margins, 107 to 85 and 28 to 20. Jackson met this challenge with a ringing veto message that blasted the Bank as monopolistic and unconstitutional. His arguments—or those of Taney, Kendall, and Donelson, who wrote the message—ranged all the way from the clear logic of the strict constructionist to the blatant appeals of the demagogue.

Biddle wrote to Clay that the veto had "all the fury of a chained panther, biting the bars of a cage. It is really a manifesto of anarchy." He even circulated it as a campaign document. With the business classes and two-thirds or more of the newspapers aroused against Jackson, the hopes of the Clay men ran high.

But the old Tennessean was wiser in the ways of the common man than Clay and Biddle and the whole army of financiers and businessmen who thought the voters would listen to reason and logic. Jackson's instincts told him that, sound or unsound, the Bank was a "Money Monster" and must be crushed, or it would crush democracy. The masses could understand his appeal, and their confidence in his judgment was unshaken.

Torchlight processions showed what they thought. The Bank spent heavily but could not stem the tide. Leading Bank Democrats, seeing the direction of the wind, hastened to make peace with Jackson. Pennsylvania, whose Democratic legislature had urged recharter, remembered only its old loyalty to Jackson. George M. Dallas, who had introduced the Bank bill in the Senate, declared for the Old Hero, "bank or no bank."

In the face of these portents of a Jackson victory, the opposition attempted to unite. Coalition electoral tickets were arranged in New York, Pennsylvania, and Ohio, with the understanding that the electors, if successful, should vote so as to bring about the defeat of Jackson. Whether this meant Clay or Wirt, no one could tell. Calhoun took no part in the election, but many of his southern friends supported Clay.

Yet the result was even more overwhelming than in 1828. Clay won his home state of Kentucky and Massachusetts, Rhode Island, Connecticut, Delaware, and 5 electors from Maryland, the only state to use the district system—a total of 49 electoral votes. Antimason Wirt had Vermont's 7. South Carolina, through her legislature, chose 11 electors who voted for John Floyd of Virginia. Jackson had 219; Van Buren, 189, as Pennsylvania's vote for vice-president went to William Wilkins.* The popular vote is difficult to estimate because of the fusion electoral tickets in some states, but Jackson's majority over both his opponents was at least 100,000 in a total vote well over 1,200,000.

State and National Conventions

The emergence of the national convention in 1832 was part and parcel of the democratizing of politics that had begun long before. Party nominations for local offices had produced the convention system in the early 1800s, when it began to supersede the more or less haphazard methods of self-nomination common in the South and the mass meeting or nomination by the candidate's friends used in the North. The Federalists, generally disdaining party machinery and democratic innovations, left to their Republican opponents the establishing of extralegal methods of voicing the will of the voters.

In the Middle States the county convention first came into general use.

* The popular vote was: Jackson, 701,780; Clay, 484,205; and Wirt, 100,715.

In New England the town (township) was the chief political unit, and the town meeting of the voters served for most purposes. But in the Middle States, where county officials were elected by the voters and party unity was necessary for success at the polls, the delegate county convention was a logical outgrowth of the local mass meetings or primaries.

In the early 1800s Delaware and New Jersey Republicans also developed the state convention. Physical obstacles to statewide meetings were not serious in these small states, and county conventions were already functioning. In Delaware Federalist use of this Republican device may help explain the persistence of Federalism after it ceased to function elsewhere.

The use of a party caucus of members of the legislature retarded the development of the convention system for state nominations in other northern states, though occasionally the caucus was modified by the introduction of delegates from counties where the party was unrepresented in the general assembly, making it a "mixed caucus."

With improvements in transportation and with the growing distrust of the masses of new voters for the undemocratic caucus system, the state convention came into its own outside the South in the 1820s. The national convention, for the same reasons, made its appearance in the 1830s to fulfill a need that the old congressional caucus and the state legislative or state convention nominations of presidential candidates could not supply.

It was representative in character; it divorced nominations from congressional control and added to the independence of the executive; it permitted an authoritative formulation of a party program; and it concentrated the party's strength behind a single ticket, the product of a compromise of personal rivalries and group or sectional interests. Despite its defects, less evident then than later, it has remained fundamentally unchanged in general structure through well over a century of usage.

Yet, compared with the modern national convention, the early nominating body showed certain irregularities or imperfections. Delegates were chosen in a variety of ways—by state conventions, district conventions, local meetings, informal caucuses—dependent on the organization and strength of the party in each state. A national convention might even recognize as delegates visitors in attendance from a state that sent no delegates.

Edward Rucker cast the entire vote of unrepresented Tennessee in the national Democratic gathering of May 1835 because he happened to be in Baltimore and was a Van Buren man. At this gathering 181 sons of Maryland appeared as delegates from that state. In the Whig national convention of 1848, the Louisiana delegates cast both their own votes and those of Texas because a Texas Whig convention had given them its proxies.

Distance or lack of interest kept some states from sending delegates to the early Whig and Democratic conventions, while the gatherings of antislavery parties were sectional in character and attracted few southerners. From the beginning, however, the major parties limited the voting strength of a state in the national convention to its electoral vote, regardless of oversize delegations or other irregularities.

With the development of a system of committees to accompany this hierarchy of conventions, all unrecognized by the laws, the party organization began its rule of politics and, indirectly, of government itself. Ostensibly this was done as the representative of the voting masses, but actually it developed into a powerful oligarchy of professionals intent on carrying elections and maintaining the party in power.

As a necessary adjunct, the party press flourished as never before. In a state capital the faithful editor of the majority organ expected to receive the public printing of the state government, just as F. P. Blair at Washington benefited from the Jackson administration. The Blair family was subsequently to become more involved in politics. In the county seats, plums in federal or state civil service or nominations for local elective offices rewarded the editor-printer of the county partisan newspaper, whose struggle for subsistence usually kept him a bare jump ahead of his creditors. In time it came to be almost a tradition in many localities that he should operate the post office for the four years following a national victory.

The Whigs, like the old Federalists, somewhat standoffish toward the masses, soon copied Democratic practices, and the later antislavery Republicans took over and improved upon the methods of both. The president found himself the chief dispenser of favors for his party. He was also its national leader, whether he relished the role or not. More than ever, the presidency became a political office, with its control the great aim of each party. Candidates were nominated by conventions of politicians who made availability their prime consideration. More often than not, the nominees were either secondary figures in public life or popular military men. Yet the results were surprisingly good, despite such dubious choices as Pierce, Buchanan, and Frémont.

An Alliance of Conservatives

Jackson's mastery of his party after his triumphant reelection forced dissenters to conform or depart. The opposition gained recruits, especially over two Jacksonian stands: his determination to use force against South Carolina in the nullification struggle of 1832–33 and his renewal of his war on the United States Bank.

Clay, forming an entente with Calhoun in the Senate, was able to end the nullification crisis with his compromise tariff, which both sides accepted. Senator Daniel Webster of Massachusetts who had stood with Jackson on nullification, turned against him when he forced the removal of government deposits from the Bank. The Senate's Great Triumvirate secured the passage of a resolution of censure and led a heterogeneous opposition to "King Andrew's executive usurpations."

Under a broad umbrella, National-Republicans, Antimasons, bank Democrats, and state-rights men, mostly southerners, drew together in a conservative alliance against this tribune of the people who was too radical on currency and other economic matters and too high-handed in using the powers of his office. They adopted the name Whig because it had been used in the American Revolution by the opposition to royal tyranny.

The Whigs insisted that they were true Jeffersonians in constitutional theory. They emphasized the supremacy of the legislative branch and criticized Jackson's free use of the veto power. In effect, they argued for an adulterated parliamentary system with a weak executive and the real power in the hands of congressional leaders. But too much can be made of constitutional theories. The Whigs, like the wealthier classes on other occasions, raised a hue and cry about destruction of the Constitution by the president because his policies threatened their interests. Executive power was dangerous because Jackson was president.

The election of 1836 was a testing time for the Whigs. It was considered inexpedient to hold a national convention, and this left the leaders in each state free to offer local favorites. In New England Daniel Webster, representing the economic views of the National Republicans, and on friendly terms with the Antimasons, had strong claims. But, as a former Federalist and the paid attorney of the United States Bank, he was too vulnerable to Democratic shafts, and his hopes elsewhere were dashed by the failure of the Pennsylvania Antimasons to endorse him.

Their state convention committed itself to General William Henry Harrison of Ohio, a hero of the War of 1812 and a man of considerable political experience, not hitherto regarded as of presidential caliber. Because of financial reverses, he was then holding the position of clerk of the courts in Cincinnati. Availability was the keynote of his candidacy, for he was popular in the West, had been a Jeffersonian in other days, and had no damning record on national questions. John McLean, kept aloof from party controversies by his position on the Supreme Court, had the support of a number of Whig leaders in Ohio and Pennsylvania; and friends in the Ohio legislature nominated him in 1835, but the movement went no further. The western states were taking up the popular Harrison.

The Democratic legislature of Tennessee furnished a candidate for the Whigs in the South when it nominated Senator Hugh L. White, only recently estranged from Jackson. The Alabama legislature took similar action, and an independent Democratic movement for White was soon under way all through the South, as he was a moderate state-rights man. Van Buren, the "Little Magician," was not popular in this section, and all Jackson's efforts could not bring him a united Democratic support. Except in the border states, where Harrison was favored, the southern Whigs endorsed White electoral tickets.

Meanwhile a Democratic national convention in Baltimore, packed with federal officeholders, had nominated Van Buren in May 1835. There was no opposition, but Jackson's choice for vice-president, Colonel Richard M. Johnson of Kentucky, barely received the two-thirds vote required. Johnson, a genial politician and war veteran, reputed slayer of Tecumseh, and long-time foe of imprisonment for debt, provided western balance for the ticket.

But he had lived with a mulatto woman, now dead, and had two daughters, whom he educated and presented socially. Such disregard of southern social conventions made him of doubtful value to the head of the ticket, and the Virginia delegation greeted his nomination with hisses.

Whig strategy aimed to defeat Van Buren by running sectional favorite sons and throwing the election to the House, where Harrison or White might be chosen. As Biddle put it, "This disease is to be treated as a local disorder—apply local remedies." The scheme failed chiefly because the might of Jackson was behind Van Buren, who received 170 electoral votes to Harrison's 73 (Vermont, New Jersey, Delaware, Maryland, Kentucky, Ohio, Indiana). White received 26 (Tennessee, Georgia), Webster, 14 (Massachusetts).*

The South Carolina legislature, hostile to White because he had voted for the Force Bill in the nullification crisis, chose eleven electors who voted for Willie P. Mangum of North Carolina. R. M. Johnson had 147 votes for vice-president, one under a majority; the northern Whig states cast 77 votes for Francis Granger of New York; Democratic Virginia gave its 23 votes to William Smith of Alabama; and South Carolina, Georgia, Tennessee, and Maryland cast 47 votes for Whig John Tyler of Virginia. The Senate, for the only time in American history, chose the vice-president, Johnson receiving 33 votes, Granger 16.

The Whigs had cause to feel encouraged. Unlike Clay in 1832, they had polled a large southern vote. They had carried two Jacksonian strongholds, Georgia and Tennessee, and three border slave states, and had given Van Buren a close race elsewhere. Furthermore, Harrison's good showing in the Ohio Valley states and in Pennsylvania, which he lost by 4,300 votes, stamped him as a good prospect for 1840. The opposition groups were on the way to becoming a party.

* The popular vote was: Van Buren, 764,176; Harrison, 550,816; White, 146,107; and Webster, 41,201.

The Panic of 1837

Within two months of Van Buren's inauguration came the collapse of the nation's overexpanded credit system—the Panic of 1837. The Whigs blamed the policies of the Jackson administration for the collapse and demanded that Van Buren take steps to solve the problems of the years of depression that followed.

Van Buren held to a laissez-faire position. The government had not caused the panic, and things would have to right themselves. He did favor an independent treasury system to protect the government from involvements with banks. In the future only gold and silver would be accepted as currency by the federal government. Not until near the end of his term did his proposal become law. Many supporters of state banks went over to the Whigs.

In New York a group of labor-oriented radicals—popularly called Locofocos—who had formed an equal-rights party, liked Van Buren's opposition to corporate monopolies and came to his support. The term Locofoco was applied gleefully by the Whigs to all Democrats for many years afterward.

Calhoun, satisfied with Van Buren's narrow concept of federal powers, returned to the Democratic Party. Little Van neither looked nor acted the part of a presidential dictator.

Van Buren's control over his party was unquestioned, and he was renominated by the Democratic national convention, meeting in Baltimore in May 1840. "Tecumseh" Johnson was denied a renomination. Reports from Kentucky indicated that he was continuing to ignore the color line in his social relations. No one was recommended for vice-president. A platform—the first in Democratic history—endorsed the Jackson-Van Buren principles and policies.

The Whigs had already held their national convention at Harrisburg in December 1839, with three candidates in the running. Clay believed that he deserved the nomination for his services to the party and had a large southern following. But important Whig politicos in New York, Pennsylvania, and Ohio regarded his long record as an inviting target for Democratic arrows. Weed in New York backed General Winfield Scott, but Stevens in Pennsylvania and the Ohio and Indiana delegation liked General William Henry Harrison, who had run well in 1836. Clay led on the first ballot, but after a number of ballots and some backstairs maneuvering, the Scott forces shifted to Harrison, and he was nominated. John Tyler of Virginia, a Clay supporter, was named for vice-president, leading to the slogan "Tippecanoe and Tyler too." Wisely, the convention made no platform.

The result at first did not seem to augur victory. Clay, disappointed as deeply as a man can be who sees the ambition of years thwarted at the moment of achievement, found liquor and profanity a temporary outlet but not a solace. "It is a diabolical intrigue, I know now, which has betrayed me. I am the most unfortunate man in the history of parties: always run by my friends when sure to be defeated, and now betrayed for a nomination when I, or any one, would be sure of an election."

Whether the friend who reported these words quoted him correctly or not, they picture the state of mind of the man who had been most instrumental in creating the party that now rejected him. He had been shabbily treated, but he should not have been surprised. The northern politicians, and behind them the conservative business interests, wanted victory. They could win by an appeal to the democratic masses. Clay was not their man.

The key to victory was furnished by the Democrats. With incredible stupidity a Baltimore newspaper correspondent disparagingly suggested that Harrison be given "a barrel of hard cider and a pension of two thousand a year, and, our word for it, he will sit the remainder of his days in a log cabin by the side of a 'sea coal' fire and study moral philosophy." A Harrisburg Whig sensed the possibilities in the statement, and the sneer became the slogan. Harrison thenceforth was "the log-cabin, hard-cider" candidate, the simple man of the frontier pitted against the New York aristocrat living in splendor amid the luxuries of the White House.

The arguments for Jackson in 1828 could now be used for Harrison, the frontier soldier. Glossed over were his aristocratic Virginia ancestry, his political activities in Ohio, his years of officeholding and officeseeking. He became the simple soldier-farmer of North Bend who would restore government to the people. His substantial country home was metamorphosed into a pioneer's log cabin.

Conventions and mass meetings, parades and processions with banners and floats, long speeches on the log-cabin theme, log-cabin songbooks and log-cabin newspapers, Harrison pictures, Tippecanoe handkerchiefs and badges, log-cabin headquarters at every crossroads, with the latchstring out and hard cider always on tap—all these devices and more were used to arouse enthusiasm that soon surpassed anything the nation had ever experienced. Crowds of unheard-of proportions turned out for Whig rallies. Ten acres of people (numbers would not suffice) were reported present at a Dayton, Ohio, jamboree.

The Democrats also held meetings and parades but, with an unaccountable display of moral rectitude, rejected hard cider and posed as the party of virtue. Democratic orators attempted to discuss the issues and—of all things—to belittle Harrison's war record when Van Buren had none. Old Andrew Jackson, on the stump in Tennessee, committed this faux pas.

Evading any expression of his bank views except to say that he favored paper money, Harrison talked in crowd-pleasing generalities at a soldiers' rally at Fort Meigs and made briefer speeches confined to Ohio. A Cincinnati committee handled all the correspondence. Whig orators assailed Van Buren's aristocracy with stories of gold spoons in the White House and a gilded coach and the trappings of British royalty.

When issues were discussed, the hard times were played up, the independent treasury was attacked, and, to alarm state-rights men, a proposal by Secretary of War Poinsett to federalize the state militia was exposed as monarchical centralization and executive usurpation. But always the Whig orators returned to the log-cabin theme. Even imposing Daniel Webster, without log-cabin nativity, claimed its virtues by association, through his older brother and sisters.

In the cotton South, Whig tactics were more moderate. Here businessmen and planters, indifferent to log cabins and much concerned about slavery, were assured that Harrison's membership in an antislavery society years before had been a youthful indiscretion, and the candidate himself declared against congressional interference with their institution. He was pictured as an antique Jeffersonian Republican in contrast with the corruptionists who controlled the Democratic Party. Clay recovered from his sulk and did yeoman service in selling Harrison's merits to the South. Even in Georgia, where a State-Rights Party had operated independently, the Whig candidate was finally accepted.

In the northern cities businessmen used economic pressure for the "Hero of Tippecanoe." Workingmen were warned of the dangers of continued low wages and unemployment if Van Buren should win; prosperity would return if he were defeated. "The subscriber will pay five dollars a hundred for pork if Harrison is elected, and two and a half if Van Buren is," So ran an advertisement in a New York paper.

But song and hard cider were better arguments than fear. One of the most popular ditties tells the story:

> What has caused this great commotion, motion,
> > Our country through?
> > It is the ball a-rolling on,
> For Tippecanoe and Tyler too, Tippecanoe and Tyler too.
> And with them we'll beat the little Van, Van, Van;
> > Van is a used-up man.

More expressive was this:

> > Old Tip he wears a homespun suit,
> > He has no ruffled shirt-wirt,wirt;
> > But Mat he has the golden plate,
> > And he's a little squirt-wirt-wirt.

Tobacco chewers would spit when they came to the "wirt."

And so Van Buren was sung and drunk out of the White House and back to Kinderhook in New York. One of the most sincerely democratic of presidents was overborne by a wave of popular enthusiasm for a log-cabin myth. Marching in the Whig ranks with simple artisans and rustic cultivators were bankers, merchants, landed gentry, mill owners, speculators—for the log-cabin cult, spreading through the land, had a. motley membership. The rich and the wellborn had at last learned that in politics the votes of the humble were not to be despised. "The Goths have taken Rome," wailed Thomas Ritchie, Virginia editor. But he did not add the bitter explanation that they had borrowed their weapons and their tactics from the Romans.

The electoral votes indicated a landslide. To Van Buren went only 60 votes (Virginia, South Carolina, Alabama, Missouri, Illinois, Arkansas, New Hampshire) out of 294. The popular vote was less conclusive: 1,275,390 for Harrison, 1,128,854 for Van Buren. Both houses of Congress were won by the Whigs. Tyler had the same electoral vote as Harrison, but R. M. Johnson had 12 fewer than Van Buren. South Carolina cast 11 for L. W. Tazewell of Virginia, while one Virginia elector voted for James K. Polk of Tennessee.

Tyler Assumes the Presidency

Harrison's death from pneumonia a month from the day of his inauguration brought John Tyler, reared in the Virginia state-rights school, into the presidency. Clay, already at odds with Harrison over patronage matters, assumed the role of Senate leader and unofficial prime minister when Congress met in special session. He offered his "American System," a program of measures covering the old trinity of banking, tariff, and internal improvements, which the Whig majorities in both Houses accepted.

Tyler, affronted at both the program, which ran counter to his constitutional scruples, and Clay's imperious assumption of leadership, vetoed a bill for a third United States Bank. A modified bank measure designed to meet his objections was then passed, but it, too, was rejected. The Whig caucus followed Clay's leadership and denounced Tyler as a party traitor, but only a watered-down version of Clay's original program was finally enacted. "His Accidency" had turned the log-cabin victory into ashes, but he had held staunchly to his principles.

But Tyler was ambitious for another term and, as an expansionist, was concerned about British interest in the Republic of Texas, still unrecognized by Mexico. After some secret negotiations he surprised the Senate with a treaty of annexation in late April 1844. That slavery existed in Texas had been a major obstacle to annexation since the birth of the Lone

Star Republic. Now, with a presidential campaign impending, a critical sectional issue confronted party leaders.

The leading candidates of both parties thought the problem had been solved when each wrote a letter for publication opposing annexation. Clay's letter, written at Raleigh, North Carolina, was more forthright, but Van Buren's wordy explanation of his position was more damaging to his prospects. Annexationists in the Democratic Party set out to keep the nomination from him, even though a majority of the delegates were already pledged to him.

Led by Robert J. Walker of Mississippi and aided by disloyal Van Buren delegates, they were able to secure the adoption of the two-thirds rule by the national convention when it met in Baltimore on May 27. Van Buren had a majority on the first ballot, but his vote declined on later trials and a deadlock resulted. On the ninth ballot a "dark horse," James K. Polk of Tennessee, former Speaker of the House and former governor of his state, was nominated.

For vice-president, George M. Dallas of Pennsylvania was the choice after Senator Silas Wright of New York, friend of Van Buren, turned down the nomination. The platform coupled the "re-occupation of Oregon and the re-annexation of Texas." It was a shrewd bid for expansionist support in both the North and the South, but the Oregon and Texas questions involved Great Britain and Texas, respectively.

England and the United States had both laid claim to the Oregon territory, and now many Americans demanded all land south of the line 54° 40′—"Fifty-four Forty or Fight."

On March 2, 1836, after a series of battles with Mexico, the territory of Texas declared itself the Republic of Texas. It later asked for admission to the United States, and this was finally achieved in 1845.

Meanwhile, the Whigs had nominated Clay and Senator Theodore Frelinghuysen of New Jersey at Baltimore earlier in May. The brief platform was vaguely conservative but did not mention the United States Bank or Texas. Clay's Raleigh letter was clear enough on the Texas issue.

Unexpectedly Van Buren had lost the Democratic nomination, and Clay faced the expansionist Polk on a platform that threatened to make heavy inroads into his southern strength. In general, the Whigs of the South had rallied loyally to Clay, and in the Senate all but one had voted against Tyler's Texas treaty. The large planters and their business allies, except speculators in Texas land, had no stomach for war with Mexico and a stirring up of sectional hatred. "The Union without Texas rather than Texas without the Union," was their slogan.

But the powerful appeal of Texas to the land-hungry small farmers and even to some planters, plus the argument of Calhoun that it was necessary to save the institution of slavery, played havoc with Clay's hopes.

He began to soften the views of his Raleigh letter and in two letters to Alabama friends made it clear that he had no objection to annexation accomplished without dishonor, without war, with the common consent of the Union, and upon just and fair terms. He would be guided as president "by the state of facts, and the state of public opinion existing at the time I might be called upon to act." The letters encouraged his southern friends, but they damaged him in the North.

Here the abolitionist Liberty Party darkened the Whig sky. It had run a candidate, James G. Birney, in 1840 but had been lost sight of in the log-cabin hullabaloo. Birney had polled some seven thousand votes. But the party had gained recruits and newspaper support since then and was becoming a threat to the major parties in close northern states, where it aimed to swing the balance of power. A national convention at Buffalo in August 1843 named Birney, now a Michigan resident, and Thomas Morris of Ohio as its ticket. When Texas became a major issue, the Liberty Party was in a difficult position. A heavy third-party vote might reduce the Whig vote in the doubtful northern states and elect expansionist Polk over Clay, committed against Texas.

The Liberty Party leaders, chiefly enthusiasts and fanatics, had little use for Clay under any circumstances; but their opposition would have mattered less had Clay not wavered on annexation. He attempted in September to return to his Raleigh letter position, undoing some of the damage. Whig hopes rose in October when the news spread that Birney had accepted a Democratic nomination for the Michigan legislature—seeming proof of a Liberty-Democratic bargain to defeat Clay. Birney attempted to explain it on the ground of purely local issues, but did openly admit his preference for Polk over Clay for the amazing reason that the latter, far more able, might lead his party to bring about annexation, while Polk was too incompetent to accomplish it.

The effect was damaging to the Liberty Party and was made more so by a forged letter, appearing in Whig newspapers a day or two before the election, in which Birney promised not to agitate the slavery question in the Michigan legislature. His refutation of it came too late. The Liberty Party lost hundreds of votes. But its power in New York still proved decisive.

Yet expansion and slavery were not the sole issues on which the election turned. Texas and Oregon might be Democratic vote-getters in the South and the West, but protectionist Pennsylvania, as important as New York in Democratic strategy, had to be propitiated in other ways. A letter from Polk to John K. Kane of Philadelphia made it clear that he favored a revenue tariff with only incidental protection, but his ardent supporters in the Keystone State used it to prove that he was as good a tariff man as Clay. "Polk, Dallas and the Tariff of '42" was their slogan.

Organized Native Americanism, based on being antiforeigner and anti-Catholic, also appeared locally in New York and Pennsylvania, with both parties angling for its support without the curse of its blessing. The Whigs had the advantage here, for the foreign-born were generally Democrats. An antiforeign American Republican Party, which had gained some local successes, endorsed Clay and Frelinghuysen. The latter had been active in Protestant evangelical movements, such as the American Bible Society and foreign missions, which weakened Whig appeal to Irish Catholics. The Democrats accused the Whigs of allying with the "church-burning" nativists, and countered by speeding up the naturalization of Irish and German newcomers in the East.

Both candidates were victims of slander and mudslinging. All Clay's chickens came home to roost. He was branded a gambler, a duelist, a profane swearer, a corrupt bargainer. Democratic newspapers printed an alleged letter of a Protestant minister who had traveled on a steamboat with him and bore witness to Clay's free use of strong language and his love of cards. Polk's character was quite exemplary, but Whig journals carried a story that a traveler had observed a gang of slaves being marched to a slave auction in Tennessee, each one branded with the letters "J.K.P." It purported to be an extract from a certain Roorback's account of a tour of the South and West. Democratic defenders of Polk exposed the story as a Whig fabrication and the name "roorback" passed into the American political vocabulary for a preelection falsehood. One way of belittling the Democratic standard-bearer was to repeat the question many Americans asked just after his nomination: "Who is James K. Polk?" Tom Corwin, popular Whig stump speaker, added, "After that, who is safe?"

The election revealed that the relatively obscure Polk had defeated his more illustrious opponent, 170 electoral votes to 105.* Clay had carried only Ohio in the expansion-minded Northwest and only the upper tier of slave states in the South (North Carolina, Tennessee, Kentucky, Maryland, and Delaware). In the East, Massachusetts, Rhode Island, Connecticut, Vermont, and New Jersey gave him their votes. The South and the West had voted for Texas and Oregon, but Polk also had Pennsylvania and New York by narrow margins. Clay needed New York's 36 electors to win. Birney had 15,812 popular votes in that crucial state. One-third of that number added to Clay's total would have meant victory. Had he not wavered on the Texas issue, he might have gained these antislavery votes.

But there is another side to the picture. His concessions to southern sentiments on Texas possibly tilted the balance to him in Tennessee. His margin there was only 113 votes. Defeat in Tennessee even with victory

* The popular vote was as folows: Polk, 1,339,494; Clay, 1,300,004; Birney, 62,103.

in New York would have lost him the election. Tyler, in throwing Texas into the campaign, had confronted Clay with a problem he could not solve, so long as the Liberty Party warred on the Whig flanks.

It was his misfortune that his presidential candidacies ran counter to the two most powerful forces in the America of his generation: Jacksonian democracy and territorial expansion. One might add a third, just beginning to build up—European immigration. Millard Fillmore, himself the losing candidate for governor of New York, wrote that the abolitionists and the foreign Catholics had defeated Clay.

While the importance of Texas had tended to give Polk's victory the aspect of a southern triumph, the result in 1844 was more nearly an endorsement of a general expansionist program. The West, as ever, was land hungry, and the Democrats had pointed the way by linking Oregon and Texas. Locofoco reformism had been diverted into a new channel that was to lead the Democratic Party southward, as Thomas Hart Benton of Missouri and Van Buren sensed; but the South was not yet in the saddle. To the West Polk was the heir of Old Hickory and was sometimes called "Young Hickory." Jackson was his mentor, not Calhoun.

President Polk and Manifest Destiny

Drab, secretive, hard-working James K. Polk was not a popular president, but he left behind him a record of accomplishing every one of his major objectives. On the domestic front, he was able to secure the restoration of the independent treasury and a lowering of tariff rates. In foreign affairs he completed the annexation of Texas, approved by joint resolution of Congress after his election. He secured a treaty for the division of the disputed Oregon country with England. His attempts to solve the Texas boundary problem and to purchase California failed, and he was largely responsible for the Mexican War, which followed the breakdown of his diplomacy. But it resulted in the addition of the vast California-New Mexico southwest to the United States. All this seemed part of "Manifest Destiny"—a belief held by many Americans that the United States should possess the entire continent.

In the midst of the Mexican War David Wilmot of Pennsylvania introduced in Congress his famous Proviso forbidding slavery in any territory to be obtained from Mexico. It passed the House but failed in the Senate. Both parties were now confronted with a serious sectional division with the election of 1848 impending.

In the Democratic camp a New York split over patronage and local issues had produced two warring factions, the Barnburners and the Hunkers. The more liberal Barnburners came out in favor of the Wilmot Proviso and appealed for antislavery support. The two factions held separate state conventions and sent separate sets of delegates to the national convention, which met in Baltimore on May 22. The convention voted, by a bare majority of two, to seat both delegations. Both rejected the solution, and New York was unrepresented.

Senator Lewis Cass of Michigan and General William O. Butler of Kentucky received the party's nominations. Cass was named on the fourth ballot. A cautious elder statesman—called a "doughface"* because he had opposed the Wilmot Proviso—he had declared for "squatter sovereignty" in a territory, which would leave the decision on slavery to the voters. The platform defended the Mexican War and praised the work of the Polk administration. Polk had refused to run for another term.

The Whigs had become critics of the Mexican War and had taken a position opposing any acquisitions of territory as productive of sectional discord. But the successful termination of the war left this program high and dry.

When they held their convention in Philadelphia on June 7, they were presented with the choice of 1840: two generals and a statesman—Zachary Taylor, Winfield Scott, and Clay, now seventy-one but still ready to battle for the prize that had eluded him so long. But a strong southern contingent and some northern politicians on the lookout for a winner were backing Taylor, and he was nominated on the fourth ballot. Millard Fillmore of New York balanced the ticket as his running mate. No platform was adopted.

Taylor, "Old Rough and Ready," a Louisiana slaveholder who had never voted, had been acclaimed for his early victories in the Mexican War, and had been ready to run as an independent when the Whigs took him over. Daniel Webster called him "an illiterate frontier colonel" and a group of antislavery Whigs prepared to bolt the nomination.

The situation seemed to call for a new antislavery party as both the major parties had ignored the Wilmot Proviso. The Liberty Party, which had already nominated John P. Hale of New Hampshire, the bolting Barnburners and their sympathizers, and many "Conscience Whigs" joined to send delegates to a convention held in a big tent in Buffalo in August. They organized the Free Soil Party, which was pledged to oppose the extension of slavery and to open the public lands to free homesteaders. Ex-president Van Buren, choice of the Barnburners, defeated Hale for the presidential nomination. A Conscience Whig, Charles Francis Adams of Massachusetts, son of John Quincy Adams, was named to run with him.

The Free-Soilers waged a strenuous campaign to attract antislavery Whigs and Van Buren Democrats. With the former they were less successful. Though the Conscience Whigs in Massachusetts and Joshua R.

* A doughface was a congressman from a northern state who was not opposed to slavery in the South.

Giddings and his following in Ohio lent aid, William H. Seward of New York and Tom Corwin of Ohio took the stump to allay antislavery dissatisfaction in Whig ranks. Van Buren's name had no attractions for northern Whigs, and many, doubting his sincerity, were persuaded that Taylor's opposition to the veto power would permit the Wilmot Proviso to become law if Congress passed it.

The Free Soil movement played havoc with the New York Democrats but did only slight damage elsewhere. Former Governor Marcus Morton of Massachusetts favored Van Buren but not the third party. Cass was popular in the Northwest, where he was not regarded as proslavery, and held most of the Democrats in line. He was the first Democratic presidential candidate from that section, and it proved loyal to him.

Both the major parties fought sectional, rather than national, campaigns. The Whigs of the South argued that southern rights were secure only if a southerner sat in the White House. The Democrats defended Cass as "safe" on slavery and warned that Taylor might die in office, bringing Fillmore, possessor of an antislavery past, into the White House. In view of what actually happened, this has a curious significance. In the North, Democrats praised Cass as faithful to northern interests and asked how antislavery Whigs could stomach Taylor. The Whig answer was to call Cass a doughface and to argue that the North would control a Whig Congress.

The election, the first to be held on the same day everywhere, gave Taylor 163 electoral votes, Cass 127. Taylor carried Massachusetts, Vermont, Connecticut, Rhode Island, New York, Pennsylvania, and New Jersey in the North; the usual Whig states in the upper South (Delaware, Maryland, Tennessee, Kentucky, and North Carolina) and Georgia, Louisiana, and Florida in the lower South. Cass carried Maine, New Hampshire, all of the Northwest (Ohio, Indiana, Illinois, Michigan, Wisconsin, Iowa), and seven slave states (Missouri, Arkansas, Texas, Alabama, Mississippi, Virginia, and South Carolina).

Taylor ran well in the usual Whig areas of the South and gained noticeably over Clay's vote of 1844 in the small-farmer sections, where his personality seemed to be reminiscent of Andrew Jackson. Pennsylvania, disgruntled over Polk's revenue tariff, and New York, lost through the Barnburner bolt, bitterly disappointed the Democrats. In New York, Taylor received 218,603 votes; Cass, 114,318; Van Buren, 120,510. A united Democracy apparently could have defeated Taylor, though it must not be forgotten that a Liberty Party vote was concealed in the Van Buren total and might, as in 1844, have held the balance. Taylor's pluralities were generally larger than those for Cass and his popular vote totaled 1,361,393 to his rival's 1,223,460 and Van Buren's 291,501.

The Free-Soilers, though their vote fell below their early expectations, had the satisfaction of holding the balance of power in eleven states and in the national House of Representatives, where they won thirteen seats. The Ohio legislature, controlled by a coalition of Free-Soilers and Democrats, sent Salmon P. Chase, Free-Soiler, to the United States Senate.

Clay's Compromise of 1850

Henry Clay, fearing that the Union was in grave danger, returned to his old Senate seat in December 1849, and offered his famous Compromise of 1850 to appease sectional grievances. In brief, it included the admission of California as a free state, the creation of two territories out of the New Mexico area, with no mention of slavery, the enactment of a stronger fugitive slave law, the abolishment of the slave trade in the District of Columbia, and the settlement of a Texas boundary dispute with New Mexico by a monetary compensation to Texas.

The southern slaveholder president had a plan of his own, more favorable to the North, and opposed Clay's proposals. But his sudden death in July 1850, as a result of gastroenteritis brought Millard Fillmore, who favored Clay's plan, into the presidency, and a bipartisan combination put the measures through Congress.

Antislavery radicals attacked the new Fugitive Slave Law, but great Union meetings in the larger northern cities better represented public sentiment. Radical southern-rights men agitated for disunion, but when a Unionist coalition captured control of a Georgia convention called to consider secession they lost heart.

The Whig national convention, held in Baltimore on June 16, 1852, adopted a platform that "acquiesced in" the Compromise measures, but sixty-six northern delegates friendly to General Winfield Scott of Virginia opposed it. The struggle for the presidential nomination went on for fifty-three ballots before Scott triumphed over Fillmore and Webster. William A. Graham, secretary of the navy, received second place on the ticket.

The Democratic national convention, opening in Baltimore on June 1, witnessed a marathon battle of three party veterans, Cass, Buchanan, and William L. Marcy, and a brash newcomer, Senator Stephen A. Douglas of Illinois. It took forty-nine ballots to convince the weary delegates that dark-horse Franklin Pierce of New Hampshire was the best solution. Veteran Senator William R. King of Alabama was named to run with him.

The platform, mostly a repetition of that of 1848, added a pledge to "abide by, and adhere to" the Compromise measures including the Fugitive Slave Law, and to resist all attempts to renew the slavery agitation. The convention had successfully surmounted all its difficulties, but the query "Who is Franklin Pierce?" was genuine, not a Whig sneer. The nominee had to be explained to the voters, though his availability could not have been higher.

Forty-seven years old, handsome, friendly, once a victim of the liquor habit but now a good temperance man, he was a fluent speaker and had no enemies to conciliate and no record to explain away. He had served in both houses of Congress without particular distinction, retiring before sectional issues became acute. He had a Mexican War record as a brave but not brilliant officer.

Every element in the party seemed to be pleased with its good-looking New Hampshire nonentity. The Van Burens and the Blairs rejoiced with the southern rights men over the defeat of the leading Compromise candidates, while Compromisers were happy that Pierce and the platform were right on the Compromise.

But the Whigs had no reason to rejoice. Southern party members were disappointed in Scott's letter of acceptance, which merely accepted the nomination "with the resolutions annexed," making no specific mention of the Compromise or the Fugitive Slave Law. To make matters worse, the warm support of William H. Seward convinced them of the candidate's unsoundness on slavery. Had not the wily New Yorker drawn poor General Taylor, himself a slaveholder, into his web? Stephens, Toombs, and a few other members of Congress formally repudiated Scott; others were silent, and nowhere in the lower South was there much enthusiasm. Some Georgia bolters, led by Stephens, ran a Webster electoral ticket; elsewhere the dissatisfied either voted Democratic or stayed away from the polls.

In the North, Webster's friends were unreconciled to Scott, and those in Massachusetts would have supported a separate electoral ticket but for the great orator's death in October. His bitterness had caused him to hope for Pierce's election. The "higher law" Whigs, as they were dubbed after Seward's Senate speech against the Compromise, were enthusiastic for Scott but not the platform. As Greeley put it, accepting the nominee, they "spit upon the platform."

Yet the Free Soil men had no use for Scott or his platform. In Ohio the *Ashtabula Sentinel* declared, "We do not desire to smuggle antislavery men or measures into the coming or any administration." The third party, under the name Free Democratic, held its national convention in Pittsburgh in August and nominated John P. Hale of New Hampshire for president and George W. Julian of Indiana for vice-president. The platform attacked slavery, condemned the Compromise and the Fugitive Slave Law, and endorsed many proposals including the free homestead policy, cheap postage, river and harbor improvements, and international arbitration. The Barnburners had gone back to the Democrats, leaving behind hardly more than the old Liberty men and some unreconciled antislavery

Whigs. Senator Chase of Ohio, after consorting with the Democrats for a year, returned to the fold. Charles Sumner, elected from Massachusetts to the Senate by a coalition of Democrats and Free-Soilers in 1851, was the eastern leader.

The campaign was issueless, spiritless, and hopelessly dull. The Whigs made a strong bid for Irish-Catholic support, as General Scott's daughters had attended church schools and one, now deceased, had become a nun. He declared in favor of citizenship for foreign-born soldiers after a year of wartime service. The Democrats retaliated with an unwise nativist letter he had written ten years before and accused him of executing German and Irish soldiers in the Mexican War. The Whigs happily discovered a clause in the New Hampshire constitution disqualifying Catholics from officeholding and blamed Pierce for it. Quotations from English newspapers approving the Democratic low-tariff attitude were reprinted in Whig newspapers to arouse anti-British feeling in Irish breasts. Pamphlets in German were circulated by Whig postmasters. Politicans were aware of the swelling tide of immigration and its political import.

Efforts of both parties to revive the tariff question and to arouse interest in foreign policies accomplished little, and the campaign degenerated further into personalities. Pierce was charged with cowardice in the Mexican War and with habitual drunkenness. Scott, an imposing figure in military regalia, was ridiculed as a pompous ass, and he almost demonstrated this in an ill-disguised electioneering tour of the North; his military career was belittled; and the dangers of electing a soldier despot were held before the voters. On this exalted plane ended one of the dullest campaigns in American history.

The Democrats triumphed by a landslide. Scott salvaged only Massachusetts and Vermont and the border Whig states of Kentucky and Tennessee—42 electoral votes. Pierce had all the rest—a total of 254. The popular vote was: Pierce, 1,607,510; Scott, 1,386,942; and Hale, 155,210. The country was voting to uphold the Compromise. The Democratic stand was clearer, and the candidate safer, on this issue. The decline of the third-party vote is additional proof of the revulsion against agitation. More businessmen and more planters voted Democratic than in any previous election, while large numbers of conservatives gave only perfunctory support to Scott or had refused to vote. The Democratic Party, divested of Jacksonian radicalism, was now safe for men of property.

The Whig party was demoralized. With its most available candidate, the party had suffered its worst defeat. Clay's Compromise had saved the Union but had wrecked the party whose foundations he had laid twenty years before. It might have passed away in any case. The growing moral sentiment against slavery, nurtured in Protestant churches, was stirring the middle classes, the backbone of Whiggery. The party was splitting apart in the North. In New England, there were Cotton and Conscience

Whigs; in New York, Woolly Heads and Silver Grays; in other places, "higher law" and "lower law" Whigs. The conservatives who sought to repair the breach between the sections were pale reflections of Clay and Webster: Fillmore, Everett of Massachusetts, Bell of Tennessee, Crittenden of Kentucky, all were thin-blooded elder statesmen. The task required dynamic leadership, and this they lacked. Whiggery had gone to seed.

V

Sectional Parties and
Civil War Politics

☆

1856-1864

IN JANUARY 1854, Stephen A. Douglas of Illinois introduced in the Senate a bill to organize the Indian country west of Missouri into a territory. This became, in its final form, the Kansas-Nebraska Act, which created two territories out of the area, with the right to decide the slavery question left to the people of each territory. This act repealed the provision of the Missouri Compromise of 1820, which had prohibited slavery north of the 36° 30′ parallel of latitude from the Mississippi River to the Rocky Mountains, with Missouri the exception. Douglas put in the repeal clause to overcome objections to the bill from some proslavery men. He was eager to get the territory organized, possibly because of his interest in having the projected Pacific Railroad built along a northern route. Whatever his motives, Douglas and President Pierce, who yielded to his persuasions, committed one of the costliest political blunders in American history.

Almost as soon as the Nebraska Bill was introduced, a group of antislavery members of Congress issued an inflammatory appeal to the people denouncing the Douglas proposal as "part and parcel of an atrocious plot" to exclude free labor from the territory and convert it into "a dreary region of despotism inhabited by masters and slaves." Mass meetings all over the North denounced "Pierce, Douglas, and Co.," and presently there was talk of a new party.

The first steps were taken in the Old Northwest. Here the Whig party was demoralized by defeat and antislavery defections; the Free Soil (or Free Democratic) Party had not lost its crusading zeal but was willing to cooperate on a moderate program; and many Democrats felt that the Polk and Pierce administrations had ignored the interests of their section as to policies and patronage, and that the South was responsible for

67

Cass's defeat in 1848. The heavy migrations into the lake regions from New England and New York and the new East-West rail connections were weakening the old economic and social ties with the South.

The first suggestion for the organization of a new antislavery party is usually accredited to a meeting in Ripon, Wisconsin, on March 1, 1854, led by Alvan E. Bovay, but other meetings were taking similar steps almost simultaneously. The name "Republican" for a new party was used by Horace Greeley in the *New York Tribune* at Bovay's suggestion, but the old Jeffersonian name was a natural one for such a party. Anti-Nebraska state and congressional tickets under various names swept the Old Northwest in the fall of 1854. But the East was another story.

The broth of nativism had been simmering for some years in eastern cities, but it boiled over with amazing suddenness in 1854. The great influx of Germans and Irish had been arousing temperance and Protestant America against the poverty-stricken, whiskey-drinking, Popish Irish and the less impecunious, beer-drinking Germans, many of whom were tabbed as atheistic Red Republicans. Both groups were Democrats, which made Whigs incline toward nativism.

The Know-Nothings

In the political confusion caused by the Nebraska Bill, Democratic factionalism in New York, and a Maine Law (liquor prohibition) movement, the secret Order of the Star-Spangled Banner burgeoned into a political party. It won some surprising local successes in the East, operating in secret and refusing to reveal its principles. This "Know-Nothing" movement soon was spreading southward, largely absorbing the homeless Whigs of that section, who looked upon it largely as a Union-saving force against agitation over slavery. The secret lodges also infiltrated the new Republican Party in the Old Northwest and threatened to dilute its antislavery principles with nativism.

But the Republicans had outdistanced the Know-Nothings by the end of 1855. They made propaganda out of the struggles of antislavery and proslavery men in newly organized Kansas. They elected Salmon P. Chase governor of Ohio and absorbed most of the Know-Nothings of that important state. They acquired the New York Whig organization of Seward and Weed, who were antinativist. And the Know-Nothings were having difficulties with the slavery issue.

In February 1856, the Know-Nothings, now calling themselves the American Party, held their national council meeting and national nominating convention at the same time. The council adopted a platform that would limit officeholding to the native-born, require twenty-one years residence for naturalization, and deny political station to anyone recognizing allegiance to a "foreign potentate, prince or power." But on slavery it lamely endorsed popular sovereignty for the territories. When the nominating convention assembled and upheld this plank, a secession of antislavery men, loosely called North Americans, followed. The majority remained and named ex-President Fillmore and Andrew Jackson Donelson of Tennessee as the party candidates.

The Republicans held an organizing convention in Pittsburgh on February 22, which set up a national committee and called a nominating convention to meet in Philadelphia on June 17. The six hundred or more delegates, plus alternates and visitors, made .the Philadelphia gathering almost a mass convention, disorderly but as enthusiastic as a religious revival. Astute eastern chieftains passed over Seward and Chase and turned to John C. Frémont, age forty-three, former army officer and famed explorer—called the Pathfinder of the West—participant in the California uprising against Mexico and, for a brief period, a senator from that state.

Conservatives, centering in the Pennsylvania delegation, favored elderly Supreme Court Justice John McLean, but the convention nominated the more glamorous Frémont, with William L. Dayton, former Whig senator from New Jersey, as his running mate. The platform declared it the duty of Congress to prohibit in the territories "those twin relics of barbarism, polygamy and slavery." Planks favoring a Pacific railroad to be built with federal aid and advocating national improvements of rivers and harbors were lost sight of in the platform's denunciations of the administration's policies in Kansas.

The seceding "North Americans" accepted both the Republican nominees after offering their own candidate for vice-president.

The Democratic national committee listened to western appeals and chose Cincinnati as the site of its national convention and June 2 as the date. The platform repeated the planks of earlier ones and added resolutions denouncing Know-Nothingism and endorsing the Kansas-Nebraska Act. Pierce wanted a renomination, and Douglas had some support, but James Buchanan of Pennsylvania, who had been minister to England and had escaped involvement in the Nebraska struggle, had friends in both sections and was the most available in all respects. The two-thirds rule delayed his nomination until the seventeenth ballot. John C. Breckinridge of Kentucky was nominated for vice-president.

An old guard of Whigs met in Baltimore in September and endorsed Fillmore and Donelson but not the American Party platform.

The course of the campaign was largely determined by the long session of Congress, from December to August, which was marked at every step by sectional and partisan bitterness. It required nine weeks to elect a Speaker because Republicans, "North" and "South" Americans, Democrats, and Republican-Americans could find no common ground. At last

Nathaniel P. Banks of Massachusetts, an American-Republican, was chosen by a plurality. Much time was consumed by the Kansas question. Long debates between "shriekers for freedom" and "subduers of freedom" produced no solution. Democratic Senate and anti-Nebraska House could not agree.

Accompanying the excitement in Congress, a series of events in Kansas culminated in the "sacking" of the town of Lawrence by a marshal's posse of which former Senator David R. Atchison of Missouri was a member— really a proslavery mob. This produced other acts of violence, all luridly misrepresented by reporters for eastern newspapers.

On May 19, while the drunken mob was in possession of Lawrence, Senator Charles Sumner of Massachusetts, eloquent, vain, stuffed with classical learning, and master of the dictionary, delivered his carefully prepared and rehearsed speech, "The Crime Against Kansas." Not content with arguments and near-obscene metaphors, he indulged in offensive personalities against Douglas and, for no apparent reason, singled out for special chastisement the elderly South Carolina senator, Andrew Pickens Butler, who was not present to defend himself. Douglas struck back with caustic comments, but Butler was avenged by his nephew, Congressman Preston Brooks.

Two days after the speech, Brooks approached Sumner at his desk in the Senate after adjournment and attacked him with a gutta-percha cane, finally breaking it over his head. Opinion differed then and afterward over the severity of the wounds; but Sumner did not reappear in the Senate for two years, going abroad in search of health. Massachusetts reelected him as a mark of its esteem.

The assault on Sumner was, next to "Bleeding Kansas," the best argument the Republicans had in 1856. A southern bully, fit product of the slavocracy, had brutally assaulted a northern senator for words used in the supposedly free forum of the Senate. When his district reelected Brooks after he had resigned as a result of a vote of censure, there was further proof of southern depravity. A leading Democrat predicted that the affair would cost his party 200,000 votes.

The campaign rivaled that of 1840 in excitement and far excelled it in importance. A major party was contesting a national election on frankly sectional grounds. An old Whig, Robert C. Winthrop of Massachusetts, now a Buchanan supporter, caustically described the Republican appeal as one-third Missouri Compromise repeal, for which northerners were largely responsible, one-third Kansas outrages, with no regard for northern provocation, and one-third "disjointed facts and misapplied figures . . . to prove that the South is, upon the whole, the very poorest, meanest, least productive, and most miserable part of creation and therefore ought to be continually teased and taunted and reviled, by everybody who feels himself better off." This antisouthern crusade with its strong moral appeal aroused the Protestant pulpit and gave a religious fervor to the Republican cause. Songs, so effective as campaign weapons in 1840, reappeared as Republican writers exhausted the possibilities of "Freedom, Freemen, and Frémont." And it must not be forgotten that northerners had been exposed to *Uncle Tom's Cabin* in print and on the stage for four years.

The Democrats, with no young hero to exploit and no crusade to conduct, appealed to the fears of conservatives and Union lovers: The elderly, colorless Buchanan typified experienced statesmanship and security for the old American order; Frémont, disunion, and possibly civil war. Toombs and Howell Cobb, the Union savers of 1850, publicly announced that the South would not submit to Republican victory. Because Fillmore could not win, Clay Whigs were urged to support Buchanan, and northern business did not need to be reminded of southern markets and investments at stake. Democratic leaders in the North forgot their earlier diatribes against the nativists and appealed to Fillmore men to make common cause with them against the specter of sectionalism. In the South, where Fillmore and Buchanan were the only contenders, the battle was sharply fought, with the "Americans" insisting that their candidate was national and at the same time sound on southern rights.

Fillmore's supporters in the North were under the disadvantage of appealing to the same general constituency as the Democrats. Had a Democrat other than Buchanan been named, their chances might have been better. Even so, they charged the Democrats with southern leanings, the Republicans with northern fanaticism, and described their own party as the truly national one. To stir up the dying embers of nativism, they concocted a story that Frémont was a Roman Catholic.* This invention, taken up by the Democrats, caused the Republicans much embarrassment because they were wooing the German-Catholic vote and a public statement by Frémont would be unwise. Friends attempted to refute the charge, but it persisted through the campaign and may have cost some Know-Nothing support.

Republican success depended on victories in Illinois, Indiana, and Pennsylvania. In these border free-states the antislavery crusade backfired. Too many voters were frightened at Republican radicalism. Attempts to arrange fusion tickets with the Fillmore men were ineffective. In spite of the combined efforts of three of the nation's shrewdest and most unscrupulous political manipulators—local managers Simon Cameron

---

* Frémont, an Episcopalian, had been married by a Catholic priest, and an adopted daughter had attended a Catholic school. His enemies went on to insist that he had been reared as a Catholic, still attended mass, and had shown his Catholicism on various occasions. Witnesses were produced to vouch for the statements.

and Thad Stevens helped by Thurlow Weed of New York—the Republicans failed to carry Pennsylvania. After all, it was Buchanan's home state, and it had never had a president.

The electoral college gave Buchanan 174 votes (Pennsylvania, New Jersey, Indiana, Illinois, California, and all the slave states except Maryland); Frémont, 114 (the remaining free states); Fillmore, 8 (Maryland). Buchanan had 1,836,072 popular votes; Frémont, 1,342,345; Fillmore, 873,053. The "Americans" were now a conservative third party, their antislavery strength having gone to the Republicans. Nativism had failed utterly as a national issue, but "Bleeding Kansas" had carried the Republicans through their critical period.

The Lincoln-Douglas Contest

The elderly bachelor president proved to be anything but the experienced physician who was to heal the nation's wounds. His administration saw the Democratic Party divided and distracted over his support of a bill to admit Kansas as a slave state under the fraudulent Lecompton Constitution, drafted by a proslavery minority. Douglas, upholder of popular sovereignty, won Republican allies in blocking the measure, but thereby damaged his chances to win southern support for the presidential nomination.

A further count against Douglas was his refusal to accept the Dred Scott decision of the Supreme Court, which, among other things, legalized slavery in the territories, as anything but a legal abstraction that would not prevent a territorial legislature from making its own decisions as to the institution. This was called the Freeport Doctrine (after the town in Illinois). Douglas defended this in his debates with Lincoln when they were contending for the Illinois senatorship in 1858. Douglas was reelected in spite of the guerrilla opposition of federal "Buchaneers."

The southern Democrats, backed by the Buchanan administration, would accept Douglas as the party's nominee only if he would accept their platform. The Democratic national convention of 1860 met in Charleston, South Carolina, on April 23, and ran on for two hectic weeks. A long and bitter struggle developed over a proposal committing the party to congressional protection of slavery in the territories, which would put federal power behind the Dred Scott decision. The plank was voted down by the Douglas supporters of popular sovereignty and a bloc of delegates from the deep South walked out, to the cheers of the crinoline galleries. The balloting for president gave the "Little Giant" a majority, but he could not get two-thirds of the original convention total. The delegates then voted to adjourn and reassemble on June 18 in the less hostile confines of Baltimore.

At Baltimore, returning seceders and some new delegates, elected to take their places, contested for seats, and the result was a second secession. Finally, the reorganized convention nominated Douglas when he had 181½ of 194½ votes. Senator Benjamin Fitzpatrick of Alabama was put on the ticket with him but later declined, and the national committee substituted Herschel V. Johnson, former governor of Georgia, for vice-president.

Seceders, old and new, met in another hall and nominated Vice-President John C. Breckinridge of Kentucky and Senator Joseph Lane of Oregon, an administration supporter, as their candidates. The "Dixiecrats" of 1860 put in their platform the principle of protection of slave property in the territories by the federal government, which, if accepted by Douglas, would have doomed the party in every free state.

Two other parties had made their nominations between the two sessions of the Democratic gathering. A Constitutional Union convention (called National Union in the invitation issued by a group of southern "American" Congressmen), meeting in Baltimore, chose veteran Whig John Bell of Tennessee over Sam Houston of Texas, favorite of the "American" contingent, and thrust upon Edward Everett of Massachusetts an unwanted nomination for vice-president. Their platform was a simple pledge to support the Constitution and the Union against all enemies at home and abroad. This was the last effort effort of graybeards of the faith of Clay and Webster to resist the sectionalism that was engulfing the major parties.

Meanwhile the Republicans had been making political hay out of the Dred Scott decision, Democratic dissensions, and the depression following the Panic of 1857, and their delegates went to Chicago on May 16 with the spirit of victory in the air. This was Chicago's first national convention, made possible by the railroad revolution of the 1850s. A specially constructed "Wigwam" held ten thousand spectators.

The platform attempted to desectionalize the party. While it favored congressional action to preserve freedom in the territories, it upheld the right of a state to determine its own domestic institutions and denounced the lawless invasion of any state (John Brown's raid from Maryland into Virginia at Harpers Ferry) as among the gravest of crimes. Brown was subsequently hanged for murder and for treason against the Commonwealth of Virginia.

The platform bid for Pennsylvania's vote with a vaguely worded endorsement of protective tariff. It satisfied the Germans with a plank opposing any abridgment of the rights of foreign-born and one favoring a homestead act for the public lands. The latter also pleased eastern labor and western pioneer farmers. Planks endorsing river and harbor improvements and federal aid for a Pacific railroad appealed to the Old Northwest and the Pacific Coast.

The need for a candidate who could carry the conservative North—Pennsylvania, Indiana, Illinois, and New Jersey, all Democratic in 1856—produced a "Stop-Seward" movement. The New York senator was leading the field when the convention opened, but politicos from the doubtful states questioned the wisdom of nominating a man whose record stamped him as an antislavery radical. Chase of Ohio was in a similar position. Edward Bates of Missouri, an old Whig, and Abraham Lincoln of Illinois were more available. In the end, the anti-Seward bloc decided to concentrate on Lincoln and secured his nomination on the third ballot. All manner of pledges, pressures, and deals went into his nominating cauldron. Senator Hannibal Hamlin of Maine was named the candidate for vice-president.

Nominally four candidates contested for the chief office in 1860. Yet in most states—excluding two or three border slave states and the Pacific Coast—it was a two-party fight: Lincoln against Douglas in the North, Bell against Breckinridge in the South. Valiant little minorities of Douglas men put electoral tickets into the field in most of the cotton states, but the great majority of southern Democrats voted for Breckinridge. The Bell-Everett ticket drew the old Whig, "American," and Unionist vote. Both Breckinridge and Bell groups professed loyalty to the South; but the "submissionists" were to be found in the Constitutional Union movement, the "secessionists" in the Democratic camp.

In the North the Bell movement attracted remnants of "Americans" and old Whigs. The failure of Fillmore in 1856 and the new-found conservatism of the Republicans caused many former Whigs such as Thomas Ewing of Ohio and Edward Bates of Missouri to support "Lincoln, the Whig," and the Whig policies in the Republican platform. The Breckinridge following in the North was little more than a corporal's guard of Buchanan officeholders seeking to destroy Douglas, even though it meant Republican success.

The real battle was between Douglas and Lincoln, with the cards stacked in favor of the "Rail Splitter." His party was united and seemed to be reasonably sure of New England, New York, Ohio, and the upper Northwest—all carried in 1856. It needed Illinois, Indiana, and Pennsylvania to win. Lincoln's Illinois residence strengthened the Republican cause in his home state and neighboring Indiana. His Whig background attracted conservatives in the Ohio Valley, and the homestead plank helped with the foreign-born.

Buchanan vetoed a modified homestead bill in the summer; southern members of Congress had voted almost solidly against it, while both Democratic platforms had ignored it. Using a pamphlet, "Vote Yourself a Farm," and speeches in German by Carl Schurz, Gustav Körner, and other popular German orators under the special direction of a "foreign department" of the national committee, the Republicans made heavy inroads into the German vote in Cincinnati, Chicago, and St. Louis. These were centers of the newer German immigration, more radical and less fixed in party affiliation than the older groups, who still clung to the Democratic Party.

In Pennsylvania and southern Ohio the tariff issue was used to win the coal and iron interests and their workingmen. The success of the fusionist People's Party in Pennsylvania in 1858 prepared the way for 1860 and a similar victory. There was plenty of money, and Simon Cameron, Andrew G. Curtin, Thad Stevens, and other experienced leaders directed the strategy.

There was not the excitement in the North that had prevailed in 1856. The Republican Party was neither so novel nor so radical, and its appeal was less emotional. Kansas had long since ceased to bleed; the territories were in little danger of ever becoming slave states; and—a strange vindication for Douglas—some Republicans even accepted popular sovereignty as a safe solution. "The operation of the natural forces of free labor and free emigration is worth a thousand Wilmot Provisos in building up free states," declared the *Cincinnati Commericial,* a powerful western Republican organ.

However, most Republican speakers and newspapers were more orthodox in favoring congressional action against slavery. The southern "intervention" idea—a congressional slave code for territories—was subjected to bitter attacks; and the South was charged with schemes to reopen the African slave trade. A well-organized campaign with numerous speakers and the usual parades and processions aroused moderate enthusiasm but no great excitement. The Wide-Awakes, drilled like military companies, marched in Lincoln-Hamlin parades. Seward overcame his bitter disappointment at his defeat and made what historian James Ford Rhodes has called "the most remarkable stump speeches ever delivered in this country." He, rather than Lincoln, seemed to be leading the party. The candidate received callers daily at an office in Springfield, was in close touch with campaign strategy, but kept a muzzle on himself.

The opposition parties thundered at the sectionalism of the Republicans and repeated the danger-of-disunion argument of 1856. This was singularly ineffective in the North. "For ten, aye, for twenty, years," taunted Seward, "these threats have been renewed, in the same language and in the same form, about the first day of November every four years. . . ." He was certain the Union was in no danger. Republican newspapers were equally sure.

But Douglas, facing certain defeat, was alarmed about the South. Unlike the other candidates, he had made speech after speech, all over the North—a new departure for presidential candidates and a shattering of old traditions. In August he turned his attention to the South, not to gain votes, for his cause was hopeless there, but to arouse national feelings and bring that section to accept Lincoln's election quietly. There is nothing finer in Douglas's career than his sturdy Union speeches in Virginia and North Carolina, where he declared that no grievance could justify secession, and that he would support the president in enforcing the laws. He returned North to campaign from New York west to Missouri, but after the unfavorable state elections in October he said to his secretary, "We must try to save the Union. I will go South." Taking a steamboat down the Mississippi to Tennessee, he spoke in Memphis, then in Chattanooga, invaded Georgia, and was in Alabama when the election took place. Threats were made against him, and a few eggs were hurled in Montgomery; but his crusade against secession went on. After the news of Lincoln's election he made his trip up the Mississippi from New Orleans a goodwill tour in an attempt to reconcile the South to a Republican administration.

Desperate efforts to unite the anti-Lincoln forces upon fusion electoral tickets characterized the closing days of the campaign in the North. Complete or partial fusion was effected in Pennsylvania, New York, New Jersey, Connecticut, and Rhode Island. The candidates for electors were apportioned among the Bell, Breckinridge, and Douglas groups, with the understanding that, if elected, they would cast their votes so as to bring about Lincoln's defeat in the electoral vote. This would throw the election to the House, where no party had a majority, but where one of the anti-Lincoln candidates might win.* A House deadlock beyond March 4 might even make Joseph Lane president, as the Senate was Buchanan-controlled, and Breckinridge's running mate, elected vice-president by that body in the event no one had a majority, would assume the presidency. The Republicans made much of this in criticizing fusion, but the danger was slight. Jefferson Davis of Mississippi wanted all three anti-Republican candidates to withdraw and unite for Horatio Seymour of New York; but Douglas refused, believing that thousands of his supporters would turn to Lincoln if he abandoned the race. In the South the Bell and Douglas men cooperated in assailing the Breckinridge "disunionists," but only in Texas was there fusion.

The South was the more troubled section in 1860, divided, distracted, fearful—the very antithesis of the antislavery picture of a section held in the grip of a malevolent, aggressive slavocracy. Conservative southern newspapers charged that Breckinridge party leaders such as Yancey of Alabama and Jefferson Davis were plotting to destroy the Union, and that their demand for congressional protection of slavery was a subterfuge to

* Actually Lincoln's chances in the House were excellent. The Republicans had fifteen of the thirty-three states and needed but two more, with Illinois and Oregon offering good prospects, especially if Douglas were eliminated.

divide the national Democratic Party. The Breckinridge following held forth on the dangers of disunity in the South and played up stories of abolitionist-slave plots, burning of houses, and poisoning of masters with distant and thinly settled Texas as the favorite locale. This fear campaign may have added votes to the southern-rights Democracy, but the large vote polled by Bell in the lower South, especially among the large slaveholders, is proof that the section was far from solid.

The election of Republican governors in doubtful Pennsylvania and Indiana in October indicated the outcome in November; but a vigorous, last-minute fight for the fusion ticket in New York held out faint hopes. Worried about disunion, the city's financial interests poured money into the campaign, but to no avail. Lincoln carried all the free states, except three of New Jersey's seven electors; Bell had Kentucky, Virginia, and Tennessee; Douglas had only Missouri and three electors from New Jersey;* Breckinridge won the remaining states, all slave and all from the lower South except Maryland and Delaware. The electoral total gave Lincoln 180, Breckinridge 72, Bell 39, Douglas 12. The popular votes were 1,865,908 for Lincoln, 848,019 for Breckinridge, 590,901 for Bell, and 1,380,202 for Douglas. But in the Senate and the House, the Republicans would be in a minority—a strong argument against immediate secession. The "Black Republican" president would have his hands tied.

Sectionalism triumphed in both North and South in 1860. The two moderate candidates, Bell and Douglas, were in a minority. Equally striking was the fact that conservative southerners preferred Bell, a southerner, over Douglas, a northerner, while in the free states the reverse was true. Even conservatives voted for a man from their own section. National parties, so long a unifying force, broke down. The sectionalists had their way. Douglas died on June 3, 1861.

A Wartime Election

Shortly after the November election, South Carolina seceded from the Union. Six other southern states followed suit and early in 1861 wrote a constitution for the Confederate States of America. The war started soon after.

The Civil War brought about a realignment of parties. Republicans and War Democrats joined in a Union Party supporting the war and the Lincoln administration. The more radical Republicans criticized Lincoln for his tardiness in making the war an antislavery crusade and for his failure to use drastic methods in putting down the rebellion and in recon-

---

* In New Jersey a fusion opposition had a small popular majority; but only three of the seven candidates received united support. Four Lincoln electors won.

structing reconquered states. But they did not carry their opposition to the polls.

The majority of Democrats held aloof from the Union Party and criticized the administration for mismanagement and corruption, violating civil liberties, and transforming a war for the Union into an abolitionist war when Lincoln issued his Emancipation Proclamation on September 22, 1862, effective January 1, 1863. A peace group led by Clement L. Vallandigham of Ohio became more aggressive after Democratic gains in the elections of 1862 and demanded an immediate end to the war and a convention to restore the Union on a compromise basis. Vallandigham's campaign for peace ended in May 1863, when he was arrested and tried before a military court for encouraging resistance to the draft. He was sentenced to prison, but Lincoln ordered him sent to the Confederacy. The exile soon made his way to Canada and ran for governor of Ohio in absentia. He was defeated overwhelmingly by a War Democrat. Gettysburg and Vicksburg had made his defeat a certainty.

Secretary of the Treasury Chase, consorting with congressional radicals and other critics of Lincoln, feuded with Secretary of State Seward, then with the influential Blair family represented in the cabinet by Postmaster General Montgomery Blair, a conservative. Chase was put into the presidential race early in 1864 by a group of friends in Washington, but Ohio and Indiana endorsed Lincoln, and he withdrew.

Some four hundred radicals, mostly Germans and abolitionists, met at Cleveland on May 31 and nominated General John C. Frémont for president in the hope of forcing Lincoln to withdraw.

The Union Party, with the administration forces in command, opened its national convention in the none too friendly city of Baltimore on June 7 in the cramped quarters of a theater. Lincoln was renominated with only the Missouri delegation opposed. It voted for General Grant. Andrew Johnson, former senator and war governor of Tennessee, a prewar Democrat, led for second place on the first ballot, and shifts of votes then nominated him. Lincoln was instrumental in his selection. The platform, praising the war president and his policies, called for the complete suppression of the rebellion and a constitutional amendment to prohibit the existence of slavery.

Democratic papers could call the two Union candidates "a rail-splitting buffoon and a boorish tailor, both from the backwoods, both growing up in uncouth ignorance," but these candidates had great popular appeal. Their vote-getting pull was underestimated by many of the party bigwigs, who were not yet ready to accept the work of the convention as final.

For three months Lincoln's reelection seemed to be in the balance. General Grant, on whose military genius the North pinned its hopes, hurled his legions against Lee; but a mounting death toll was the only result. He then settled down for his long siege of Petersburg. General

Sherman was making little headway against Atlanta, and a terrible despondency fell upon the North. In July, General Early dashed up the Shenandoah Valley, and for a day Washington seemed at his mercy. Greenbacks fell below forty cents on the dollar.

The radicals renewed their war on the president by issuing the "Wade-Davis Manifesto," a criticism of his moderate reconstruction policy (which had been applied in Tennessee, Louisiana, and Arkansas) and a reply to his pocket veto of a radical measure of Senator Ben Wade of Ohio and Representative Henry Winter Davis of Maryland. The two vented their spleen in the manifesto with a large bloc of Republican senators and representatives in sympathy with them. They called the veto a "studied outrage on the legislative authority," charged that Lincoln held the electoral votes of the reconstructed rebel states at his dictation, and warned him to confine himself to his executive duties—"to obey and execute, not make the laws."

Chase had offered to resign late in June when miffed over a trivial patronage difficulty, and the president had surprised him by accepting his resignation. Now his hopes rose as defeatism threatened to engulf the North. If a new pilot were needed, he was ready. Radical leaders were not prepared to commit themselves to a particular candidacy, but in August an undercover movement centered in New York set about securing the withdrawal of both Lincoln and Frémont and the immediate calling of another national convention. Vindictive spirits such as Wade and Davis, the erratic Greeley, the critical Sumner, the moderate John Sherman of Ohio, Governor Andrew of Massachusetts, the friends of Chase, and many practical politicians agreed that Lincoln must go. Even those good friends of the administration, Thurlow Weed and Henry Raymond, chairman of the national committee, whose *New York Times* was the only avowed administration organ in that city, began to despair. Lincoln seemed certain to be a one-term president.

In the midst of this season of intrigue and gloom, the Democrats held their national convention in Chicago on August 29, with high hopes of victory and a popular candidate at hand. On the first ballot, with but slight opposition, General George B. McClellan was nominated. Military authorities credit "Little Mac" with organizing ability and a certain cautious type of generalship; but his insufferable egotism, his contemptuous attitude toward the president and the War Department, and his inability to act when action was required had caused his removal late in 1862. He had two assets, his popularity with soldiers of the Army of the Potomac and his grievances against the administration, upon which he placed the full responsibility for his military failures. Democratic politicians, eager for a soldier candidate, found him a ready tool, and he became the party nominee on a platform that pronounced the war a failure and declared in favor of immediate efforts "for a cessation of hostilities with a view to an ultimate convention of the States, or other peaceable means" to restore the Union. Attacks upon the subversion of civil liberties, the exercise of unconstitutional powers by the administration, and military interference with elections in the border states were included in the brief platform, along with a resolution praising the soldiers and sailors and promising to protect and care for them.

The peace plank reflected the influence of the indomitable Vallandigham, who had quietly returned from Canada and became a delegate to the convention from his home district. George H. Pendleton, an Ohio congressman, was nominated to run with McClellan. The combination of a war hero and a peace platform seemed to be well contrived to attract united Democratic support for the ticket in the face of a quarreling, disunited Union Party.

But on September 1 an event revolutionized the whole political situation. General Sherman captured Atlanta, key to the lower South, and broke the military backbone of the Confederacy. The Gulf States were cut off from Richmond, and Lee's fate was sealed. The tight-lipped Sherman, who had no use for politics and politicians, had inadvertently proved to be a master politician. As northern crowds cheered and rejoiced, Lincoln's star rose again, and the radicals hastened to make their peace.

All talk of a second convention was dropped. The *New York Tribune* pronounced for Lincoln on September 6. Chase, by mid-September, was ready to go on the stump. Wade and Davis, seeking a way to cover their retreat, were induced by their radical colleague, Senator Chandler of Michigan, to accept the removal of Blair from the cabinet as a peace offering. Lincoln, with the game in his hands, might have rejected Chandler's proposal, but the postmaster general, unpopular even with many good Lincoln men, had become a liability to the administration. The president requested his resignation, and he promptly and graciously acceded, showing his loyalty to his chief by speaking soon afterward before a great Lincoln meeting in New York City. Wade and Davis, appeased, went on the stump, but it was reported that Davis would not mention Lincoln's name.

Frémont's withdrawal was almost simultaneous with Blair's resignation, and Chandler believed it was due to his own indefatigable efforts. But Frémont had already made his decision, regardless of the status of Blair. His candidacy had become hopeless, and he was seeking a way out. Efforts to sound out McClellan and possibly make a deal with him had been ignored. Sullenly acquiescing in the inevitable, this overrated man withdrew in the interest of Union success but in a final bitter fling declared that the Lincoln administration was "politically, militarily, and financially a failure," and "that its necessary continuance is a cause of regret to the country." Thus ungraciously the once-popular Pathfinder passed into political oblivion.

Fate dealt Lincoln a final trump, no longer needed, in his game with the radicals: Chief Justice Taney died on October 12. Chase, eagerly desirous of Taney's office, next in importance to the presidency itself, must have felt keenly humiliated at seeking it from the man he had so often criticized and belittled. His friends, however, ate humble pie for him and pressed his candidacy. Lincoln, amused at the situation, waited until after the election. Then he duly appointed Salmon P. Chase to the highest judicial position, and on the fourth of the following March received the oath from the solemn-visaged Jovian chief justice, whose pettiness of spirit had so gravely marred his public career.

General McClellan, facing a united and harmonious Union Party, saw his own candidacy threatened with shipwreck between the militant peace faction and the less militant war supporters. Vallandigham, still antiwar and fierce for peace, importuned the candidate not "to insinuate even a little war" into his letter of acceptance as it would cost him two hundred thousand votes in the West. He stated on September 6 at a public meeting in Dayton, Ohio, that the convention "meant peace, and it said it."

But eastern Democrats, conscious of the war prosperity their section was enjoying and seeing the political appeal to the soldiers of a war stand, pressed the general to insist on restoration of the Union as a condition of peace. August Belmont, New York financier and chairman of the Democratic national committee, warned McClellan that he must emphasize this point.

Bedeviled by such conflicting opinions, Little Mac wrote his letter of acceptance several times, at first with a decided swing toward the viewpoint of an armistice without conditions, then back to an unconditional Union stand. The final draft gave cold comfort to the peace men. "I could not look in the faces of my gallant comrades of the army and navy who have survived so many bloody battles," he wrote, "and tell them that their labors and the sacrifices of so many of our slain and wounded brethren had been in vain—that we had abandoned the Union for which we have so often periled our lives." The candidate had repudiated the platform, and the War Democrats were satisfied.

But the peace element, deeply disappointed, gave a grudging support or remained away from the polls. Vallandigham reluctantly stumped for the ticket, but a group of western peace Democrats attempted to put another candidate into the field. A meeting in Columbus, Ohio, chose Alexander Long, a Cincinnati member of Congress, but he refused to run.

The inconsistencies of the Democrats made their campaign a two-faced affair. A *McClellan Campaign Songster* contained both war and peace songs. To the tune of "Dixie" crowds were expected to sing:

> For rebel traitors we've a halter,
> They falsely swore at freedom's altar
>> Cheer away, cheer away,
>> Cheer away, cheer away.
> We've tried all means to keep 'em quiet,
> Shot and shell their only diet,
>> Cheer away, cheer away,
>> Cheer away, cheer away.

And on another page, to the air of "The Battle Cry of Freedom," they could chant,

> We'll extend the hand of peace,
> That this wicked war may cease,
> Shouting McClellan, boys, and freedom.

Politicians have been notoriously adept at riding two horses, but a bloody civil war compelled men to take sides. The strain on party loyalties was a heavy one. The Democratic effort to play both sides became untenable when the Union Party harmonized its differences, and military success cleared the air.

Democratic prospects, so bright in August, faded with the first frosts of autumn. Following the fall of Atlanta came the successes of Sheridan in the Shenandoah Valley while Grant's tentacles slowly and relentlessly extended around Petersburg without relaxing their grip. Cheered on by a season of victory in the field, radicals and conservatives alike worked for Lincoln and the Union Party, and officeholders and government contractors filled Chairman Henry J. Raymond's campaign chest. On Election Day Lincoln carried all the loyal states except Kentucky, Delaware, and New Jersey. He had 212 electoral votes to McClellan's 21. The new vice-president was Andrew Johnson. The popular majority of the Union Party was four hundred thousand*—an amazing refutation of the dire predictions of radicals and Democrats but a few weeks before.

Before counting the electoral vote on February 8, Congress adopted the Twenty-second Joint Rule, whereby no electoral votes objected to in joint session should be counted except by concurrent votes of both houses. This was to ensure the rejection of the electoral votes of Louisiana and Tennessee, newly reconstructed under the president's plan. Elections had not been held in the other seceded states.

---

* Lincoln had 2,218,388 popular votes; McClellan, 1,812,807.

VI

Grant and Hayes

☆

1868-1876

WITH THE ASSASSINATION of Lincoln on April 14, 1865, Vice-President Andrew Johnson became president. The involved story of the struggle between Johnson and the radical leadership in Congress boils down to Johnson's stubborn insistence on a moderate policy toward the defeated South and the determination of a congressional oligarchy to keep ex-Confederates out of power and create Republican bastions in the former Confederate states. In the end, military rule and a process of readmission, including compulsory Negro suffrage, became the congressional solution. Congressman Thaddeus Stevens from Pennsylvania and Senator Charles Sumner of Massachusetts tried to remove Johnson as a dangerous obstacle to the success of their program, but the impeachment proceedings against him failed of conviction by a margin of one vote. Perhaps the major contribution of the Johnson administration was the purchase of Alaska from Russia in 1867 by Secretary of State William H. Seward. It seems amazing today that many Americans then referred to the purchase as "Seward's folly" or "Seward's icebox."

The Question of Greenbackism

Radical reconstruction was certain to be a major issue in the campaign of 1868, but "greenbackism" was becoming its rival in both parties. The greenbacks, issued without gold backing because of the stresses of war financing, were being called in, but pressure from western farmers stopped the progress of this deflation in 1868. Instead, there was a growing demand for the payment of war bonds with new issues of paper money instead of gold as the treasury had promised. The problem was embarrassing to both parties, for it tended toward an east-west division.

The "National Union Republican" party solved the problems of Negro

83

suffrage and the greenbacks at its national convention at Chicago, May
20–21, by some skillfully evasive planks. The platform declared that
Negro suffrage in the reconstructed states was necessary to protect the
loyal men of the South, but in the North it properly belonged to the
people of the states. The currency plank favored the payment of the
national debt according to the letter and spirit of the laws without defining either. The platform defended the reconstruction policy of Congress
and catalogued the misdeeds of Andrew Johnson.

General Ulysses S. Grant was the unanimous choice to head the ticket,
but it took five ballots to give Speaker Schuyler Colfax the vice-presidential nomination.

Having been deprived of Grant, a prewar Democrat, by the Republican convention, the Democrats were confronted with a concerted movement by eastern leaders to nominate a radical Republican, Chief Justice
Salmon P. Chase. His ambitious daughter, Kate Chase Sprague, was his
manager. But more orthodox Democrats were in the race, and a wide-
open battle got under way when the national convention opened its sessions in newly built Tammany Hall in New York on July 4. The platform
assailed radical reconstruction and approved a greenback plank, a concession to western demands. But the western favorite, George H. Pendleton
of Ohio, who led on the early ballots, was blocked by eastern opposition,
and a long deadlock developed. Just when it seemed that Chase might be
offered as the solution, a stampede was started to nominate the chairman
of the convention, Horatio Seymour, former governor of New York. Seymour protested, but on the twenty-second ballot he became the nominee.
Francis P. Blair, Jr., of Missouri was named to run with him. He had
recently written a strongly worded letter suggesting the use of force to
disperse carpetbag governments in the South, a political blunder, as it
was used against him in the campaign.

The campaign of the Democrats bogged down almost from the start.
Seymour and the eastern leaders did not repudiate the greenback plank,
but their evasions indicated their feelings. The candidate aroused no
enthusiasm in the inflationist West, and the plank did not help. Although
Seymour's letter of acceptance virtually repudiated Blair's letter, it did
not prevent the Republicans from playing up the issue and declaring that
Blair would rule the administration if Seymour won. They even charged
that the Democrats would try to pay the Confederate debt. Instead of
campaigning aggressively on the reconstruction issues, the Democrats
were thrown on the defensive and were unable to make headway.

Money and propaganda generally were with the Republicans,
although wealthy Democrats such as August Belmont, Cyrus H.
McCormick, and Samuel J. Tilden did their best. Tariff benefits, land
grants to railroads, and the Republican currency position induced the
Astors, the Vanderbilts, Jay Cooke, and others of wealth to give freely to

the campaign chest. The metropolitan newspapers and the leading week-lies—*Harper's*, the *Nation*, the *Independent*, and *Leslie's*—were mostly Republican and conservative in their economic views, though radical enough toward the South.

Old Union party conservatives and Johnson men had to make a hard choice between the radical-sponsored Grant and the orthodox Democrat, Seymour, whose party bore the stigma of Copperheadism. The word *Copperhead* was used to refer to Confederate sympathizers. President Johnson himself tardily endorsed Seymour, though he made no speeches, and his cabinet was badly divided. Chief Justice Chase was friendly toward Seymour but hostile to Blair, and held aloof from expressions of opinion. The conservative Republican senators who had voted for Johnson in the impeachment proceedings remained Republican despite the torrent of denunciation from party organs. Had they been forced to choose between Seymour and an out-and-out radical, many conservatives might well have preferred the Democrat; but Grant's reputation as the strong, silent sol-dier—he refused to make speeches—the moderation of his past views and actions, and his "Let us have peace" statement induced most of them to take him on faith.

The general trend of the October state elections toward the Republi-cans produced a movement, started under cover earlier, to have both Sey-mour and Blair withdraw. The national committee would then select a new ticket, with Chase presumably to head it. Alexander Long and some other Chase men were involved, while the *New York World* called for Blair's resignation and, by inference, Seymour's as well. But the national committee did not countenance the move, the eastern leaders were hostile, and the party newspapers disapproved almost unanimously.

One effect of the October reverses was the appearance of Seymour on the stump, actually against his wishes. He was an excellent speaker, and it was felt that he might stir the admittedly lagging spirits of the Demo-crats. He covered the Middle West as far as Chicago, returning through Pennsylvania. He criticized the Republicans as violators of the Constitu-tion and emphasized the moderate, peaceful character of his own party's views. It was a fine futile attempt to undo the damage done by Republi-can misconstruction of Blair's position.

A Narrow Popular-Vote Victory

The November results verified the October forecasts. Grant and Colfax had 214 electoral votes; Seymour and Blair, 80, with the popular vote running 3,013,650 to 2,708,744.* Seymour had New York, New

---

* Florida chose electors through the legislature; Virginia, Mississippi, and Texas, still under military rule, did not vote. Thirty-four states took part in the election.

Jersey, and Oregon from the North, Delaware, Maryland, and Kentucky from the border, Georgia and Louisiana from the South.

Grant's victory rested on two pillars that Democrat campaigning could not overturn: the widespread popular confidence in the man and the operation of radical reconstruction. The former gave him the North; the latter, the South. The effect of Negro suffrage is evident. Without the black vote Grant would have had a smaller popular vote than Seymour, though possibly an electoral majority because of his strength in the white-voting North.

To Republican leaders the value of the Negro vote was clear. But it was needed in the North as well as in the South, and this required a constitutional amendment. The retiring Congress, disregarding the statement of the Republican platform that control of the suffrage in the North could be safely left to the states, passed the Fifteenth Amendment, providing that the right to vote should not be denied or abridged on account of race, color, or previous condition of servitude. With Republican legislatures already chosen in the great majority of states and subject to party control, ratification was possible without giving the voters a chance to express themselves at the polls. Twelve state legislatures ratified the amendment within a month. Within a year three-fourths of the states had ratified,* and Negro suffrage was made compulsory everywhere, with the Republican Party the beneficiary.

Grant Versus Greeley

Grant's government was rife with corruption. For example, Vice-President Colfax was involved in the Union Pacific Railroad scandal, and some of Grant's friends and his brother-in-law conspired to corner the gold supply. The eventual corrective action by Secretary of the Treasury Boutwell resulted in a financial panic referred to as Black Friday, September 24, 1869. Even Grant's private secretary was involved in an organized effort to defraud the government of taxes on liquor.

In addition, widespread dissatisfaction with Grant's harsh policy toward the South, together with his failure to bring about tariff reductions and civil service reform, caused a Liberal Repulican movement to get under way to defeat him at the polls in 1872. Reformers of all stripes and some dissatisfied politicians met at Cincinnati on May 1, 1872, to name candidates and draw up a platform. Its variegated composition caused some difficulties, but a platform was adopted that endorsed the three war constitutional amendments, universal amnesty and local self-

---

* Texas, Virginia, and Mississippi were required to accept it as a condition of reconstruction. They were not readmitted until 1870.

government for the South, civil service reform, and a speedy return to specie payments for greenbacks.

The practical politicians, however, succeeded in manipulating the convention, burdened with too many candidates, to bring about the nomination of Horace Greeley, long-time editor of the *New York Tribune*, over Charles Francis Adams, minister to England during the Civil War, and the choice of eastern reformers and intellectuals. B. Gratz Brown, governor of Missouri, where the Liberal movement had started, was made the vice-presidential choice. He had had a hand in Greeley's nomination.

The Democratic convention swallowed the bitter dose when it met at Baltimore on July 9. Greeley and Brown became its candidates on the Cincinnati platform, although the New York editor had been flaying Democrats all his journalistic life. A group of bitter-enders revolted and nominated Charles O'Conor of New York at a Louisville meeting in September. He rejected the nomination, but electoral tickets were run under his name in twenty-three states.

The regular Republican Party leaders and eastern business and finance were satisfied with Grant and wanted the Hero of Appomattox renominated. The Republican convention in Philadelphia on June 5 complied without a dissenting voice. Senator Henry Wilson of Massachusetts replaced Vice-President Colfax as Grant's running mate. The platform pointed with pride to the party's past and paid lip service to civil service reform.

Appalled at Greeley's nomination, many of the Liberals found Grant more acceptable. But Carl Schurz, senator from Missouri, who had inaugurated the Liberal movement in that state and had presided at the Cincinnati convention, and Lyman Trumbull, one of the candidates for the nomination, urged support for Greeley as the only practical course.

Two Unfit Candidates

The campaign was a strange one. Never in American history have two more unfit men been offered to the country for the highest office. The simple soldier, inexperienced in statecraft, impervious to sound advice, and oblivious to his own blundering, was pitted against the vain, erratic, reforming editor, whose goodness of heart could not make up for his sad lack of judgment. The man of no ideas was running against the man of too many. Intelligent voters, in perplexity, might well have preferred Grant and the evils that went with him to Greeley and evils they knew not of. But many a good American saw no problem involved in the choice. The indomitable Grant of Civil War days was resurrected by press and politicians to save the blundering, ineffectual Grant of the White House.

The legend prevailed, but not against the real Greeley. His foibles and eccentricities were exaggerated and cruelly ridiculed so that the country saw him in grotesque caricature. Thomas Nast's cruel pencil in *Harper's Weekly* held him up to ridicule in cartoons so merciless that even George William Curtis, the editor, protested.

Yet it was so easy to laugh at Greeley. His appearance was anything but imposing or dignified. He was usually in a long linen duster that covered wrinkled clothes; a white hat concealed his frontal baldness but not the long silver locks at the back; metal-rimmed spectacles were hooked over his ears; and a fringe of whiskers framed his smooth, round face like a miniature fur piece. A friendly observer might have detected a resemblance to Franklin, but the savage Nast cartoons made him more like a nearsighted German professor with the heavy body of a peasant, the mind of a fool, and the vanity of a child. Partisan editors dragged forth choice morsels from old files of the *Tribune* to reveal his inconsistencies and eccentricities. The courageous humanitarian editor was forgotten, and a scarecrow Greeley appeared in his place. Democratic and Liberal papers savagely attacked Grant, shouting Caesarism and corruption, but the silent soldier quietly enjoying the summer at Long Branch played the role his managers had marked out for him, without speeches. How could a caricature contend against him?

Yet even Grant could not have won in the face of a great depression. This would have torn the legend to shreds. Fortune smiled on the Republicans, however, and prosperity continued another year. Business, pleased with Grant and his party, contributed liberally to the campaign coffers. A disciplined party organization, with the patronage of the federal government and most of the states at its disposal, did the rest. The Liberals, poorly organized and embarrassed for funds, could hardly have won against such odds, even with a stronger candidate.

Greeley's strong points proved to be of slight value. His long record of friendliness to the workers did not draw a heavy labor vote, for labor was not well organized and was politically impotent. His antislavery record and equal-rights principles failed to attract the black vote, though Sumner gave his blessing. Gratitude toward the Republican Party and fear of the Democrats outweighed the appeals of these two veteran defenders of the black man.

The North Carolina state election in August indicated the probable defeat of the Liberals, but it remained for Pennsylvania, Ohio, and Indiana, vitally important "October states," to settle the question. Greeley went on the stump for several weeks in a remarkable oratorical campaign before large crowds. To the surprise of most people he spoke with dignity, breadth of vision, and restraint, exhibiting none of the eccentricities for which he had been lampooned. But the results were not evident on election day. Pennsylvania and Ohio went Republican and, while Indiana elected the popular Hendricks governor, the majority of the legislature and most of the congressmen were Republican. The Liberals lost hope, and thousands of their Democratic allies failed to vote in November.

Grant Reelected

Grant carried every northern state and most of the carpetbag South; Greeley had three border states (Missouri, Kentucky, and Maryland), Tennessee, Texas, and Georgia. Louisiana, according to the official returning board, was apparently carried by the Liberal-Democratic coalition; but a Grant returning board reported different results, and Congress rejected both sets of electors. It also threw out three Georgia electoral votes for Greeley because the electors had voted for a dead man.* Arkansas, carried by Grant, was thrown out on a technicality. The coalition had made a poorer showing than Seymour in 1868. Grant's popularity seemed to be greater than ever.

For Greeley the result was fatal. His wife died October 30; he was crushingly defeated on November 5; reports came to him soon afterward of a movement to deprive him of the *Tribune*; and on November 29 he was dead. "The poor white hat!" said Harriet Beecher Stowe. "If, alas, it covered many weaknesses, it covered also much strength, much real kindness and benevolence, and much that the world will be better for."

The Liberal-Republican movement disappeared with Greeley's defeat. Loosely organized and dependent upon the Democrats for most of their votes, the Liberals collapsed under the shock of a disastrous defeat. Represented in Congress by a mere handful, with no patronage to sustain them, they could not preserve their separate identity.

Despite seeming failure, the Liberal-Republican movement did not live wholly in vain. It was an honest attempt to end the vexatious southern question, whose very existence imperiled any reform movement. Not until federal interference in the South ceased and local self-government was restored could the attention of the voters, northern and southern alike, be directed to the new America that had come into existence.

* Greeley died before the electoral college met, and so the Liberal-Democratic electors voted for other choices. The official vote, accepted by Congress, was as follows: Grant, 286; Hendricks of Indiana, 42; B. Gratz Brown of Missouri, 18; Charles J. Jenkins of Georgia, 2; David Davis of Illinois, 1. Henry Wilson had the same vote as Grant, but the Liberal-Democratic electors scattered their votes for vice-president, Brown receiving 42, seven others dividing the remainder. The popular vote, including Arkansas and the more official of the Louisiana returns, gave Grant 3,598,235, and Greeley, 2,834,761. O'Conor, straight-out Democrat, received 18,602; James Black, Prohibitionist, 3,371.

In Grant's second term the country realized this truth, and the policy of President Hayes in 1877 vindicated the Liberal position. The Amnesty Act of 1872, which restored political and voting rights to almost all former Confederates, was due to Liberal pressure, and the alignment of southern conservatives in a united front was aided by the national Democratic-Liberal coalition. The Liberal movement also infused a reform leaven into the old Copperhead Democracy and committed it to acceptance of the finality of war amendments, thus closing the books on the past. It loosened party ties in the West and made that section more receptive to the appeal of agrarian reformers.

Perhaps the most significant accomplishment of the Liberal movement was the creation of a group of independents who, held together by a common interest in civil service reform and honesty in government, would play a notable part in the battles of the next twenty years. The Liberals had failed as party organizers, but the spirit of reform did not die with Greeley.

A Time for Reform

The years of Republican rule seemed about to end as the time for choosing Grant's successor drew near. The Panic of 1873 and the six years of hard times that followed destroyed the Republican prosperity argument, while appalling revelations of corruption in the national government seemed to demand the overthrow of the party in power. Impervious to criticism, Grant was willing to run again but was clearly not wanted.

When the delegates to the Republican convention came to Cincinnati on June 14, 1876, a reform candidate seemed to be the party's only hope. Nevertheless, Senators Oliver P. Morton of Indiana and Roscoe Conkling of New York, party stalwarts, and popular Speaker James G. Blaine, recently tarred by a "Mulligan Letters" scandal, had strong delegate support. (A James Mulligan had charged that Blaine, while Speaker of the House, had been involved in shady dealings with railroad interests.)

To prevent a Blaine nomination (Conkling was a bitter enemy), spoilsmen and reformers joined in support of innocuous Rutherford B. Hayes, governor of Ohio, whose reputation was unblemished and whose war record was excellent. He was nominated on the seventh ballot. The platform was vaguely reformist and said little about Grant's policies. Representative William A. Wheeler of New York was the vice-presidential choice.

The optimistic Democrats assembled in convention in St. Louis on June 27 with a reformer candidate far in the lead, Governor Samuel J. Tilden of New York. He received the necessary two-thirds of the votes on the second ballot. His chief rival, Thomas J. Hendricks of Indiana, was named to run with him. The platform was a stirring indictment of Republican misdeeds but sidestepped the greenback issue, which the depression was bringing to the front.

Samuel J. Tilden was a veteran in New York politics, from the days of Martin Van Buren, but his earlier interests were in party management rather than officeholding. Acclaimed for his part in exposing and prosecuting the Tweed Ring, he was elected governor in 1874, and showed a high order of ability as a reform administrator. (During the 1860s and 1870s, "Boss" William M. Tweed, in conjunction with Tammany Hall, controlled New York City.) That he could carry New York, essential to Democratic success, was a powerful argument for him, although Bayard, Thurman, and Hendricks were better known.

Yet he was a strange choice. Sixty-two years old, unmarried, in rather poor health, this coldly intellectual, secretive corporation lawyer was far removed from the popular concept of a crusading knight of reform. Worst of all, he was a multimillionaire, having amassed his fortune in part through skill in reorganizing insolvent railroads. Such a man might give a clean, efficient administration to the country and relieve the South of carpetbag misrule, but his political and economic tenets were thoroughly conservative. The temple of business would suffer no profanation from a Tilden in the White House. He and Hayes, if not two peas from the same pod, at least gave indications of coming from the same parent vine.

The problem of the greenback Democrats, it was hoped, had been solved through the nomination of the friendly Hendricks for second place and through Hayes's outspoken stand against inflation. But, with both parties unfriendly, the extreme inflationists launched the Independent, or "Greenback," Party, a threat to Democratic unity in the West. Tilden's letter of acceptance, intended to harmonize differences, hurt him in the East, where concern was also expressed over the possibility that Hendricks, an avowed greenbacker, might become president if the none-too-robust head of the ticket did not live out his term.

Hayes, in accepting the Republican nomination, went beyond the party platform. He definitely favored resumption of specie payments, a policy of noninterference with the South, "thorough, radical, and complete" reform of the civil service, and a single term for president. Republican politicians were taken aback, and Grant was annoyed at the implied criticisms of his policies; but reformers were enthusiastic. Schurz took the stump and frequently wrote letters of advice to Hayes; the former Liberal-Republican organs, Bowles's *Springfield Republican*, Halstead's *Cincinnati Commercial*, and Whitelaw Reid's *New York Tribune*, extolled the virtues of the candidate in contrast with the delinquencies of Grant; and most of the eastern reformers also expressed faith in the nominee. Joseph

Pulitzer in the *New York World*, angry at reformer support of Hayes, could find but one reason: "Hayes has never stolen. Good God, has it come to this?"

The Conkling-Morton-Chandler group, saddled with a reformer candidate, made the best of the situation by working for party victory and ignoring Hayes, whom they did not even consult about the national chairmanship. With a better appreciation of the realities of politics, they saw that the reform issue was an admission of Republican guilt and was playing directly into Tilden's hands. A political newcomer, Colonel Robert G. Ingersoll, acclaimed for his nominating speech for Blaine, was put on the stump and drew huge crowds all the way from Maine to the Mississippi River, "waving the bloody shirt," that is, stirring up war emotions, as it had never been waved before and assailing the Democratic Party as the party of treason and rebellion. A South Carolina riot in July in which several Negroes were slain served to point the moral of southern depravity and to show the dire consequences to be expected if the southern-controlled Democratic party came into power.

This stirring of old hatreds reached such a stage that late in the campaign the Democratic national chairman, Abram S. Hewitt, forced from the excessively cautious Tilden a public declaration against any payment of Confederate debts, any compensation for loss of slaves, or any recognition of damage claims of disloyal persons, a touchy point.

Republican orators assailed Tilden's private character, charging that he was a railroad wrecker, a grasping penny pincher, an income-tax evader, a sham reformer, and—Ingersoll added—a dried-up, old bachelor, as bad as Buchanan. Zach Chandler, Republican chairman, managing the Hayes campaign with no illusions about reform, collected large sums from federal officeholders and concentrated on New York and Indiana, to the neglect of other states. "A bloody-shirt campaign, with money, and Indiana is safe," wrote one party leader in a letter that got into the newspapers; "a financial campaign and no money, and we are beaten." Hayes, aware of the straits of the party in these two states and even in Ohio, came down from his pedestal and urged Blaine to play up in his speeches the dread of a solid South and rebel rule to distract people's thoughts from hard times. Nor was he averse to stirring up anti-Catholic prejudices against Tilden, whose record was combed to provide some evidence. The secret anti-Catholic, antiforeign "Order of the American Alliance" endorsed Hayes.

Tilden's "barrel," as depicted by the cartoonist Nast, was supposed to finance the Democratic campaign; but this was far from the case. The candidate kept a tight hold on his purse strings, offended Chairman Hewitt and the organization managers by his indifferent attitude toward their arduous work, and failed to supply funds that might have made safe the three doubtful southern states—South Carolina, Louisiana, and Florida.

As it was, the national headquarters centered its efforts and funds on New York and Indiana and did a good job. The South was left to shift for itself —a fatal error.

In the October state elections Indiana was Democratic by a small margin, Ohio, Republican by a slightly larger plurality. The Democrats were encouraged. Indiana, New York, and a solid South would mean victory. Betting odds favored Tilden, while Hayes calmly prepared himself for an unfavorable verdict, though worried over the possibility of a disputed outcome.

Early returns indicated before midnight of November 7 that Tilden had been elected. New York, Indiana, Connecticut, and New Jersey had gone Democratic, and while there was some uncertainty about the "solidity" of the South, Tilden could spare two southern states and still win.* Republican headquarters in New York closed up, and Chairman Chandler, discouraged at reports from Louisiana and Florida, went to bed. Hayes admitted his defeat in his diary, and nearly all the Republican papers gave up hope.

In the early hours of the morning of November 8, while the editors of the *New York Times,* staunchest of Republican organs, debated whether to concede Tilden's election, a message came from Democratic state headquarters asking for the *Times* estimate of the electoral vote. This indication of Democratic uncertainty encouraged the editorial staff to hold out a little longer. The *Times,* without basis, thereupon claimed Louisiana and South Carolina for Hayes, but left Oregon, New Jersey, and Florida in doubt. John C. Reid, managing editor, then hastened to the Fifth Avenue Hotel headquarters of Chairman Zach Chandler, picking up an ally on the way, William E. Chandler of New Hampshire, national committeeman and lobbyist.

The two aroused the exhausted, uncomprehending national chairman and secured his permission to send telegrams alerting party leaders in South Carolina, Florida, and Louisiana to the fact that the national outcome depended on holding these states. Without this prod, they might have accepted as final the reported returns. Agents well supplied with money were soon heading southward, and National Chairman Chandler, belatedly aware of the situation, announced that Hayes had 185 electoral votes; Tilden, 184.

Everything seemed to depend on the official count in the three doubtful states, and both sides sent "visiting statesmen" south to watch the count.

The situation in the three states was similar. The Republicans, control-

---

* The popular vote is difficult to determine accurately because of disputed returns. Figures cited by the Congressional Quarterly in *Presidential Elections Since 1789* are as follows: Hayes, 4,034,311; Tilden, 4,288,546; Peter Cooper (Greenbacker), 75,973; and Green Clay Smith (Prohibitionist), 6,743.

ling the state governments and the election machinery, had relied upon the Negro masses for votes and had practiced frauds as in the past. The Democrats used threats, intimidation, and even violence, when necessary, to keep Negroes from the polls; and where they were in a position to do so they resorted to fraud also. The firm determination of the whites to overthrow corrupt carpetbag rule contributed to make a full and fair vote impossible; carpetbag hold on the state governments made a fair count impossible. Radical reconstruction was reaping its final harvest.

In Florida a small Tilden majority was wiped out by a Republican-controlled election board, and the Hayes electors received the official certificates. In South Carolina Hayes had a small margin of the popular vote, though the Democrats elected Wade Hampton governor and carried the legislature. In both states the Democratic electoral candidates claimed the election and cast their votes for Tilden, though officially the Republicans had the better case.

In Louisiana a Republican election board, by throwing out the votes of whole parishes where there was any evidence that violence or intimidation had affected the result, changed a Tilden majority into a Hayes margin of some 3,500 votes and awarded the governorship and legislature to the Republicans. Three members of the board later received federal offices from Hayes. In Oregon, carried by the Republicans, the Democrats contested an electoral vote on a technicality.

A Democratic House and a Republican Senate had to decide which of the double sets of electoral votes from the disputed states should be counted. Twenty votes were involved.

The Constitution states that the president of the Senate shall, in the presence of the two houses, "open all the certificates, and the votes shall then be counted." Did this confer any power on the presiding officer to decide which votes should be counted or rejected when double sets of returns came from a state? Most authorities were inclined to answer in the negative, and this was in accord with all the precedents, though Hayes personally held to the other viewpoint. Senator Ferry of Michigan, a Republican, presided over the Senate (Vice-President Wilson was dead) and would doubtless act in the interests of his party. But, granted the right of the two houses to decide such matters, how could a Republican Senate and a Democratic House of Representatives be expected to agree?

A joint committee of the two houses, after long discussion, evolved a plan for an Electoral Commission to consist of five senators, five representatives, and five Supreme Court justices. The two houses were to elect their representatives (in each case, three from the majority and two from the minority); four justices (two from each party) were designated in the bill, and they were to choose a fifth, presumably David Davis, of uncertain political affiliations. This electoral commission was to have final authority in the cases of double sets of electoral votes, unless both houses agreed to overrule it. The plan was accepted by large majorities, most of the opposition coming from die-hard Republicans. The Democrats felt certain that such a commission could not be so partisan as to award all the disputed votes to Hayes—and Tilden needed only one to win. Without arbitration, the cards were stacked in favor of the Republicans, who controlled the executive (and the army), the Supreme Court, and the Senate.

Democratic hopes were suddenly dashed to the ground on the very day the bill passed the lower house. News of a startling character arrived from Springfield, Illinois. The preceding day, a coalition of Democrats and independents in the Illinois legislature had elected Justice Davis to the United States Senate, rendering him unacceptable for service on the Electoral Commission. Fortune seemed to reserve her smiles for the Republicans through these years; but in this case asinine blundering by Illinois Democrats would seem to be a more logical explanation. National Chairman Hewitt and the congressional leaders, intent on getting the Electoral Commission bill passed, realized too late the dangers in the Illinois situation.

There was still the possibility that the judicial members of the commission would show the fair-mindedness of true judges and not the spirit of partisans. At least the fifth justice, on whom the burden of the final decision must rest, would surely realize the gravity of his position and put aside partisan considerations. That unfortunate individual, chosen by the four justices already on the commission after Davis became disqualified, was Justice Joseph P. Bradley. Bradley had the approval of Democratic leaders as he appeared to be the most independent of the remaining members of the Court, all of them Republican.

The electoral count began before the two houses on February 1, with a great crowd present in the hall of the House of Representatives. When Florida was reached, objections were raised against the certificates of both Republican and Democratic electors, and the problem went to the Electoral Commission. The first and most important matter for it to settle was whether it should go behind the returns. After long arguments by eminent counsel, it was voted, eight to seven, that the commission was not competent to receive evidence that was not submitted to the two houses in joint session. In other words, the regularity of the certificates would be considered, but not the proceedings and measures in Florida responsible for them. After such a decision, arguments were futile. Regularity was with the Republicans, and the commission, eight to seven, awarded the Florida votes to Hayes, with Bradley casting the deciding vote.

The Democratic House rejected the commission's decision in the Florida case; but the Republican Senate upheld it, and so it was final accord-

ing to the law. Similar verdicts in the Louisiana, Oregon, and South Carolina cases gave Hayes their disputed electoral votes. House and Senate
separated to vote on each disputed state.

While the South Carolina case was under consideration, an alarming
possibility developed. Democratic die-hards in the House were ready to
inaugurate a filibuster that would prevent resumption of joint sessions
and completion of the count before March 4. What would then happen,
no one could say. Civil war might begin. But the danger was more apparent than real.

Actually, negotiations had been under way for many weeks to take
care of such a situation. William Henry Smith, general agent of the Western Associated Press, acting for the Hayes inner circle, had established
contacts with important southern conservatives, chiefly former Whigs, and
reached a tentative agreement with them that would ensure their support
for the peaceful acceptance of Hayes as president. As finally worked out,
the terms of the bargain included assurances that Hayes would live up to
his letter of acceptance and bring to an end federal support of carpetbag
rule; that at least one cabinet post, and other patronage favors, would go
to southern conservatives; that Hayes would favor federal aid for education and internal improvements in the South, including a government sub-
sidy for the Texas & Pacific Railway. The lower Mississippi Valley was
eager for a rail connection with the Far West, but the panic had stalled
the project. Thomas A. Scott, president of the Pennsylvania Railroad, was
interested in the Texas & Pacific and played a part in the consummation
of the bargain.

Hayes made these commitments cautiously, through intermediaries. In
return, he received promises of equal rights and fair treatment for southern Negroes and assurances that the electoral count would proceed unob-
structed. He also believed that a coalition to elect James A. Garfield
Speaker of the new House might be arranged. Southern Democrats, especially those of Whig background, saw more loaves and fishes for their
neglected section in a deal with the Hayes men than in a resolute stand
beside their intransigent northern colleagues. Hayes had once been a
Whig.

The well-known conference in late February in Wormley's Hotel in
Washington, long supposed to have produced the solution to the filibuster
threat, actually was only a last-minute meeting to reassure worried southerners that the terms already agreed upon would be respected. A number
of persons participated in the negotiations at various stages, including the
indefatigable William Henry Smith, General Henry Van Ness Boynton, a
Washington correspondent, Andrew J. Kellar of the *Memphis Avalanche*,
Major E. A. Burk of Louisiana, Tom Scott's Pennsylvania Railroad lobby,
several conservative southern members of Congress, and a group of Ohio
friends of Hayes. Although not involved in the deal, Speaker Randall and

National Chairman Hewitt also worked to prevent delays in completing the count of the electoral votes. In the early hours of March 2 the two houses finished their tabulation: Hayes had 185 electoral votes; Tilden, 184.

Hayes arrived at the capital that day and took the oath of office privately the next evening at the White House, because March 4 was a Sunday. On Monday, with due ceremony, he was formally inaugurated.

VII

Reform and Tariff
Elections

☆

1880-1892

HAYES, committed to a single term as president, determined the political course of his party by two actions. He removed the federal troops from Louisiana and South Carolina, after which the Democrats evicted the carpetbag governments from those states, angering Republican "Stalwarts," who termed Hayes supporters "Half-Breeds." He attempted to reform the civil service system by presidential edict and clashed with Senator Roscoe Conkling of New York when he removed Chester A. Arthur and Alonzo B. Cornell from the top federal posts at the port of New York. Both were important cogs in the Conkling machine, and the angry boss tried to get their successors rejected by the Senate. He lost out after a long battle.

The New York Colossus, determined to recapture the White House for the true-blue Republicans, decided that Grant, recently returned from a leisurely trip around the world, should run again. Grant was willing. Conkling controlled New York, J. Donald Cameron accounted for Pennsylvania, and John A. Logan, for Illinois. Those against a third term supported Blaine, John Sherman of Ohio, and some favorite sons.

When the convention opened in Chicago on June 2, a dramatic clash ensued between Conkling and James A. Garfield, Sherman's manager and leader of the anti-Grant forces. Conkling was defeated in an attempt to secure the adoption of the unit rule, which would have suppressed anti-Grant minorities in the three large Grant states. When the balloting began, Grant led with 304 votes, but this was far from the 378 votes needed for the nomination. After thirty-five ballots the Blaine and Sherman forces combined and made Garfield the nominee on the thirty-sixth. Over Conkling's objections, Chester A. Arthur, the recently removed collector of the port of New York, accepted the offer of the Garfield forces to run for vice-president. Except for a condemnation of Chinese immigration, the platform merely rephrased the planks of 1876.

The Democratic convention met in Cincinnati on June 22 with Tilden out of the picture, presumably because of impaired health. The brief platform endorsed "tariff for revenue only"—a blunder—opposed Chinese immigration, and deplored the "great fraud" of 1876–77. On the first ballot for president, nineteen persons received votes, with General Winfield S. Hancock of Pennsylvania in the lead. He had less than one-fourth of the total but received the nomination on the second ballot, almost by default. There was little enthusiasm for any of his rivals, and his soldier record was a major asset. Former Congressman William H. English, a banker with a "barrel," completed the ticket. His residence in doubtful Indiana helped his cause.

A Campaign Devoid of Issues

The campaign of 1880 was barren of issues and devoid of drama. Labor troubles and farmer unrest had subsided, though the Greenback Party, headed by General James B. Weaver, tried to keep the embers alive. Neither major party had a program, and only on the tariff question was there any divergence. The Republicans waved the bloody shirt rather feebly and talked of southern disfranchisement of Negroes and the power the white South would exercise in a Democratic administration. The Democrats did not overlook the "fraud" of 1876–77 and repeated the old charges of Republican corruption, though the honest administration of Hayes gave these small weight.

The reformers, or Independents, again seemed to be in a position to decide the election. Both platforms had endorsed civil service reform, but more to the point were the records of the candidates. Here Garfield's garments were slightly spotted. As the recipient of a share of stock in the Crédit Mobilier, which had been exposed in Grant's administration, he had collected $329 in dividends. His explanations of this and of a large attorney's fee in a Washington paving-contract scandal satisfied even the impeccable Nation and G. W. Curtis's Harper's Weekly. Schurz added his praises as well.

But Garfield's letter of acceptance was not the positive statement on civil service reform the reformers expected, and during the campaign he seemed to cater to the machine leaders. In spite of this, the Independents turned down Hancock, with an unblemished record, apparently because of his lack of experience in government. Sneers at his imposing physique —"a good man weighing two hundred and forty pounds"—and Nast's cartoons portraying his naïve ignorance were the extent of Republican assaults on the man.

Conkling was the chief Republican problem. Arthur, Cameron, and Logan did their part but "Lord" Roscoe sulked in his tent. Garfield visited the East in August to appeal for financial support, and secured Jay Gould's help. Thomas C. Platt and other New York Stalwarts conferred with the candidate and apparently received some general assurances about patronage. Conkling did not appear, but his lieutenants were satisfied and went to work. In September he went on the stump in New York for the Republican cause, if not for Garfield.

Maine startled Republican leaders by electing a Democratic-Greenback governor in September, and fears were felt for Indiana and Ohio. Conkling then went West to speak; Grant joined him, making a seven-minute speech at Warren, Ohio, and the two, with a number of retainers, were maneuvered into a brief call on Garfield in his home, at Mentor. Out of this call later grew Platt's story that the grateful candidate rushed out in the rain to embrace Conkling and pledge him control of New York appointments. Historians have given little credence to the "treaty of Mentor." Garfield was not given to making rash pledges, particularly to the domineering New Yorker.

Conkling also spoke in Indiana, where the situation was serious. Money as well as oratory flowed like water in the Hoosier State, where S. W. Dorsey, secretary of the national committee, had things in his hands. The fears of business and industrial leaders were played upon with a belated use of the Democratic "tariff for revenue only" plank. Hancock denied that the Democrats would not protect the manufacturer and declared with much truth that the tariff was "a local question." Republicans seized upon this as an example of the General's ignorance and ridiculed his views. The Greenback character of the Maine outcome was a further argument used by Republicans to draw money from reluctant financiers, for Garfield's record was consistently anti-inflationist. At the candidate's own suggestion John D. Rockefeller was importuned to bring his Standard Oil agents into line for the Republican ticket in Indiana. In the end Republican money and organization carried the October state elections in Indiana and Ohio, foreshadowing success in November.

At this juncture appeared the forged Morey letter, a desperate attempt to turn the Pacific Coast against Garfield. The letter, addressed to "H. L. Morey of the Employers' Union, Lynn, Massachusetts," and apparently signed by the Republican candidate, approved of Chinese immigration "until our great manufacturing and corporate interests are conserved in the matter of labor." Garfield learned of its existence on October 20 and at once declared it a forgery; but *Truth*, the New York paper publishing the letter, insisted on its genuineness. Doubtless it injured him in the Far West, where the Chinese question was a vital issue, though every effort was made to show that the letter was simply a campaign lie for political effect.

A Republican Victory

Democratic hopes were dashed on Election Day when the Republicans carried the entire North and West except New Jersey, Nevada, and five of California's six electors. Garfield had 214 electoral votes; Hancock 155. However, the victor's popular plurality was small.* The Democrats took what little consolation they could from the "solidity" of the South: every former slave state had voted for Hancock.

The leading factors in the Republican victory were prosperity, the support of the business and financial interests, and the improvement in reputation of the party during the Hayes administration. That it was a party victory rather than a personal one was shown by the Republican majority in the lower house, the first in six years. In the Senate two Independents held the balance of power and divided between the two parties, creating a tie on organization questions and giving Vice-President Chester A. Arthur the deciding vote. In effect, party government was restored in 1880 after a six-year deadlock.

Garfield Assassinated

Garfield appointed Conkling's Half-Breed enemy, James G. Blaine, secretary of state and did not satisfy Conkling with some other appointments. But open war began when he made a Blaine henchman collector of the port of New York. Conkling fought the nomination with characteristic verbal violence and abuse, but when the appointment was about to receive Senate confirmation, he and his colleague, "Me, Too" Tom Platt, resigned and went to Albany to ask the legislature to vindicate their stand by returning them to Washington. They were turned down, but Garfield did not live to enjoy his triumph. On July 22, 1881, a mentally unbalanced office seeker shot the president in the back in the Washington railway station. Garfield died from the wound on September 19. Vice-President Arthur became president, and Blaine resigned.

Arthur was a pleasant surprise as president. He displayed independence and good judgment and made a record that seemed to warrant his nomination in 1884. The Pendleton Act to reform the civil service was passed in 1883, certain vetoes were generally praised, and in his appointments, he did not give special preference to Stalwarts. But the Half-Breeds wanted Blaine, and even among the Stalwarts, with Conkling out of power, there was the feeling that Blaine's turn had come. The reform

* Garfield, 4,446,158; Hancock, 4,444,260; James B. Weaver, Greenback, 305,997; Neal Dow, Prohibitionist, 9,674.

group preferred Senator Edmunds of Vermont to Arthur, and John Sherman of Ohio and John A. Logan of Illinois had their friends.

The Republican convention met again in Chicago, on June 3. To the customary platform generalities was added a stronger protective tariff plank. In spite of delegate and gallery enthusiasm for Blaine, it took four ballots to nominate him. John A. Logan, Illinois Stalwart, received second place on the ticket.

The Democrats, confronted with Blaine and Logan, needed a reform candidate to draw the Independent vote. One appeared in 1882 when Grover Cleveland was elected governor of New York. His record at Albany won the reformers but antagonized the Tammany machine headed by John Kelly. Kelly controlled part of the New York delegation but was muzzled by the unit rule.

A generally harmonious convention assembled in Chicago on July 8. "Cockeyed" Ben Butler turned up with two third-party nominations, but his past party shiftings and southern remembrance of his wartime rule of New Orleans eliminated him from serious consideration. His attempts to amend the platform were voted down. That document was long, platitudinous, and on the tariff question, verbosely ambiguous. But reform was too important an issue to be sidetracked by tariff, currency, or any other controversial question, and the platform's indictment of Republican misdeeds was well stated.

Ill-timed attacks on Cleveland by Tammany henchmen were greeted with hisses, and the galleries roared their approval of Bragg of Wisconsin when he said that Cleveland's friends "love him most for the enemies he has made." The New York governor was far in the lead on the first ballot and received the necessary two-thirds on the second. Hendricks of Indiana, Tilden's running mate, a soft-money westerner, balanced the ticket. He was not a reformer.

The campaign for Cleveland was a double-headed affair in which the forces of darkness and of light joined hands. On the side of darkness were Daniel Manning, Democratic boss of the Empire State; William C. Whitney, a wealthy young lawyer of tremendous energy and proper Wall Street connections; and Senator Arthur P. Gorman of Maryland, an astute, hard-headed politician who headed the national executive committee (a figurehead, ex-Senator William H. Barnum of Connecticut, was chairman of the national committee). These unregenerate partisans collected a larger campaign fund than usual from a segment of business and from Democratic state and municipal officeholders, made terms with recalcitrant or sulking local bosses, and used methods on occasion that might not have commended themselves to the candidate had he been fully informed. Their problem was to get every real or half-hearted Democrat to the polls. On the offensive they joined hands with the Independents in vicious attacks on Blaine.

The Mugwumps

Schurz, heading a separate organization with a small, poorly manned office in New York City, led the Independents, popularly called Mugwumps, and the Republican bolters into battle. (Mugwump was an Algonquin Indian term meaning "big chief.") Among these forces of light were many eminent American intellectual leaders: President Charles W. Eliot and almost the whole Harvard faculty, Henry Ward Beecher, James Freeman Clarke, Thomas Wentworth Higginson, and the veteran civil service reformers Godkin and Curtis. The important periodicals *Harper's Weekly*, the *Nation*, and *Puck*, and independent or Republican papers including the *Herald, Times, Evening Post* and *Telegram* in New York, the *Transcript, Herald*, and *Advertiser* in Boston, the *Springfield Republican*, the *Brooklyn Union*, the *Times* and the *Record* of Philadelphia, and the *Times* and *News* of Chicago, were anti-Blaine.

Yet many Republicans who had opposed Blaine before the Chicago convention now became mute or openly conformed. The whip of party regularity brought those looking to the future into line. Congressman Henry Cabot Lodge, young Massachusetts aristocrat, refused to sacrifice his seat to principle and stated that bolting would "destroy all the influence and power for good I possess." His fellow Harvardian Theodore Roosevelt, after weeks of uncertainty, returned from a Dakota ranch to speak for Blaine; earlier, as a New York State assemblyman, he had found much about Cleveland to commend. Senator Edmunds of Vermont was harder to move. Toward the close of the campaign he made one speech for his party but refused to mention Blaine's name. But Blaine's old enemy, Roscoe Conkling, in a reputed reply to requests for his support, was devastating: "I do not engage in criminal practice." His home county, usually Republican, was carried by Cleveland.

The Mugwump fire was centered on the Republican candidate's record, particularly the Mulligan letters. In 1869, Blaine, Speaker of the House, after helping secure renewal of a land grant for an Arkansas railroad, worked with a Boston broker, Warren Fisher, to sell its bonds. When they declined in value Blaine refunded the money to investors by secretly selling the nearly worthless bonds to the Union Pacific at a high price. Letters supplied by Fisher's bookkeeper, James Mulligan, to a House committee in 1876 were secured by Blaine on a pretext and not returned. Instead, he read extracts to the House and made a brilliant, if disingenuous, defense. There the matter rested until Blaine's nomination in 1884 revived the old charges. Worse even was a new batch of letters uncovered during the campaign, including a draft of a letter exonerating him that he himself had written and sent to Fisher to copy and mail back.

On it in his own hand was the significant request, "Burn this letter." The request had not been carried out, and the draft letter had not been sent. Both now appeared in print to humiliate the candidate.

Bernhard Gillam, the cartoonist of *Puck,* who outdid Nast of *Harper's Weekly* in vindictiveness, stamped the Republican candidate unforgettably in the public mind as the "tattooed man," marked on his body with "Bribery," "Mulligan Letters," "Little Rock," and other unpleasant reminders of his record.

The unrestrained abuse of Blaine drew a savage retaliation from Republican sources that might well have been deadly had it been better timed. In July the *Buffalo Evening Telegraph* gave the world the sordid story of Mrs. Maria Halpin. The prepossessing widow, employed in a Buffalo store in the early seventies, had been on intimate terms with several men. When a son was born to her in 1874 she named Cleveland as the father. He accepted the responsibility, perhaps to shield the others involved, and made some financial arrangements for the child. Eventually, because of the mother's misconduct, he had the boy placed in an orphanage, from which he was adopted by a good family. Few people knew of the matter until it appeared in print in 1884.

Jubilant Republican papers printed all the details, and many partisan Protestant ministers preached sermons against moral laxity and the danger of placing men of debauched character in high office. Cleveland astonished friends and enemies alike by admitting his sin and offering no excuses. His confession threw the Democratic-reformer camp into confusion. But the witty comment of a clever anonymous Chicagoan at a New York conference of Mugwumps let sunlight through the dark clouds. Let Blaine, he argued, whose private life was blameless, be remanded to private life, and let Cleveland, whose public life was a model of integrity, be kept in public life. Two famous Protestant ministers, James Freeman Clarke and Henry Ward Beecher, championed Cleveland; and Republican charges of gross immorality began to lose their weight. By Election Day the Halpin affair had become no more effective than any stale gossip after the truth has been clearly revealed. Cleveland's frankness was refreshing after Blaine's dissembling evasions of the Mulligan letters.

As the contest drew to a close, Republican strategists, alarmed at the situation in the Middle West, violated Republican precedents and put Blaine himself on the stump. His tour stirred the Republican masses as he preached on the benefits of protective tariff and dilated on his favorite theme, the dangers of rebel rule. In less spectacular fashion, Colonel W. W. Dudley, commissioner of pensions, and a hundred special examiners appeared in Ohio and Indiana to pressure the soldier vote.

If the Middle West, except Indiana, seemed to be safe by mid-October, New York was not, and the pleadings of Blaine's managers—or, perhaps, some inexorable fate—called him back to his destruction. The New York situation was complicated. John P. St. John, former Republican and governor of Kansas, was campaigning in New York as Prohibition candidate for president; and Frances E. Willard and the Woman's Christian Temperance Union, angry at contemptuous treatment accorded to a temperance petition at the Republican national convention, were supporting him. Temperance advocates, usually Republican in the past, might be drawn to St. John to punish Blaine just as the abolitionists had punished Clay in 1844. To offset this danger, the Republican national committee was secretly financing Ben Butler, the Antimonopoly-Greenback candidate, in an attempt to draw Democratic votes from Cleveland. John Kelly of Tammany was suspected of secret friendliness toward Butler.

Tied up with the Tammany and Butler problems was the Irish vote. Blaine was of Irish descent. His mother was a Roman Catholic, a cousin was the mother superior of a convent, and he himself had long exhibited a tendency to twist the British Lion's tail, to the edification of all good Irish. The *Irish Nation* and the *Irish World* of New York endorsed him, and a great meeting of Blaine Irish-Americans was held on July 28. Cleveland, son of a Presbyterian minister, had no particular appeal to the sons of Erin except as traditional Democrats. The Republicans, calling the Mugwumps and Democrats free-traders, dubbed him the "British candidate," whose success would imperil American industries. The *Irish World,* speaking for the more vociferous "professional" Irish-Americans, charged that all the great British dailies were opposed to Blaine.

Rum, Romanism, and Rebellion

To New York City came Blaine with the scales so evenly weighted that a straw might unbalance them. On the morning of October 29 he spoke to a group of Protestant ministers at the Fifth Avenue Hotel. In welcoming the candidate, Samuel D. Burchard, a Presbyterian minister, carved his niche in history with one asinine sentence: "We are Republicans and don't propose to leave our party and identify ourselves with the party whose antecedents have been rum, Romanism, and rebellion." Blaine did not catch the remark and made no mention of it in his reply.

A shorthand reporter took it down, turned it in to Chairman Gorman at Democratic headquarters, and within a few hours "Rum, Romanism, and Rebellion" was doing its work. Newspapers and handbills carried the story of Burchard's insult to Roman Catholics and Blaine's apparent acquiescence. No explanation could undo the damage. Enough Irish votes were probably lost to change the result in New York.

As if this were not enough for one day, Blaine was again victimized in the evening by supposed friends. Unwisely, and against Chairman Elkins's advice, he attended a dinner at Delmonico's given by the wealthiest men in the city. Present were John Jacob Astor, Jay Gould, Cyrus W. Field, Russell Sage, Levi P. Morton, and many other millionaires. The solitary reporter present (from Jay Gould's Associated Press) heard Blaine extol the tremendous increase in the country's wealth under Republican rule. Then all went into a private room (with the reporter excluded) and discussed campaign funds. Next day a *New York World* cartoon pictured "Belshazzar Blaine and the Money Kings" dining in splendor on "Monopoly Soup," "Lobby Pudding," "Navy Contract" and "Gould Pie," while a starving workingman and his wife appealed in vain for food. In a year of hard times, the reaction of labor to the incident was bound to be unfavorable.

Cleveland made two formal speeches—in Newark, New Jersey, and in Bridgeport, Connecticut—and attended a great celebration in Buffalo. On the Saturday before the election he reviewed a parade of forty thousand in New York City, listening to the tramping thousands chanting "Blaine, Blaine, James G. Blaine, the Monumental Liar from the State of Maine," and "Burn this letter, burn this letter, kind regards to Mrs. Fisher," while the marchers held lighted matches to sheets of paper. Twice in this same week Blaine had had his innings when the Republican hosts paraded past him roaring "Blaine, Blaine, James G. Blaine, O-O-O-hi-O, No-No-No Free Trade," though some were not above chorusing "Ma! Ma! Where's my pa? Gone to the White House, Ha! Ha! Ha!" Not since 1840 had Americans worked so hard at politics.

A Democrat Elected President

As the returns came in on the night of November 4, it was evident that New York would decide the outcome. Cleveland had the solid South, Indiana, Connecticut, and New Jersey, a total of 183 electoral votes; Blaine had the rest, except New York, 182 in all; New York's 36 were in doubt. The weather had taken a hand at the last minute, and a driving rain in upstate New York, "good weather for Democrats," made it hard for the farmers to get to the polls. Blaine was the loser thereby, for more Democrats lived in the cities.

This was the first Democratic presidential victory in twenty-eight years. Cleveland's plurality in New York was 1,149 in a total vote of 1,167,169.* The scales had indeed been tipped against Blaine by a straw. But what was the straw? Was it the much publicized Burchard remark, or

---

* The popular vote was as follows: Cleveland, 4,874,621; Blaine, 4,848,936; Butler, 175,096; St. John, 147,482. In New York the vote was: Cleveland, 563,154; Blaine, 562,005; Butler, 16,994; St. John, 25,016. The electoral vote was 219 for Cleveland, 182 for Blaine.

the banquet of the millionaires, or Conkling's ill will, or the unexpected strength of St. John, who polled 25,000 votes, or Butler's poor showing, or the rain of November 4, or some other fortuitous circumstance? Blaine believed that the suppression of the southern Republican vote had forced the party to depend on New York, and that the Independents, the Prohibitionists, and the Burchard remark accounted for that state. Better known is his message to Murat Halstead: "As the Lord sent upon us an ass in the shape of a preacher and a rainstorm to lessen our vote in New York, I am disposed to feel resigned to the dispensation of defeat that flowed directly from these agencies."

More fundamental were two factors that accounted for heavy Democratic inroads into Republican strength everywhere in the North. One was the failure of Republican economic appeal in a year of much unemployment and business stagnation. The other was the Independent, or Mugwump, uprising. The reform groups held the balance of power in the four northern states carried by Cleveland and reduced the Republican vote in other states. But for their activity in New York, Blaine would have won by such a margin that preacher, Prohibitionists, and rainstorm combined could not have changed the result.

The parties had not come to grips over economic issues. Both sides had ignored or touched lightly such matters as labor unrest, farmer problems, public-land policies, railway regulation, the growth of monopolies, and even tariff reform. The evasion was deliberate but not at all strange. Why should party leaders, whose function was to carry elections, attempt to formulate programs upon which few people were agreed? Third parties had tried and failed dismally. Reform in government was regarded by thousands of honest Americans as necessary before other reforms could come. For years corruption and a vicious spoils system had been undermining confidence in democratic government. The election was a contest to see whether a sentimental loyalty to a party in power that had long promised reform but had performed slowly and half-heartedly for its own presidents, and whose candidate was now suspect, should triumph over a party whose chief pledge was a candidate of unquestioned integrity with a record to match. The majority of the voters decided that the party that had saved the Union should no longer misgovern it.

Cleveland, a neophyte in national politics who was confronted with a Republican Senate, learned as he went along. Neither party spoilsmen nor reformers were satisfied with his handling of appointments, but civil service reform did make some progress. He antagonized the Grand Army of the Republic (GAR) by vetoing several hundred private pension bills and by an order, later rescinded, to return to their states captured Confederate battle flags.

Cleveland's ideas of economy and the application of business principles to government were affronted by the growing surplus in the federal treasury, chiefly from tariff revenues. Protectionist Democrats helped Republicans in blocking bills to revise the tariff, but Cleveland devoted his entire message to the problem in 1887 and committed his party to a policy of rate revision to reduce the surplus.

The First Tariff Campaign

The task of the Democratic national convention, assembled in St. Louis on June 5, was the easiest that had confronted the party since 1840. The platform contained a long statement on the tariff, which, in spite of its ambiguities, was taken to mean an endorsement of a downward revision policy. A separate resolution approved the moderate Mills bill, pending in the House of Representatives. Cleveland's record was the real platform. He was renominated by acclamation; former Senator Allen G. Thurman of Ohio became his running mate.

The Republicans came to Chicago on June 19, jubilant over Cleveland's commitment of his party to a lower tariff. Blaine would have been renominated but for a formal declination he sent from Italy to the chairman of the national committee. A flock of favorite sons got into the race and fourteen persons received votes on the first ballot. John Sherman of Ohio, making his third effort, had 229 votes. Judge Walter Q. Gresham of Indiana, hope of the unbossed, was second with 111. But bosses Matthew S. Quay of Pennsylvania, Tom Platt of New York, and some lesser lights seemed to determine the nomination after the deadlock forced an adjournment over the weekend. In any case, on the eighth ballot on Monday, ex-Senator Benjamin Harrison of Indiana was chosen. He was Ohio-born, had been a Civil War brigadier, was the grandson of a president, had no scandals to cover up, and was a faithful Presbyterian. Levi P. Morton, New York banker and businessman, represented the East on the ticket.

The platform contained an uncompromising protective tariff plank and promised to dispose of the surplus revenue with increased appropriations for defense, pensions, and public works.

The Republican campaign manager was Matthew S. Quay, who had succeeded the Cameron dynasty in the boss-controlled state of Pennsylvania, and whose organization methods were thorough and unscrupulous. Colonel W. W. Dudley, former head of the pensions bureau, was campaign treasurer. Money was presently raised on an unprecedented scale. John Wanamaker, Philadelphia merchant, acted as liaison officer to tap the vast resources of American business. Heading an advisory committee of businessmen, he was soon engaged in what came to be called cynically "frying out the fat." Mark Hanna, businessman-politician, raised more than $100,000 in northern Ohio. A key figure was James M. Swank of

Pennsylvania, head of the American Iron and Steel Association, which, with kindred organizations, sent hundreds of thousands of pamphlets to propagandize the partially industrialized Middle West on the merits of protection. No longer were officeholders expected to carry the chief burden of financing a national campaign. If businessmen felt that the security of their investments depended on Republican control, they must expect to pay a good, stiff price for it.

Harrison, a small man, aristocratic in bearing, aloof and difficult in personal contacts, called "Kid Glove" Harrison in Indiana, made surprisingly effective public addresses from his Indianapolis front porch. His good Civil War record was contrasted with Cleveland's having hired a substitute, and helped to make the GAR, already angry over the pension vetoes, into a Republican auxiliary.

It remained for Blaine, however, to quicken Republican heartbeats with his compelling eloquence, to give to a dry tariff argument a dramatic touch, to expose the British Lion and the Confederate Brigadier hiding behind the Democratic free-trade ramparts. It was a memorable tenth of August when Blaine rode up New York harbor on a tender amid a din of whistles, horns, band music, and frantic cheers to throw his spellbinding energy into the rather apathetic campaign. Tens of thousands greeted him, and other tens of thousands fought to hear him in Indianapolis and elsewhere in the Middle West in October. Finishing in doubtful Connecticut and New York, he had done more for Harrison than he could have done for himself.

Meanwhile, what of Cleveland? With Congress on his hands all summer and far into October, he had little time for campaign matters. His one public appearance was to read his letter of acceptance. The campaign was left to his managers, William H. Barnum of Connecticut, chairman of the national committee as in 1884, and Calvin S. Brice, chairman of the executive committee, a wealthy railroad financier and Wall Street speculator with a home in Ohio. Neither had any interest in tariff reform— Barnum being a member of the Iron and Steel Association—and neither had the president's interests closely at heart. The American Free Trade League headed by David A. Wells circulated pamphlets by the thousands; the American Tariff Reform League operated after a fashion in the Middle West; Godkin, Curtis, William Graham Sumner, Henry George, and others engaged in a campaign of education; but the heavy weight of the moneybags unbalanced the scales against them. Most of the old Mugwump papers remained loyal to Cleveland, but civil service reform attracted little attention. The scandal of 1884 was not revived. Cleveland had married in 1886, but stories did circulate that he beat his young wife and was drunk on the presidential yacht.

As in 1884, New York and Indiana were the key states. In the Empire State, Governor David B. Hill, candidate for reelection and no friend of

Cleveland or reform, had the strong backing of Tammany and the urban liquor interests. He was indifferent to Cleveland's fate, and Republican Boss Platt was willing to sacrifice his own party's candidate for governor, Warner Miller. A deal was apparently cooked up between three local machine leaders in the metropolis and the Republican organization. Harrison and Hill benefited at the expense of Cleveland and Miller. The *New York Times* and loyal Cleveland men charged that Hill himself was a party to the deal. The bolting of German Republicans, opposed to Miller's antiliquor position, may have been a factor. At least Harrison carried the state, and Hill won the governorship.

Bribery and Corruption

In New York corruption may have affected the result; in Indiana it was the deciding factor. That state no longer held its state elections in October, but a Republican poll sixty days before the November election showed the Democrats ahead. National headquarters then came to the relief of the state organization. "Divide the floaters into blocks of five," wrote Treasurer W. W. Dudley to Indiana lieutenants. "Put a trusted man with the necessary funds in charge of these five and make him responsible that none gets away and that all vote our ticket." This letter, put into Democratic hands by a railway mail clerk, created a sensation. Chairman Quay denounced it as a forgery, and Dudley brought libel suits—later dropped—against newspapers printing it. But stories of floaters, locked up the day before the election, then marched to the polls with Republican ballots in their hands and as much as fifteen dollars each in their pockets, have been well authenticated. Never had that considerable number of poor Hoosiers who were accustomed to turning a dishonest dollar at the polling places been so well rewarded. Afterward, an investigation was launched into Dudley's activities; but he threatened to "explode a lot of dynamite" if he were made the scapegoat, and a federal judge saw fit to dismiss the case. At all events, Indiana voted for Harrison by the scant margin of 2,348.

More widely used than direct bribery was the fear appeal. Industrialists warned employees of wage cuts and unemployment if Cleveland should win. Although he did not advocate free trade, it became the bogy of Republican orators; and such a good friend of labor as Henry George played into their hands by preaching its benefits while speaking for the Democrats.

Anti-British sentiment was stirred up by the publication of a letter from Sir Lionel Sackville-West, the British minister, to "Charles F. Murchison" of California, favoring Cleveland over Harrison. "Murchison," a Republican, posed as a former British subject writing for advice. The stupid minister was at once dismissed, but the episode may have cost Cleveland some Irish votes.

The election was close, but the outcome was clear by midnight. Harrison had the 36 electoral votes of New York by a margin of about 13,000. Cleveland lost Indiana but carried Connecticut and New Jersey. The rest of the North and West went Republican as in 1884, though in most cases Cleveland ran better than before and had a popular plurality of 90,596.* The unrepresentative electoral system gave him only 168 electoral votes to Harrison's 233.

Cleveland's courageous if inexpedient tariff stand made him the leader of his party and, in defeat, its most popular figure. He had ended its halting expediency and had given it an issue. More important, his four years in office had finally given the lie to the old cry that rebels would rule if the Democrats won. The party of the Copperheads had at last attained respectability.

The Second Tariff Campaign

Party rule returned with Harrison. The president and both houses of Congress were Republican. Blaine became secretary of state and Thomas B. ("Czar") Reed, Speaker of the House. The promises of the platform of 1888 were carried out by the passage of the highly protective McKinley Tariff Act and liberal appropriations for defense and pensions. This policy disposed of the treasury surplus but was not popular, and coupled with a farmer uprising, product of droughts and falling farm prices, produced a disastrous Republican defeat in the midterm elections.

Party bosses Quay, Platt, and J. S. Clarkson of Iowa were dissatisfied with Harrison for personal and patronage reasons and attempted to prevent his renomination at the Republican convention, which met in Minneapolis, in the discontented farm belt, on June 7, 1892. Secretary of State Blaine resigned suddenly three days before the convention met without giving any reasons. The anti-Harrison alliance offered him as their candidate, but Harrison was renominated with 535 1/6 votes out of 905 cast. Blaine had 182 5/6, and William McKinley, without being a candidate, received 182 votes. Whitelaw Reid of the *New York Tribune*, a longtime foe of Platt, was nominated for vice-president. The platform reaffirmed the tariff position of 1888 and defended the measures of the Republican Congress.

---

* Cleveland had 5,534,488 popular votes; Harrison, 5,443,892; Clinton B. Fisk (Prohibitionist), 249,813; Alson J. Streeter (Union Labor), 146,602. A United Labor candidate polled 2,818 votes in New York and Illinois, and an "American" candidate had 1,591 in California. Socialist and scattering votes totaled 7,006. Other totals vary slightly from these.

Eastern business interests, alarmed at the farmer revolt, looked to the Democrats to nominate Cleveland, who could be trusted to stand staunchly against free silver and agrarian radicalism. The New York Democratic machine backed Senator David B. Hill, who avoided commitments on issues by saying, "I am a Democrat," but Hill had slight support outside his home state. William C. Whitney managed Cleveland's preconvention campaign skillfully, and the former president was nominated on the first ballot at the national convention, which opened at Chicago on June 21. Adlai E. Stevenson, a silver Democrat and former first assistant postmaster general, was named for the vice-presidency, a peace offering to the free-silver advocates.

The platform committee's moderate tariff plank was revised on the convention floor to commit the party to a tariff for revenue only. The currency plank denounced the Sherman Silver Purchase Act of the Republicans as a cowardly makeshift but otherwise was as evasive as the Republican plank.

The Populist Party

A formidable third party, product of a swelling farmer discontent in the West and the South, was launched in Omaha on July 2. Delegates from various farmer, labor and other liberal organizations adopted with wild enthusiasm a platform that condemned the major parties for engaging in sham battles, and demanded a national paper currency along with the free coinage of silver, a graduated income tax, government ownership of railroad, telegraph, and telephone systems, and other reform proposals of a radical character. The convention nominated for president James B. Weaver of Iowa, who had been the Greenback candidate in 1880, and for vice-president James G. Field of Virginia, a coupling of Union and Confederate generals. The new party called itself the People's Party but was better known by the term Populist.

Except where agrarian discontent fed the fires of Populism, the campaign was the dullest in many years. Honest, bearded Benjamin Harrison confronting honest, mustached Grover Cleveland in a tariff debate was a repeat performance that did not inspire parades with torches or the chanting of campaign ditties. Neither candidate appeared on the stump, Harrison because of Mrs. Harrison's illness and subsequent death, and Cleveland out of respect for his rival's sad affliction. The Democrats, out of power, could assail Republican tariff policy without clarifying their own position. Cleveland's acceptance letter made it clear that he was no theoretical free trader—a necessary precaution, as the extreme tariff plank declaring that protection was unconstitutional was a boon to Republicans picturing the dangers of Democratic radicalism. The Republicans also had to defend their spending policy against charges of waste and extravagance, while the Sherman Silver Purchase Act suited neither silver men nor gold advocates.

The argument that labor benefited from protection received a stunning blow when a great strike occurred in the Carnegie steelworks in Homestead, Pennsylvania. Wage reductions were the ostensible cause, but the company's desire to break the power of the steel workers' union soon became evident. After much violence and bloodshed, the strike ended in failure; but its lesson was clear. A prohibitive tariff wall might confer huge profits on monopolistic industries, but labor would get little enough. Cleveland's letter of acceptance hammered this point home. Labor troubles in other places added to Harrison's woes.

The "fat-frying" tactics of 1888 worked poorly in 1892. Industrialists contributed to the Republican campaign, but the amounts apparently were smaller. The McKinley Tariff rates were so high that the moderate reductions to be expected from the Democrats were not alarming. Spending for corrupt purposes, however, was not much in evidence.* The secret Australian ballot, already adopted by thirty-three states in 1892, made vote-buying more difficult. Voters might still be bribed, but it was harder to check on their fidelity.

Another aspect of this dull campaign was the lethargy of the professional politicians. Quay, Platt, and Clarkson, the active leaders of 1888, were still sulking, and did little. Hanna of Ohio worked chiefly to advertise the virtues of William McKinley by having him speak for Harrison and the tariff all the way from Iowa to Maine. Blaine, stricken by disease and the shock of the sudden death of his son Emmons, was in no condition to play his customary part. He visited Whitelaw Reid at his country estate in New York and read a ten-minute address to a crowd of citizens from the neighboring towns, his only speech of the campaign. He came to Washington shortly before the election, was cordially received by Harrison, and walked home from church with him. Within three months he was in his grave.

In the Democratic camp the indefatigable Whitney handled the campaign efficiently, without blunders. The central organization was small, and finances for a time troubled him; but his Wall Street contacts helped bring in the necessary funds. The biggest problem was Grover Cleveland. Promises of jobs and favors were foreign to his nature, and he could not forgive his enemies. In the midst of the campaign he broke with Henry Watterson, the powerful Kentucky editor; and the two were never reconciled. When Whitney undertook to gain the good will of the Hill machine, Cleveland would make no pledges as to patronage. Sensing a

---

* Tabulations of campaign expenditures since 1860 list those of 1892 as the largest in any campaign to that time. However, the estimates are largely guesswork.

national victory, Hill and his cohorts fell in line and worked for the party, if not the candidate.

Whitney also advised Cleveland to take a more sympathetic attitude toward silver, as the newly organized Populists were charging him with subservience to the eastern money power. A vague sentence in his letter of acceptance about remedying "the wants of our people arising from the deficiency or imperfect distribution of money circulation" was the limit of his concession. However, Democratic state organizations in half a dozen western states where the Republicans had the upper hand joined forces with the Populists and gave twenty-two electoral votes to Weaver, the third-party leader.

Although late indications pointed to a Democratic victory, the margin was surprising. It was a near landslide. Cleveland had the South, the doubtful northern group—New York, New Jersey, Connecticut, and Indiana—and normally Republican Illinois, Wisconsin, and California (except one elector). He also had 5 of Michigan's 14 (a Democratic legislature had districted the state for electors) and 1 from Ohio, where a Democratic elector, oddly enough, led the ticket, followed by 22 Republicans. Fusion in North Dakota produced one Cleveland elector also. The totals were: Cleveland, 277; Harrison, 145; Weaver, 22. The popular vote gave the victor a substantial margin.* Fusion arrangements with the Populists in some states gave Weaver many Democratic votes. In New York, Cleveland had a plurality of more than 45,000; but the Empire State for once did not decide the result. The Democrats would have won without it.

The verdict was too decisive to be explained by anything except a widespread revulsion against Republican policies and an abiding confidence by voters of all classes in the integrity of Grover Cleveland. Had the four years that followed brought prosperity and domestic peace, he might have retired in 1897 with the popularity of a Coolidge. But the financial panic of 1893, followed by business collapse, unemployment and labor troubles, farmer discontent, and the strife of classes and sections brought out in a cruel light his fundamental conservatism, the negative character of his virtues, and the inflexibility of his mind. He saw only the necessity of resisting discontent; he did not know how to allay it. In the end his party was torn apart, and his leadership repudiated.

---

* The popular vote was as follows: Cleveland, 5,551,883; Harrison, 5,179,244; Weaver, 1,024,280; John Bidwell, Prohibitionist, 270,770; Simon Wing, Socialist Labor, 21,163. Forty-four states participated in the election, six having been admitted since 1888. Kansas, Idaho, Colorado, and Nevada chose Populist electors. North Dakota, carried by a Democratic-Populist coalition, gave Weaver and Cleveland each an electoral vote, while 1 Republican elector was successful. One Weaver elector was chosen in Oregon. A joint electoral ticket was defeated in Wyoming.

VIII

McKinley and Bryan

☆

1896-1900

THE COUNTRY seethed with discontent during the depression following the Panic of 1893. Cleveland insisted on upholding the gold standard at all costs, to the anger of the inflationist silver-coinage forces. Labor was aroused over the federal government's drastic actions in the Pullman Strike in Chicago. The Supreme Court was sharply criticized for its five-to-four decision that the income tax (in the Wilson-Gorman Tariff of 1894) was unconstitutional.

The People's Party, advocating free coinage of silver among its list of reforms, was threatening to swallow the Democratic Party in the farmer-silver West and was challenging its control of the South. Democratic silver advocates such as veteran Congressman Richard P. Bland of Missouri and young William Jennings Bryan of Nebraska set to work to convert their party to free silver and make it a farmer-labor vehicle that might absorb Populism and unite South and West against the conservative East. The Republican Party gained ground in the midterm elections of 1894, but was also divided into "Gold Bugs" and "Silver Bugs."

The Republicans faced the currency problem first. Their national convention opened in St. Louis on June 16, 1896, with a new operator displacing the old state bosses at the controls.

Marcus A. Hanna, wealthy Cleveland business leader, was better known as a fund raiser than a political manager when he formed an alliance with William McKinley, northeastern Ohio congressman, author of the Tariff Law of 1890, war veteran, and experienced campaigner for public office. Hanna worked and spent to elect McKinley governor of Ohio for two terms and then planned a preconvention strategy to get him the presidential nomination. He operated so skillfully that "he had the South practically solid before some of us waked up,"—Boss Platt's version. The old bosses encouraged favorite-son candidacies, but Hanna's lieutenants, such as Charles G. Dawes in Illinois, won delegates for McKinley over local favorites.

Republicans Favor Gold

Hanna handled the currency problem skillfully. McKinley had been a "straddle bug" on the issue but reluctantly agreed to a gold plank. When the eastern leaders arrived, Hanna created the impression that he was not committed to the gold standard and seemed to capitulate to their demands as the convention opened. Actually his close associates had already drafted the gold plank that went into the platform. As adopted, it opposed the free coinage of silver except by international agreement that "we pledge ourselves to promote and until such agreement can be obtained the existing gold standard must be preserved."

A free-silver substitute offered on the floor of the convention by Senator Henry M. Teller of Colorado was tabled, 818½ to 105½. Then followed a secession of twenty-four delegates and some alternates, nearly all from the silver-producing mountain states.

The platform blamed Democratic policies for the panic and depression and promised protective tariff to right things. It foreshadowed the imperialism of the next few years by its statements on foreign policy, but these were overlooked in the tumult over silver.

The balloting for president gave McKinley 661½ votes; Speaker Thomas B. Reed, 84½; Quay, 61½; Levi P. Morton of New York, 58; William B. Allison of Iowa, 35½; and Donald Cameron of Pennsylvania, 1. Garret A. Hobart of New Jersey, a loyal member of the McKinley organization, was nominated for vice-president.

Democrats Reject "A Cross of Gold"

The Democratic national convention opened in Chicago on July 7. The silver men were in control, but the credentials committee strengthened their hold by seating the Bryan delegation from Nebraska and awarding four Michigan seats to silver men. The resolutions committee presented a silver majority report and a gold minority report to the convention. David B. Hill of New York led the gold debaters. It was Bryan's good fortune to be the closing speaker on the silver side. His famous effort appeared to be extemporaneous, but he had tried out parts of the speech on smaller audiences in his preconvention campaigning for silver, and only the arrangement was improvised. His magnificent voice reached every part of the great hall, and the audience responded "like a trained choir," he wrote afterward. He concluded with the sentence that has given the speech its name. "You shall not press down upon the brow of labor this crown of thorns, you shall not crucify mankind upon a cross of gold."

The majority report was upheld, and an endorsement of Cleveland's administration voted down. The platform declared for the free and unlimited coinage of silver at the ratio of sixteen to one without waiting for the aid or consent of any other nation. It criticized the Supreme Court sharply for declaring the income tax unconstitutional, opposed the importation of foreign labor, favored arbitration of labor disputes, and denounced the use of injunctions by federal courts and federal interference in local affairs—a reference to the recent Pullman Strike. Other resolutions demanded enlargement of the powers of the Interstate Commerce Commission and condemned President Cleveland's bond sales to banking syndicates. Such a platform seemed anarchistic to conservative easteners, and 178 delegates refused to vote on the balloting for president.

Richard P. Bland of Missouri, veteran silver leader, and Senator Henry M. Teller of Colorado, bolting Silver Republican, had been regarded as the favorites in the large field of candidates, but Bryan's electrifying speech had altered the situation. It took five ballots to dispose of instructions and pledges. On the fifth ballot Bryan had 652 of the 930 votes in the convention. He had celebrated his thirty-sixth birthday on the preceding nineteenth of March.

For the vice-presidency Arthur Sewall of Maine, a shipbuilder, railroad director, and bank president—and yet a silver advocate—was named on the fifth ballot over John R. McLean of Ohio.

With their silver thunder stolen by the Democrats, the People's Party, meeting in St. Louis on July 22, had a hard choice between independent action and expediency. The latter won. Bryan was endorsed, but a separate candidate, Thomas E. Watson of Georgia, was named for vice-president. The platform was much more radical than the Democratic, but Bryan did not have to accept it. Thus the Populists became "Popocrats."

The bolting Silver Republicans and a National Silver Party also joined the coalition by endorsing Bryan.

The Gold Democrats held a convention in Indianapolis on September 2 and nominated General John M. Palmer for president and General Simon B. Buckner of Kentucky for vice-president. By this strategy Cleveland, Carlisle, and other conservatives avoided voting Republican. But David B. Hill, who did not bolt, was quoted as saying, "I am still a Democrat, very still."

The action of the Democratic convention had upset the Republican plan of campaign. Expecting to throw the responsibility for the depression and the blunders of Cleveland's administration on the Democratic Party and to advocate a return to a higher tariff as the way of economic

salvation, the party of McKinley and Hanna had counted on an easy victory over a disorganized foe.

But the Democrats had repudiated the Cleveland administration, had
set up a standard to which all the forces of discontent were invited to
repair, and were threatening to sweep the upper Mississippi Valley from
its Republican moorings with a far more plausible method of curing the
hard times than Republican tariff policy. It was now poor strategy for the
Republicans to center their guns on Cleveland as it would only antago-
nize the Gold Democrats, whose support was worth attracting. Instead,
McKinley was forced to defend the existing gold standard, for which he
had little heart, and place less emphasis on protection, in which he thoroughly believed. To make concessions to silver now would only play into
Bryan's hands.

The People Visit a Candidate

McKinley determined his own role in the canvass. A fluent public
speaker, he could talk generalities more impressively than any man then
in public life. His formal friendliness had none of Harrison's chill, and his
solid figure and careful dress—with wing collar, starched shirt, long, dou-
ble-breasted coat, white vest, and red carnation—convinced audiences
that they were looking at a statesman before he uttered a word. As a candidate for lesser offices, he had pleaded his own cause. But a presidential
candidate, he felt, must remain in dignified waiting until the voters made
their decision. He then devised a curious compromise. He might not go to
the people, but the people might come to him. The idea of delegations
and committees calling upon the candidate was familiar enough, but the
excursions to Canton in 1896 amounted to mass pilgrimages. People came
by the thousands in special trains—farmers, merchants, GAR posts, railroad workers, religious and racial groups, and many others, often with
their expenses paid—to see McKinley and listen to a few well-chosen
remarks or, in the case of large delegations, a formal address of some
length.

Nothing was left to chance. McKinley would have no "Rum, Romanism, and Rebellion" upset his careful planning. He invited the chairman
of every visiting group to Canton ahead of time and asked him to submit
his remarks in writing. These were carefully edited, unfortunate or
embarrassing expressions deleted, and sometimes whole sections rewrit-
ten. Then, on the appointed day, the chairman would take his delegation
to McKinley's home, recite his prepared speech to the appreciative candidate, and listen to a most felicitous response on the significant issues of
the campaign, particularly attuned to the interests of the group of listen-

ers. The speeches in this "front-porch" campaign appeared, of course, in the newspapers and added to McKinley's stature as a candidate.

Hanna's management problem was not easy. No longer was it one of raising sufficient funds to buy floaters in Indiana and deal with venal Tammany politicians in New York. The East seemed to be safely Republican, but every state west of Pennsylvania was listening to the silver siren. To win on such an extended front would require organization and propaganda on a large scale. Money must be provided by the wealthy East if business and financial leaders wanted to save their system from the deluded "anarchists" of the midlands.

The sums Hanna demanded seemed to be excessive in a period of business distress; but the wave of enthusiasm for Bryan immediately following his nomination, and the united front established by the silver groups, frightened bankers and businessmen and made Hanna's task easier. James J. Hill, railroad magnate, introduced him to Wall Street, and the money began to pour in. Ability to pay, not generosity, determined the contributions. For banks the assessment was fixed at one-quarter of 1 percent of their capital. Life insurance companies contributed liberally, as did nearly all the great corporations. The Standard Oil Company gave $250,000 to Hanna's war chest. The audited accounts of the national committee revealed collections of about $3,500,000. Charles G. Dawes, who handled all funds at the Chicago headquarters, recorded in his diary a total of $1,962,325.59 spent in Chicago. He estimated the New York total at $1,600,000.00. The wild guesses by unfriendly writers of $10,000,000 to $12,000,000 seem to be impossibly large.

Very little of this disappeared into the capacious pockets of grafting politicians. Hanna demanded results, and from the national headquarters in New York City and the well-organized regional headquarters at Chicago he directed his army of workers with admirable efficiency. A group of veteran political strategists managed the New York headquarters, but he entrusted the more important Chicago center to aggressive younger men including Henry C. Payne of Wisconsin, Charles G. Dawes of Chicago, W. T. Durbin of Indiana, and Cyrus Leland, Jr., of Kansas.

Pamphlets and leaflets by the millions were sent out from Chicago, some of them in seven or eight foreign languages, to catch the interest of voters of all classes, creeds, and nationalities. Everything from boilerplate matter for small-town newspapers to McKinley buttons for schoolboys poured out of Hanna's mill, while billboards along country roads carried the likeness of "The Advance Agent of Prosperity." Some fourteen hundred speakers were available to preach the Republican gospel in the doubtful areas.

But as the campaign grew in heat and bitterness, ugly aspects appeared for which Hanna had no direct responsibility. Men of wealth, alarmed at the enthusiasm aroused by Bryan and taking at face value the extreme utterances of Populist orators, fought back with powerful economic weapons in an attempt to coerce, where persuasion might fail. Labor, the uncertain partner in Bryan's poorly constructed farmer-labor coalition, was threatened with loss of employment in case Bryan won. Buyers gave orders for materials subject to cancellation if McKinley lost. In some cases workers were told not to report Wednesday morning after election unless McKinley won. Such methods, coupled with the steady pounding away at the workingman with the prosperity argument, made of little account the efforts of those champions of the downtrodden, Governor Altgeld of Illinois, Eugene V. Debs, and Henry George.

In farming areas pressure of a different sort was attempted. Reports went around that agents of the great insurance companies, large holders of farm mortgages, were promising extensions at lower rates of interest if McKinley were elected. This was used to offset the boon of easier credit supposed to come when free silver went into effect.

Bryan's campaign was almost a one-man show. The "Boy Orator of the Platte" was a novelty in American politics. The "Cross of Gold" speech had made him a popular hero, and Americans clamored to see and hear him. A front-porch campaign was out of the question. The only sensible strategy was to send him around the country to carry his message to the largest possible number. There followed the most famous stumping tour in American history.

Bryan Tours the Country

His first trip East was made early in August to receive formal notification of his nomination in New York City. The thousands that jammed Madison Square Garden wanted a fiery, fighting speech, a challenge to battle against the powers of mammon. Instead, the candidate read a carefully phrased but tiresome treatise on the economics of the currency question, while they squirmed and perspired, and some even departed. Opposition newspapers—nearly the whole metropolitan press—ridiculed the performance as a false alarm, and even the friendly *New York Journal* admitted that the audience was disappointed. Bryan had used a manuscript because he was in "the enemy country" and felt that he must make no slips in this keynote speech. This was a mistake. He had missed a great opportunity to arouse the eastern masses. Men of wealth slept more soundly after this.

The return trip provided opportunities for numerous speeches in upstate New York, Pennsylvania, and the Middle West as far north as Milwaukee. Bryan then made the most extensive trip of the campaign, a speaking tour all the way from Nebraska to Maine, and from the upper

South to the Canadian border. The Middle West, the great battleground, received most attention. The trip ended in Lincoln, Nebraska, his home town, the Sunday before the election. He devoted Monday, November 2, to his home state, addressing twenty-seven audiences on that day. Altogether, by his own estimates, he covered 18,009 miles and made some 600 speeches to possibly 5,000,000 persons. Fears that his magnificent voice would not hold out led to all manner of throat treatments—compresses, gargles, cough drops; but finally he discarded them all and found his vocal chords in fine condition at the end of his oratorical marathon.

Democratic difficulties centered around money and the fusion of the silver forces. The paltry $650,000 with which they tried to match Hanna's millions was the smallest fund since Hancock's campaign of 1880. But for the contributions of a group of wealthy silver-mine owners, the campaign chest would have been insignificant. On the other hand, donations from the Republican national committee solved in part the financial problem of those Democrats who had bolted and nominated Palmer and Buckner.

Securing the cooperation of all the silver forces was an awkward problem. Three organized parties—Democratic, Populist, and National Silver, each with its national committee—and a group of Silver Republicans were supporting Bryan and attempting to preserve their separate identities at the same time. The Populists even had their own vice-presidential candidate, Tom Watson, and a platform that Bryan did not accept. This duality was solved by the nomination of joint electoral tickets of "Popocrats" with part of the electors apportioned by Bryan and Sewall and part to Bryan and Watson. In 26 states where division was agreed upon, Sewall had 198 possible electoral votes to Watson's 78. Watson naturally resented this arrangement as it rendered his defeat certain. Even if Bryan won, he would finish third and the Senate would choose from the two highest, Hobart and Sewall.

Yet no other course was possible. Except in Louisiana, Arkansas, and North Carolina, the Democrats of the South rejected fusion, forcing the Populists to accept their tickets. In a few states separate electoral tickets for Bryan and Watson were nominated, but they had no effect on the election.

Fusion on state and congressional tickets was far more complicated and was not always achieved. In the South the Populists tended to work with the Republicans; in the West, with the Democrats, though the independent Silver Republicans followed their own course, and fusion became confusion in the mountain states.

The Bryan campaign headquarters, despite limited funds, sent out a considerable amount of literature. The best-known piece used by either side was *Coin's Financial School.* A primer of the silver question first published in 1894 by William H. Harvey, a lawyer then living in Chicago, it recited in simple dialogue the merits of free coinage of silver, leaving the gold advocates in its pages utterly confounded. The cracker-box philosophy of the little book struck home in a period of hard times and gave it a circulation of several million.

A Partisan Press

One of Bryan's greatest handicaps was lack of newspaper support in the larger cities. The Republican press, the independent journals, the influential weeklies such as *Harper's Weekly*, the *Nation*, and the *Independent*, and most of the larger Democratic papers in the metropolitan centers were against him. In New York City only William Randolph Hearst's *Journal* was loyal; even Pulitzer's *World* joined the bolters. Not again until 1936 was there such a journalistic phalanx on one side of a great political contest.

Near-hysteria seemed to grip the conservative East by autumn, and a campaign of fear and hate broke loose that outdid in vituperation the most rabid utterances of the Populists. Bryan was derided as a boy orator and a political faker; but more effective was the cartoon representation of him in *Harper's Weekly* as a huge silver dollar with Governor Altgeld of Illinois, the "anarchist," hiding behind him. Altgeld had outraged conservatives by pardoning the anarchists imprisoned for the bombing in Haymarket Square in 1886, in Chicago. Bryan was now linked with Altgeld and Debs, the Pullman strike leader, in a trinity of subversive infamy. Theodore Roosevelt compared them in a campaign speech to "the leaders of the Terror of France in mental and moral attitude"; and he declared in an unguarded moment in a private conversation later made public that he expected to meet Altgeld and his followers "sword to sword on the field of battle." The metropolitan Protestant pulpit entered the campaign, and many eminent reverend figures, including T. De Witt Talmage and Charles H. Parkhurst, upheld the cross of gold.

Against the tide of abuse and denunciation Hearst's *New York Journal* retaliated in kind. Its cartoonist, Homer Davenport, pictured Hanna invariably as a bloated plutocrat stamped with dollar signs, and McKinley as his puppet. Alfred Henry Lewis wrote articles so offensive that Hanna, unaccustomed to this political infighting, considered court action; but he decided that this might be just what Hearst wanted.

McKinley Wins

As Election Day approached, close observers could see that the result was no longer in doubt. After weeks and weeks of careful work the great Hanna organization had everything in hand. The Middle West, the battleground, was safe. Historians have usually given some credit to a fortuitous circumstance. The wheat crop of 1896 was a bumper one, yet a heavy foreign demand in the fall brought a sharp rise in price. This came without free silver and may have helped the Republican argument for gold; but the higher wheat prices seem to have benefited speculators rather than farmers, and prices of other products continued to slump.

Before midnight of November 3, Bryan knew that he was beaten. The Middle West as far as Minnesota, North Dakota, and Iowa had gone Republican, as had the East, the southern border states of Delaware, Maryland, West Virginia, and Kentucky, and California and Oregon on the Pacific Coast. McKinley had 271 electoral votes to Bryan's 176. Bryan had the South and the newer western farming and mining states, admitted after 1860, except North Dakota, and also one elector each from California and Kentucky.

McKinley had 7,108,480 popular votes; Bryan, 6,511,495 including fusion electoral tickets.* Both houses of Congress were Republican by safe margins.

Bryan had failed to corral the industrial workers. The cities outside the South and the silver-mining West were nearly all Republican. Hanna had sold the prospects of prosperity and good wages to labor, though pressure and intimidation played a part. Bryan's farm vote fell short of his expectations. The debt-burdened and impoverished followed him; the better off, as so often in the past, voted Republican. The rural South and the silver-mining states did as expected, but his margin of victory in the distressed Populist belt was small, for cities and towns voted against him. In the older Middle West he shared the farm vote with McKinley, but in the rural parts of the East he failed badly. He lost every county in New England and carried but one in New York. He ran proportionately better in the seaboard cities than in the neighboring country districts. His effort to unite South and West was too late by at least two decades. Industrialism and urbanization, spreading westward, even had outposts beyond the Mississippi, while the older farm states were almost as conservative as the East.

The People's Party had been swallowed by the Democratic Party; but it had liberalized the older organization in the process, and while its reform program was forgotten in the din raised over silver, the best features were to be revived and accepted later by the major parties. Even free silver was vindicated in a way, for unexpectedly large increases in the world's gold supply provided the currency expansion Bryan and the "Popocrats" were demanding.

* John M. Palmer, Gold Democrat, had 133,435; Joshua Levering, Prohibitionist, 125,072; Charles E. Bentley, National Party (Prohibition seceders), 19,363; Charles H. Matchett, Socialist Labor, 36,356.

McKinley Again Nominated

The violent shift of American political issues from domestic problems to foreign relations made McKinley's term of office very different from what he had expected. The Spanish-American War, the acquisition of Puerto Rico and the Philippines, the annexation of Hawaii, and the demand for an interoceanic canal tell the story of the breakdown of isolation and the emergence of America as a world power. The angry voices of the Leases, the Donnellys, and the other prophets of Populism fell on deaf ears as prosperity returned and imperialism took over the political stage. The Gold Standard Act of 1900 seemed to settle the currency problem, and Republicans gave the new Dingley Tariff much of the credit for the good times.

The Republicans held their convention in Philadelphia on June 19, 1900, with everything but the vice-presidential nomination planned in advance by the president and Mark Hanna. The gold standard, the Dingley Tariff, the Spanish-American War, and the fruits of the new adventure in glory were extolled in the long platform. McKinley refused to express a preference for a running mate, and after his own nomination by acclamation, the delegates took matters out of Hanna's hands by nominating Theodore Roosevelt, governor of New York, and "Rough Rider" hero of the Spanish-American War. Behind the scenes Boss Platt of New York, who wanted to keep Roosevelt from another term as governor, and Boss Quay of Pennsylvania, who had some scores to pay with Hanna, helped manipulate the stampede. Roosevelt had been reluctant to run but, to Hanna's annoyance, decided to accept the nomination.

The Democrats again turned to Bryan, still the popular hero to the masses of Democratic voters. The chief problem faced by the national convention at Kansas City on July 4 was endorsement of free coinage of silver. Bryan insisted on it over the opposition of eastern delegates and some of his own friends and had his way. The platform attacked Republican imperialism and the administration's policies toward Cuba, Puerto Rico, and the Philippines, and demanded more stringent antitrust laws. Bryan was renominated with much enthusiasm, and former Vice-President Adlai Stevenson was named as his running mate.

The Populists were divided. A fusion group and some Silver Republicans endorsed Bryan, but a middle-of-the-road group ran independent candidates. A newly formed Socialist Party nominated Eugene V. Debs.

Although insistent that free silver go into the platform, Bryan did not plead for it in his campaign but made imperialism the paramount issue, with the trust question second in importance. He attempted, as in 1896, to make it a struggle between democracy and plutocracy, but the class and sectional appeal was less evident in 1900. He appeared rather as the defender of American liberal traditions in opposing an imperialism that would exploit weaker peoples, "civilize with dynamite and proselyte with the sword." He promised in his notification speech in Indianapolis before fifty thousand people to set up a stable form of government in the Philippines and then to give the people independence under American protection. The strong religious strain in Bryan came to the surface repeatedly in his assaults upon the immorality of holding weaker peoples in subjection. "The command 'Go ye into all the world and preach the Gospel to every creature' has no Gatling-gun attachment," he shouted. Imperialism had no warrant in the Bible, he insisted, and he flung scriptural citations at the Republicans with the fervor of a traveling evangelist.

However, the Democratic candidate began to shift his emphasis as the campaign went on. The dangers of imperialism were not arousing the voters. The woes of the little brown brothers, whom unsympathetic American soldiers were "civilizing with a Krag" (a rifle), were not like the woes of the debt-burdened agrarians four years earlier. Then Bryan had voiced magnificently the demands of impoverished Americans for a more abundant life, and his words had struck home. In 1900 he was preaching sermons to well-fed audiences on the right of self-determination of faraway Filipinos. His appeal was not much more exciting than that of a returned foreign missionary seeking funds for Christianizing the heathen. "It sounded like music, and it read like the prophets of old," was one listener's comment on a Bryan speech.

But it was not stirring the masses. Bryan sensed this, and began to play up the trust question and the need to curb special privilege. This was a note more in keeping with the Bryan of 1896 and, under more propitious circumstances, might have been powerfully effective. But Americans, relaxing from the stresses and strains of the depression years, were content for a season to enjoy the fruits of prosperity without examining too closely the warped and misshapen tree that produced them. Bryan was on the right track, but he had chosen the wrong moment.

His plan of campaign, like that of 1896, involved a long speaking tour, and large crowds turned out. In the East he was particularly well received. Richard Croker, head of Tammany, had become a Bryan convert—from reading the candidate's book, The First Battle, so he said—and the Tammany braves made the welkin ring when the Nebraskan descended on Madison Square Garden. "Great is Tammany," said Bryan, "and Croker is his prophet." But the Gold Democrats were still hostile. Had Bryan abandoned free silver, most of them would have supported him, for nearly all were anti-imperialists. Instead many voted for McKinley, as in 1896.

Cleveland apparently did not vote. He refused to say a word that could be construed as an endorsement of either candidate, despite all manner of requests that he commit himself. While bitter toward "Bryanism," he could not swallow "McKinleyism." Richard Olney, Judson Harmon, William L. Wilson, and J. Sterling Morton—all former members of his cabinet—and the veteran editor, Henry Watterson, chose Bryan as the lesser evil. "I am going to shut my eyes, hold my nose, vote, go home and disinfect myself," wrote Morton to his old chief.

Among Republican anti-imperialists the problem was equally difficult. Andrew Carnegie, Senators Hoar and Hale, and many other old-fashioned Republicans found Bryan's silver views and his reputation for instability sufficient justification for a vote for McKinley. Thomas B. Reed, eased out of the Speakership and now retired from politics, took refuge in a stony and embittered silence. Carl Schurz, despite his lifelong advocacy of sound money, accepted Bryan, though with a wry face. George S. Boutwell, secretary of the treasury under Grant and now heading the Anti-Imperialist League, and Erving Winslow, the league's secretary, gave loyal support to the Nebraskan, but Republican bolters were not very numerous. It is doubtful whether the omission of the silver plank would have drawn many of these Republican anti-imperialist conservatives to Bryan. He repelled them in too many other ways. In the end, the difficulty of uniting Gold Democrats, Bryan Democrats, Populists, Silver Republicans, and anti-imperialists on one ticket was too great to be overcome.

Hanna's management of McKinley's campaign involved fewer problems than in 1896. His organization functioned efficiently and collected approximately $2,500,000, principally from big business interests pleased with McKinley's policies and fearful of Bryan's antitrust program. The party machine under Hanna had become a systematic, well-organized business that could be trusted to conduct a campaign honestly and efficiently. No special favors were granted, as a Wall Street group discovered when its ten-thousand-dollar contribution was returned because it had strings attached to it.

Roosevelt Joins the Campaign Trail

McKinley was now more than ever averse to descending from his pedestal, and so the defense of the administration was turned over to the hero of San Juan Hill—known to the average man as "Teddy," though Roosevelt thoroughly disliked the nickname. His tours were a grand success. In part, he followed Bryan's trail; and the duel of these two rabblerousers gave color to a campaign that was otherwise apathetic. Bryan preached—Roosevelt shouted. The Nebraskan quoted Scripture—the

Rough Rider waved the flag. The great Democratic leader was an artist with words—his Republican rival was a better tub-thumper. Roosevelt's voice, often cracking into a high falsetto, began to give way toward the end; but he waved his arms and pounded his fists and at least impressed his audiences with his tremendous vigor and his certainty as to what was right. References to "my opponent" made it almost seem as if Roosevelt himself were running for the presidency.* No vice-presidential candidate had ever before stolen the show from the head of the ticket.

Hanna had become a successful stump speaker since 1896, and the organization functioned so efficiently that he could devote some time to campaigning. People wanted to see the bloated, dollar-decorated ogre of the hostile cartoons, and there were many requests for him. Invariably he captured his audiences. A genial, unaffected soul, he spoke to a thousand in the same informal manner that he talked to three or four. He would talk on whatever came into his head at the moment, and his listeners liked it. In 1900 he confined most of his attention to South Dakota and Nebraska, home states of his particular enemy Senator R. F. Pettigrew, bolting Silver Republican, and of Bryan. His invasion of South Dakota partook of the nature of a private vendetta, for Pettigrew had attacked the validity of his election to the Senate. McKinley, dubious about the undertaking, sent an emissary to dissuade the national chairman. Hanna, discovering who had sent his caller, answered angrily, "Return to Washington, and tell the president that God hates a coward." Sensitive over this reflection on his judgment, he considered resigning as chairman, but his old loyalty soon reasserted itself. However, he went ahead with his tour.

Accompanied by Victor Dolliver of Iowa and Senator Frye of Maine, Hanna stumped the Populist belt by special train. Large crowds gathered at every stop, and occasionally he was heckled. At one place a sign read: "*Populist Farmers, Beware! ! !* Chain Your Children to Yourselves or Put Them Under the Bed. *Mark Hanna Is in Town.*" But his good humor, his sallies of rough wit, and his blunt, straightforward style of speaking won admirers everywhere and helped dispel the bogyman belief where it was most strongly held. It was disarming to the crowds of farmers at little railroad stations to hear the generalissimo of plutocracy in his own defense. In a tour lasting one week he made seventy-two speeches.

In declaring that there was but one issue in the campaign, "Let well enough alone," Hanna touched upon the strongest argument of the Republicans. Economic conditions were so much improved that "the full dinner pail" became the slogan of party orators and newspapers. Only in a limited sense was the election a referendum on imperialism.

---

* Mrs. Bryan, in the joint memoirs of herself and her husband, inadvertently refers to his defeat "by Mr. Roosevelt" in 1900.

McKinley and Roosevelt Elected

The defeat of the Democrats was greater than in 1896. McKinley had 292 electoral votes to Bryan's 155, compared with the earlier 271 to 176. He added Kansas, Nebraska, South Dakota, Utah, Wyoming, and Washington to his total, more than making up for the loss of Kentucky. The silver states, Colorado, Idaho, Montana, and Nevada, remained loyal to the Democrats, but the entire agricultural West was again Republican. Bryan had the South as before, though West Virginia, Maryland, and Delaware on the border were still Republican. The popular vote was: McKinley, 7,218,039; Bryan, 6,358,345.* The former had exceeded his total of 1896, while Bryan had declined proportionately. Hanna was delighted. Even Nebraska was Republican, and Pettigrew lost his Senate seat from South Dakota.

But on September 6, 1901, six months after his second inauguration, McKinley was assassinated at the Pan-American Exposition in Buffalo. Theodore Roosevelt, the "Rough Rider," the "hero of San Juan Hill," became the twenty-sixth president of the United States.

* The other candidates had these totals: Woolley, Prohibition, 209,004; Debs, Social Democratic, 86,935; Malloney, Socialist Labor, 40,900; Barker, Populist ("Middle-of-the-Road"), 50,340; Ellis, Union Reform, 5,693.

IX

Progressivism and War

☆

1904-1916

McKinley's assassination brought "that damned cowboy" (Mark Hanna's description) into the presidency and shifted party leadership from Hanna and the standpatters to the energetic, pugnacious, reforming "TR." The latter responded to a growing progressive sentiment for ending the capitalist-politician partnership in the temple of government by instituting antitrust suits and asking for legislation for more effective regulation of railroads and large-scale business enterprises. Hanna avoided a clash with the president, but his death in 1904 removed the only possible obstacle in Roosevelt's path to the nomination for another term.

The Republican national convention in Chicago, June 21–23, was a tame affair. The platform pointed with pride and promised a continuance of the McKinley-Roosevelt policies, but left it to the candidate to clarify its generalities. The 994 delegates nominated Roosevelt by acclamation and put Senator Charles Warren Fairbanks of Indiana, a staid conservative, on the ticket with him.

The Democratic convention met in St. Louis on July 6. The conservative Democrats, with Bryanism twice turned down, wanted a safe-and-sane easterner on a conservative platform to draw business support and turn the tables on the Republicans, afflicted with a problem child as unpredictable as he was uncontrollable. A dearth of northern governors and senators forced them to turn to the bench. Judge Alton B. Parker of the New York Court of Appeals seemed to be the best solution. Journalist William Randolph Hearst offered himself with a reform program but did not fit the situation. Parker was nominated on the first ballot over Hearst and some favorite sons. Bryan conducted a battle for a liberal platform and secured a strong antitrust plank and some other liberal commitments.

The platform's silence on the gold standard evoked a telegram from Parker pledging himself to uphold it and offering to decline the nomination if this was unsatisfactory to the majority. Bryan and his following were incensed, but the convention voted that the gold standard had been omitted because it was not an issue and that Parker's views did not preclude him from accepting the nomination.

The convention nominated wealthy eighty-year-old Henry Gassaway Davis of West Virginia for vice-president. From Republican sources came this gibe at the Democratic ticket—"an enigma from New York and a ruin from West Virginia."

The convention had not actually healed the breach in the party. The Bryanites were angry and, without bolting, gave only a perfunctory support to Parker. Bryan took the stump, but his purpose was to retain his hold on the masses of Democrats and to recover control of the party after the election. He was shrewdly demonstrating his regularity to teach the bolters of 1896 a lesson in loyalty. Ten days before the election he announced in the *Commoner*, for many years his personal organ, his intention of reorganizing the party "along radical lines."

The general management of the Democratic campaign was in the hands of Thomas Taggart, chairman of the national committee and Indiana's shrewdest politician, with William F. Sheehan of New York at the head of the executive committee. But the hoped-for support of the business interests did not materialize. August Belmont, Thomas F. Ryan, Daniel S. Lamont, and a few other loyal Democrats helped, but Republican businessmen were not to be weaned away from the party that had protected their interests. E. H. Harriman, J. P. Morgan, George J. Gould, James Stillman, H. C. Frick, the Standard Oil interests, and a number of other wealthy corporations and individuals contributed liberally to the Roosevelt cause.

Big Business Supports Roosevelt

The Republican candidate knew big business was supporting him; but Cornelius N. Bliss, treasurer of the national committee, kept his own books on the more than two million he raised, and Roosevelt showed no unseemly curiosity.* His attitude toward the trusts had not changed, but he maintained a discreet and dignified silence during the campaign, sticking to the presidential tradition of abstaining from speech-making. His excessively long letter of acceptance reviewed the measures and policies of his administration and invited the opposition to make them the issues.

That even a huge campaign chest could have elected Parker is highly improbable. Regardless of the fact that the Democratic platform was more liberal, the voters tended to regard Roosevelt as the dynamic pro-

* Not until the investigations of the Clapp Committee of the Senate in 1912 was the extent of corporation contributions revealed, although much had been surmised before this.

gressive and Parker as the cautious conservative. Even if Parker had attempted a vigorous offensive, it would have spoiled the picture of the well-balanced, dignified judge who was to save the nation from the erratic, spectacular "TR." The Democratic candidate belonged in the Republican camp, conducting a front-porch campaign, while Roosevelt, given the leadership of the opposition, would have been freed from his inhibitions and could have assailed Wall Street, the trusts, and the corruptions of boss rule with sledge-hammer blows. The labels were mixed in 1904.

The achievements of Roosevelt were so generally popular that Democratic guns had to be leveled at methods rather than measures. Even the much criticized "rape of Panama" was an asset to Roosevelt. To the average man it meant merely that the canal, talked about for a quarter of a century, would be built at once instead of encountering further delays. Old issues were devoid of interest, while Roosevelt's trust prosecutions deprived the Democrats of ammunition in that area. Of necessity they assailed the man and his methods. Bryan attacked him for sword-waving and militarism, and Henry Watterson called him "as sweet a gentleman as ever scuttled a ship or cut a throat." More staidly the Parker Constitutional Club of eminent New York lawyers pointed to Roosevelt's "arbitrary usurping of legislative functions" and his "massing enormous power in his own hands," and called for a man of "safe tendencies."

The dull campaign furnished only one lively incident, near the close. Joseph Pulitzer of the *New York World*, with his keen perception of realities, pointed to Republican Chairman Cortelyou's former headship of the Department of Commerce and Labor, containing the Bureau of Corporations, which had been strangely inactive since its creation. Did the corporations, pouring money into the campaign, assume that they were buying protection? Pulitzer called on Roosevelt to make public the contributions of big business. The Republican candidate was silent, but when Parker, rather belatedly, repeated the insinuations about Cortelyou and the Bureau of Corporations, Roosevelt angrily termed the charge a wicked falsehood. The campaign closed on this triumphantly righteous note.

Roosevelt did not deny the fact of corporation contributions, though not informed by Cortelyou and Bliss of their extent. In one case at least he was personally responsible. Alarmed at the prospect of defeat for the Republican state ticket (and possibly the national ticket) in New York because of local issues, he invited Edward H. Harriman, the railroad magnate, to the White House and asked him to raise funds to save the day. Harriman returned to New York and raised $250,000, which he turned over to Treasurer Bliss. Over a year later he wrote to a friend explaining his relations with Roosevelt.

In April 1907, the letter, sold by a discharged employee, appeared in the *New York World*. Roosevelt, angry over Harriman's hostility toward

railroad legislation and cynical remarks about his ability to buy legislatures and courts, flamed at this revelation of their former relations. "I
never requested Mr. Harriman to raise a dollar for the presidential campaign of 1904," he stormed, insisting that the story was utterly false. The
money was for the *state ticket*. Roosevelt seemed to be arguing that
$250,000 spent on behalf of the state ticket would have no influence on the
outcome of the national election in the Empire State.

Roosevelt Elected President

But no revelations of corporation connection with the Republican
campaign could have saved the Democrats. Roosevelt had captured the
popular imagination, and nothing short of a complete economic collapse
could have prevented his election. Even in that contingency he might
have escaped by blaming Wall Street. Not since Jackson had there been
such a popular hero. The king could do no wrong. And so Judge Parker
went down to defeat on November 8 by a record-breaking margin in the
popular vote. Roosevelt had 7,626,593, Parker, 5,082,898.° Only the South
remained loyal to the Democrats—Missouri, West Virginia, and Maryland
(popular vote) were lost. Roosevelt had 336 electoral votes to 140 for
Parker, the largest majority since the Grant-Greeley election of 1872,
when the South was under carpetbag rule. Both houses of Congress were
Republican by large majorities. The Democratic conservatives' bid for
power had been a disastrous failure.

Roosevelt celebrated his astounding triumph with an amazing blunder. On election night he issued this statement: "The wise custom which
limits the president to two terms regards the substance and not the form,
and under no circumstances will I be a candidate for or accept another
nomination." This most energetic of presidents, barely forty-six years of
age, was relegating himself permanently to the painful estate of an ex-
president at the expiration of his term. In effect, he was notifying the
party leaders in Congress that his power to reward and punish was of
limited duration. For so astute a politician the statement was inexcusable.
Exuberance over his great victory had betrayed his judgment. The club of
a possible third term (in his case actually a second elective term) would
have served him well in dealing with a recalcitrant Congress in the years
to follow. And in 1912 he was made painfully aware of this entirely
unnecessary pledge when he chose to run again.

° Maryland gave Roosevelt one electoral vote, Parker the rest. Delaware was consistently Republican from 1896 to 1936, except for 1912. The vote of the minor parties
was as follows: Swallow, Prohibition, 258,596; Debs, Socialist, 402,489; Watson, People's, 114,051; Corregan, Socialist Labor, 33,156. Debs's vote had risen from 86,935 in
1900 to 402,489—a surprising increase, indicating a growing protest against the conservatism of the major parties.

Roosevelt Nominates Taft

Roosevelt's second term did not produce the results he had expected. The Hepburn Act—extending the powers of the Interstate Commerce Commission over railroad rates—a Meat Inspection Act, and a Pure Food and Drugs Act were major achievements, but the Senate, led by Nelson W. Aldrich of Rhode Island, and the House, under Speaker Joseph Cannon, blocked further Roosevelt reform measures, especially after the Wall Street panic of 1907.

To stop rumors that he wanted a third term and to provide a successor after his own heart, Roosevelt decided to back Secretary of War William Howard Taft of Ohio, who had been a federal judge and the first civil governor of the Philippines. The southern delegates, usually chosen by federal officeholders, were easily drawn into the Taft-Roosevelt fold, and in the northern states only a group of favorite sons, called the "Allies," offered opposition.

Chicago was again the scene of the national convention, which opened on June 16, 1908. The problem of 223 contested seats, mostly from the South, was solved in Taft's favor in most cases. A proposal to reduce southern representation—the party's rotten borough system—was defeated by a narrow margin. The platform, far too long for what it contained, declared for revision of the tariff, strengthening of the antitrust law, conservation of natural resources, and a more elastic currency.

A last-minute attempt to stampede the convention for Roosevelt had gallery support of forty-six minutes, but Chairman Henry Cabot Lodge stopped it with the roll call. Taft had 702 votes and the opposition 277. Veteran Congressman James S. Sherman, an arch-conservative member of Speaker Cannon's inner circle, was New York's choice for vice-president; he was nominated with 816 of 979 votes cast.

Having tried Parker and conservatism, the Democrats were ready for Bryan again, when the delegates assembled in hospitable Denver on July 7. A progressive platform, largely the Commoner's own handiwork, included downward revision of the tariff, more teeth in the antitrust laws, an income tax, direct election of United States senators, and restrictions on the use of injunctions in labor disputes. A seventy-minute demonstration greeted the presentation of Bryan's name. The one ballot gave him 888½ votes to 59½ for Governor John A. Johnson of Minnesota and 46 for Judge George Gray of Delaware. John Worth Kern, an Indiana Bryanite, was nominated for vice-president.

The usual array of minor parties presented candidates, and a new one appeared. The Socialists again offered Eugene V. Debs with high hopes of another large gain in voting strength. The Socialist Labor Party named

August Gillhaus, and the Prohibitionists, Eugene W. Chafin. The feeble remnant of Populists made their last stand, led by the veteran agrarian Tom Watson. The new party was the Independence Party, a Hearst-financed, one-ring circus with Thomas L. Hisgen as candidate and Hearst as ringmaster. Its platform, occupying ground between the Democrats and Socialists, was decidedly progressive. Hearst had not yet tossed overboard the liberalism of his early years, though his recent dealings with Tammany had made progressives view him with suspicion.

The Republican campaign got under way slowly. Taft, burdened with his judicial temperament, would have preferred a front-porch affair but was persuaded that stumping was necessary to counteract the appeal of Bryan. Frank H. Hitchcock, his manager, withheld the Republican fire for the closing weeks, and as late as September Bryan and Taft seemed to be running neck and neck. Then Taft went on the stump, Hearst attempted to expose men prominent in both parties, Roosevelt started a debate by letter with Bryan, and the tepid campaign warmed up a little.

Hearst had secured letters from the files of the Standard Oil Company revealing that Ohio Republican Senator Joseph B. Foraker and Governor C. N. Haskell of Oklahoma, treasurer of the Democratic national committee, had had intimate connections with the great oil trust. Foraker defended himself by showing that his dealings with Standard Oil were on a purely business basis; but the fact that a United States senator, in a period of bitter public feeling toward trusts, had sought favors from the most hated of the species was enough to damn him. Roosevelt, with the Hepburn bill and the Brownsville affair* fresh in his memory, was eager to destroy Foraker and urged Taft not to appear with him at a public meeting. Foraker solved the problem for Taft by staying away, but Roosevelt was not satisfied. "He ought to throw Foraker over with a bump," he wrote to his son-in-law. "I have decided to put a little vim into the campaign by making a publication of my own."

His "publication" was an interview attacking Bryan for retaining Haskell as campaign treasurer and showing that Taft, by contrast, had refused to have dealings with Foraker long before. Then followed a lively public controversy between Bryan and Roosevelt. Bryan went back to 1904 to show that the president's hands were not clean of corporation assistance. He charged that the trust magnates were supporting Taft and demanded publicity for all contributions. Charges and countercharges followed, with Haskell resigning as treasurer in the midst of the controversy.

* Brownsville, Texas, had been mysteriously shot up on the night of August 13, 1906, presumably by black soldiers of a United States infantry regiment stationed there. One man was killed and another wounded. The evidence of guilt was not very clear, but the president dismissed three companies from the service on the ground that the men not guilty had refused to expose the culprits. Foraker defended the soldiers in the Senate and criticized Roosevelt. The two men clashed bitterly at a banquet of the Gridiron Club, famed Washington press club.

The question of publicity of campaign contributions, raised by Bryan, was an awkward one. He had announced earlier that a $10,000 limit would be placed on individual contributions and that the names of donors of more than $100 would be made public. The Republicans were embarrassed, but Taft declared that the law of New York State, which required a statement of receipts and expenditures after the election, would be observed. This was less frank than the Democratic position but was in advance of earlier methods. Roosevelt privately protested to the Republican campaign treasurer, George R. Sheldon, against reported requests for funds from John D. Archbold of Standard Oil and Edward H. Harriman. Sheldon responded with the disagreeable information that Standard Oil money had been accepted in 1904, contrary to Roosevelt's wishes. Neither party was particularly well financed in 1908, though as usual the Republicans fared better than their rivals.

Apart from the interest injected by Roosevelt, the campaign dragged. Trusts, tariff, and currency developed no sharp differences. Taft declared that the ambiguous Republican tariff plank meant revision downward, which seemed to place the parties rather close together on this question. Samuel Gompers, head of the American Federation of Labor, endorsed Bryan because of the anti-injunction plank in his platform, but there was little evidence of any pronounced swing of labor to the Democrats.

Bryan found that Roosevelt's liberalism had cut the ground from under his feet in the West, while the East, as in his earlier campaigns, saw no reason to change its Republican allegiance. He was no longer the glamorous "Boy Orator of the Platte," but a middle-aged political preacher whose ideas, fed to Chautauqua audiences year after year, had become a familiar story. Roosevelt had altered his opinion of the Nebraskan for the better since 1896 and now spoke of him as "a kindly man and well meaning in a weak way; always provided that to mean well must not be translated by him into doing well if it would interfere with his personal prospects. But he is the cheapest fakir we have ever had proposed for president." Yet a conservative Republican of the McKinley stamp would have found this "fakir" a formidable opponent. The country was turning liberal, but Roosevelt had postponed the day of reckoning for his party by giving it the habiliments of reform.

Taft Elected

November 3 wrote finis to Bryan's efforts to be elected president. He had 6,406,801 votes to Taft's 7,676,258.* His total was larger, but his per-

* The minor parties had these totals: Debs, Socialist, 420,380; Chaffin, Prohibition, 252,821; Hisgen, Independence, 82,537; Watson, People's, 28,376; Gillhaus, Socialist Labor, 14,018.

centage was slightly smaller, than in 1896 or 1900. His popular vote was far above Parker's in 1904, but his electoral defeat was almost as bad, for he had only 162 to Taft's 321. He had the usual southern bloc plus 6 of Maryland's 8 electoral votes, Kentucky, newly admitted Oklahoma, Colorado, Nevada, and his home state, Nebraska. The rest of the North and West and Missouri, West Virginia, and Delaware went Republican as in 1904. Judged by the total vote, the Democratic Party was no better off than it had been when Bryan ran before. It had merely recovered the ground lost by Parker.

But there were bright spots in the Democratic picture. Bryan's vote was less sectional and better distributed than before. In five states carried by Taft, Democratic governors were chosen. In several other states Republican state candidates ran far behind the head of the ticket. The progressive movement was spreading eastward. Unless the dominant Republicans recognized reform demands, a reviving democracy under new leadership might serve the purpose of the progressives.

The Republican Party Splits

Beginning with the Payne-Aldrich Tariff, Taft antagonized the progressive Republicans by his measures and actions and by the aid and comfort he gave to the standpat elements in the party. Roosevelt, returning from an African hunting trip, was soon campaigning for progressive Republicans and drawing away from Taft. His speeches and editorial comments in the *Outlook* clashed with Taft's basically conservative views and policies and brought on the break in 1912.

Progressive Republicans, fearing that Senator Robert M. La Follette of Wisconsin, their original choice, could not defeat Taft, put pressure on Roosevelt to run after La Follette had suffered a temporary breakdown. Roosevelt was easy to persuade and the battle of 1912 was on. The president and the ex-president, now bitter rivals, stumped the important states having primaries, and soon name-calling prevailed over discussions of principles. The net result of a dozen primaries gave Roosevelt 278 delegates; Taft, 48; La Follette, 36. In the convention states, the organizations gave Taft most of the delegates. The Roosevelt forces, charging fraud and trickery, especially in the southern states, sent contesting delegates for 254 of the 1,078 seats.

The Taft forces, controlling the national committee, gave the seats to their claimants in most cases. This was the situation when the national convention opened its sessions in the Coliseum in Chicago on June 18. The test vote, taken on electing a temporary chairman, was 558 to 501 for the Taft choice, Elihu Root, who also became permanent chairman.

Defeated in the credentials committee and on the floor of the convention, the Roosevelt forces refused to participate further in the proceedings.

Taft was renominated with 501 votes. Roosevelt received 107; La Follette, 41; Cummins, 17; Hughes, 2; not voting 349. Vice-President James S. Sherman was also renominated. A rather liberal platform had been adopted and forgotten.

The convention was one of the most disorderly on record. The pro-Roosevelt galleries added to the tumult with boos and whistle imitations of steamrollers. Roosevelt came to Chicago to direct the strategy and told reporters he felt like a bull moose. This animal of the north woods became the symbol of his cause.

The bolting Rooseveltians called for a new party, and on August 5 more than two thousand delegates came to Chicago to nominate Roosevelt and Governor Hiram Johnson of California as their candidates. The platform included almost every reform the progressive movement had spawned or inherited.

The convention could have been mistaken for a religious revival as delegates and galleries sang "Onward Christian Soldiers" and the stirring "Battle Hymn of the Republic." Roosevelt gave his Confession of Faith. He was standing at Armageddon and battling for the Lord (his earlier description of his cause). The party took the name Progressive, but Bull Moose was the more popular term.

The delegates of the jubilant, yet worried, Democrats came to Baltimore to make their nominations on June 25. The progressive-conservative division was present but less serious for a party long out of power and now in sight of the promised land.

Bryan created a turmoil at the opening session by opposing the national committee's choice of Alton B. Parker for temporary chairman. He lost by 579 votes to 508, but he had stirred up outside sentiment for the progressive cause. Bryan served on the resolutions committee and helped write a progressive platform. After the preliminary work of the convention was out of the way, he offered a resolution that the convention declare itself "opposed to the nomination of any candidate for president who is the representative of or under obligation to J. Pierpont Morgan, Thomas F. Ryan, August Belmont, or any other member of the privilege-hunting and favor-seeking class." After great uproar and confusion the resolution was adopted by a large majority. Belmont and Ryan were delegates.

In the preconvention struggle Speaker Champ Clark of Missouri had bagged the most delegates. His house record and his strong western support seemed to vouch for his liberalism, but state machines tended to line up for him, and Hearst's newspapers sang his praises.

Democrats Nominate Woodrow Wilson

Governor Woodrow Wilson of New Jersey, former president of Princeton, had made a fine record as governor after dumping the bosses and ranked next to Clark in delegate strength. He had ditched his early conservative sponsor, Colonel George Harvey of *Harper's Weekly*, and stood out as the leading progressive contender. Governor Judson Harmon of Ohio, who had been attorney general under President Cleveland, and Oscar Underwood of Alabama, floor leader of the House of Representatives, were respected conservatives but did not fit the situation or suit Bryan. Of the favorite sons, only Governors Thomas Marshall of Indiana and Simeon Baldwin of Connecticut were placed in nomination at the convention.

On the first ballot Clark had 440½; Wilson, 324; Harmon, 148; Underwood, 117½; Marshall, 31; Baldwin, 22; William Sulzer, of New York, 2; Bryan, 1; not voting, 2. On the tenth ballot New York shifted from Harmon to Clark, giving the latter a majority. A Clark victory parade lasting an hour proved to be premature. A Wilson-Underwood agreement to hold out kept Clark well short of the required two-thirds. On the fourteenth ballot Bryan surprised the convention by announcing his intention to change his vote from Clark to Wilson because Clark might be under obligation to the interests represented by the New York delegation then voting for him.

The convention adjourned over the weekend after twenty-six ballots with the deadlock unbroken. Thousands of telegrams poured into Baltimore on Sunday demanding the nomination of Wilson. The battle continued into Tuesday when the July heat, the strain on delegate pocketbooks, and the shift of Roger Sullivan, boss of Illinois, to Wilson brought it to an end. On the forty-sixth ballot the New Jersey governor received the nomination. Underwood would not accept second place, and it went to Governor Marshall of Indiana on the second ballot. He was the choice of the Wilson managers.

The platform, adopted after the nominations, was moderately progressive, favoring tariff reduction, more effective antitrust measures, banking reform, the passage of constitutional amendments for an income tax, and direct election of United States senators.

The campaign of 1912 really ended with the three conventions. Woodrow Wilson's liberal views and aggressive campaigning soon made it clear that he would poll the normal party vote; and it would be sufficient to elect him, regardless of any other consideration. Had the Democrats nominated a conservative, a Progressive tidal wave might have carried Roosevelt to victory. Fortunately they had named their strongest man. Wilson,

an easterner and once a conservative, had won the liberals by his courageous course as New Jersey's governor and had received the blessing of
Bryan. Yet he steered clear of extremes and conducted a campaign that
kept him safely between the conservatism of Taft and the radicalism of
Roosevelt.

A Portrait of Wilson

To nullify the fiery aggressiveness of Roosevelt, Wilson was put on the
stump. Curiosity drew many to see what a professor-politician was like,
and they were pleasantly surprised. The tall, homely, long-jawed candidate was no owlish, dry, remote scholar but a skillful phrasemaker, occasionally witty, always clear and convincing, who knew what he wanted to
say and said it well. In dealing with issues he dwelt on tariff and trusts;
but he was more concerned with the regeneration of politics through a
spiritual awakening. This sometimes worried his friends. Like the evangelist's appeal to "get right with God" and thus solve all mundane problems, it hardly seemed to come to grips with the hard facts of life.

Roosevelt battled with devils and had a weapon to slay each one. Wilson's faultless sentences pleaded for a "New Freedom," but his listeners
too often were more inspired and uplifted than enlightened. Rather
naïvely, he proposed to destroy private monopoly and restore competition,
thus making business free and giving to every man the just rewards of his
talents. Roosevelt termed such ideas "rural toryism." The Progressives'
program of government regulation was more realistic. Yet, as president,
Wilson came far nearer the Progressive position than his speeches forecast.

Samuel Gompers supported Wilson. The anti-injunction plank in the
Democratic platform pleased him, and he also developed a great admiration for the candidate. The appeal of the Progressives' program of social
justice failed to overcome union labor's doubts of Roosevelt himself and
the segment of big business in his camp.

Campaign Funds

The party campaigns were managed much as in the past. William F.
McCombs, manager of Wilson's preconvention campaign, became Democratic national chairman. Suffering from ill health, he had to leave much
of the work to William G. McAdoo, with whom he often disagreed. Henry
Morgenthau handled Democratic finances efficiently, ending the campaign with a cash balance. Nearly 90,000 persons contributed
$1,159,446.33. Wilson warned the party treasurer not to accept contribu-

tions from certain dubious sources, and one gift was returned to avoid embarrassment to the candidate.

The Progressive chest was better filled than a third party had any right to expect.* Supporting Roosevelt were a few men of wealth such as Frank Munsey, magazine publisher, and George W. Perkins, once a partner of J. P. Morgan and an important figure in the International Harvester Company and other large corporations. Without their financial backing Roosevelt might have refused to run. Perkins, chairman of the executive committee, managed the campaign. Senator Joseph M. Dixon of Montana, although chairman of the national committee, was relegated almost to a figurehead role. The Democrats accused Roosevelt of favoring the International Harvester Company and the United States Steel Corporation during his presidency by not prosecuting them under the Sherman Act, and much was made of his intimacy with Perkins.

Charles D. Hilles, Taft's private secretary, was chairman of the Republican national committee, and George R. Sheldon, a New York banker, was treasurer. Business, angry at Taft's trust prosecutions, gave niggardly.† Taft made few speeches, as his cause was recognized as hopeless. In his acceptance speech he made an able defense of his administration but revealed his essential conservatism by picturing the dangers of socialism and the destruction of American institutions if either of his opponents triumphed.

Other Third Parties

The usual third parties appeared: the Socialists with Debs again as candidate; the Socialist Labor group with Arthur E. Reimer; and the Prohibitionists with Eugene W. Chafin. The Socialists, despite dissension at their national convention between conservatives and direct actionists, conducted an aggressive campaign. The unrest that had produced the progressive movement in the old parties helped their cause, and a number of victories in local elections encouraged them to believe that 1912 would bring a great increase in their vote, even though the new third party would attract many radicals.‡

The campaign drew to its close without the excitement that the convention struggles had seemed to foreshasow. The most dramatic incident

---

* The national committee reported receipts of $676,672.73, disbursements of $665,500.00, and liabilities of $5,714.31.

† Receipts were reported at $1,076,391.51; disbursements, $1,076,548.57. These and the figures reported for the other parties were filed with the clerk of the House of Representatives in accordance with the act of 1910.

‡ Milwaukee had a Socialist mayor and a Socialist Congressman, Emil Seidel and Victor Berger, elected in 1910. In 1912 it was estimated that 1,141 Socialists held elective offices in the nation.

occurred on October 14 in Milwaukee when an insane man attempted to assassinate Roosevelt. The bullet entered the right side of his chest and lodged in a rib. Showing his usual fortitude, Roosevelt delivered his scheduled speech without medical treatment. Although the wound proved to be not too serious, it ended his speaking tour. Both Taft and Wilson telegraphed their regrets and suspended campaign activities until he recovered. On October 30 he addressed a great New York gathering at Madison Square Garden, where the faithful showed their loyalty in the shadow of defeat.

Wilson Wins

On November 5 the Democrats were successful for the first time since 1892. Wilson had 435 electoral votes; Roosevelt, 88 (Michigan, Minnesota, Pennsylvania, South Dakota, Washington, and 11 of California's 13); and Taft 8, (Utah, Vermont).* Wilson polled 6,293,152 popular votes, to 4,119,207 for Roosevelt and 3,486,333 for Taft. This made Wilson a minority president; but it would be a mistake to assume that he would have lost if he had had only one major opponent. In the two-party battle of 1910 the Democrats had won a majority in the House and had elected governors in several Republican states. The tide had not changed in 1912, and Wilson was to be victorious in 1916 when conditions were much less favorable.

The surprising increase in the Socialist vote from 420,380 in 1908 to 900,369 gave clear proof of the country's swing to the left. The liberalism of Roosevelt and Wilson kept the Debs total from being greater. The Prohibition vote, which had been around 250,000 for two campaigns, dropped to 207,972 in 1912. Reimer, Socialist Labor, had 29,374.

The new Congress was Democratic: the Senate 50 to 44, not counting 1 Progressive and 1 vacancy; the House 291 to 144. Of the 144, only about 15 were Progressives, though many others had been elected with Progressive assistance. The situation was much the same in the various state legislatures, thus placing the new party under a serious handicap. With few officeholders and almost no patronage, it was not in a good position to establish itself as a major party. But much depended on what happened to the Democrats under Wilson's leadership.

Two constitutional amendments were ratified in 1913, the Sixteenth, authorizing taxes on incomes, and the Seventeenth, providing for popular election of United States senators.

Wilson's "Moral Diplomacy" and his "New Freedom" programs provided a type of leadership for the Democratic Congress that seemed to

* Vice-President Sherman, running with Taft, died on October 30. The eight Republican electors cast their vice–presidential votes for Nicholas Murray Butler.

hark back to Jefferson. The strong-willed president had to his credit by October 1914, a notable group of progressive laws dealing with tariff, banking, and trusts. But the problems that followed the outbreak of World War I dwarfed all domestic issues, and the progressive movement lost its momentum. His handling of neutral rights drew the fire of German-Americans and Irish-Americans at one extreme and ardent sympathizers with the Allies such as Roosevelt at the other. His tardiness in advocating military preparedness measures was a further count against him.

The Republicans Reunite

Republicans and Progressives began to draw together in 1914, and the Progressive vote fell off badly. Roosevelt, now concerned about war problems and national defense, was willing to return to his old allegiance if a suitable candidate were offered for 1916. The usual flock of favorite sons, mostly undistinguished conservatives, appeared on the scene, but not one of them seemed to fit the situation. A man was needed who was not involved in the battle of 1912, who had not offended Roosevelt, and who had a record that was completely blank on controversial issues. Justice Charles E. Hughes, a member of the Supreme Court since 1910 and a former governor of New York, was the answer. He preserved a sphinx-like silence, but important leaders took care of his interests. When the convention met in Chicago on June 7, it was Hughes against the field.

The Republican platform assailed Wilson's foreign policy as one of "shifty expedients" and "phrasemaking" and promised an honest neutrality and the protection of American rights, but did not clarify the party's position on these points. It criticized Wilson's policy toward business and offered a strong national defense plank.

The Progressive Party was holding its convention in Chicago at the same time, and a committee conferred with a Republican committee as to candidates, but no agreement could be reached.

The Republican convention proceeded to ballot and nominated Hughes on the third trial. Former Vice-President Fairbanks was named to run with him. Derisive Democrats suggested "Win with Whiskers" as a slogan, referring to the hirsute adornments of both candidates.

The Progressive convention delegates, who had been held in restraint by George W. Perkins and other compromisers, broke loose and nominated Roosevelt, with John M. Parker of Louisiana as his running mate. Roosevelt's reply was a conditional refusal. His final decision would be determined by the attitude of Hughes on the vital questions of the day. The convention adjourned in an atmosphere of bitter resentment, leaving the party's future course to the determination of its national committee.

When, after a conference with Hughes, Roosevelt announced his definite withdrawal, the Progressive national committee voted against a separate ticket.

Wilson Renominated

The Democratic convention, meeting in St. Louis on June 14, was a ratifying rather than a nominating body. Wilson was renominated with one dissenting vote and Vice-President Marshall by acclamation. The platform recited the accomplishments of the administration, favored preparedness, had a strongly worded Americanism plank, and endorsed woman suffrage by state action. The delegates yelled loudest and longest when speakers stressed the peace theme. A significant statement in the platform praising Wilson's diplomatic victories ended with the words "and kept us out of war."

Hughes, asserting his prerogative as the party's nominee, selected as campaign chairman William R. Wilcox of New York City, a man not well known to party leaders. Cornelius N. Bliss, Jr., served as treasurer of the national committee. Wilson displaced William F. McCombs with Vance McCormick of Pennsylvania as chairman of the Democratic national committee, while Henry Morgenthau looked after finances, and Robert W. Woolley directed publicity. On the whole the Democratic campaign was handled much better than the Republican, although it was not so well financed.

Pacifism Versus Militarism

Hughes was one of the country's finest legal minds, but the task assigned to him was an impossible one. A man of force and sincerity, he was not gifted in equivocating; but any other course would cost votes. His dilemma on the major issues of foreign policy was a cruel one. He had to criticize Wilson's handling of Mexican difficulties and his failure to compel respect for American rights at sea. This provoked Democratic charges that Hughes's more vigorous policy might lead to wars with Mexico and Germany, which, of course, he must disprove. German-Americans and many pacifists believed that Wilson had dealt too harshly with Germany; the friends of the Allies, as represented by Roosevelt, charged him with spinelessness. Hughes had to satisfy both groups. The Democrats could insist that Wilson had preserved peace; no one knew what Hughes might do. On preparedness the Republican candidate was more effective, for Wilson had been tardy in advocating defense measures. But his conversion and the steps taken satisfied most voters. Americans were not military-minded, and in some quarters the Hughes-Roosevelt position smelled of the militarism charged against the Kaiser.

Among domestic questions, only the tariff offered a safe issue, for Wilson's accomplishments in other respects were hard to attack. But a war boom had ended the recession of 1914, and Republican warnings of bread lines to come under the Underwood Tariff fell flat. Hughes blundered in criticizing the Adamson Act, which authorized an eight-hour day for railway trainmen without a change in pay from their former ten-hour day, enacted in September 1916 at Wilson's suggestion to avert a nationwide rail strike. Without opposing the eight-hour day in principle, he assailed Wilson for submitting to a pressure group. His forthright stand was taken in speeches in Ohio, headquarters of the Railway Brotherhoods. Organized labor, already suspicious of Hughes, swung sharply to Wilson, and Ohio proved to be a crucial state.

A Blunder in California

An inadvertent blunder probably cost him the vote of California. Here Governor Hiram Johnson, Roosevelt's running mate in 1912, was a candidate for the Republican nomination for United States senator and was bitterly opposed by an Old Guard faction headed by National Committeeman William H. Crocker. Johnson, of course, was supporting Hughes and, as governor, might have been expected to preside at a Hughes meeting or confer with the candidate when he arrived in California in August. Crocker, however, made all the arrangements and kept the two men apart, even though at one time they were in the same hotel. This unnecessary snub was repaid in full when Johnson won the senatorial nomination and was elected in November by 300,000 votes, while Hughes lost the state by 3,773. Like the Reverend Burchard in 1884, Crocker achieved the unenviable distinction of defeating his own candidate. But Hughes ought to have realized the dynamite in the situation and made it a point to conciliate Johnson.

Despite the bogging down of the Hughes campaign shown by the decline in betting odds from two to one to ten to seven, the Republicans expected to win. The return of the Progressives, and the German-American and Irish-American resentments toward Wilson seemed to insure Democratic defeat.

But the strategy of the Democrats was to view the East as lost and center their efforts on the states west of Pennsylvania. They had two powerful appeals. One was Wilson's progressive accomplishments. Progressives who put principles ahead of loyalty to Roosevelt came trooping into the Wilson camp, especially west of the Mississippi.

The other appeal was, "He kept us out of war," one of the most effective slogans ever used in a campaign. It did tremendous damage to Hughes away from the eastern seaboard, particularly in farming sections with pacifist and isolationist leanings, and in the woman-suffrage states of the West. Roosevelt became a Democratic asset in this connection. His belligerent utterances were quoted and coupled with a statement of Hughes that he and Roosevelt were in complete accord. A pre-election Democratic paid advertisement carried this appeal:

> You are working, not fighting!
> Alive and happy, not cannon-fodder!
> Wilson and peace with honor?
>   Or
> Hughes with Roosevelt and war.

This must have been galling to Roosevelt, who was not happy in his support of the "bearded iceberg" and was reported to have remarked that Hughes was the kind of man who would vote for Wilson.

Wilson, with Congress in session all summer, could not campaign then. Later he yielded to party leaders and spoke in Omaha, Indianapolis, Chicago, and Cincinnati, key points in Democratic strategy. Speeches in Buffalo and New York City just before the election were concessions to the feeling that New York must not be abandoned without a struggle. A great parade headed by Sheriff Alfred E. Smith preceded the final rally at Madison Square Garden, where thousands, unable to get in, clamored for a sight of the president. The enthusiasm was metropolitan only; the state voted for Hughes.

Wilson Reelected

The campaign closed with the Democratic candidate much stronger than at the beginning but with Wall Street still betting on Hughes. The returns up to midnight, November 7, bore out this view. Even the Democratic papers in the East conceded defeat. As the returns from the Middle West came in with only Ohio for Wilson, the president privately admitted to a feeling of relief that the great burden of office had been lifted from him. A great Democratic "victory" banquet given by Henry Morgenthau for party leaders and cabinet members at the Biltmore Hotel in New York that night was a "morguelike" affair, while rejoicing Republicans serenaded Hughes at the Astor with two bands. Toward morning, as word came from the West, doubt succeeded certainty. Minnesota and California were the last to report, and not until Thursday afternoon was it known that Wilson had the latter state. This elected him, regardless of Minnesota, which finally went to Hughes by a plurality of fewer than four hundred votes.

Wilson had 277 electoral votes, Hughes 254. The popular vote was in Wilson's favor, 9,126,300 to 8,546,789.* The new House of Representatives was almost evenly divided between Republicans and Democrats, while the new Senate was Democratic by 10 votes, instead of the former 16. Clearly it was a Wilson rather than a Democratic Party victory. His liberalism and his avoidance of war received a vote of confidence. Other factors were incidental. Among them were the failure of the Republicans to get a solid German-American vote, the poor strategy of Hughes and his managers, the swashbuckling of Roosevelt, the effect of the Adamson Act, the apparent swing of the Mormon voters of Utah and neighboring states to Wilson, the peculiar California situation, and the support given to Wilson by the woman-suffrage states of the West.

The alignment was singularly like that of 1896 with one or two signifi- cant exceptions. Wilson had the solid South and the border states except Delaware and West Virginia (which gave Hughes 7 of its 8 votes); all the trans-Mississippi West except Oregon, Minnesota, South Dakota, and Iowa; and Ohio and New Hampshire east of the Mississippi. Hughes had the remaining area from New England westward to South Dakota, including the great industrial and older farming sections. He carried sub- stantially the McKinley states of 1896 with two fatal exceptions, California and Ohio.

Hughes and the Republicans in a sense were fortunate in defeat. The Democrats had to bear the chief responsibility for American entry into the war. If Hughes had won, he could scarcely have avoided doing what Wilson did in 1917. Yet the Democrats then could have thrust upon him and his party the blame for what followed. It might have given the war a partisan aspect and engulfed the Republicans in the great revulsion of 1920. Luck was really with them in 1916, for to the successful peace candi- date fell the momentous decision to make war.

Wilson took the oath of office on March 4, 1917, and on April 6 the United States declared war against Germany, thus entering World War I.

---

* The minor parties were as follows: Benson, Socialist, 589,924; Hanly, Prohibi- tion, 221,030; Reimer, Socialist Labor, 15,284. The sharp decline in the Socialist vote was due probably to the party's extreme antiwar position, which was confused in the popular mind with pro-Germanism, and to the attractions of Wilsonian liberalism for many radicals and pacifists.

X

Republican Ascendancy

☆

1920-1932

WHEN GERMANY'S unrestricted submarine warfare brought the United States into the war, politics, it was said, had been adjourned for the war. But the political truce did not last. Already badly strained, it broke down in 1918 when Wilson appealed to the country for a Democratic Congress. The election gave both houses to the Republicans.

The Issue of the League of Nations

This weakened Wilson's hand in the diplomatic game in Paris and in his own country when he asked for approval of the Treaty of Versailles. The Senate's rejection of the treaty containing the League of Nations, in part because of Wilson's refusal to accept reservations or make concessions, made the League an issue in the presidential election. His physical breakdown, the result of a stroke, left his party leaderless as the campaign of 1920 approached.

Difficult economic and social readjustments and a general postwar disillusionment provided grist for the Republican mill when the party's delegates assembled in Chicago, June 8–12, 1920. Henry Cabot Lodge, Wilson's chief opponent in the battle over the League of Nations, was both temporary and permanent chairman, and senatorial colleagues held key positions. The platform assailed Wilson and his works, but it took a vague, meaningless plank on the League of Nations to keep moderates and irreconcilables from staging a floor fight.

Three candidates had conducted extensive campaigns for delegates: General Leonard Wood, Governor Frank Lowden of Illinois, and Senator Hiram Johnson of California. The heavy spending of Wood and Lowden became liabilities, and Johnson was an extreme isolationist on the League of Nations. Several favorite sons, seeing a deadlock in prospect, set up their lightning rods. Among the better known were Governor Calvin Coolidge of Massachusetts and Senator Warren G. Harding of Ohio. The latter's campaign manager, Harry M. Daugherty, predicted that the nomination would be decided for a deadlocked convention by a little group in a smoke-filled hotel room "about eleven minutes after two o'clock" in the morning, and his candidate would be the lucky man.

On the first ballot Wood, Lowden, and Johnson led in that order, but after four ballots Lodge adjourned the convention until the next morning. That night, a long conference, or succession of conferences, did the work. Lodge and his senatorial confreres looked over the field and decided that Harding was the man. He possessed a pleasing personality, a handsome figure, was not assertive, and would work well with congressional leaders.

Next day, the deadlock ran on for a few ballots while Lowden passed Wood; then the shift toward Harding began. He received the nomination on the tenth ballot on Saturday afternoon.

The delegates gagged at the senatorial clique's choice of Senator Irvine Lenroot of Wisconsin for vice-president and nominated Governor Calvin Coolidge of Massachusetts, who was persona non grata to Lodge but was acclaimed for his role in putting down a Boston police strike.

The Democrats assembled in San Francisco on June 28 and passed a Wilsonian platform that endorsed his course on the League of Nations and defended his conduct of the war. William G. McAdoo, recently resigned as secretary of the treasury, and Attorney General A. Mitchell Palmer of Pennsylvania, "Red-hunter" extraordinary, were the leading candidates, but Governor James M. Cox of Ohio was more available as he carried no Wilson administration burdens. Several local favorites had delegate support. It took forty-four ballots before the deadlock ended with Cox's nomination. The vice-presidential choice was made quickly. New York seemed to require representation on the ticket, and Cox suggested Franklin D. Roosevelt, assistant secretary of the navy, who was named by acclamation. Charles Murphy, Tammany boss, did not care for Roosevelt but let Cox have his way.

The Republican campaign as managed by the efficient and tireless national chairman, Will H. Hays of Indiana, was a model of vote-catching banality. "Americanism" and "Getting back to normalcy" constituted its sum and substance. The first—which no one has ever been able to define —implied that Wilson had put the rest of the world ahead of his own country. The Republicans would reverse this. The second nostalgically promised a return to some less-troubled past, though no one could be sure just when Americans had lived in a state of "normalcy."

At least Harding was the ideal candidate to present this dose of soothing syrup to an angry and disillusioned electorate. Modest, unassuming, given to making speeches that consisted of "an army of pompous phrases moving across the landscape in search of an idea," he seemed to the typi-

cal good resident of small town and countryside to be a man who understood the ways of his fellow-men and would work with them to find solutions for their problems. Except for a few carefully prepared major
speeches that skillful ghost writers provided, he campaigned from his
front porch in Marion, Ohio, uttering pleasantries to visiting delegations
after the McKinley pattern but less studied, more informal, more human.

One problem stumped Harding and almost baffled his speech writers.
This was the League of Nations. He had voted for the League with the
Lodge reservations attached, and this position was supported by Hughes,
Taft, Root, Hoover, and other party bigwigs in varying degrees. But the
irreconcilables had blood in their eyes and demanded repudiation of the
League. Harding tried to emulate the vagueness of the platform; but the
task proved to be far too great for his powers of circumlocution, and
George Harvey and Richard Washburn Child came to the rescue. The
result was a long and involved speech in which the candidate seemed to
favor a world court of justice and an "association" of nations for conference in place of the Wilsonian League. Even these vague proposals were
not to be final, for he promised to consult "the most experienced minds of
this country" before presenting his plans to other nations. Late in the
campaign, still confused, the candidate seemed to wobble more to the isolationist side, though thirty-one distinguished Republicans signed a public
appeal urging his election as the only way to bring the United States into
"an effective league."

A 1923 magazine article, written with White House approval, stated
that Harding had never had any intention of having the United States
enter the League of Nations. Apparently he had convictions and was
merely concealing them during the campaign.

Lesser Republican speakers, unable to follow their leader along the
tightwire, felt free to flay Wilson's League as a superstate dangerous to
American sovereignty. Voters of Irish, German, and Italian ancestry, hostile to the Treaty of Versailles for various reasons, joined in the clamor
against American involvement. In the upper Mississippi Valley, where the
peace appeal had worked for the Democrats in 1916, isolationism was
now rampant.

Cox put up a brave battle against heavy odds. Soon after the nomination he and his running mate, Franklin D. Roosevelt, called upon the
pathetic figure in the White House and assured him they would stand
with him on the League. As Cox had not been involved in the Senate
battle, such a pledge seemed to be inexpedient; but he refused to be a
trimmer. Then he went on the stump, speaking in all parts of the country.
He attempted to revive the progressivism of the prewar days, in which he
had played a notable part in his home state; but the country was in no
mood for reform. George White, Democratic national chairman, was hampered by finances and apathy in building up an effective organization.

The Democratic national committee spent $1,470,000 compared with the Republican $5,417,000; but no amount of money could have saved Cox. The swing was to the right.

In this campaign appeared the first large-scale attempt to poll the electorate in a presidential election. The *Literary Digest*, a well-known weekly devoted to presenting newspaper opinion in digest form, undertook the task through millions of postcards. Its methods overemphasized middle-class sentiment, but this was not evident when the Republican trend was so general.

The whispering that sometimes disgraces a presidential campaign appeared in 1920. The most sensational story was the allegation that Harding had Negro ancestry. Circulars purporting to prove it by affidavits and a family tree appeared mysteriously on doorsteps and even in the mails. The authorship could not be clearly established. It had an Ohio origin but was widely circulated shortly before the election.

A Republican Landslide

On November 2 a tidal wave engulfed the Democratic Party. Harding carried the entire North and West including Oklahoma; the border states of the South except Kentucky; and Tennessee from the solid South—its first lapse from Democratic orthodoxy since 1872. He had 404 electoral votes to Cox's 127. The popular vote was divided as follows: Harding 16,133,314; Cox, 9,140,884; Debs, Socialist, 913,664; Christensen, Farmer-Labor, 264,540; Watkins, Prohibition, 188,391; Cox, Socialist Labor, 30,418. With more than 60 percent of the total vote and a plurality of nearly 7,000,000, Harding shattered all records. In the new House of Representatives, more than 300 of the 435 members were Republicans. In the Senate 59 were Republicans, and only 37 Democrats.

In 1920, it has been said, the voters voted their resentments. Champ Clark, from Missouri, defeated after twenty-eight years in Congress, snarled one word at a newspaperman who asked the cause of the landslide: "Wilson!" It was not the broken man in the White House that the voters were repudiating but Wilson as the symbol of things they wanted to forget. The intoxication of patriotic sacrifices for high ideals and the exhilaration of war prosperity were over. The year 1920 was the morning after. The world was out of joint, and the American people, in their disillusionment, sought a victim. The election was not, as Wilson had hoped, a "great and solemn referendum" on the League. Without the League as a factor, the result would have been much the same. Americans were homesick for the hopeful, sane, and secure world of 1914. Perhaps an average man such as Harding could restore that "normalcy." But the president-elect was looking beyond that. He wanted to go back to McKinley.

The 1920 election was the first presidential election in which women could vote. The Nineteenth Amendment had gone into effect in August of that year. In the preceding year, the Eighteenth Amendment—the Prohibition Amendment—was ratified by the states in January. The "wets" continued their actions against this amendment, and it was finally repealed in 1933 by the Twenty-first Amendment.

Harding's administration followed a generally conservative and isolationist course, but the nation had not yet reached the port of normalcy when he died on August 2, 1923, of a heart attack while on a western trip. Vice-President Calvin Coolidge became president.

Harding's two years in office had seen scandal and corruption. Two Senate investigations exposed former Secretary of the Interior Albert B. Fall as corruptly involved with two large oil producers (the Teapot Dome scandal). There were also some questionable activities of the "Ohio Gang" (Harding's friends and associates, including Attorney General Harry M. Daugherty). Coolidge saw that prosecutions were instituted in the oil cases and asked for Daugherty's resignation. The Ohio Gang had already departed.

Coolidge Nominated for President

With the Harding inheritance disposed of and business booming, the Republican nomination of 1924 came to the shrewd, silent Yankee politician with only a dissenting murmur from a band of Wisconsin La Follette irregulars. Cleveland's first national convention, opening on June 10, was a cut-and-dried affair. Economy and tax reduction were emphasized in the platform, which was also anti-League of Nations and pro-World Court. Corruption was passed over as affecting both parties, and punishment of the guilty was demanded, but the platform condemned attempts to besmirch the innocent and undermine confidence in the government. This was a slap at nosy investigators.

Senator William E. Borah refused to be considered for vice-president, and former Governor Lowden of Illinois was nominated. He declined the honor, and General Charles G. Dawes, also of Illinois, banker and author of a reparations plan for defeated Germany, was then nominated.

The Democrats spoiled whatever chance they had to make use of the Harding scandals by staging a bitter cat-and-dog fight at their national convention, held in Madison Square Garden in New York on June 24. The eastern Democrats, largely urban, wet, and Catholic, were aligned against their brethren of the more rural, dry, Protestant hinterlands.

The revived Ku Klux Klan, anti-foreign, anti-Catholic, anti-Jewish, and anti-Negro, had infiltrated the Democratic Party in many parts of the South and West and exerted its influence over a considerable bloc of delegates. When the platform was reported, a bitter battle developed over the question of denouncing the Klan by name or by implication. The advocates of the milder plank won by a narrow margin, but the cleavage continued into the struggle for the nomination. Governor Alfred E. Smith of New York represented the antiprohibition, Catholic East; William G. McAdoo of California, the dry, Protestant West. But the situation was complicated by the presence of a considerable number of favorite-son candidates and some potential dark horses who waited for the leaders to destroy each other.

McAdoo was well in the lead and hoped to reach a majority, after which he expected the Smith forces would concede the two-thirds. He was unsuccessful, and the struggle dragged on through 103 ballots. In sheer weariness the convention finally accepted John W. Davis, nominally of West Virginia, a conservative lawyer, who had been ambassador to Great Britain, and who practiced in New York City. The violent partisanship of the galleries for Smith angered the McAdoo partisans and helped prolong the deadlock. Proposals were made to hold closed sessions and even to move the convention to Kansas City.

Governor Charles W. Bryan of Nebraska, brother of William Jennings Bryan, was nominated for vice-president.

The convention had lasted from June 24 to July 9, and its proceedings had been covered by radio, which did not help the public image of the Democrats.

The La Follette Group

Dissatisfied liberals, seeing an opportunity for a farmer-labor movement, turned to Senator Robert M. La Follette, who had at last decided to break with the Republican Party. A gathering of farmer, labor, and liberal groups in Cleveland on July 4 named him for president and Burton K. Wheeler, Democratic senator from Montana, who had conducted the Daugherty investigation, for vice-president. The platform, prepared by La Follette, declared that the great issue before the people was the control of government and industry by private monopoly. It endorsed public ownership of the nation's water power, important natural resources, and railroads, and favored constitutional amendments to permit Congress to reenact a law over a judicial veto and to provide for popular election of federal judges, abolition of injunctions in labor disputes, direct nomination and election of presidents, a popular referendum on declarations of war, outlawry of war, and a drastic reduction of armaments.

The Conference for Progressive Political Action, active since 1922, launched the La Follette candidacy, and it had the support of the American Federation of Labor, the Railway Brotherhoods, the Socialist Party, and other left-wing farmer and labor groups, as well as intellectuals of liberal stamp as represented by the *New Republic* and the *Nation*. La Follette and Wheeler made an active campaign, but there was no party organization and little money back of them, and labor did not prove to be of much assistance. Their chief hope was to carry enough states in the upper Mississippi Valley, where farmer discontent centered, to throw the election to the House.

The Republicans, blessed with a campaign fund of more than $4,000,000, a popular candidate, an able manager and organizer in the person of William M. Butler, and a return of prosperity—even farm prices went up in 1924—had no very serious problems. A fear that La Follette's strength in the farm states might prevent an electoral majority led the party leaders to center their attack on the independent candidate. They played up his economic radicalism and his proposal to take away the judicial veto of the Supreme Court in order to frighten conservatives into voting for Coolidge rather than Davis, thus making certain that the election would not go to the House. Prosperity and satisfaction with the status quo made Republican success almost certain in any case. Had Harding lived, the exposures of corruption might have been awkward to meet; but with Coolidge in office the situation was completely changed. The slogan "Keep Cool with Coolidge" expressed the sentiments of a majority of the electorate.

The Democrats, having used up their energies at the convention, had none left for the campaign. Clem Shaver of West Virginia became national chairman at Davis's request, but he was not well known to party leaders and was hampered by lack of funds and by organization problems. Expenditures were about $1,100,000. Davis went on the stump and made able speeches assailing Republican corruption, but could not overcome Democratic lethargy or draw Republican fire. Labor was cold toward the Wall Street lawyer, and the Bryan West refused to be stirred by the speeches of the aging Commoner. The Klan question drifted into the background and had slight effect on the election. Prohibition had become a matter of law enforcement, and both major parties, of course, gave it lip service.

Coolidge Elected President

The *Literary Digest* poll predicted a Coolidge victory, and the prediction was more than verified in November. Coolidge had 382 electoral votes; Davis, 136; La Follette, 13 (Wisconsin). West Virginia, Kentucky, Missouri, Maryland, and Delaware followed the lead of the entire North and West in going Republican. Only the South (including Oklahoma) was Democratic. Coolidge's popular vote was 15,717,553; Davis had

8,386,169; La Follette, 4,814,050. Several minor-party candidates polled insignificant votes.

The outcome was less sweeping than in 1920 but still decisive enough. Both houses of Congress were Republican by safe majorities. La Follette had run second in eleven western states. He had been favored by those farmers who were not satisfied with Coolidge prosperity, and his antiwar stand had not been forgotten in German communities. In California and the Pacific Northwest, thousands of liberal Democrats preferred him to Davis. East of the Mississippi, liberal, labor, and socialist support accounted for a heavy urban vote. But admiration for the Wisconsin veteran and disgust with the old parties could not, of themselves, create a new party. The basic groundwork of local organization was not laid, and the Progressive movement of 1924 passed into history.

This campaign marked the last stumping appearances of two old warriors of liberalism, La Follette and Bryan. Both died in 1925. La Follette bequeathed his Wisconsin organization and his principles to his sons, but Bryan had all but blotted out the memory of his battles against plutocracy by his later crusades against the liquor traffic and the teaching of evolution.

Republicans Nominate Herbert Hoover

Coolidge had his difficulties with Congress in his second term. The disputes ranged from tax reduction to farm relief and government operation of water power on the Tennessee River. But his renomination seemed certain, for the stock market was booming and his personal popularity was still great. Quite suddenly, on August 3, 1927, he announced from his summer residence in the Black Hills of South Dakota, "I do not choose to run for president in 1928."

This opened the way for Secretary of Commerce Herbert Hoover, of California, who had long been making plans, and soon his personal organization was engaged in a delegate hunt. The "Great Engineer" had as his assets his achievements as director of Belgian relief and later as food administrator in World War I, and the special administrative tasks he had carried out while secretary of commerce. He lacked Coolidge's blessing, but only a mediocre crop of favorite sons opposed him, and the nomination was practically settled when the Republican convention began its sessions in Kansas City on June 12. His only threat, a "Draft Coolidge" movement, had made no headway.

Farm discontent was becoming a problem, and the vagueness of the plank in the platform caused a floor fight, but the attempt to amend it was defeated overwhelmingly. The drys were satisfied with a plank declaring for vigorous enforcement of the Eighteenth Amendment. Earlier, Hoover had referred to prohibition as "a great social and economic experiment, noble in motive and far-reaching in purpose." The rest of the platform recited the Harding-Coolidge accomplishments and promised to continue along the same lines. "Rugged individualism" was one of his slogans.

It took only one ballot to make Hoover the party's choice. The nomination of Charles Curtis of Kansas, Senate floor leader, to run with him was also decided by a single ballot. Curtis had criticized Hoover as not a genuine Republican, but Senator Borah of Idaho had insisted that the Kansas veteran be chosen.

Democrats Nominate a Roman Catholic

The Democrats were now ready for Alfred E. Smith of New York. Son of Irish immigrant parents, newsboy, clerk in a fish market, and holder of minor political offices, Smith had emerged from his Tammany cocoon to become an important figure in his state and to win the governorship in 1918. Defeated for reelection by the Harding landslide, he was returned to the office in 1922 for three more terms. Backed by certain wealthy eastern Democrats and by city-controlled state organizations, Smith was able to overcome the handicaps of his Catholic faith, his antiprohibition stand, and his Tammany upbringing, and to ride toward the nomination in 1928 with only some local favorites in his path.

The convention opened on June 26 in Houston, drawn there by the money and efforts of Jesse Jones and the desire of the Smith men to appease the South.

Prohibition troubled the platform makers, but they ended up with a plank criticizing the Republican record and promising an honest effort to enforce the Eighteenth Amendment. The farm relief and tariff planks did not differ sharply from the Republican efforts. For the third time Franklin D. Roosevelt, who in 1924 had called Smith the "Happy Warrior," presented his name to a Democratic convention, and this time success crowned his effort. Smith was ten votes short of the required two-thirds on the only roll call, and changes quickly put him across. Next day, Senator Joseph T. Robinson of Arkansas, permanent chairman of the convention, became the choice for vice-president. He was a dry, a Protestant, and a southerner. Smith startled the convention in its closing moments with a telegram reiterating his belief in "fundamental changes in the present provisions for national prohibition." The drys regarded this virtual repudiation of the platform pledge as a challenge in the coming campaign.

The minor parties presented candidates as usual, but only Norman Thomas, named by the Socialists, was in a position to cut into the major party vote. A man of high intelligence and fine character and a forceful speaker, he had naturally inherited the mantle of Debs and could appeal to dissatisfied liberals; but, as the campaign went on, most of these turned to Smith, and Thomas had a disappointingly small vote.

The Republican organization was quickly set up. Dr. Hubert Work of Colorado resigned as secretary of the interior to be national chairman, and Joseph R. Nutt of Ohio was treasurer. Jeremiah Milbank, a New York banker, served as contact man with Wall Street. A huge campaign fund was raised, and the national committee spent more than $6,000,000, a record-breaking total; but the general prosperity made collecting money less difficult than in some other campaigns.

Hoover's acceptance speech, delivered in the stadium of Leland Stanford University, played up Republican accomplishments and the prosperity issue. In this and later speeches he talked optimistically of the coming abolition of poverty and want, praised rugged individualism, and opposed state socialism. His radio addresses, solid, humorless, and often boring, reiterated his basically conservative tenets.

Charles E. Hughes in the East and Senator Borah in the midlands displayed more voter appeal than the candidate. Hughes stuck to prosperity and Republican achievements in the East, where prohibition was unpopular. Borah, the bellwether of the Republican progressives, used prohibition, farm relief, and Tammany Hall in the depressed farm belt and did much to allay farmer discontent. Only Senator Norris, the veteran Nebraska progressive, and the La Follette group in Wisconsin refused to follow him. Norris, satisfied with Smith's stand on government operation of hydroelectric power at Muscle Shoals, Alabama, bolted Hoover in a speech that also paid his respects to the religious intolerance that was engulfing all other issues.

Smith was his party's most dynamic figure and its best campaigner. After a set acceptance speech in Albany on August 22, he took to the road and covered a large part of the country with major addresses. Radio enabled him to reach a nationwide audience without exhausting his voice in short speeches at a series of train stops. Disdaining careful preparation, he spoke from notes scrawled (but well organized) on the backs of envelopes. Each speech was confined to a particular subject, designed for a particular locality: for example, farm relief at Omaha; prohibition at Milwaukee; religious intolerance at Oklahoma City. His captivating personality, his ready wit, his pungent expressions, and his brown derby won the visible audiences and stamped him as one of the most colorful campaign speakers in the history of American politics. An old, popular song, "The Sidewalks of New York," was revived to add the final touch. Not one serious slip did he commit through his free, extemporaneous method of speech. Unfortunately, he was less successful over the radio—or "raddio" as he called it. His voice had a rasping quality, and listeners caught occasional grammatical lapses while missing the appeal of his personality.

Smith's campaign was the best financed in Democratic annals. John J. Raskob of Delaware, lately a Republican but a personal friend of the Democratic nominee, managed it. An official of General Motors and a millionaire, he gained business support for the party; but he lost some votes, for he was both Catholic and wet. Senator Peter G. Gerry of Rhode Island helped direct the political strategy. James W. Gerard, ambassador to Germany under Wilson, was treasurer of the national committee. A Wall Street banker, Herbert H. Lehman, acted as chairman of the finance committee and was aided by Jesse Jones of Texas. This setup enabled the national committee to collect and spend $5,342,000. But clearly the election was not determined by the size of the war chests. Had Raskob spent twice what he did, the result would have been much the same. The Democrats were faced with an impossible problem.

Boiled down to its lowest terms, the difficulty was twofold: to combat the prosperity appeal and to overcome the triple objections to Smith, namely, his "wetness," his religion, and his Tammany associations. In the wet East, when Smith attempted to appeal to antiprohibition feeling, he was confronted with the prosperity argument. In the farm belt, when he pointed to the depressed condition of the farmer and virtually endorsed the McNary-Haugen plan, Borah answered with charges of "wetness" and Tammany and promises that Hoover, the miracle man, would come nearer to solving the farm problem than the inexperienced city politician. Thus prosperity served the Republicans where it existed; where it fell short, emotional appeals to bigotry and prejudice took its place.

In the Democratic South the Republicans kept in the background and let the anti-Smith Democrats, or "Hoovercrats," fight their battle. The real force in the anti-Smith movement was Bishop James Cannon, Jr., of the Methodist Episcopal Church South, who appealed to his large following to vote against rum, Romanism, and Tammany, and helped organize the rural South for Hoover. A Colonel Horace Mann operated in the background with funds from Republican sources. The Anti-Saloon League, the Woman's Christian Temperance Union, the Ku Klux Klan, and other dry or Catholic-baiting organizations joined in the hue and cry.

Catholicism an Issue

Though Smith boldly met the religious issue in his Oklahoma City speech and attempted to bring his accusers into the open, he could do little to combat the "whispering" that made the campaign one of the dirtiest in American history. Tales went around of Catholic projects to bring the Pope to the United States to reside if Smith were elected, and pictures of the governor at the entrance of the new Holland Tunnel under the Hudson were circulated in the rural South with the amazing explanation that the tunnel was to be extended under the Atlantic to the basement of the Vatican! A story was fabricated that Smith was so drunk on a certain public appearance that it took two men to support him, though different versions made the occasion of this lapse vary considerably. Evidence pointed to a common source for this invention but denials of authorship met his efforts to run it down.

In the East liberals without party affiliation who had followed La Follette in 1924 tended to swing to Smith, as he clarified his views by his speeches in contrast with Hoover's more evasive but generally conservative attitude. The *Nation* and the *New Republic* and Professor John Dewey spoke for this group. The Scripps-Howard League of independent newspapers expressed a preference for Hoover at the start of the campaign but grew more lukewarm toward the close, though nominally for him. Labor, to judge from the expressions of its leaders, was divided, though Smith seemed to have more endorsements.

Hoover Elected

On November 6 this bitter campaign ended in another great Republican victory. Hoover had the East with two exceptions, the entire West, the border South, and Texas, Florida, North Carolina, Tennessee, and Virginia from the old "solid South." He had 444 electoral votes; Smith had 87, carrying but eight states: Massachusetts and Rhode Island, where his antiprohibition stand and his religion were assets, and South Carolina, Georgia, Alabama, Mississippi, Louisiana, and Arkansas. Even New York was lost by more than 100,000 votes. He had persuaded Franklin D. Roosevelt to help the Democratic cause by running for governor. The latter, stricken by polio in 1921, surprised by carrying the state in the face of the tremendous Republican sweep.

The popular vote was nearly 8,000,000 above that of 1924. Hoover received 21,411,991; Smith, 15,000,185. The vote of the minor parties was unusually small. The Socialist vote for Thomas was but 266,453, the poorest showing since 1900.* Smith had the consolation of knowing that he had polled the largest vote ever given to a Democratic candidate, and that, despite the electoral vote, he had run far better than Cox in 1920 or Davis in 1924. He had received a large urban vote, carrying New York, Boston, Cleveland, St. Louis, and San Francisco, and running well in other large cities. A dry, Protestant candidate would have held the south-

---

* The others were as follows: Foster, Communist, 48,170; Reynolds, Socialist Labor, 21,608; Varney, Prohibitionist, 34,489; Webb, Farmer-Labor, 6,390.

ern electoral votes but would have done far worse than Smith in the East and probably but little better in the West. No Democrat could possibly have won, and none but Smith could have gained such a large popular support.

The Democrats could thank their lucky stars for the defeat of 1928. Had they won, the Great Depression would have descended upon them as relentlessly as it did upon Hoover, and the Republican dogma that prosperity was a GOP (Grand Old Party) monopoly would have become so established in the popular mind that no Democrat could have overcome it for another generation. The Great Engineer was the unfortunate man in 1928, not his defeated opponent. The Happy Warrior would not have remained happy very long in the White House after 1929.

The Great Depression

The stock market crash in October 1929, and the spread of the Great Depression changed the political picture, as depressions always do. Hoover's acceptance of the high Smoot-Hawley Tariff and his reluctance to use federal power to meet the emergency caused liberals in his party to turn against him. When he did act, as in setting up the Reconstruction Finance Corporation and in providing federal loans to the states for relief purposes, his critics charged that his measures were always too little and too late. Yet neither progressives nor old-line party regulars, who had never cared for him, attempted to prevent his renomination.

The 1932 Republican convention met in Chicago on June 14 in an artificially cooled new stadium. It proved to be a spiritless affair. A floor battle over the prohibition issue created the only excitement. The Hoover administration offered an evasive plank that proposed to submit to the people a substitute for the Eighteenth Amendment that would seem to return control of the liquor traffic to the states but under some kind of federal supervision. A dissenting minority report favored outright repeal. The administration won a sharply contested floor battle. The other planks of the platform were largely defenses of the Hoover record. The continuance of the depression was attributed to events in Europe.

Hoover was renominated with 1,126½ votes to 13 for Senator Blaine of Wisconsin and 10½ for four others. There was some opposition to the renomination of Vice-President Curtis, but he was only 19¼ votes short of a majority on the roll call, and Pennsylvania then put him over the line.

The optimistic Democrats had been smelling victory since their midterm success of 1930, which included capture of the House of Representatives. Candidates were numerous enough, but Governor Franklin D. Roosevelt, two-term governor of New York, took an early lead. His campaign manager, big, genial James A. Farley, established friendly contacts with hundreds of local leaders all over the West and South. Speaker John N. Garner, who added California to his Texas support, some favorite sons, and a dark horse or two, such as Newton D. Baker of Ohio, did not seem able to stop the Roosevelt bandwagon until Al Smith entered the race. He had broken with Roosevelt for personal reasons and became his strongest opponent, rounding up a considerable bloc of eastern delegates.

The Democrats and a "New Deal"

The convention opened in Chicago on June 27 and soon was engaged in a battle over the permanent chairmanship. The Roosevelt forces won, electing Senator Thomas J. Walsh of Montana over Jouett Shouse, choice of the national committee controlled by the Smith-Raskob leadership of 1928, by a vote of 626 to 528. The platform recommended outright repeal of the Eighteenth Amendment. It favored reduction in expenditures, a balanced budget, a revenue tariff and reciprocal trade agreements, and an extension of federal action along a number of lines to meet depression problems, particularly unemployment. This last included a series of public works. The vague farm plank included extension of cooperatives and control of crop surpluses, among other proposed remedies.

Of broader appeal were promises to enforce antitrust laws and to regulate more effectively public utilities, holding companies, and the stock market. The overtones of a resurgent liberalism were present in the platform, and it challenged Hoover's rugged individualism.

The first ballot gave Roosevelt 666¼; Smith, 201¾; Garner, 90¼; 7 others lesser numbers. Adjournment came after 3 ballots, with Roosevelt 88 votes short of the required two-thirds. Next day Garner consented to take second place, California and Texas shifted to Roosevelt, and he had the nomination with 945 votes. Garner became his running mate without opposition.

On the final day the victor broke precedent by flying to Chicago and accepting the nomination in person. He pledged himself to a "New Deal" for the American people with the nation listening on the radio.

Depressions produce a bumper crop of protest parties and extremist movements, some of which never get beyond the name stage. In 1932 twenty-one different parties had their names on the ballots in various states, and several others claimed an existence that was not in evidence on Election Day. In the end none of the new movements reached the strength of the older third parties, all of whom offered candidates as usual.

Of the others that did not expire before Election Day, Coin Harvey's "Liberty" Party made the best showing. Harvey, forgotten since 1896, raised the inflationist banner again, but few flocked to it. However, he had a larger total than that once-famous leader of the jobless of the nineties, General Jacob S. Coxey of Massillon, Ohio. Coxey, candidate of a Farmer-Labor remnant, did not get on the ballot in most of the states. Some other protest parties were confined to a single state.

The "Brain Trust"

The Democratic campaign was well planned and well managed. James A. Farley naturally became national chairman and handled affairs from his New York headquarters directly through the state organizations, without special regional or branch headquarters. Charles Michelson took care of publicity. An efficient corps of assistants worked with Farley, and the "brain trust"—experts selected for their knowledge of public problems but lacking in political experience—came on the scene to advise the candidate and help him in the preparation of important addresses. The charter members were Raymond Moley, Rexford G. Tugwell, and Adolf A. Berle, Jr., all from Columbia University, and Justice Samuel J. Rosenman. According to Moley, the group was concerned exclusively with policy-planning and had nothing to do with campaign management or tactics. Roosevelt's major speeches were prepared from materials compiled and interpreted by this "brain trust." That a candidate should seek guidance from unbiased experts on difficult problems, chiefly economic in character, was indeed an innovation in a political campaign. Unlike Harding, Roosevelt did not recite what others had written. He used the ideas of others but, according to Charles Michelson, was a better phrasemaker than anybody around him.

Roosevelt conducted a vigorous offensive with twenty-seven major addresses from coast to coast. His purpose was not only to give the lie to whispers about his physical condition but, more important, to play the role of a New Deal Messiah, particularly in the midwestern farm belt where riots against mortgage foreclosures and forced sales indicated the temper of farm voters.

His sympathetic approach attracted George N. Peek, Henry A. Wallace, and other farm leaders to his camp and was a factor in the bolt of Senators Norris, Hiram Johnson, Bronson Cutting of New Mexico, and Robert M. La Follette, Jr. Norris was more interested in his friendliness toward public ownership of electric power. Borah preserved a sullen silence toward both candidates.

In the East the conservative Smith-Raskob wing of the party had to be conciliated. Roosevelt and Smith cooperated in obtaining the nomination of Herbert Lehman for governor of New York, and then the man with the brown derby went on the stump to make antiprohibition speeches. Tammany also fell in line, and the urban East seemed united behind Roosevelt.

The Republican organization was headed by Everett Sanders, former Indiana congressman and secretary to President Coolidge. As in 1928, Joseph R. Nutt and Jeremiah Milbank handled finances. Hoover had intended to make only three or four set speeches, but alarming reports of Republican defections—Maine went Democratic in September—forced him to take the stump. In ten major speeches and many brief talks at train stops, he exhibited a sturdy fighting spirit, in contrast to his ignoring of Smith in 1928. Despite fears of his advisers, he was treated everywhere with respect, except in Detroit, where there were some catcalls and boos from the sidewalks.

Republicans hoped that the depression would begin to lift and prosperity peep around the corner in time to save them, but Fortune refused to favor them this time. There was left only the argument that things would be worse if the Democrats won. "Grass will grow in the streets of a hundred cities," warned Hoover in his final speech in a moment of emotional strain unusual with him. But the old fear argument had lost its potency. With better psychology his opponent was offering the more abundant life to the "forgotten man."

Neither party was blessed with a huge campaign chest. The Republicans as usual were better off, but the depression had reduced some of their chief sources of revenue. At one time Hoover had to take personal direction of the job of collecting funds to stave off a financial breakdown. About $2,900,000 was spent, against receipts of $2,650,000. The Democrats collected $2,379,000 and spent $2,246,000, without allowance for a large deficit incurred in the preceding four years. Both national committees continued heavily in debt after the campaign was over.

The Influence of Radio

Radio was a more powerful factor in 1932 than in 1928. The major speeches of both candidates and many broadcasts by lesser figures reached millions of listeners and challenged the significance of newspapers and other forms of publicity. The direct appeal of candidates to voters sitting in their homes and unmoved by crowd psychology compelled greater care in the preparation of speeches and a special technique in presentation. Here the Democrats showed to advantage. The heavy, monotonous seriousness of Hoover's speeches made listening an effort. Roosevelt, by contrast, was at his best when heard over the air. The deep, mellow tones of his voice, a cheerful warmth of personality, and a skill in interjecting light, humorous touches into his speeches made his broadcasts the most effective type of propaganda the Democrats used.

The result was almost foreordained. Republican money, organization, and propaganda could not meet the deadly realities of the Great Depression. The difference between the two candidates was not so much in specific issues as in methods of approach. Hoover stood on his record and could promise little more than continuance along the same lines. Roosevelt, critical of the president's conservatism, could offer an open mind and a willingness to try new paths. The country had soured on Hoover and felt that any change would be for the better.

Roosevelt Elected

On November 8 the Republicans went down to a crushing defeat. Roosevelt had 472 electoral votes; Hoover, 59. Pennsylvania, Delaware, Maine, New Hampshire, Vermont, and Connecticut constituted the Republican total. In the popular vote Roosevelt had a plurality of more than 7,000,000.* The Democrats had more than 70 percent of the House and a margin of 22 votes in the Senate. Such Old Guard leaders as Watson of Indiana, Smoot of Utah, and Moses of New Hampshire were defeated. As in 1920 the voters had voted their resentments; but this time the Republicans were the victims. The Socialist vote approached the total Debs had received in 1920; but on the whole the minor parties made a poor showing for a depression year.

The discontented had chosen the Roosevelt road, which offered some hope of immediate relief, rather than unfamiliar third-party bypaths and blind alleys. It remained for the Democrats to prove that they had made no mistake.

* Roosevelt, 22,825,016; Hoover, 15,758,397; Thomas, Socialist, 883,990; Foster, Communist, 102,221; Upshaw, Prohibition, 81,916; Harvey, Liberty, 53,199; Reynolds, Socialist Labor, 34,028.

XI

The New Deal Landslide

IN THE INAUGURAL ADDRESS on March 4, 1933, President Franklin Delano Roosevelt encouraged the nation by saying, "The only thing we have to fear is fear itself." He subsequently began a comprehensive program to help the country recover from the depression.

The CCC (Civilian Conservation Corps), started in 1933, consisted of about 2,000 work camps for youths, who were given food, clothing, shelter, and wages. Their work consisted mainly in helping to develop, repair, and conserve the country's natural resources. Another job program—for adults—was the WPA (Works Progress Administration), begun in 1935. Industry and agriculture were covered by the NRA (National Recovery Act) and the AAA (Agricultural Adjustment Administration), respectively.

Also in 1933 there was the FDIC (Federal Deposit Insurance Corporation), which guaranteed the savings of bank depositors. In 1934 the SEC (Securities and Exchange Commission) was formed to regulate stock exchanges. And in 1935 the Social Security Act provided for unemployment insurance and old-age pensions.

Perhaps the most innovative act was the creation in 1933 of the TVA (Tennessee Valley Authority) to develop electric power, control floods, and prevent soil erosion.

Roosevelt's appointment in 1933 of Frances Perkins as secretary of labor is also noteworthy. Miss Perkins, the first woman to hold a cabinet post, remained in that office until she resigned in May 1945, soon after Roosevelt's death.

Nevertheless, the Republicans began to recover hope as 1936 approached. Millions were still unemployed; lavish government expenditures had not restored prosperity; the budget was unbalanced, and the national debt was mounting; taxes and government restrictions alarmed businessmen; many conservatives saw constitutional government in danger.

There were signs also of restiveness in Congress. Although the passage of a comprehensive Social Security Act marked the high-water mark of the reform program, Roosevelt suffered his first defeat in the Senate when his proposal for American entry into the World Court failed by seven votes to attain the required two-thirds. The Wheeler-Rayburn bill to regulate public utilities had its drastic "death sentence" provision for holding companies modified because of conservative pressure, though in the main the administration was satisfied with the measure. These straws seemed to indicate a weakening of the Roosevelt magic and a possible conservative revival.

Unpromising Republican Candidates

The Republican problem was to find a suitable candidate. Hoover was a liability; the Senate Old Guard had been almost wiped out; the insurgents were generally disqualified as bolters in 1932 or supporters of New Deal measures; hardly a Republican governor of a strategically important state was left. Never had the material been so unpromising. Three names were considered: Charles L. McNary and Arthur H. Vandenberg, senators from Oregon and Michigan, and Alfred M. Landon, governor of Kansas. Neither senator was well known outside his home state; McNary was badly located geographically, and both had voting records that indicated liberal tendencies.

The party regulars found Landon the most suitable. The Kansas governor had been an oil producer—a fact that would appeal to businessmen. He had twice carried an important farming state and presumably would run well in the farm belt, where Republican losses had been heavy. He had once followed Theodore Roosevelt and was regarded as mildly progressive, which would suit the liberal element. A group of Kansas friends, including John D. M. Hamilton, national committeeman, Roy A. Roberts of the *Kansas City Star*, and William Allen White, provided backing and publicity, and the Hearst papers began to praise him.

Who else was there? Colonel Frank Knox, publisher of the *Chicago Daily News* and an old Bull Mooser, jumped into the race and showed plenty of energy but aroused no popular support. Belatedly and unexpectedly Borah decided to run, but the regulars would not even consider him.

The Landon backers, playing up their candidate as a western reincarnation of Calvin Coolidge, mellowed by a progressive heritage and a Kansas environment, came to the Republican national convention in Cleveland on June 9, 1936, with the nomination sewed up. Senator Frederick Steiwer of Oregon was temporary chairman of the convention, and Congressman Bertrand H. Snell of New York, permanent chairman. Hoover aroused the most enthusiasm with a speech that emphasized the dangers threatening the American way of life and the need for the party to conduct "a holy crusade for liberty."

The platform required a great deal of work to satisfy conflicting interests. Senator Borah adopted a threatening attitude with demands for liberalism on domestic policies and isolationism in foreign relations. Eventually a compromise platform was adopted without opposition.

An Attempt to Answer the New Deal

It began with the solemn preamble: "America is in peril. The welfare of American men and women and the future of our youth are at stake. We dedicate ourselves to the preservation of their political liberty, their individual opportunity and their character as free citizens, which today for the first time are threatened by government itself." Then followed an indictment of "the New Deal administration" (all through, the term "New Deal" was used instead of "Democratic") for misdeeds and usurpations. All Americans, regardless of parties, were invited "to join in defense of American institutions." The preservation of constitutional government and the American system of free enterprise came first in the list of pledges. Then followed statements of policy on various problems.

Unemployment was to be solved by encouragement of private business and removal of hampering government regulations; relief was to be returned to local control with federal grants-in-aid; more adequate old-age pensions were offered in place of the Social Security Act; protective tariff with flexible provisions to promote international trade was recommended; further devaluation of the dollar was opposed, New Deal finance condemned, and a balanced budget promised. A thirteen-point agricultural section of the platform accepted, with some qualifications, most of the administration farm program, and even insisted that the New Deal had taken over the Republican policy of soil conservation and land retirement. Collective bargaining in labor disputes was promised, and state laws and interstate compacts to protect women and children in industry. Extreme isolationism characterized the statements on foreign relations. Even the World Court was condemned.

The convention cheered for half an hour a telegram from Governor Landon approving the platform but favoring a constitutional amendment to permit states to enact legislation necessary to protect women and children as to hours, wages, and working conditions, if this could not be attained within the Constitution (a Supreme Court decision setting aside a New York minimum wage statute had aroused a storm of criticism). Landon also declared himself for a stable currency expressed in terms of gold, and for the application of the merit system to all administrative positions below the rank of assistant secretary. This display of independence received generally favorable comment, though Borah, who had left the convention, was displeased with the gold-standard pronouncement.

Landon Nominated

Landon was nominated almost without opposition after half a dozen nominal favorite sons released their delegates.* He received 984 votes; Borah, 19 including 18 of Wisconsin's 24. Knox's preconvention campaigning won him the vice-presidential nomination when Senator Vandenberg refused to be considered. John D. M. Hamilton of Kansas, who had presented Landon's name to the convention and had managed his delegate hunt, naturally was chosen for the post of national chairman.

Landon's acceptance speech, in Topeka on July 23 before fifty thousand persons, was preceded by a picturesque pageant of frontier days, emblematic of the candidate's background; and an enthusiastic and apparently united party approved of the general tenor of his remarks. But the pageant, not the candidate, provided the color. He appeared as a sincere, uninspiring conservative, rather than as the wielder of the sword of Theodore Roosevelt. It remained for the Republicans to prove that the country needed his type, an average man of substantial virtues without Coolidge's narrowness or Franklin Roosevelt's dangerous "charm."

Roosevelt Renominated

The Democratic convention, in Philadelphia in the Municipal Auditorium, June 23–27, 1936, was an utterly useless performance, except for the hotels, restaurants, and stores of the Quaker City. Platform and candidates were predetermined, and the delegates came merely to ratify; yet the program was spread over five days. Chairman Farley called the convention to order and gave the opening address; Senators Alben W. Barkley of Kentucky and Joseph T. Robinson were the presiding officers. The most significant action taken was the abrogation of the century-old two-thirds rule, as recommended by the convention of 1932. The only opposition was in the rules committee, where the vote was 36 to 13.

Senator Robert F. Wagner presented a White House platform that paraphrased the Declaration of Independence with its self-evident truths, proclaiming that farmers, workers, businesspeople, and the youth of the nation had been returned to the road to freedom and prosperity, and promising, "We will keep them on that road." A recital of accomplishment was offered as evidence.

Unemployment was declared to be a national problem, to be met in a

* These were Senator Vandenberg, Senator L. J. Dickinson of Iowa, Governor Harry W. Nice of Maryland, Frank Knox, Robert A. Taft of Ohio, and Walter E. Edge of New Jersey.

national way. While more than five million had found employment through "our stimulation of private enterprise," a continuation of work relief was promised where needed. Republican proposals to solve national problems by state action were derided. The Democrats promised to deal with them by federal legislation within the Constitution or, if this proved impossible, by a "clarifying amendment" to give Congress and the states the necessary powers, within their respective jurisdictions. The financial measures of the administration were defended, and a balanced budget was promised at the earliest possible moment, as relief requirements declined and national income increased.

The party pledged itself to continue the "Good Neighbor" policy in Latin America, to take the profits out of war, and to guard against involvement in any war anywhere. The World Court and the League of Nations were not mentioned. The platform closed by defining the issue as one between a party that would regiment the people in the service of privileged groups and an administration dedicated to the establishment of equal opportunity for all.

After the adoption of the ready-made platform came a marathon of oratory. To make the convention last, Farley had planned that each state, territory, and dependency should have a seconding speaker after Judge John E. Mack had presented the president's name. Over the air waves, hour after hour, flowed a seemingly endless stream of banal oratory that listeners could tune off, but which the delegates had to endure. Forty-nine men and eight women participated. At the end Roosevelt and Garner were safely nominated without opposition. The enthusiasm for Roosevelt was tremendous, but the oratorical relay was indefensible.

At Franklin Field that night, June 27, President Roosevelt delivered his acceptance speech to an assemblage estimated at one hundred thousand, while the whole country listened in. Though for the most part he spoke in terms of exalted idealism, his denunciation of "economic royalists" sounded the keynote of a campaign that was to carry the war into the enemy's country.

Third-Party Candidates

On June 19, Congressman William Lemke of North Dakota, a nominal Republican but an agrarian radical, announced his presidential candidacy on a "Union Party" ticket. He received the endorsement of three minor prophets of discontent: the Reverend Gerald L. K. Smith, self-proclaimed leader of a Share-the-Wealth Movement started by Senator Huey P. Long of Louisiana, who had made himself virtual dictator of that state before he was assassinated; Father Charles Coughlin, a Detroit Catholic priest with a large radio following that he tried to organize into a Union for

Social Justice; and Dr. Francis E. Townsend, whose proposal for pensions of two hundred dollars a month for the retired, dependent elderly had produced thousands of Townsend clubs. This troika pulled in somewhat different directions and did not agree on a platform, although they gave their support to Lemke.

The older minor parties had candidates as usual. The Communists embarrassed the Democrats by following the "party line"—later changed —of "a united front against Fascism," meaning the Republicans.

The Country Now Divided into Economic Groups

The campaign soon revealed that the country was dividing less along traditional party lines and more according to economic groups than at any time since 1896. Roosevelt was supported by the leaders of the American Federation of Labor and its new rival, the CIO (Congress of Industrial Organizations), which combined the skilled and unskilled workers of an industry. In the political field their support was made effective by an organization known as Labor's Nonpartisan League. John L. Lewis, though not the official head, was its real organizer. The farmers, less united in sentiment, seemed to be still favorable to the New Deal in the great grain-growing regions, once Republican strongholds. The La Follettes, Norris, the Minnesota Farmer-Laborites, and other western progressives cooperated with the Democrats on the presidential ticket, while Senators Borah and McNary campaigned for themselves, not for Landon. Thus the party of Roosevelt appeared as a farmer-labor combination, as Bryan had attempted to make it in 1896, and as it had been in Jackson's day, though the labor partner then was a pygmy compared with 1936.

Backing the Republican cause was big business as represented by the Liberty League, the NAM (National Association of Manufacturers), and other organizations, numerically small but financially powerful. There was general expectation among Republicans that the smaller-business-people and the professional groups—the upper-middle class—would be with them as in the past. Dislike and fear of New Deal spending and regimentation were evident here.

The conservatism of the party also drew Democratic allies, unable to stomach New Deal liberalism. The conservatives, calling themselves "Jeffersonian Democrats,"* included such impressive names as John W. Davis, Alfred E. Smith, James A. Reed of Missouri, Bainbridge Colby (Wilson's secretary of state), and former Governor Joseph B. Ely of Massachusetts. Unfortunately for the Republicans, these figures were hardly

* A conference of bolting conservative Democrats, held in Detroit on August 7, took this name.

more than museum pieces, imposing to gaze upon but useless as vote-get-ters. In fact, the Toryism of the Republicans cost them far more votes through defections on the left than were gained from recruiting on the right.

The Republican management seemed to be liberally supplied with funds, though it ended the campaign with a budget badly out of balance. It spent nearly $9,000,000—a new record for campaign expenditures. This did not include sums raised and spent by the Liberty League and by state committees. Such names as Hearst, Guggenheim, Rockefeller, Du Pont, Pew, and Vanderbilt among Republican contributors indicate the party's financial backing.

Yet money alone could not solve the problem. A strategy had to be devised to recover the populous East and Middle West, long Republican but rendered doubtful by the popularity of the New Deal with labor and farmer. Relying upon the past conservatism of this area, the Republican general staff began a vigorous assault upon the New Deal and all its works. Criticisms of its spending policy, its farm-relief measures, its atti-tude toward business, its currency program, its disregard of the Constitu-tion, and Roosevelt's failure to keep some of his platform promises of 1932 filled Republican newspapers, were the meat of hundreds of speeches, and reached millions of voters over the air waves. These attacks were made more pointed by charges that the New Deal was collectivistic and even communistic.

Toward the close of the campaign a concerted attempt was made to use the Social Security Act against Roosevelt. To alarm wage earners, the act was assailed as a "pay reduction" measure. Many employers assisted the Republican cause with explanations designed to influence their employees. Some used bulletins in factories and slips in pay envelopes, reminiscent of the tactics of 1896. The net effect was to sharpen the class alignment and make labor more resentful toward such pressure and more pro-Roosevelt than before.

The Republican organization functioned badly. Chairman Hamilton, inexperienced in national politics but filled with enthusiasm for his task, found the state and local organizations in bad shape, their morale broken by the succession of defeats since 1930. The national chairman, assuming the role of a traveling salesman, went around the country making the acquaintance of local leaders, stirring them to action, and delivering speeches for Landon at the same time. The national headquarters at Chi-cago became a huge propaganda machine manned by super salespeople and pouring forth every possible type of publicity for the Republican cause. Much of this was wasted because of bad management and bun-gling tactics.

Chairman Farley's Democratic machine reached its peak in 1936. For-tified by victory and the possession of offices, and stimulated by the chairman's unceasing vigilance, the Democratic organizations, national, state, and local, left nothing to chance. Numerous reports from party workers to the New York headquarters, tabulated, checked, and analyzed by Emil Hurja, gave the national chairman a clear picture of the battle at every stage and enabled him to adapt his tactics to the immediate situation.

The hostility of big business reduced the number of large contributors and compelled the Democrats to rely upon a larger number of small gifts than in the past. Half a million individuals gave to the Democratic campaign fund, more than a third of the total amount being accounted for by gifts of less than $100. Labor organizations—a hitherto untapped source of funds—were heavy contributors. A new device, continued after 1936, was the holding of Jackson Day dinners all over the country on January 8, with tickets selling as high as $100 a plate but graded down to fit the pocketbooks of the faithful who attended in the provinces.* The campaign expenditures by the national committee amounted to $5,194,000. Like the Republicans, the Democrats had the assistance of auxiliary organizations whose outlays added materially to the total cost.

The Democratic strategy was not cautiously defensive but a vigorous assault on the forces of reaction. The "economic royalists" and "Tories" behind Landon, "the straw man," received the major brunt of the attack. The support given by Hoover, Hearst, former Governor Smith, and the Liberty League was offered as concrete evidence of the reactionary character of the opposition.

But the strongest argument in the Democratic repertory was the contrast between 1932 and 1936. Even conceding that the glittering prosperity of the 1920s had not returned, they argued that conditions had improved immeasurably under Roosevelt, that old abuses had been removed, confidence had been restored, and that farmer, laborer, and businesspeople were better off. Against this the Republican cry that the Constitution and the American way of life were in danger fell flat.

Both candidates took the stump. They centered their attention on the Middle West but appeared also in the East, and Landon made a foray to the Pacific Coast. Roosevelt aroused far greater mass enthusiasm. In Chicago five miles of streets were almost impassable for the presidential car, and a hundred thousand people packed the stadium to hear him. His oratorical cleverness and his role of crusader against plutocracy made him the greatest political attraction since Theodore Roosevelt, and Bryan had charged and countercharged. Landon, utterly lacking in magnetism and mediocre as a speaker, did not appear to advantage on the stump; and he was further handicapped by a poor radio voice.

The power of radio to overcome unfavorable newspaper publicity was

* Another device, much criticized, was the sale of the *Book of the Democratic Convention*, with the president's autograph, at $100 or more per copy. Its sale was continued after the campaign to help pay off the national committee's deficit.

clearly shown in this campaign. No candidate since Bryan in 1896 had had to fight such a powerful array of newspapers as confronted Roosevelt. To the normal Republican journalistic preponderance outside the South were added the Hearst chain, the *Baltimore Sun,* and the *St. Louis Post-Dispatch.* In the fifteen largest cities the newspaper alignment was 71 percent for Landon, as measured by circulation figures. In Chicago it was eight to one in his favor, but Roosevelt's majority was almost two to one. The press, with its savage editorial denunciations of the New Deal—comparable to the anti-Bryan violence of 1896—its warped news stories, and its misleading headlines, played a rather sorry part in the campaign.

The whispering, or undercover, campaign that has so often disgraced American politics appeared chiefly in the form of stories about the president's sanity. In 1932 it was his physical condition; in 1936, his mental state. It was "whispered" at country clubs and across bridge tables that his mind had been affected by his siege of infantile paralysis; and medical authorities were cited to prove that his symptoms foreshadowed mental collapse. In addition, the divorces in the Roosevelt family and Mrs. Roosevelt's manifold activities offended the sensibilities of middle-class Roosevelt haters and were used as propaganda wherever possible. Among the overly well fed, the most astonishing reason offered for opposing the president was that he was a traitor to his "class."

The various polls, with one notable exception, pointed toward a Roosevelt victory. But the huge postcard poll of the *Literary Digest,* so successful in its prophecies in the past, indicated a large Landon electoral majority. Its failure to give due weight to the different groups and classes in the voting population was its undoing.

On the other hand the careful "sampling" methods of the American Institute of Public Opinion, headed by Dr. George Gallup, and similar techniques used by *Fortune* magazine and by Archibald M. Crossley were completely vindicated by the result in November. But they too underestimated the size of the Roosevelt victory, as did all the polls and the major prophets except Chairman Farley. With Emil Hurja's figures before him, Farley created amusement among Republicans by extravagantly claiming all the electoral votes for Roosevelt except those of Maine and Vermont.

The Roosevelt Tidal Wave

On November 3 he was found to be exactly right. Roosevelt had 523 electoral votes; Landon, 8 (Maine and Vermont). In the past, Maine had been regarded as a guide to an election, with the slogan, "As Maine goes, so goes the nation." The victors now changed this to, "As Maine goes, so goes Vermont." Not since the reelection of President Monroe in 1820 had a winner come so near to a clean sweep. Roosevelt's share of the popular vote, 60.8 percent, was slightly more than Harding's in 1920; his plurality was eleven million votes.* Lemke's poor showing indicated the end of the Union Party. Father Coughin's German and Irish-Catholic isolationists had provided much of his support. The Townsendites and Huey Long's old following had gone elsewhere. The other minor parties likewise had fared badly. The Socialist vote was the smallest since 1900.

The House had 333 Democratic members out of the total membership of 435; the Senate, 75 Democrats out of 96; and a host of Democratic candidates for state and local offices rode to victory on Roosevelt's coattails. In 1932 the verdict had been anti-Hoover; in 1936 it was pro-Roosevelt. The New Deal's good works had built up a powerful farmer-labor-Negro coalition and had cut heavily into Republican middle-income strength. Urban solidarity for Roosevelt was without precedent. The Democratic tide had receded somewhat in the trans-Mississippi West, and nationally the Republicans carried more counties than in 1932. But the loss of the cities was fatal. Labor, whether of native or of immigrant stock, voted its economic interests.

The result was a complete repudiation of the Toryism that had governed the Republican Party's strategy despite the new leadership. The old myths and the old slogans had failed to convince. Standing by the Constitution, defending the American way of life, and calling New Dealers Communists would not supply food for the unemployed, higher farm prices for debt-burdened agrarians, or security for the wage-earners. So the masses of voters had seemed to reason. No Republican could have defeated Roosevelt, but a more intelligent leadership in the years before 1936 might have averted the complete debacle. This was the lesson for 1940. The emaciated frame of the Grand Old Party needed both vitamins and calories.

The Master Politician Slips a Little

The second Franklin Roosevelt administration began on January 20, 1937,† with inauguration ceremonies marred by a cold, drenching rain. The president served notice in his address that the New Deal was not completed, that much remained to be done while one-third of the American people were "ill-housed, ill-clad, ill-nourished." The era of good feelings that followed his nearly unanimous electoral victory was a mirage

---

* Roosevelt had 27,747,636; Landon, 16,679,543; Lemke, Union, 892,492; Thomas, Socialist, 187,785; Browder, Communist, 79,211; Colvin, Prohibition, 37,668; Aiken, Socialist Labor, 12,790.

† The change from March 4 was effected by the Twentieth Amendment, the work of Senator Norris, which eliminated the lame-duck session of Congress by fixing January 3 as the date for each new Congress to begin to function, and set January 20 as the date for the new president and vice-president to be inaugurated.

that vanished with the meeting of the new Congress. Harmonious inaction had no place in the Roosevelt lexicon. The New Deal was to be implemented further by reform legislation dealing with the still difficult problems of economic maladjustment.

But a serious obstacle to reform was the conservative Supreme Court, without a single Roosevelt appointee. Six of the nine members were past seventy, making it the oldest Supreme Court in American history. In the preceding two years it had overturned seven basic New Deal laws, usually by split decisions based on "personal economic predilections," according to Justice Stone. Roosevelt, strengthened by the popular verdict of 1936, now proposed to liberalize the Court by adding a justice for each justice past seventy. The result was the bitterest battle of his career. A group of conservative Senate Democrats charged him with "court packing" to build up his own power, and defeated the proposal with Republican support.

However, during the struggle the Court, influenced by Chief Justice Hughes, began to uphold New Deal social legislation; and the resignation of conservative Justice Van Devanter broke the hold of the septuagenarian majority. Politically Roosevelt had suffered a major setback. The Court issue had split the Democratic Party in Congress, and the effects were evident later at the polls, even though most of his domestic program fared well enough. Acts affecting labor, farmers, and housing rounded out his reform program.

More serious in general effects than the Court fight was a business recession in 1937–1938. It produced an increase in federal spending and gave weight to the charge that the New Deal had failed to bring about a sound recovery. An epidemic of sit-down strikes by unions under the newly organized Congress of Industrial Organizations alarmed businesspeople and farmers over the radicalism let loose by the New Deal.

With the political skies more clouded than at any time since 1932, Roosevelt set out to punish the conservatives in his own party in the primaries of 1938. In this "purge," he went on the stump in several states to bless for renomination senators who had stood with him and to defeat those who had opposed his measures. His failure to defeat Millard E. Tydings of Maryland and Walter F. George of Georgia was a blow to his political prestige.

The elections of 1938 produced a Republican revival. Eighteen states turned against the Democrats and increased the Republican membership in the House of Representatives from 89 to 170 against 262 Democrats, and in the Senate from 17 to 23 against 69 Democrats.*

A bipartisan conservative bloc could now offer an effective opposition.

---

* There were three independents in the House and four in the Senate.

One of the achievements was the Hatch Act of 1939 prohibiting political activities by federal administrative officials, except a few top-ranking ones. In 1940 a more stringent act included state officials paid wholly or in part with federal funds and limited a party's campaign expenditures to $3,000,000.

But foreign problems now overshadowed domestic issues. Hitler had invaded Poland in September 1939. World War II had begun.

XII

"That Man" Again

AMERICAN POLITICS, for nearly two decades, had been more isolationist than American policies. Since 1920, foreign problems had not entered into presidential elections and had not divided the parties in Congress. Though the United States participated actively in various international conferences, it drew back from cooperation with the League of Nations when aggression threatened war. A series of drastic neutrality acts in the 1930s, backed by both parties, attempted to insulate the nation from foreign wars by cutting off American arms, loans, and shipping from all belligerents, with the unintentional effect of encouraging aggressors. Roosevelt was not satisfied with this solution, but public sentiment was against him. Domestic questions were far more pressing, in any case.

At the outbreak of World War II Americans were strongly anti-Hitler; but not until the collapse of France in June 1940, was there alarm at the prospect of a dictator victory. All aid for England short of war and an immediate American rearmament program were major policies on which Roosevelt and most Americans agreed. But Republicans soon realized that this might mean a third term for him, and the hostility of some turned from the New Deal to his "warmongering." A convention divided in opinion on foreign policy and uncertain as to its nominee for the first time since 1920 gathered in Philadelphia in late June.

The elections of 1938 had produced a new crop of hopefuls, though nearly all were too untried and inexpert to do battle with the master politician in the White House. Senator Robert A. Taft of Ohio and District Attorney Thomas E. Dewey of New York City were the leading contenders. Senator Taft, son of a president, had a sharp mind, came from an important, doubtful middle-western state, and had the assistance of a wealthy family; but he was a colorless, uninspiring speaker, too orthodox to attract independents and liberals, and seemed to be reaching for the grand prize before he had won his spurs in the upper house. Nevertheless, by avoiding primaries and working with the practical politicians, he bagged a goodly number of delegates and had strong second-choice support.

Dewey's aggressive handling of the district attorney's office in New York and his close race against Governor Lehman marked him as a man with a future. He showed surprising strength in several state primaries, but it was freely predicted that his delegate support would melt away after the early ballots. Aspiring New Yorkers, by tradition, should reach the White House by way of Albany.

Among favorite sons, Charles L. McNary of Oregon, Senate floor leader, and Arthur H. Vandenberg, senator from Michigan, had the most experience. They did not attract much outside support, though a deadlock might enhance their chances.

Wendell L. Willkie as Candidate

A few days before the convention a great deal began to be heard about Wendell L. Willkie. Indiana-born and formerly of Ohio, he lived in New York City and had made his way in the business world through his ability as a utilities lawyer until, in 1933, he became head of Commonwealth & Southern Corporation, a large holding company. Long opposed to the federal Tennessee Valley Authority, he had finally sold a subsidiary company in that area to it and declared a truce with the government. He had been a Democrat until 1938 and had even served on a Tammany Hall committee, but had never held public office. At first sight this was not a promising background for an aspirant for the Republican presidential nomination.

But Willkie had assets that his rivals lacked. A big, tousle-headed man in the prime of life—he was forty-eight—he had a dynamic personality, supreme self-confidence, a wisecracking sense of humor, skill in extempore speaking, a disarming frankness, and an ability to win friends. Of small-town upbringing, he had the look of the stalwart middle-western self-made man that old-fashioned Americans had long regarded as one of the most wholesome products of their land of opportunity. That he was no politician was entirely in his favor. Business and professional people, wearied of the New Deal and dubious over the ability of any politician candidate to defeat Roosevelt, trooped into the Willkie camp, for here was one of their own sort. Big business approved but wisely kept in the background, for its support would be a liability.

Who first suggested Willkie's name is a matter of dispute; but the men who organized his candidacy were Oren Root, Jr., a young lawyer and a grandnephew of Elihu Root, and Russell Davenport, managing editor of Fortune magazine. Blank petitions were sent out to be circulated, Willkie clubs sprang up in different parts of the country, literature about the new man was soon in demand everywhere, and the encouraging popular response made his backers redouble their efforts. Delegates already elected were made aware of the Willkie candidacy by the pressure of business and professional people in their own communities, who were organizing Willkie clubs and creating a backfire hard to resist with a barrage of last-minute letters, telegrams, and declarations for Willkie.

But the regular Republicans were not ready to hand over the party leadership to a man whose coating of Republicanism had hardly had time to dry. A hundred congressmen representing some twenty states held a caucus and demanded that the convention name a man "whose personal views and public statements present an opportunity for a clear-cut vote on foreign and domestic issues in harmony with the Republican record in Congress." His utilities record was played up as a grave liability, and a strong isolationist group objected to his support of Roosevelt's foreign policy. There was much talk of a "Stop Willkie" movement, and a Taft-Dewey ticket was rumored as the solution.

The youthful Governor Harold E. Stassen of Minnesota opened the convention in Philadelphia on Monday, June 24, 1940, with a stirring keynote speech assailing the Roosevelt administration for its failure on the fronts of national preparedness, "fifth column" activities, domestic economic welfare, and governmental effectiveness and integrity. Joseph W. Martin, Jr., of Massachusetts, Republican floor leader in the House of Representatives, as permanent chairman followed with another assault on the New Deal record. On Tuesday night former President Hoover had his moment of glory; but the hopes of friends that he might stampede the delegates and win the nomination were dimmed by his performance. He was still the Hoover of old. He was warmly applauded and then dropped from consideration as a candidate.

The platform, much briefer than usual, began with an arraignment of the Roosevelt administration and then pledged the Republican Party to "Americanism, preparedness, and peace." It promised an adequate national defense and condemned the "explosive utterances" of the president as imperiling peace. The controversial plank on aid to Britain promised "the extension to all peoples fighting for liberty, or whose liberty is threatened, of such aid as shall not be in violation of international law or inconsistent with the requirements of our own national defense." This statement left the candidate plenty of leeway later.

Unemployment was to be solved by encouraging private enterprise; relief was to be turned over to the states with federal grants-in-aid; social security was to be extended to groups not yet covered, with the states controlling the administration. The right of free organization and collective bargaining was guaranteed to labor, but the National Labor Relations Act was to be amended to provide "true freedom for, and orderliness in, self-organization and collective bargaining."

The farm planks, as in 1936, received much attention. In effect, they promised to continue existing benefit payments until expanding business and greater consumer buying power took care of overproduction. Easier credit, encouragement of cooperatives (referring to farms), better tariff protection, and a condemnation of reciprocal trade agreements were also thrown into the agricultural hopper. Business was wooed with promises of economy, encouragement of investment, an end of the president's control of the currency, and a minimum of federal competition. A constitutional amendment limiting a president to two terms was also endorsed.

The general tone was friendly to business, but the party asked to be taken on faith. Other than currency control, no pledge was made to repeal or modify seriously any major acts of legislation of the Roosevelt administrations.

With the platform out of the way on Wednesday afternoon, the nominating speeches were in order. In a flood of oratory, Dewey, Frank E. Gannett of New York, Taft, Willkie, Hanford MacNider of Iowa, Vandenberg of Michigan, H. Styles Bridges of New Hampshire, McNary of Oregon, Governor Arthur H. James of Pennsylvania, and Governor Harlan J. Bushfield of South Dakota were placed in nomination. When Representative Charles A. Halleck of Indiana offered Willkie the galleries shrieked approval; but whistles, boos, and heckling from delegates pledged to other candidates indicated a resentment at the outside pressure for the "utilities tycoon." This hostility grew more intense as the balloting went on and threatened to bring about a coalition movement in favor of a true-blue Republican.

The first ballot, on Thursday afternoon, ran almost as predicted. Dewey led with 360; Taft had 189; Willkie, 105; and 11 others divided the rest of the thousand votes.* The next three ballots saw Dewey's support decline to 250 votes; while Taft went up to 254 and Willkie to 306. On the fifth ballot, Willkie reached 429 and Taft 377, while Dewey, who had released his delegates, dropped to 57. With the shift of Kansas and most of New York to Willkie on this ballot the bandwagon hove in sight. Desperately the Taft leaders tried to rally the straight-out party men; but the avalanche of letters and telegrams, the excellent publicity for the businessman candidate, and the roars of the galleries had done the work. The "amateurs" were cleverer than the politicians. When Vandenberg released the Michigan delegates on the sixth ballot and they shifted to Willkie, the battle was practically over. Pennsylvania then decided for him, and other delegations changed their votes before the count was officially announced, to make the nomination unanimous.

Next day, after several of the presidential aspirants refused to be considered, second place on the ticket went to Senator McNary, who reluctantly accepted. His western residence, his post as floor leader in the

* These were as follows: Vandenberg, 76; James, 74; Chairman Joseph Martin, 44; MacNider, 34; Gannett, 33; Bridges, 28; Capper, 18; Hoover, 17; McNary, 13; Bushfield, 9.

Senate, and his liberalism as attested by his support of a number of New Deal measures made him an excellent choice.

Willkie, who had been in Philadelphia conducting his own campaign —as had his chief rivals—came before the convention and was received like a conquering hero. Overnight the old-line politicians forgot their bitterness and began to sense that the delegates might, after all, have done a shrewd piece of work. As a businessman Willkie would have the backing of the financial overlords, which meant a well-financed campaign; as an ex-Democrat he was satisfactory to Democrats opposed to the New Deal and to a third term; and his middle-western background might help the party where help was badly needed. His vulnerable spot—his record as a utilities lawyer and official—might be offset by the argument that he was an able administrator, and that he had not amassed a great fortune by dubious practices. Had the Republicans at last found a challenger who could fight it out on even terms with the "champ" himself?

The Democrats and the Chicago Anticlimax

That the 1,094 delegates who assembled at Chicago on Monday, July 15, would nominate President Roosevelt for a third term was a foregone conclusion. For several months the "Draft Roosevelt" movement had been eliminating any possible competitors. The president's silence had had a sharply deterrent effect on candidacies, and the few primaries where opposition showed itself indicated an overwhelming sentiment for the man in the White House. The liberal groups had no alternative. No one in the administration had developed any degree of popular strength and, if Roosevelt refused to run, the choice promised to fall upon an old-line Democrat, such as Hull, Farley, or Garner. But there was another angle. Mayor Kelly of Chicago, Mayor Hague of Jersey City, and other local organization leaders, in bad repute with liberals, saw in the president their best bet to save their state and local tickets. In state after state the organizations lined up for the man on whose coattails they had been riding to victory since 1932. Only he could check the Republican tide that had swept away several states in 1938 and was threatening to engulf even more in 1940.

Vice-President Garner, refusing to await the president's decision, let it be known in December 1939, that he would be a candidate. In March, Postmaster General Farley, apparently no longer in the president's confidence, announced that his name would be presented in the Massachusetts primaries, though it was not clear whether the Farley delegates would remain loyal if Roosevelt decided to run. Senator Wheeler of Montana and Senator Tydings were regarded as potential anti-Roosevelt candidates, but neither had any strength outside his own state. Secretary of State Cordell Hull was popular among the rank and file and might have been named if Roosevelt had withdrawn. But there was no strictly New Deal candidate except the president himself. He had failed to groom a successor.

The Chicago convention opened with the stage set for the president's renomination. Harry Hopkins, former head of FERA (Federal Emergency Relief Administration) and of the WPA, established headquarters at the Blackstone Hotel to direct proceedings, but the regulars resented his presence and almost got out of hand on the final day, when the balloting for vice-president began. Speaker William B. Bankhead delivered the keynote speech as temporary chairman, and Senator Barkley was chosen as permanent chairman. Both were good party men, loyal to Roosevelt, and their speeches were strong defenses of the administration's foreign and domestic policies.

Barkley closed his speech with a message from the president—a tense moment, for some believed he would yet renounce the nomination. But the words from the White House merely indicated that the president had no wish to be a candidate again, that "all the delegates are free to vote for any candidate." This did not change matters, and the forty-five-minute demonstration that greeted Barkley's announcement indicated clearly what the convention would do.

The resolutions committee, headed by Senator Robert F. Wagner of New York, had some difficulty with foreign affairs, but ended with a watered-down compromise pledging the party against participation in foreign wars or sending military forces to fight outside the Americas except in case of attack. This was a concession to Senator Wheeler and the isolationists. Stressing the problems created by the world crisis, the platform contended that the Roosevelt administration had strengthened democracy by taking defensive measures against aggression, by increasing economic efficiency, and by improving the welfare of the people. Aid to Britain was promised in a plank that pledged "all the material aid at our command consistent with law and not inconsistent with the interests of our own national defense" to peace-loving and liberty-loving peoples wantonly attacked by ruthless aggressors.

The sections dealing with agriculture and labor recited the accomplishments of the preceding seven years with pledges to continue along the same general lines. The platform took direct issue with the Republicans by opposing local control of federally financed work relief. It promised to extend the Social Security Act to cover new groups and to strengthen the unemployment insurance system.

A long section on "capital and the businessman" was chiefly a defense of New Deal policies. Electric power received separate consideration because of the Republican candidate's record as a utility executive and an opponent of public power. The Tennessee and Columbia river projects were offered as proof of the success of hydroelectric plants under government ownership and operation.

A brief flurry occurred when Congressman Elmer J. Ryan of Minnesota offered a resolution against a third term. A roar of boos and shouts of disapproval from the delegates turned it down without a roll call. The platform was then accepted as presented by the resolutions committee.

As soon as it was out of the way on Wednesday night, Senator Lister Hill of Alabama presented the name of President Roosevelt in a dramatic speech. A sweaty demonstration, twenty-three minutes long, ensued, with the cheers led by one of Mayor Kelly's henchmen from a basement microphone. The venerable Senator Carter Glass of Virginia then nominated James A. Farley; but his remarks were none too well received, particularly his reference to Jefferson's refusal of a third term. Maryland offered Senator Tydings, and Texas, Vice-President Garner, while the delegates and galleries listened with ill-concealed impatience. Senator Wheeler's name was not presented, though he had established headquarters in Chicago. On the first ballot Roosevelt had 946-13/30 votes; Farley, 72-9/10; Garner, 61; Tydings, 9-1/2; Cordell Hull, 5-2/3. Before the result was announced, the nomination of Roosevelt was made unanimous. Farley received a great ovation as he withdrew his name, as it was known that he planned to resign from the cabinet and from the national chairmanship.

Next day, unexpectedly, there broke out the only real battle of the convention. From Washington came the word that Secretary of Agriculture Henry Wallace was the president's choice for second place on the ticket. Smoldering dissatisfaction blazed into open revolt. Primarily it was directed at New Deal control of the convention, and the rebels were orthodox, old-line regulars. They resented the prominence of Hopkins and others and refused to believe that Wallace, once a Republican and reputed to be a star-gazing idealist, was a proper choice. Southern Democrats of conservative cast wanted a southerner on the ticket, and friends of Farley and Garner saw an opportunity to strike a blow at the New Deal crowd. The galleries, eager for a fight, cheered for the insurgents, who presented Speaker Bankhead of Alabama. A movement for Paul V. McNutt, social security administrator and former governor of Indiana, stalled when the tall, handsome favorite of the crowd withdrew his name in the face of roars of "No" and declared for Wallace. One ballot unofficially gave Wallace 627-7/10 votes, Bankhead 328-2/3, and McNutt 66-19/30, and several others scattering support. The nomination of Wallace was then made unanimous.

The secretary's Iowa residence and his responsibility for the administration's farm policies were regarded as assets in appealing to the farm belt, long Republican but pro-Roosevelt since 1932. The Republican revival of 1938 seemed to require that the Democratic vice-presidential nominee be from this region.

The last act of the delegates was to listen to a calming radio address by the president, delivered just after midnight of the long Thursday session. He declared that he had not desired a third term but insisted that the world crisis forced personal considerations into the background. He would not have time, he said, because of the pressure of his work, "to engage in purely political debate," but would "never be loath to call the attention of the nation to deliberate or unwitting falsifications of fact, which are sometimes made by political candidates."

The Battle of America

Willke's acceptance speech, delivered on August 17 before a huge crowd at his old home in Elwood, Indiana, shocked right-wing Republicans. He accepted the major objectives of the Roosevelt foreign and domestic policies and confined his criticisms chiefly to methods. He advocated an economy of production as opposed to one of scarcity, which he charged upon the New Deal, without calling for the repeal of any significant New Deal measure. On foreign policy he rejected isolationism and promised to "outdistance Hitler in any contest he chooses."

On the whole, Willkie's strategy was sound. The Toryism of 1936 would not be repeated in 1940; nor would he accept the equally fatal position of the isolationists, which would have opened the way to Democratic charges of appeasement and Hitlerism. His courageous endorsement of the pending Selective-Service Law (military conscription), opposed by the majority of Republicans in Congress, was a case in point. Ambiguous silence or open opposition would have pleased the party regulars, but he refused to compromise with his convictions. Thus the issue was eliminated from the campaign.

Willkie also indicated his intention of controlling the management of his campaign by relegating Chairman Hamilton of the national committee to a post of executive secretary and placing in the chairmanship Joseph W. Martin, Jr., who had presided over the convention. Martin's task was not easy. The untamed candidate often ignored the professionals and listened to the amateurs, and the campaign broth had too many cooks. Raising funds was turned over to a leading industrialist, Tom M. Girdler, head of Republic Steel Corporation, who had the confidence of business but had an antilabor record that was a source of embarrassment in the campaign. Willkie announced at the outset that his campaign expenditures would be kept strictly within the $3,000,000 limit prescribed by the new Hatch Act.

The first speech was on September 17 in Coffeyville, Kansas, where

Willkie had once taught school. The "battle of America" was his theme—the battle to save democracy at home against concentration of power in one man. Then followed as arduous a campaign as any since Bryan's famous stumping tours. Covering 34 states, he traveled an estimated 30,000 miles by rail, air, and automobile to deliver 540 speeches. Perhaps 12,000,000 people turned out to see and hear him. His deep voice grew strained and husky, but he never spared it. He was the despair of his throat specialist, for he held forth in his private car between platform appearances. His inexperience in politics cropped out sometimes in indiscreet statements that had to be qualified or explained away afterward. But his unfailing good humor, his abundant vitality, and his vigorous style of speech were increasingly effective in arousing enthusiasm as the campaign progressed and he developed greater adeptness in presenting his case. Over the radio he was a better speaker than Landon; but a sloppiness of diction and a clumsiness of phrasing reduced the effectiveness of his appeal somewhat.

The Republican organization was assisted by several auxiliary groups, separately financed, the most important being the "Associated Willkie Clubs" and the "Democrats for Willkie." Thousands of "amateurs" gave their services to Willkie Clubs to prepare and mail literature, telephone to voters, and perform other political labors usually left to the professionals. Middle-class housewives, discovering a sudden interest in politics, worked in relays at the telephones in Willkie headquarters to warn women voters about the dangers of war and the third term. The "Mothers of America," financed by the Republican national committee, presented emotional radio appeals on behalf of Willkie and peace.

In some of the more doubtful states local Republican organizations raised and spent large sums, ostensibly for state and local tickets, thus evading the limitations of the Hatch Act. In Pennsylvania, for example, a survey after the election revealed that the Republicans had spent $2,500,000 through state and local organizations and volunteer clubs, an astonishing amount even for a state accustomed to freehanded spending in primaries and elections. Wide use of every form of political advertising and propaganda testified to the size of the Republican Party's war chest and the elaborateness of the Willkie setup.

Meanwhile, the Democrats were having their troubles. The coldness of many regulars toward the New Deal element made the problem of a successor to Farley as national chairman an awkward one. But Roosevelt found a reasonably satisfactory solution. He chose Edward J. Flynn of New York City, a successful lawyer of independent means and for years political boss of the Bronx. He had long been close to both Roosevelt and Farley, who was to continue as state chairman. Thus it was hoped that the soreness in evidence at Chicago might be removed. Flynn lacked his predecessor's wide acquaintance among politicians of the hinterland and did not essay the role of traveling salesman; but he managed the campaign competently from his New York headquarters. In any case, the grand strategy was in the hands of Roosevelt.

That some conservative Democrats would repudiate the New Deal leadership seemed to be certain, and with the no-third-term tradition as a convenient bridge, a long procession was soon crossing over to the Willkie camp. The wisdom of naming a former Democrat as Republican standard-bearer seemed to be amply justified; but observers pointed out that nearly all of the more prominent bolters were either former "greats" or lame ducks who had lost influence in the party. Among them were former Governors Smith of New York, White of Ohio, and Ely of Massachusetts, former Senator Reed of Missouri, former Representative John J. O'Connor of New York, and Senator Edward R. Burke of Nebraska, who had just been defeated for renomination. Such Senate conservatives as Glass and Byrd and Tydings, and the isolationists Wheeler of Montana and Bennett Champ Clark of Missouri silently acquiesced in the Roosevelt candidacy, Clark even giving a half-hearted endorsement of the national ticket in a belated radio speech. Vice-President Garner neither spoke nor voted.

In every locality newspapers carried stories of lifelong Democrats who were repudiating the national ticket. These were usually business or professional people and not active figures in the party organization. Despite the heat and the bitterness of the struggle, Democratic insurgency was far less extensive than in the Hoover-Smith campaign of 1928. Among the rank and file it was more in evidence in rural than in urban districts.

Independent Voters for Roosevelt

As a partial offset to conservative defections a group of liberals set up a committee of "Independent Voters for Roosevelt." The veteran progressive, Norris of Nebraska, and Mayor La Guardia of New York were the leaders, with Thomas G. Corcoran the chief organizer. Willkie's headship of a great utilities holding company and his battle with the Tennessee Valley Authority made him anything but satisfactory to Norris and the friends of public power. Mayor La Guardia, Fusionist opponent of Tammany, threw his fiery energy into the Roosevelt cause. The American Labor Party of New York also endorsed the president. In Wisconsin, Robert M. La Follette, Jr., who had cooled toward the administration and was opposing its foreign policy, ran for reelection to the Senate with his state Progressive Party's backing. Fighting for his political life against a Republican trend, he decided for Roosevelt on domestic issues and won the backing of liberal Democrats. Dorothy Thompson, influential columnist, who had been critical of the New Deal, supported Roosevelt on foreign policy.

The president in his acceptance speech had indicated the line of argument to be followed in the campaign, but the brunt of the battle was to be left to the vice-presidential candidate. Wallace centered his attention on the doubtful farm belt; but the growing enthusiasm aroused by Willkie required that the Democrats play their trump card, and so Roosevelt went before the voters to inspect national-defense projects from Maine to Virginia and west to Dayton, Ohio. Though his brief remarks were in a nonpartisan key, huge crowds turned out at all stops to cheer him. Republican newspapers frothed at this further evidence of Rooseveltian hyprocrisy.

In the closing days of the campaign the president threw off all disguise and made five major political addresses in key cities of the East and the Middle West. His entry into the campaign did much to restore Democratic morale, which had been shaken somewhat by the Willkie trend of some of the polls and by the tremendous barrage of Republican propaganda.

Equaling the Civil War and free-silver campaigns in bitterness and emotional pitch, the struggle of 1940 tended to become one of highly charged appeals to prejudices, traditions, class hatreds, and partisan bigotry. Sound and fury made rational discussion of concrete issues impossible.

Magnifying Roosevelt's refusal to respect the no-third-term tradition into an assault upon constitutional government, Republican newspapers and orators proclaimed that dictatorship was imminent and democracy itself in dire peril. Willkie himself solemnly declared that if the administration were restored to power for a third term, "our democratic system will not outlast another four years." Obsessed with dislike of the man in the White House, Republicans forgot that they would have rejoiced if Calvin Coolidge had consented to stand for another term in 1928, and that in their ranks were many old-timers who had done their best to put Theodore Roosevelt in the White House for a third term in 1912. Several Democratic senators and the Progressive La Follette found themselves compelled to eat their own words, as they had supported a resolution against a third term in 1928.

The Democrats met the third-term argument with much talk about the grave emergency and the dangers of swapping horses in midstream "until we reach the clear sure footing ahead"—as Roosevelt phrased it in his Cleveland speech. Hurling back at his critics the dictatorship cry, he attacked the "unholy alliance" of Communists and "Girdlers" who were trying to weaken democracy in America and "to destroy the free man's faith in his own cause." The Democrats invoked Washington's authority to offset Republican quotations of Jefferson's familiar anti-third term sentiments. Had not the Father of His Country once written that he saw no reason for "precluding ourselves from the services of any man, who on some great emergency shall be deemed universally most capable of serving the public"? Yet the third-term issue was a difficult obstacle for the Democrats to hurdle. Americans are pronounced traditionalists in their political thinking, and the Republicans were defending an old tradition. Their appeal was simple and emotional and irrational, and therefore all the more difficult to combat.

In the closing stages of the campaign the Republican offensive centered on the war issue and the closely related problem of national defense. Willkie had endorsed the Roosevelt policy of all possible aid to the democracies, and favored immediate rearmament and the compulsory military service law. Both candidates declared that they would not send American boys to Europe to fight except in defense of American liberty. Republican propaganda, however, charged that Roosevelt was the war candidate, and used the air waves and the newspapers to appeal to the mothers of America to save their boys from slaughter on foreign battlefields by voting Republican. Roosevelt partisans denied that he was a warmonger and countercharged that leading Republicans were isolationists and Hitler appeasers. As to national defense, the pot called the kettle black by pointing to the spots on its record.

A dramatic incident of the campaign was John L. Lewis's radio address on October 25 urging labor to vote for Willkie and pledging himself to retire from the headship of the CIO if Roosevelt won. He charged that the Democratic Party had broken faith with labor, that Roosevelt was aiming at war and dictatorship, that the administration had failed by every test, and that Willkie's election was imperative to the country's welfare.

Lewis's plea won support from some left-wing leaders in the CIO including Harry Bridges, under fire as a Communist; but the heads of the larger unions generally repudiated his stand and reaffirmed their support of Roosevelt. Most of the leaders of the rival American Federation of Labor, then bitterly hostile to Lewis, were already strongly pro-Roosevelt. The presence of Tom Girdler, Ernest T. Weir, and other antiunion industrialists in the Willkie camp detracted from the effectiveness of the Lewis appeal to labor.

Minor parties received slight support from labor and farmer in 1940. The crazy-quilt Union Party of 1936 had not survived. Father Coughlin tried to take his following over to Willkie, but his support was regarded as a liability. The Republican candidate denounced racial and religious intolerance and offered cold comfort to budding Fascist groups. The Socialist Party convention in Washington in April adopted a strongly isolationist and antiwar platform, opposing even economic aid to any belligerent. Norman Thomas was again its nominee.

The Communist Party, weakened in membership and even more in prestige by the Stalin-Hitler pact of 1939, offered Earl Browder for president. It declared against any participation in the "imperialist war," opposed military preparations, and in general followed the party line laid down from Moscow. Browder, sentenced to prison for misuse of a passport, was out on bail; but his campaign activities were sharply circumscribed.

The Socialist Labor and Prohibition parties also nominated candidates but attracted little attention and few votes.

The Verdict

The polls, scientific and otherwise, which attempted to predict the result, were in such sharp disagreement that even veteran political analysts were bewildered. The American Institute of Public Opinion—the Gallup poll—issued a final statement on the eve of the election giving Roosevelt 198 electoral votes, Willkie 59, but leaving 274 doubtful! Roosevelt, it conceded, might have 52 percent of the total popular vote, but because of the heavy concentration of Democratic strength in the South this might not mean electoral success. *Fortune* magazine's survey gave Roosevelt 55.2 percent of the popular vote but admitted that Willkie might squeeze through with an electoral majority. Two other nationwide samplers of opinion predicted a decisive Willkie victory. Chairman Flynn's claim of 427 votes for Roosevelt seemed to be the customary exaggeration of a party manager.

But the verdict on November 5 went beyond even Flynn's expectations. Roosevelt had 449 electoral votes to Willkie's 82. The Dakotas, Nebraska, Kansas, Iowa, Colorado, Indiana, Michigan, Maine, and Vermont constituted the Willkie total. Roosevelt's popular vote was 27,263,448; Willkie's 22,336,260.* The victor's 54.7 percent of the popular vote was lower than it had been in 1932 (57.4) and 1936 (60.8). The Democrats added slightly to their House majority but lost three Senate seats.

Isolationist Republicans took the election of seventeen Republican governors in thirty-four state contests as proof that Willkie was weaker than his party. But the Republican representation in the House was proportionately less than its presidential vote, though in many states the arrangement of districts overrepresented the rural voters.

Willkie ran better in the western wheat and corn states than anywhere else. His persuasive philosophy of an expanding economy, with farm subsidies if needed, struck the right note. Farmers, unhappy over government restrictions even with benefit payments, complained about laborers loafing on the WPA while farm workers were hard to get, were alarmed at

---

* Minor party totals were: Thomas, Socialist, 116,827; Babson, Prohibition, 56,685; Browder, Communist, 48,548; Aiken, Socialist Labor, 14,883.

continuing treasury deficits and, especially in German-American localities, suspected Roosevelt of maneuvering to involve the nation in the war.

But the Democrats retained most of their urban support. Republican charges that reliefers decided the election ("You can't beat Santa Claus") were apparently refuted by the equally heavy Roosevelt vote of employed labor. Prolabor policies and various New Deal benefits weighed heavily with the city voters. The swing of Polish-American, Jewish, and other anti-Hitler elements to Roosevelt overcame losses among voters of German and Italian ancestry, where emotions overruled economics.

The role of the press came in for much comment. Roosevelt lost the *New York Times*, the *Cleveland Plain Dealer*, the Scripps-Howard chain, and other supporters of 1936, while some nominally Democratic organs were lukewarm. Yet in the face of a heavy Republican journalistic preponderance, he had carried every city of more than 400,000 population except Cincinnati, sometimes without a single friendly newspaper. Was urban journalism, having evolved into a few big-business corporations, reflecting corporation character? Was Roosevelt, because of his radio appeal, especially in his "fireside chats," too overshadowing to be much affected by editorial arrows or editorial praise?

XIII

And Again

PRESIDENT ROOSEVELT, fortified by his great victory at the polls, continued and extended his policy of making the United States the arsenal of democracy. Though supported by Wendell Willkie, he encountered a growing isolationist opposition from men of such divergent views as Senator Burton K. Wheeler, Democrat, of Montana; Senator Gerald P. Nye, Republican, of North Dakota; Robert E. Wood and Robert Young of the business world; John L. Lewis of the United Mine Workers; Charles A. Lindbergh of aviation fame; Colonel Robert R. McCormick of the *Chicago Tribune;* Norman Thomas, Socialist leader; and the La Follettes. Most of them were affiliated with an America First Committee. Embarrassingly friendly to them were the followers of Father Coughlin and the Reverend Gerald L. K. Smith and, for a time, the Communists.

Roosevelt's major congressional victory came over his proposal to lend or lease war materials to any nation whose defense the president deemed vital to the defense of the United States. A few isolationist Democrats and the great majority of Republicans in Congress opposed the measure, yet the alignment was as much sectional as partisan. The upper Mississippi Valley, represented largely by Republicans, was more isolationist than other sections.

Hitler's attack on Russia strengthened the isolationists for a time. England, it seemed, was now safe from invasion, and Americans felt a sense of relief. When the president sent American forces to occupy Iceland and used the navy to patrol the western Atlantic in order to protect Lend-Lease shipments against submarine attacks, America Firsters sharply criticized him for drawing the nation closer to the abyss of war. In Congress the opposition to extending the one year of service of drafted men was so great that it carried in the House by the bare margin of one vote. Yet by November the president was able to secure the passage of a measure freeing American merchant ships from the restrictions of the Neutrality Act and authorizing their arming. The final House vote showed 53 Democrats and 137 Republicans in opposition. Attacks upon American destroyers had altered the situation. Aid to England was too vital to American defense to permit pretensions to neutrality to stand in the way.

Pearl Harbor—
America Enters the War

The Japanese attack upon Pearl Harbor on December 7, 1941, closed the mouths of administration critics. The war came to America, and from an unexpected quarter. The long months of negotiation with Japan had not prepared Americans for a Pacific war. Politics had not been involved, the isolationists had been strangely indifferent to the dangers in the Far East. The tardiness of the administration in stopping shipment of war materials to Japan had evoked as much criticism from its friends as from its foes. Consequently, when the blow fell at Pearl Harbor, isolationists and interventionists joined forces in support of the war, though a few of the former felt that Rooseveltian diabolism was behind the whole thing. As in 1917, politics was adjourned.

The months of discouragement and defeat made 1942 another 1862. The war machine was slow in getting under way, and criticisms of men and methods, of wartime restrictions, of price controls and labor difficulties appeared in Congress and in the newspapers. With the allies everywhere on the defensive in the summer, except in the Solomon Islands, where progress was dishearteningly slow, the war seemed to stretch endlessly into the future. Roosevelt was berated as a dictator and was berated for not using his vast powers more effectively.

The midterm elections aroused slight interest, and political analysts predicted little change in the composition of Congress. They were wrong. The Republicans gained ten seats in the Senate and forty-seven in the House, which they almost captured.* New York, Ohio, Pennsylvania, Michigan, Minnesota, and California elected Republican state tickets. In a light vote the nation had almost repudiated the administration.

One effect of the setback was the organization by CIO leaders of a Political Action Committee in July 1943, with Sidney Hillman in charge, to get labor to the polls through organization and propaganda at the household level. It soon showed its power in state primaries, even in the conservative South. The PAC was a virtual Democratic auxiliary.

The swing to the right in 1942 was reflected in the relations of the president and the new Congress. The administration had its way on Lend-Lease renewal, extension of the Reciprocal Trade Agreement Act, war appropriations, and other nondomestic measures; but taxation, food subsidies, antistrike bills, soldier voting, and proposals to do away with poll taxes provoked sharp controversies, in which the wishes of the White

---

* The House had 222 Democrats, 209 Republicans, 2 Progressives, 1 American Labor, 1 Farmer-Labor. In the Senate were 57 Democrats, 38 Republicans, 1 Progressive.

House were often ignored or overriden. A bloc of southern conservatives led by Senator Harry F. Byrd of Virginia usually voted with the Republicans.

Dewey and Bricker

The elections of 1942 provided the Republicans with three possibilities for president in 1944, all governors of states: Thomas E. Dewey of New York, John W. Bricker of Ohio, and Harold E. Stassen of Minnesota. Bricker and Stassen were reelected, but Dewey's victory was his first. A fourth availability was General Douglas MacArthur, in command in the Southwest Pacific. Over all these hung the shadow of Wendell Willkie, whose ambitions had not been destroyed by the verdict of 1940, and who seemed at first to be in a strong position to determine the future course of the party.

Dewey, well known since the 1940 convention, added to his popularity by the leadership he displayed in Albany. He avoided campaigning and primary battles by refusing to announce his candidacy, though delegates pledged to him were generally successful in state primaries. A public address in April made it clear that he had abandoned his earlier isolationist views and favored a strong United Nations to prevent future wars. When the convention met, MacArthur and Willkie were already eliminated, and the only remaining opposition was from Bricker and Stassen.

The MacArthur movement had never got beyond the talking stage. The general was regarded as willing, but organization and popular support failed to materialize. The publication of some correspondence with a Nebraska congressman brought from MacArthur a statement that he was not a candidate for the nomination; but this did not eliminate the possibility of a draft. On April 30, 1944, when the Dewey bandwagon had begun to roll, a second statement withdrew his name with finality.

Wendell Willkie was the problem child of the GOP. The party regulars had never accepted him as a genuine Republican, and they blamed him for the 1940 defeat. The isolationists had never liked him, and his support of Lend-Lease in 1941 brought forth a chorus of denunciation. The *Chicago Tribune* charged that international bankers, together with the "champagne and caviar liberals of the East," had brought about his nomination.

Willkie visited England during the "blitz," endeared himself to the British, and in 1942 made a trip around the world as an unofficial emissary of President Roosevelt. His book describing the journey, *One World*, was an immediate best-seller; but it damned him for the more orthodox Republicans, who resented both his internationalism and his increasingly liberal viewpoint. Although critical of New Deal methods, he seemed to be determined to liberalize the Republican Party by committing it to New Deal objectives.

Willkie's downfall was due in part to his rashness—or courage—and in part to his lack of political skill. His enemies were strongest in the isolationist Middle West; yet he decided to risk his candidacy for the Republican nomination by entering his name in the Wisconsin, Nebraska, and Oregon presidential primaries. Confident that the voters were with him, he went to Wisconsin and conducted an aggressive campaign. The primary election, on April 4, was a major defeat for him, Dewey's supporters sweeping the field. Before the Nebraska primaries, Willkie announced his withdrawal from the race. He had lost not only the nomination but also his influence in shaping party policies. A series of newspaper articles in which he advocated a decidedly liberal platform received no consideration in the national convention. He was not even accorded the courtesy of an invitation to address the delegates, a snub that many of his supporters answered with Roosevelt ballots in November.

Stassen and Bricker did not profit from Willkie's withdrawal. The party regulars who had backed Dewey to kill off the 1940 standard-bearer now found the New Yorker too far in the lead to be stopped. Stassen had entered the United States Navy, but Senator Joseph H. Ball, an anti-isolationist from his own state, conducted a campaign to draft him for the nomination. Poor showings in Wisconsin and Nebraska practically eliminated him. Bricker, the only remaining avowed candidate, crossed the country in a quest for delegates, hammering hard at New Deal bureaucracy and mismanagement but suggesting an alternative only in general terms. An aura of old-fashioned Republicanism emanated from the broad-shouldered, handsome Ohioan, and Old Guardsmen and isolationists took him to their hearts. William Allen White caustically called him "an honest Harding" (a gibe that he credited to Alice Roosevelt Longworth); but his friends saw a kinship with McKinley in his cautious party regularity and his ability to work with the men who ran the organizations. Party leaders liked him, and business approved; but Dewey seemed to be stronger with the voters.

The Republican convention, held in Chicago June 26–28, was marked by the utmost harmony. The 1,057 delegates listened to Governor Earl Warren of California, the temporary chairman, at the first night session and elected Joseph W. Martin, Jr., of Massachusetts, permanent chairman the next day. The platform, presented by Senator Taft of Ohio, had been in preparation since September 1943, when a preliminary meeting of party leaders at Mackinac, Michigan, had organized eight committees to study different aspects of party policy and offer recommendations. The resolutions committee of the convention was thus in a position to write the platform with commendable speed. The delegates accepted it unanimously.

This rather lengthy document committed the party to a prosecution of the war to total victory and promised "responsible participation by the United States in postwar cooperative organization" to maintain peace, with the qualification that any agreement or treaty should receive Senate approval. A section on domestic policy pledged the party to end government competition with private industry, to promote stable employment through private enterprise, and to avoid regulation of farmers, workers, businesspeople, and consumers; it warned the country that four years more of New Deal policy would centralize all power in the president and endanger the Republic. A broad social security program was endorsed, with emphasis on federal aid and state or local control.

As in 1940 the labor and farm pronouncements did not take issue with the New Deal measures but criticized methods and administration. A special bid for the Negro vote appeared in planks favoring a fair employment practices commission, antilynching legislation, and a constitutional amendment abolishing poll taxes. Equal rights for women and the opening of Palestine to unrestricted Jewish immigration were other vote-catchers.

The Dewey leaders sought to give Governor Warren of doubtful California second place on the ticket but struck a snag when he positively refused it. This opened the way for Governor Bricker, and before the balloting began he appeared before the delegates to endorse Dewey and withdraw his name from consideration for first place. He was warmly applauded. Senator Ball withdrew Stassen, and Dewey, placed in nomination by Governor Dwight R. Griswold of Nebraska, became the convention's all-but-unanimous choice—one stubborn Wisconsin delegate insisted on voting for MacArthur. Bricker, whose popularity had been steadily mounting, then received the vice-presidential nomination. Dewey came at once to Chicago and accepted the honor of leading the Republican forces. He pledged his utmost efforts to winning the war and declared against any change in its military conduct, but assailed the incompetence of the administration and charged that it was unfit to achieve a lasting peace. His reference to "stubborn men grown old and tired and quarrelsome in office," sounded the keynote of his acceptance. He minimized the differences between isolationists and internationalists and emphasized the "broad area of agreement" between the two extremes of isolation and a superstate.

The convention was a cut-and-dried affair. The delegates showed little spontaneous enthusiasm as they listened to the customary partisan oratory, highlighted by Herbert Hoover's quadrennial appearance as the prophet of gloom and Mrs. Clare Boothe Luce's emotional interpretation of the feelings of "GI Joe" and "GI Jim." The drafting of Dewey was carefully prearranged by his board of strategy, and the delegates chose him not from any personal attachment to a magnetic leader but from the belief that the shrewd, competent New York governor was their best bet.

The candidate knew that he would be drafted, and so he carefully prepared his acceptance speech in advance. He made a good impression, and the delegates adjourned in an optimistic mood. From the outside came one discordant note. Wendell Willkie did not like the platform. Some Republicans began to wonder if they hadn't slapped him down too hard. He still had a following.

Roosevelt's Fourth Nomination

The Democratic picture was not encouraging in the early months of 1944. Conservative southerners could not defeat Roosevelt's fourth nomination, but there was a danger that they might withhold their support at the polls. Party conventions in Texas, South Carolina, and Mississippi named electoral tickets that were not pledged to the national nominees. Demands were made for the restoration of the two-thirds rule, the elimination of Wallace for vice-president, and the recognition of white supremacy. Senator Byrd was the dissenters' favorite for the presidential nomination.

For the great majority of Democrats, Roosevelt was the only choice. New Dealers and machine politicians were agreed on this point, and public opinion polls offered further proof. The new national chairman, Robert E. Hannegan of St. Louis, secured a statement from the president, made public before the convention met, that he would accept another nomination. This left only the question of his running mate to be settled.

Chicago also entertained the Democratic convention. The 1,176 delegates assembled on July 19, with Governor Robert S. Kerr of Oklahoma as temporary chairman delivering the keynote speech. He charged the Republicans with isolationism and Old Guard domination and answered Dewey's "tired old men" charge by citing the ages of Stalin, Churchill, and top-ranking American military leaders. Senator Samuel D. Jackson of Indiana succeeded Governor Kerr in the chair. Two delegations from Texas created a problem, which was solved by seating both and dividing the vote. Thirty-three delegates and alternates of the "regulars," who were anti-Roosevelt, walked out, but many later returned to their seats.

The platform of 1,360 words, less than one-third the length of the Republican, cost the drafting committee many hours of labor to iron out difficult points but was generally acceptable in the end. It declared that the Democratic Party stood on its record in peace and war, and summed up the major accomplishments. It pledged American membership in an international organization with the power to use armed force to prevent aggression and to preserve peace. It endorsed an international court of justice, the Good Neighbor policy, the administration's trade policies, the Atlantic Charter, and the opening of Palestine to unrestricted Jewish immigration. These commitments on foreign policy were more definite than the Republican stand, but there were no sharp differences. A post-war domestic program was outlined to appeal to ex-servicemen and women, farmers, labor, and businesspeople; but this was hardly more than an assurance that all would be well with all of them.

In one respect the Democratic platform fell short of the Republican. The race-relations declaration was watered down to a vague statement that "racial and religious minorities have the right to live, develop, and vote equally with all citizens and share the rights that are guaranteed by our Constitution," and that Congress should protect these rights. The poll tax and the fair employment practices commission were not mentioned.

The much-advertised southern revolt began to peter out. Senator Barkley presented Roosevelt's name, and a Florida delegate offered Senator Byrd for the nomination. The one ballot gave Roosevelt 1,086 votes, Byrd 89, and James A. Farley 1. Most of the Byrd vote was from seven southern states, and even there it was only a minority. Twelve of the Texas "regulars" voted for Roosevelt, despite the "walkout" of their faction. The victor was nominated by a larger margin than in 1940. He was so obviously the choice of both party leaders and Democratic voters that the cry of "synthetic draft" fell flat. Roosevelt accepted by radio from a Pacific Coast naval base, emphasizing the dangers of entrusting the government to "inexperienced and immature hands," and to those who had opposed Lend-Lease and international cooperation, and who had led the American people down to "the abyss of 1932."

Truman or Wallace

The real drama of the convention came next day when the vice-presidential nomination was made. Henry Wallace seemed to be the popular choice in 1944. By his speech seconding the nomination of Roosevelt he won the admiration of galleries and radio listeners alike; but he hurt his own chances by his declarations against the poll tax and for educational and economic equality "regardless of race or sex." Roosevelt earlier had given Wallace the kiss of death by expressing a preference for him but a readiness to let the convention decide about second place. National Chairman Robert E. Hannegan, after the convention met, made public a letter from the president approving either Senator Harry S Truman of Missouri or Justice William O. Douglas, of the Supreme Court, for second place. War Mobilization Director James F. Byrnes of South Carolina had wanted to run, but he suited neither the Political Action Committee nor Roosevelt. Northern state machines were lining up for Truman, and southern conservatives preferred him to Wallace. The convention, after Roosevelt's acceptance speech, showed signs of getting out of hand and possibly stampeding to Wallace when Chairman Jackson adjourned it until the next day at Hannegan's insistence. Behind Wallace were the labor leaders Philip Murray and Sidney Hillman, Senators Guffey of Pennsylvania and Pepper of Florida, and Governor Arnall of Georgia, a southern liberal.

The outwardly confused situation brought out twelve nominations. The first ballot gave Wallace 429½ votes and Truman 319½, while a flock of favorite sons held the rest. On the second ballot Truman reached 473 and Wallace 477½; but before the result could be announced Alabama and Indiana dropped their favorites for Truman, and a procession of other states followed suit until his total reached 1,031 of the 1,176 convention votes. His victory was a triumph for the organization people as opposed to the liberal-labor group. Yet Truman was at least acceptable to Hillman and his labor following, and had the support of southern conservatives who wanted Wallace stopped.

The Minor Parties

The minor parties appeared as usual, but radical reforms aroused slight interest in wartime. The Socialist, Socialist Labor, and Prohibition parties nominated candidates* as in the past, but the Communists, who had abandoned their opposition to the war after Hitler attacked Russia, dissolved as a party in May 1944, and formed the Communist Political Association. In New York they formed a segment of the American Labor Party. A seceding conservative wing of that party formed the Liberal Party; but both groups supported Roosevelt, as did the Farmer-Labor Party of Minnesota, which joined forces with the Democrats in that state. An America First Party held a convention in Detroit on August 30 and nominated Gerald L. K. Smith for president and Governor Bricker for vice-president. Bricker indignantly rejected the dubious honor, for Smith had shown Nazi sympathies, and the platform was anti-Jewish, anti-Negro, and extremely isolationist. In most states the America Firsters did not appear on the ballot.

The War Election

Both campaigns were managed by newcomers, but they were not amateurs. Democratic Chairman Robert E. Hannegan had lined up the organization leaders in the vice-presidential battle in Chicago, and he worked with them in the campaign. Hillman, Murray, and the labor

* The Socialists nominated Norman Thomas of New York; the Socialist Labor Party (also called the Industrial Government party), Edward A. Teichert of Pennsylvania; and the Prohibition Party, Claude A. Watson of California.

group continued the PAC but allied with it a "National Citizens Political Action Committee" appealing to liberals of all shades and not limited in its spending by the Smith-Connally Act. The PAC's most effective work was in getting the labor vote to the polls. A series of simple leaflets, prepared by writers and artists at its New York headquarters, appealed to the workers to register and vote. Some of these abandoned any pretense of nonpartisanship, and one, entitled "Lest We Forget," contained a photograph of an unemployed man selling apples in front of a "Hoover Club" in 1932, with an inset showing a large red apple and a picture of Dewey conferring with Hoover. Nearly ten million such leaflets and pamphlets went out every week in the closing stages of the campaign to CIO unions and through their fourteen thousand locals to the members. Clubs, speeches, radio programs, and even doorbell ringing helped arouse labor from the lethargy of high wages and war prosperity. Democratic organization leaders welcomed the PAC as an ally and worked with it.

Herbert Brownell, Jr., manager of Dewey's campaign for governor, handled his preconvention campaign with assistance from Edwin F. Jaeckle, New York state chairman, and J. Russel Sprague, national committeeman from New York. These three continued to direct the national campaign, Brownell heading the national committee. John Foster Dulles was Dewey's adviser on foreign policy. This grandson of a secretary of state had had considerable diplomatic experience in his earlier years, and his law practice had had international connections. Republican contacts with the business world were maintained through James S. Kemper, chairman of the finance committee and a former president of the United States Chamber of Commerce, who had shown marked isolationist sympathies.

The moneybags of business were opened to the Republicans as in 1936 and 1940. The legal limitation of national campaign expenditures to $3,000,000 did not prevent heavy contributions to state campaigns and independent organizations. The totals, according to the Senate Campaign Expenditures Committee, almost equaled the record level of 1936. The United Republican Finance Committee for Metropolitan New York collected $1,629,451 and spent $1,260,593; the Pennsylvania Republican Finance Committee, $1,252,700 and $939,934. The PAC's receipts for the entire country were $1,405,120; its expenditures $1,327,775. The Du Pont and Pew families together gave more than $200,000 to the Republican chest. The Democrats collected $22,000 from the Marshall Fields and $20,680 from the Andrew J. Higgins family of New Orleans. The Republicans spent nearly twice as much as the Democrats, with expenses of local candidates not reported to the Senate committee.

The campaign opened late and was comparatively brief. Much depended, as in 1864, on the military situation. A summer of victories in France was followed by an autumn stalemate but with ultimate allied victory not too far off. This was probably more favorable to Roosevelt than to Dewey. It was no time to swap horses.

Dewey's speechmaking began in Philadelphia on September 9 and covered a large part of the country outside the South. He made no platform appearances, kept secret the exact train route on his western swing, and aimed his brief, well-phrased speeches at the radio rather than the visible audiences. His general themes were a more efficient administration, an end to the quarreling and bickering of the "tired, old men," better relations with Congress, a durable peace settlement, and jobs for all through the stimulation of private enterprise. He assailed the administration for inadequate preparedness, for burdening labor, agriculture, and business with unnecessary and conflicting restrictions, for planning to keep men in military service to prevent unemployment, and for consorting with Communists.

The last charge was the basis of an eleventh-hour fear campaign. Sidney Hillman of the PAC was linked with Earl Browder, Communist leader, as "Hillman, Browder, and Co.," a Communist conspiracy controlling the PAC. The attacks upon Hillman as "foreign-born" and "Russian-born" came close to anti-Semitism, as when a leading New York newspaper referred to his "rabbinical education." The admonition, "Clear it with Sidney," was the favorite Republican slur, for Roosevelt had allegedly made this remark with regard to the Democratic vice-presidential nomination before the Chicago convention. It became a stock gibe in Republican campaign speeches, and Hearst newspapers had "Sidney" limerick contests. This concentrated assault on an important labor leader, with its scarcely veiled Ku-Kluxism, gave Roosevelt the opportunity in his final speech to slash at the Republicans as enemies of the foreign-born, and gave the PAC a publicity that probably helped it in getting lethargic labor to come to the polls.

Roosevelt limited his campaign to two dinner addresses and three public speeches, all broadcast, and three special radio talks. Rumors about ill health seemed to be disproved by the vigor of his campaigning.

On foreign policy the two candidates were close together. Both upheld the Dumbarton Oaks plan for a world security organization, and both favored empowering the American representative on a security council to act in an emergency to enforce peace. But Dewey was embarrassed in his criticisms by his party's record on defense and foreign policy and by the isolationism of a considerable segment. Though he courageously repudiated the candidacy of Hamilton Fish for reelection to Congress from New York, he had to accept the support of the *Chicago Tribune* and its middle-western satellite papers and to endorse his party's candidates generally, despite their deviations from his stands on major policies.

On October 8 Wendell Willkie died suddenly without revealing how he had intended to vote. Some of his Republican and independent sympathizers announced for Roosevelt. These included Russell Davenport, his 1940 preconvention manager; Bartley C. Crum, head of the California Willkie Committee; Gifford Pinchot of Pennsylvania; Daniel A. Poling, nationally known Baptist minister; and Walter Lippmann, columnist. A surprise bolter was Senator Ball of Minnesota, a Stassen supporter at the Republican convention. Although the newspaper preponderance was heavy for Dewey, two independent newspapers that had been hostile in 1940, the *St. Louis Post-Dispatch* and the *New York Times*, favored Roosevelt.

As in Roosevelt's earlier campaigns, the Democrats depended on radio to offset newspaper hostility, but Dewey's deep voice and clear diction made him the strongest opponent the old Democratic master of air technique had faced.

The two second-place nominees concentrated on doubtful areas. Bricker thundered at bureaucrats and "Hillman, Browder, and Co.," and worked to keep the party regulars in line. Truman's plain, uninspired speeches were helpful in appeasing the Democratic disgruntled. Henry Wallace also stumped for the ticket and was especially effective with the Negro voters.

Political forecasters and professional takers of polls had a hard time. The size of the soldier vote, the number of disfranchised migratory workers, and the apparently narrow margins between the candidates in the large states forced them to hedge their predictions with many qualifications, so that they had slight value. The usual conclusion was that Roosevelt had a narrow popular lead, but the electoral vote might go otherwise. Unusually heavy registration in several large cities dampened Republican hopes somewhat.

Roosevelt Wins a Fourth Term

The early returns on November 7 indicated another Roosevelt sweep, which became greater as the urban vote was reported. The electoral landslide—432 to 99—represented a popular plurality of approximately 3,600,000 votes in a total vote of 47,974,819. Despite the fact that several millions in the armed services had not been able to vote, the total was surprisingly near the 1940 vote of 49,840,443. The percentages of the popular vote were 53.4 (25,611,936) for Roosevelt and 45.9 (22,013,372) for Dewey.* Roosevelt's plurality was 1,300,000 less than in 1940, when he polled 54.7 percent of the total vote.

* Minor parties polled 0.7 percent of the total: Thomas, Socialist, 79,000; Watson, Prohibition, 74,733; and others, 195,778.

Dewey carried Ohio, Wisconsin, and Wyoming, which had gone for Roosevelt in 1940. He lost Michigan, which Willkie had carried, but won the other Willkie states: Maine, Vermont, Indiana, Iowa, the Dakotas, Kansas, Nebraska, and Colorado. Both houses of Congress were Democratic by substantial margins.

Roosevelt's greatest losses in the popular vote were in the South, where they did not matter. He ran better than in 1940 in the important states of New York, Illinois, Michigan, and Minnesota. His electoral vote in the North and West was so large that he could have won without the South, as in his other victories.

The soldier vote was not a decisive factor. In the few states that tabulated it separately it was more heavily pro-Roosevelt than the civilian vote, giving point to the earlier fears of some Republicans that a uniform federal ballot would work to their disadvantage. The Republican radio appeal, "End the war quicker with Dewey and Bricker," may have influenced civilian voters, but soldiers on the fighting fronts had little interest in politics, and many who could have voted did not.

Roosevelt retained most of his labor and urban black support in the North but lost ground in the farm belt. The draining away of farm labor by industry and the draft, difficulties in getting machinery, rationing requirements, price ceilings, and other restrictions angered individualistic farmers, who felt that labor was pampered by the government. In Kansas, Nebraska, Iowa, and the Dakotas, where Hoover's name still aroused bitter memories, farmers were now almost as critical of his successor. In some communities this was an expression of a latent antiwar feeling.

The fundamental explanation of Roosevelt's fourth victory was the war. The majority felt that it was too great a risk to drop the pilot. "Without a doubt the desire to play it safe was the determining factor in the election," stated a leading Republican newspaper. "Roosevelt's leadership represented a known quantity that had every prospect of going on to victory." "He would have won," commented another, "if we had never heard of the PAC and if Dewey had received the solid Republican vote."

In spite of his fourth sweeping victory, Roosevelt soon encountered trouble in the new Congress. The Senate held up his appointment of Henry Wallace as secretary of commerce in place of Jesse Jones until the lending powers of the Reconstruction Finance Corporation were separated from the Commerce Department. Certain southern Democrats, angry at the removal of Jesse Jones, were again cooperating with the Republicans.

In foreign relations, however, the president's leadership was unchallenged. He played his cards skillfully, including leading Republicans in the American delegation to draw up a United Nations charter. Arthur Vandenberg, once an isolationist, was a delegate and helped steer his

Republican colleagues in the Senate to acceptance of American support of a world organization for peace.

But Roosevelt did not live to attain his objectives. On April 12, 1945, with military victory in sight, he was stricken by a cerebral hemorrhage and died in the "Little White House" in Warm Springs, Georgia. Vice-President Harry S Truman then became the thirty-third president of the United States. The war in Europe ended on May 7, 1945, and the war in the Pacific on September 2, 1945, after the dropping of the first atomic bomb on Hiroshima, Japan, on August 6, and a second one on August 9 on Nagasaki.

XIV

The Great Surprise

LIKE HARDING, Harry S Truman had come to the presidency from the Senate and was a party regular; but the resemblance went no further, in spite of his unpromising background as a cog in the notorious Pendergast Kansas City machine. Eight years as presiding judge of the Jackson County Court and his Pendergast connections had helped him to the United States Senate in 1934. In 1940, after the boss and his chief henchmen had been sent to prison, he won renomination in the primary only after a bitter fight and rode to victory in the election on Roosevelt's coattails.

The early Senate record of the modest, earnest, industrious Missourian, whose personal integrity was untouched by his political background, was that of an undistinguished administration supporter. In 1941 Senator Truman, disturbed at evidences of waste in the government's construction program for the new army, secured the creation of a special Senate committee to ferret out graft and inefficiency in the huge national defense program. The committee, headed by Truman and assisted by an able, young attorney, Hugh Fulton, did its work so well that the mild-mannered, colorless Senator's reputation was made.

After the passing of the numbing shock of personal loss that had swept the nation at Roosevelt's death, many reasoned that it was all for the best. Roosevelt had been the crisis statesman, a man fitted to meet great emergencies; his successor, an average man, might handle more effectively the prosaic but difficult tasks that would come with peace. Then, too, the bitter enmities that FDR had aroused might now be stilled; no one held any grudges against Truman.

The new chief executive set about taking advantage of his political honeymoon. As senator and as vice-president, Truman had been disturbed at the widening gap between White House and Capitol Hill. Now he was in a position to do something. Cooperation was to be his keynote. Personalized government was at an end. He expected to operate through the established departments, not through "palace" advisers, and to consult the wishes of Congress. An era of good feelings seemed at hand. Little parties with Senate cronies were in order.

Cabinet changes, however, were soon found desirable. Stettinius, Morgenthau, and Ickes were replaced by Truman appointees. Henry Wallace resigned in September 1946, after a speech criticizing the "get-tough-with-Russia" policy of the State Department. The departure of these Rooseveltians seemed to symbolize the declining New Deal influence in the administration.

Left-of-Center Truman

In policies, the president was happily tagged as "a little to the left of center." He would try to harmonize the party by following a middle course of moderate liberalism without abandoning the major Roosevelt objectives. On foreign policy he was at first quite successful. Congress accepted the Bretton Woods Pact for an international bank and the United Nations Charter in the summer of 1945 with but slight isolationist opposition. A year later the British loan agreement carried, but 155 votes were cast against it in the House, chiefly by Republicans. Generally speaking, on international issues the Democratic majority held together fairly well; the Republicans were divided, with a varying group of isolationists opposing administration measures. The role of Senator Vandenberg, now committed to international cooperation, was increasingly important in holding Republicans in line.

On domestic questions, the president soon discovered that Roosevelt's policies, rather than his methods, had created the coalition of Republicans and southern Democrats. Appeasement did not work. When he pressed for action on public housing, extension of the Office of Price Administration (OPA), full employment, a permanent fair employment practices commission, and other Rooseveltian proposals, he was checkmated by the bipartisan alliance that had blocked his predecessor on so many occasions. The battle against inflation was lost when the president, after one veto, was forced to accept an unworkable OPA that virtually ended price control. Administration bills, when not defeated outright, were killed in committee or by filibuster, or were passed in mangled form. Truman's honeymoon had ended.

Industrial unrest—the product of rising prices, postwar maladjustments, and labor's fears of losing its "top-dog" position—produced an epidemic of strikes and, consequently, demands for antistrike legislation. President Truman estranged labor by a proposal to draft strikers during the brief railroad strike of May 1946; but later he vetoed the sharply restrictive Case bill, passed by the coalition in Congress.

Republicans Gain in Congress

This year of turmoil turned into the year of jubilee for the Republicans. Shortages of consumer goods, soaring prices, inability of returning veterans to find homes, anger of farmers and businesspeople at the remaining controls, labor resentments and unrest, middle-class fears of Communism, all went into the brew the Republicans were concocting. "Had enough?" was their slogan. It was more than enough. No program was necessary. The voters were looking for a scapegoat, and the Truman administration was it. The meat shortage—really a strike of livestock interests and meat packers—became so acute that President Truman lifted all controls in October. It made little difference. The Republican sweep could not be checked. When the votes were counted on November 5, the GOP had a margin of 28 in the House and 2 in the Senate and had nearly all the governorships outside the South. Even Missouri elected a Republican senator and turned down the president's choice for the House from his home district. The Republicans could now legislate to "end controls, confusion, corruption, Communism," as they had promised.

The rejoicing Republican majorities placed experienced leaders in charge of Congress. Joseph W. Martin, Jr., became Speaker, and Charles A. Halleck of Indiana, Republican floor leader of the House, and hardboiled conservatives became committee chairmen according to the rule of seniority. Arthur H. Vandenberg became president pro tempore of the Senate and remained the guide on foreign policy; Taft headed the steering committee, which planned party strategy, and took for himself the chairmanship of the Labor and Public Welfare Committee. The bipartisan line on foreign policy was continued, though restive Republican isolationists voted against aid to Greece and demanded an end to loans to European nations. Economy and tax reduction ran into the threat of Russian expansion in Europe and Asia.

The dire economic situation of western Europe and the growing American fear of Russia led Congress to accept the administration's plan to aid economy recovery, proposed by Secretary of State George Marshall. Only a little group of isolationists rejected Senator Vandenberg's pleas and voted against it. On other matters, as the 1948 election approached, president and Congress battled for political advantage. Six presidential vetoes were overridden by the Eightieth Congress. The Republicans could boast of tax reduction, a cut in the budget, and the Taft-Hartley Act restricting labor; Truman could blame Congress for the failure of his civil rights and anti-inflation proposals, and could point to congressional inaction on housing, minimum-wage extension, and other social welfare measures. The fact that many southern Democrats had followed the Republican line made no difference to the president. He calculated shrewdly that the administration must stay left of center and play up Republican Toryism in order to hold together the Roosevelt liberal-labor following. Safe seats and seniority had placed in key positions stand-pat Republicans who saw no need to make concessions to reform; and Truman made the most of this. He called the Eightieth Congress the worst in American history.

Dewey's Comeback

Meanwhile presidential candidates were trooping across the stage. Governor Dewey, triumphantly reelected in New York in 1946, had the edge in popularity among the voters in the public opinion polls; but isolationists were hostile, and party regulars preferred Senator Taft. Taft's leadership in Congress had enhanced his reputation. More in the nature of liabilities were his generally conservative and isolationist record, his forthright but sometimes inept public utterances, the pronounced opposition of organized labor, and his lack of voter appeal. Harold E. Stassen of Minnesota, the first to announce his candidacy, appealed to the more liberal elements, the internationalists, and the younger voters, especially the war veterans; but the men who ran the state machines were unfriendly to him. Vandenberg did not avow his candidacy but was regarded as a "draft" possibility if a deadlock occurred. Earl Warren, governor of California, was popular on the Pacific Coast and was in the favorite-son category.

Two war heroes were mentioned: General Douglas MacArthur, military administrator of Japan, and General Dwight D. Eisenhower, chief of staff, who was soon to become president of Columbia University. A "Draft Eisenhower" movement seemed to be stirring some popular interest, but he disposed of it in January 1948, with an unequivocal refusal to run. General MacArthur took the other tack. In March he announced that he would accept any public duty to which he might be called. A MacArthur organization was soon engaged in an active delegate hunt.

Party organizations dominated the choice of delegates in the majority of states; but where presidential primaries existed the results were surprising. Stassen captured 19 of Wisconsin's 27 delegates and polled more than 40 percent of Nebraska's vote. MacArthur, winning only 8 delegates in Wisconsin and ranking fifth in Nebraska, was finished as a contender. The support of Hearst newspapers, of some top figures in World War I veterans' organizations, and of a few men of wealth had done him more harm than good.

Governor Dewey, who had taken Stassen too lightly, now turned his attention to the Oregon primary and devoted three weeks to arduous campaigning in that state. The result, late in May, was an impressive victory. Stassen, already damaged by his failure to break Taft's hold on Ohio, was relegated to third place. There seemed to be a genuine possibility that the front runners would kill each other off.

An enthusiastic horde of Republicans converged on Philadelphia late in June to see "the next president" nominated, while millions of Americans across the country listened in and other millions along the eastern seaboard watched the proceedings through the miracle of television. Dwight H. Green, governor of Illinois, gave the keynote speech as temporary chairman, and Speaker Martin followed him in the chair. Speeches from party notables included, as in previous conventions, the wisecracking sarcasms of Mrs. Clare Boothe Luce and the portentous solemnities of Herbert Hoover.

Long hours of committee wrangling produced a platform sufficiently innocuous to suit all elements in the party. A group of isolationists lost the fight to tone down the strong internationalist section, which had Vandenberg's approval. It endorsed collective security and support of the United Nations and approved of the bipartisan foreign policy. It upheld aid to peace-loving nations "within the prudent limits of our own economic welfare"—a virtual endorsement of the Marshall Plan. A cautiously qualified statement in favor of federal aid for slum clearance and low-rent housing dealt with a problem upon which Congress had refused to act. The Taft-Hartley Act was called "a sensible reform of the labor law," but another paragraph pledged "continuing study to improve labor-management legislation." On civil rights the platform was emphatic—it favored legislation against lynching and poll taxes and for "equal opportunity to work."

Other planks condemned the mismanagement of the Truman administration and praised the record of the Republican Congress but proposed no important changes in government policies. The philosophy of the New Deal was attacked, without recommendations for repeal of specific measures. Men and methods were criticized.

In seven hours of oratory, parading, and carnival revelry the names of all the candidates were presented to the convention. The Taft demonstration was the longest; the Stassen parade, the most colorful; but the Dewey bandwagon drive did not depend on ballyhoo. Behind the scenes the efficient Dewey managers rounded up the votes. Senator Edward Martin of Pennsylvania announced for the New York governor on Tuesday, carrying with him a majority of that state's delegates. Representative Halleck then followed suit with Indiana, and rumors of other defections in favorite-son delegations multiplied. In alarm Taft, Stassen, and representatives of Vandenberg and Warren tried to arrange an anti-Dewey coalition before the balloting; but the Dewey blitz forged ahead. Senator Leverett Saltonstall withdrew as the choice of Massachusetts, and New Jersey was reported as ready to join Dewey on the second ballot.

The first ballot revealed that Dewey had 434 of the necessary 548 votes. Taft had 224; Stassen, 157; Vandenberg, 62; Warren, 59; and there were half a dozen others. The second ballot showed results of the careful work of the Dewey machine. The New Yorker gained most of New Jersey, a majority from Iowa, and stray votes from other states to reach 515, just 33 short of a majority. A recess, conceded by the confident Dewey forces, revealed the hopelessness of the coalition efforts. Before the third ballot, all the other candidates withdrew in favor of Dewey, who then received a unanimous nomination. He accepted soon afterward in a brief speech evidently prepared well beforehand.

A night of conferences by Dewey and invited supporters produced a decision to name Governor Warren for vice-president. Warren was reluctant but agreed after promises that the office should have more authority than in the past. The delegates obeyed the mandate from Dewey headquarters and Warren was named by acclamation. The nomination of the big, friendly California governor seemed to ensure Republican success in the Far West and recognized that section's growing importance in national elections. Yet it was a snub for the Middle West, which had been accustomed to representation on Republican national tickets since the days of Lincoln. Warren's views on public questions were close to Dewey's, and the work of the convention was a bitter disappointment to old-fashioned Republicans whose opinions were well voiced by Colonel Robert McCormick and the *Chicago Tribune*.

Truman and Barkley

Democratic prospects seemed to be so hopeless in the early summer of 1948 that a concerted movement developed to put aside Truman for Eisenhower. City bosses, disgruntled New Dealers, discouraged labor leaders, and southerners angry over civil rights agreed on one thing—the certainty of defeat if Truman ran. Only Eisenhower was thought to be popular enough to stem the Republican tide. Hoping against hope, they pressed the case for the hero of World War II up to the week before the convention. Then Eisenhower settled the matter with a positive refusal. Some turned to Justice Douglas of the Supreme Court; but when he was equally adamant, opposition to Truman evaporated, except from some die-hard southerners who intended to go down fighting and who already were considering a bolt.

The Philadelphia convention met on July 12, with two problems: a running mate for Truman, and a civil rights plank. The first was solved without much difficulty. The president preferred Justice Douglas, a decided New Dealer. When Douglas would not permit his name to be offered, Senator Alben W. Barkley, the temporary chairman, came into the picture. The seventy-year-old Kentucky spellbinder settled the matter by his keynote address, a homely, fighting speech that shook the convention out of its lethargy and produced a spontaneous demonstration that lasted for half an hour. After that, no one else was considered for vice-president. President Truman, New Dealers, and southerners were in accord. Barkley would be a decided asset in a slugging campaign.

The Question of Civil Rights

After electing Sam Rayburn of Texas permanent chairman and listening to an array of speakers, the delegates considered the platform. It contained a rather vague endorsement of equal rights for racial minorities, to be guaranteed by Congress to the limit of its constitutional powers. This started the fireworks. A southern state-rights minority report, two other southern amendment proposals, and a stronger civil rights statement drafted by Hubert H. Humphrey, Jr., mayor of Minneapolis and candidate for the United States Senate, were offered from the floor. A bitter debate followed. As was expected, the southern proposals were beaten overwhelmingly. More surprising, with the eloquent Humphrey leading the battle, the strongly worded northern substitute plank carried by a vote of 651½ to 582½. New Deal liberals, determined to take the party "out of the shadow of states' rights and into the sunlight of human rights," and northern state machines, concerned over possible Negro defections, joined forces to put it over. In effect, the convention repudiated the southern conservatives who had been making common cause with the Republicans in Congress on domestic questions for many years.

From the purely political angle, the decision was sound. The party could not afford to risk the populous northern states in order to hold in line the electoral votes of two or three, or at most half a dozen, southern states. After all, most of the southerners were not going to bolt, though the issue was a touchy one. Nor were all of them die-hard conservatives. When the shouting was over, only Mississippi and half of the Alabama delegation walked out, defiantly waving a Confederate flag.

In addition to the strong civil rights statement the platform incorporated the chief recommendations of President Truman that Congress had largely ignored: measures to control inflation, federal housing and education programs, national health insurance, increased social security benefits, repeal of the Taft-Hartley Act, and retention of price supports for farm products.

Then followed the nominations. Truman had 947½ votes on the only ballot for president; Senator Richard Russell of Georgia, 263; Paul V. McNutt, ½. Barkley had no opposition for second place.

President Truman came from Washington to accept the nomination and delivered a militant speech shortly before 2:00 A.M. that did much to dispel the defeatism that had enshrouded the convention. He announced that he was calling "that worst Eightieth Congress" into special session to give the Republicans a chance to carry out their platform pledges.

Two more conventions named candidates that month. The anti-Truman southerners, denying that they were bolters, met in Birmingham on July 17 and nominated Governor J. Strom Thurmond of South Carolina for president and Governor Fielding L. Wright of Mississippi for vice-president on a state-rights and anti-race-equality platform. In spite of appeals to the emotions and prejudices of the white South, these sectionalists—called Dixiecrats—drew in few nationally important southern Democrats. But the bolters had control of the state organizations in several states and could compel the regular Democratic presidential electors to support Thurmond. This would force the Truman electors to run as independents with slight chance of success. The Dixiecrats aimed to defeat Truman, even though Dewey's civil rights position was just as unsatisfactory.

While the Dixiecrats preempted the extreme right, a new party appeared on the left—not a wing of seceding Democrats but a hybrid of radicals and nonparty liberals of all shades of opinion. In December 1947, Henry Wallace had accepted the invitation of a group called the Progressive Citizens of America to run for president. A national convention, meeting in Philadelphia on July 22, organized the Progressive Party and nominated Wallace and Senator Glen Taylor of Idaho as its candidates. Wallace appeared at a great mass meeting at Shibe Park to accept the nomination on a platform that attacked the Marshall Plan, called for disarmament and the destruction of atomic-bomb stockpiles, and demanded equality of treatment for all minority groups. It was a gathering, in large part, of idealistic young voters who, gazing through the tinted glasses of peace and equal rights and alarmed at the Cold War and the revival of the draft, could not see the Communist pattern of the platform and the skillful management of the party-liners in the convention's proceedings. Early in August a Communist Party convention endorsed Wallace and adopted a platform very similar to that of the Progressive Party.

Congress, called into special session by Truman, refused to act on most of his program. The Republican majority denounced his action as a political move—which it was—and adjourned after passing weak housing and anti-inflation bills that were hardly more than gestures for campaign purposes. The cast-iron conservatism of the house leadership played into Truman's hands. He could now go on the stump and repeat his charges against the Eightieth Congress with even more emphasis.

But Truman's plight seemed to be hopeless. The Dixiecrats were certain to win some southern electoral votes. Wallace would cut into Democratic strength in New York and possibly other states of the East and the Middle West. If Dewey polled the normal Republican vote he would move into the White House. And there was no evidence that the Republican trend of 1946 had been reversed. As a result, the Democratic leadership fell into a defeatist lethargy, and Truman and a few loyal supporters had to bear the brunt of the campaigning. The national chairman, J. Howard McGrath, was confronted with a lack of funds and a disorganized party, and had one of the most difficult tasks a campaign manager had ever faced.

Truman's Whistle-Stop Campaign

Truman, undaunted by the odds against him, traveled 31,000 miles in a "whistle-stop" campaign and spoke to some 6,000,000 people. He hammered away at the record of the Eightieth Congress, blaming it for price and rent rises and the housing shortage (an appeal to salaried workers and veterans) and for the Taft-Hartley Act (an appeal to labor). For farmers, he pointed to years of prosperity under Democratic rule and warned of the dangers of an end of price supports if the Republicans won. For the conservation-minded West, he emphasized the benefits of a liberal federal policy and the threats to reclamation projects from congressional cuts in appropriations. Thus he offered both performance and promise. Late in the campaign, he shifted to the civil rights issue in speeches in the East and the Middle West where large minority groups—Negroes, Jews, foreign-born—were tempted by the Wallace lure. This put a strain on southern Democrats, but traditional party loyalty had to take care of the Thurmond threat.

The president's speeches were homely, down-to-earth, hard-hitting talks of an average man aimed at the average person. A little group of faithful aides assisted him, and their planning belied the caustic comment of a newspaperman: "With Truman's staff, Robert E. Lee couldn't carry Virginia." All the working journalists were puzzled by the large crowds that turned out to see the president, and wondered at the apparent warmth of their greeting. But did this mean votes or merely admiration for a little guy who didn't know when he was licked?

The Dewey Campaign

On the Republican side the campaign was managed by the same efficient methods that had brought Dewey the nomination. Representative Hugh D. Scott, Jr., of Pennsylvania was national chairman, but Governor Dewey and his experienced general staff directed the strategy. Dewey's speeches stressed the need for an administration that would promote national unity and the cause of world peace. He promised to "work for peace through the United Nations and by every honorable means wherever the peace is threatened." At home, he would promote both social progress and individual freedom. He avoided concrete commitments that might create trouble in his own party and might prove embarrassing after election. His task, with victory seemingly assured, was not to win friends but to keep from alienating people. His deep voice, excellent for radio, poured out polished, faultless sentences, correctly inflected and uttered with a confident assurance that carried conviction. Truman appeared as an inept fumbler beside him; but the Republican candidate's speeches seemed to flow over his audiences, not into them. He seemed to be the cool, cautious champion; Truman, the fighting challenger. Dewey chose to let his wild-swinging opponent defeat himself, rather than to take chances by trading punches; but it made the campaign singularly dull. Dewey was a machine with a cellophane cover, said one observant critic.

Dixiecrats Campaign

In the South the Dixiecrats conducted a vigorous campaign. They controlled the state committees in Alabama, Mississippi, South Carolina, and Louisiana, where their electors ran as the regular Democratic candidates. In Alabama the ballot listed no Truman electors. In other parts of the South, Thurmond-Wright electoral candidates ran as independents and threatened to give Virginia, Florida, and Tennessee to the Republicans. Loyal Truman Democrats believed that the Southern Rights movement had financial support from northern business interests with southern connections, and that state rights, rebel yells, and Yankee dollars worked in harmony for Republican victory.

Henry Wallace provided the thunder on the left. His invasion of the South to preach equal rights produced some acts of rowdiness where it defied Jim Crow regulations, but his political importance was in the urban sections of the East and the Middle West. Wherever his name appeared on the ballot, it lessened Democratic chances of victory. Likewise, it pointed up the Communist issue for the major parties. The Un-American Activities Committee of the House of Representatives, under Republican control, unearthed sufficient evidence of Communist espionage and other operations to create a good deal of concern, and Republican speakers made much of Communist infiltration. Dewey, however, opposed outlawry of the Communist Party. Truman criticized the inquisitorial methods of the investigators and called their allegations "a red herring" to divert attention from more important matters. Wallace's candidacy actually did the Democrats a good turn. It attracted radicals of all shades and freed Truman of the taint of their support. But there were fears that he would need these votes to win the close states.

All the leading polls, the political analysts, and the important newspapers predicted a Dewey victory, though some conceded that Truman's fighting campaign had stirred lagging Democratic spirits, and that control of the next Senate was in doubt. The cautious *New York Times,* on the basis of reports of its correspondents, gave Dewey 305 electoral votes, Truman 105, and Thurmond 38, with 43 votes doubtful. The president himself forecast in mid-October: Truman, 229 votes; Dewey, 109; Thurmond, 8; doubtful, 189.

On the night of November 2 the early returns put Truman in the lead, but Republican headquarters remained optimistic. These were urban votes that would be nullified by later returns from rural districts. Quite the reverse happened. Truman's popular lead increased as the western states reported, but there was uncertainty about the electoral votes. The election might go to the House. The *Chicago Tribune* appeared with a front-page headline that read "Dewey Defeats Truman." Not until 11:14 A.M. on Wednesday, after California and Ohio had gone into the Truman column, did Dewey concede defeat. The electoral results were 303 votes for Truman, 189 for Dewey, 39 for Thurmond. Dewey had carried Maine, New Hampshire, Vermont, Connecticut, New York, Pennsylvania, New Jersey, Maryland, and Delaware in the East, Michigan and Indiana in the Middle West, North Dakota, South Dakota, Nebraska, and Kansas in the farm belt, and Oregon on the Pacific Coast. Thurmond had South Carolina, Alabama, Mississippi, and Louisiana, and one Tennessee elector who violated his Truman pledge. Truman carried the remaining twenty-eight states.

The states from Ohio westward and the upper South provided most of his votes, but the surprising thing was the wide distribution of his strength. But for the Wallace candidacy he might have carried New York, Michigan, and Maryland; and Thurmond certainly cost him 39 electoral votes in the South. Dewey's percentage of the popular vote (45.1) was a little under that in 1944 (45.9). Truman had 49.5 percent; the minor parties, 5.4 percent.*

Various explanations were offered for the incredible result: farm prosperity and farmer distrust of Easterner Dewey; labor's weight in the cities; Truman's whistle-stop campaign, stressing the record of the Eightieth Congress; Dewey's failure to come to grips with the issues; Republican overconfidence and consequent failure to get out a full vote; an unusually

---

* The popular vote was as follows: Truman, 24,105,587; Dewey, 21,970,017; Thurmond, 1,169,134; Wallace, 1,157,057; Thomas, Socialist, 138,973; Watson, Prohibitionist, 103,489; Teichert, Socialist Labor, 29,038; Dobbs, Socialist Workers, 13,614.

strong crop of Democratic candidates for the Senate and for state governorships, which aided the national ticket; the failure of Thurmond and
Wallace to do what the pollsters had predicted.

Political analyst Samuel Lubell has argued convincingly that the very
instability of a majority coalition may be a source of strength. Disaffection
on the left may strengthen loyalties on the right, and vice versa. In 1948
the Wallace candidacy took the blight of radicalism from Truman's shoulders and eased the return to the fold of some isolationist and other anti-
Roosevelt groups such as farm-belt German Catholics and urban Irish.
The Democratic Catholic vote in some areas exceeded the turnout for Al
Smith in 1928. The Dixiecrat seceders also did Truman a good turn by
proving to northern Negroes that he was sound on civil rights. But the
urge to preserve, if not to advance, the various gains of the Roosevelt
years was basic in the Democratic miracle, and Truman made the most of
it. In a sense Roosevelt won his greatest victory after his death.

The most heartening thing about the election was the stubborn independence of the voting majority in defying the bandwagon psychology
created by polls, newspaper opinion, and the near-unanimous verdict of
the political pundits. These samplers of opinion were quite crestfallen,
and the laughter over their discomfiture tempered the disappointment of
the defeated. Never again would an election be regarded as settled until
the votes were counted.

One other lesson was not so well learned. For a few hours after the
polls closed on November 2 it had seemed possible either that Dewey
would have a majority of the electoral votes, though second in the popular vote, or that the election would go to the House of Representatives for
lack of an electoral decision, with the ultimate verdict in doubt. Fortunately, later returns ended the danger of a perversion of the popular will.
But in Congress, up to 1979, efforts to alter or abolish the antiquated,
undemocratic electoral college produced only debates and disagreement.
Liberals and conservatives in both parties were badly divided over the
merits of several reform proposals.

The Fair Deal Fails

Truman had been triumphant running on his "Fair Deal" program,
and with both houses again Democratic he had the right to expect the
legislators to register the verdict promptly. But the old pattern reappeared. Republicans, despite their platform pledges, aided the antiadministration southern senators in blocking civil rights legislation. The story
was repeated with other administration measures, and the fruits of the
great victory of 1948 were lost. Particularly bitter to Truman supporters

was their inability to repeal the Taft-Hartley Act, as pledged to labor in the campaign. On this issue the coalition won in both houses.

Although the president failed to secure enactment of a large part of his domestic program, he did secure the renewal of the reciprocal trade agreements, continued appropriations for the European Recovery Program, and ratification of the North Atlantic Security Pact. Senator Vandenberg lined up most of the Republican senators for the bipartisan foreign policy. But the victory of the Communists in China in 1949 and the outbreak of war in Korea in June 1950, saddled the administration with a set of liabilities so potent that Republican hopes rose to a new high by 1952.

The North Korean Communist invasion of South Korea produced in Congress a temporary united front against aggression, but this soon broke down. The initial United Nations failure in stemming the North Korean sweep, the glaring unpreparedness of the American military arm, the nullification of General MacArthur's later successes by Communist China's entry into the struggle, the long stalemate that ensued, the heavy American casualties and increased defense expenditures, the removal of MacArthur by President Truman for alleged interference in policy matters, and a widespread belief that past State Department blunders in China were responsible for the Communist triumph in that country were factors that did not need Republican oratory to raise doubts in the minds of many Americans as to the wisdom of administration policies. The war also created a state of alarm in which fears of the Communist menace within the United States mounted.

Even before the Korean crisis Alger Hiss, a former state department official, had been convicted of perjury for denying that he had used his position in the State Department in the late 1930s to further Communist ends. Other cases involved leading Communists in conspiracy charges, and some underlings were caught betraying atomic energy secrets. This helped set the stage for congressional investigations to determine the extent of Communist infiltration in government departments. Republican Senator Joseph R. McCarthy of Wisconsin made the headlines by blanket charges that the State Department harbored Communists.

Secretary of State Dean G. Acheson became McCarthy's chief target, and other Republicans soon joined in the hue and cry. Although President Truman had instituted a system of loyalty checks of administrative employees, Red-hunting critics were not appeased; and the Communist issue loomed large on the political horizon, with the Korean War a constant reminder of the ever-present Russian menace. Communist pressure in Greece and Turkey eventually led to the Truman Doctrine (May 1947) "to help people who are resisting attempted subjugation." The "Cold War" had started.

On the domestic front the administration struggled with increased consumer prices, ineffective controls, heavier tax burdens, wage freezes and labor unrest, the slow pace of rearmament, and presently, exposure of corruption in governmental departments. The last was, politically, far and away the most serious. Congressional investigations dug out details of shady deals, of activities of influence peddlers, of tax frauds, and of other unsavory transactions by officials in the Bureau of Internal Revenue, the Justice Department, and the Reconstruction Finance Corporation. "Mink coats," "deep freezers," and "five percenters" hit the newspaper headlines and were used in Republican campaign propaganda to remind the voters of the "mess in Washington." Unlike the Harding scandals, the Truman frauds were entirely below the cabinet level, though some top officials were guilty of bad appointments and of woeful blindness to the doings of responsible subordinates. Truman was compared with Harding in his inclination toward "government by crony" and in his slowness to see the faults in his friends. His belated housecleaning did little to undo the political damage resulting from the exposures.

The midterm elections, before the full impact of exposures of corruption and Communism had been felt but after reverses in Korea, brought a decided slap at the administration. Gains put the Republican Party within two seats of control of the Senate, and the Democratic majority in the House was greatly reduced. The Democrats were better off in Congress than in 1946, but there were ominous aspects. Among the defeated in the Senate were Scott W. Lucas of Illinois, majority leader; Francis J. Myers of Pennsylvania, majority whip; and two long-time important committee chairmen, Millard Tydings of Maryland and Elbert Thomas of Utah. Tydings's defeat was attributed chiefly to the tactics of Senator McCarthy in the Maryland campaign, later the subject of a Senate investigation. Most significant of the Republican victories was that of Senator Taft, who was reelected by a landslide in the face of labor opposition. After this resounding popular endorsement, "Mr. Republican" could not overlook the White House in his plans for 1952.

XV

"I Like Ike"

SENATOR TAFT announced in September 1951, that his intentions were serious, and he embarked upon as strenuous a delegate hunt as a candidate had ever undertaken. The sparse-haired, bespectacled, scholarly-looking Ohio statesman with the dry, metallic voice was not a good rabble-rouser, but in his own way was an effective campaigner. His intelligence, earnestness, command of facts, and unrelenting partisanship made sympathetic listeners overlook his lack of humor and imagination. Believing that the party had lost too many times with "me too" candidates, he took issue with every major Truman policy and gave the voters his version of true Republicanism.

To his standard came party wheel horses, courthouse politicians, isolationists, Asia Firsters, and small-town and country Tories, especially the elderly. Middle-western state machines and the southern skeletons, as before, lined up for "Mr. Republican." Where the party was well entrenched—New England excepted—and where it was weakest, Taft was favored.

General Eisenhower Enters the Race

But internationalists and liberals could see no hope in Taft's line. He was calling the primitive Republicans to arms; but independents and anti-Truman Democrats would look askance at a man who had been an isolationist, a defender of McCarthy, a critic of organized labor, and an extreme conservative. The East, doubtful Michigan and Minnesota, and the farther West were at stake. Truman's humorous comment that Taft was his favorite Republican candidate had a point. The anti-Taft forces, however, were at a disadvantage within the Republican Party, where independents and Democrats had no voice. Only an outstanding man would have a chance against him. And so General Dwight D. Eisenhower ("Ike") was urged to make the race.

This popular leader in World War II, after a brief tenure as president of Columbia University, had been placed in charge of the European defense system of the North Atlantic Treaty Organization (NATO). A nominal Republican, he had, like Grant, a popularity that transcended party lines. A group of anti-Taft Republicans—Governor Dewey, Senators James H. Duff of Pennsylvania, Frank Carlson of Kansas, and Henry Cabot Lodge of Massachusetts—launched a "Draft Eisenhower" movement to put pressure on the reluctant general, who was still in Europe. In January 1952, he permitted his name to be entered in the New Hampshire primary, and an organization headed by Senator Lodge undertook to transmute popularity into delegates. Financial backing was expected from big-business sources. Metropolitan newspapers and the largest news weeklies were friendly.

Two lesser figures also offered themselves. Harold Stassen decided to try his luck again, and Earl Warren, elected for a third term as governor of California, was the Pacific Coast's choice. Here and there a voice was lifted for General MacArthur after his dismissal by President Truman, but his "martyrdom" served his party's interests better than his own.

The preferential primary results were indecisive and somewhat sectional. New Hampshire, voting first, gave Eisenhower a clear margin over Taft and Stassen, but direct clashes between the two top candidates were avoided in most of the other primary states. Sometimes "write-in" campaigns were attempted to show popular support. Stassen and Warren also complicated matters. In general, Taft showed greater strength in the Middle West although he lost six Wisconsin delegates to Warren, and Eisenhower ran better in the East, although he almost took Minnesota from Stassen by write-in votes.

Eisenhower, at the insistence of his managers, resigned as NATO commander and returned home in June to strengthen his cause by direct appeal. His first speech was in Abilene, Kansas, his boyhood home. After this initial plunge, he began to act more like a candidate. Speeches and conferences with party leaders and delegates in key states followed. His statements on issues drew the fire of the Taft men—"five-star generalities," the *Chicago Tribune* called them—but the warmth and sincerity of his personality meant more for his cause than what he said. He was still a tyro in politics, but the voters more than once have favored a candidate unsoiled and unspoiled by the evils of politics. His propaganda played him up as the people's choice, Taft as the politicians', and pointed to opinion polls as proof.

Though the Eisenhower movement made surprising headway, Taft led in pledged delegates when the convention met in the International Amphitheater in Chicago on July 7, 1952. But the uncommitted delegates, including Michigan and Pennsylvania, the contested seats from the South, and the Warren and Stassen blocs held the answer for the two front runners. Taft had one decided advantage—control of the national committee. That body chose Walter S. Hallanan of West Virginia as temporary chairman of the convention, former Speaker Martin as permanent chairman, General MacArthur as keynoter, and Herbert Hoover for an evening address. Not one of them favored Eisenhower. More important was the power of the national committee to rule on contested seats and then to make up the temporary roll. A situation like that of 1912 seemed to be shaping up, for some seventy seats were in dispute.

Taft's Final Try

The national committee, with television cameras carefully excluded, heard arguments over the contested seats. Georgia, Louisiana, and Texas were the key states. Here the Republican organizations were, in effect, closed clubs that hand-picked delegates to national conventions and controlled the patronage when there was any. These had been lined up for Taft, and it was assumed that local and state conventions would be the usual cut-and-dried affairs.

Unexpectedly, Eisenhower Republicans had turned up in force at the local primary meetings or caucuses and in many instances had elected their slates of delegates to district and state conventions. Charging that these interlopers were not true Republicans, the Taft regulars sometimes had walked out and chosen their own delegates at closed caucuses. The party committees, being pro-Taft, denied recognition to the Eisenhower delegates whenever Taft claimants appeared. Such tactics split state and district conventions and produced two sets of delegates to Chicago. The national committee, after wrestling with various compromise proposals, ended by giving a large majority of the disputed seats to Taft. This was 1912 again.

The matter now came before the opening session of the national convention on a routine motion to adopt the rules of the 1948 convention. This would have permitted the delegates from each contested state occupying temporary seats to vote on all matters except their own seats. The Eisenhower strategists countered with a substitute that delegations opposed by more than one-third of the national committee should not vote on the credentials of any other delegation. The key vote came on a proposal to exempt seven Louisiana delegates from the operation of the rule. After a bitter two-hour debate, the Taft forces lost by a margin of 110 votes. The substitute then carried.

The credentials committee, under Taft control, now heard all contests for seats in the glare of television cameras. This exposure of southern dirty linen did the Taft cause no good. The convention rejected the committee's report on the Georgia contest, 607 to 531, and the Eisenhower delegates were then seated in all cases. The bitterness displayed in the debate by the usually well-mannered Republicans was almost unparalleled. At one stage impassioned Senator Everett M. Dirksen of Illinois, pointing at Governor Dewey, in the New York delegation, assailed him for leading the party down to defeat in the past. This produced a roar of boos. The internationalist East and the isolationist Middle West were locked in a battle for control. To a degree, it was the large urban centers versus the smaller places and the countryside.

While the credentials committee struggled over the contested seats, the convention endured speech after speech by Taft-selected party celebrities, highlighted by the oratory of General MacArthur and Herbert Hoover at evening sessions. MacArthur's dramatic passages did not quite meet expectations; Hoover, now seventy-seven, was more appealing with his jeremiads than in the past. Before the balloting he endorsed Taft.

After voting on the contested seats the convention received the platform with such noisy inattention that Chairman Martin had to take a hand with a sharp reproof. The resolutions committee had ironed out the controversial issues, and the convention accepted the result with a voice vote. The document of six thousand words contained mostly denunciations, with some carefully qualified pledges as to future action. The foreign relations plank, written by John Foster Dulles, rejected both isolationism and the Truman policy of containment of Communism, accepted collective security and foreign commitments with the reservation that they should not endanger the economic health of the United States, and promised equal treatment of Asia and Europe. It spoke of making the nation again a "dynamic, moral and spiritual force" and ending "the negative, futile and immoral policy of containment."

Communism and corruption in the administration were condemned, and an improved national defense was promised with economy and tax reduction. A long section on agriculture covered "a farm program aimed at full parity prices." A civil rights section was a little less emphatic than in 1948, putting more weight on state action. Except for approval of the extension of social security, the platform leaned strongly toward state rights and opposed government in business. It favored eventual local control of federal water projects, opposed "Federal socialistic valley authorities," declared for state ownership of lands and resources beneath offshore waters, and proposed changes in public-land policy in favor of individual and local interests. It condemned federal compulsory health insurance and upheld the Taft-Hartley Act, but left the door open for possible amendments to improve it.

The votes on the contested seats had foreshadowed defeat for Taft. The unpledged Pennsylvania and Michigan delegations, controlled by Governor John S. Fine and National Committeeman Arthur E. Summerfield, respectively, had voted with the Eisenhower forces. The Stassen and Warren blocs were also anti-Taft and seemed certain to go to Eisenhower on the presidential balloting if he should come close to a majority. The result of the one ballot for the nomination was even more favorable than the strategists for Eisenhower had expected. He had 595 (9 short of a majority); Taft, 500; Warren, 81; Stassen, 20; MacArthur, 10. Minnesota, which had already cast 9 votes for Eisenhower, now added the rest of its votes to his total; other states followed until he had 845. Taft had 280; Warren, 77; and MacArthur, 4. Senator Bricker of Ohio then sorrowfully moved that the nomination be made unanimous. Taft's third and last attempt had fallen short.

In a sense Taft had defeated himself. He had relied too much on party regulars and organizations, and these had overreached themselves in the South. The time-honored, if shabby, methods of corralling delegates there gave the Eisenhower leaders an opportunity to occupy high moral ground in refusing to compromise with sin. When the television cameras invaded the hearings of the credentials committee, they confirmed—to the uninitiated—the villainies of the hardened professionals in delegate grabbing. A crusade against Democratic corruption by a candidate nominated through such methods would have been unconvincing.

Yet there were hardened professionals and shrewd manipulations on the victor's side. Governor Dewey, still a power, was unrelentingly anti-Taft. Herbert Brownell, Jr., who had directed Dewey's campaigns, pulled the strings behind the scenes at Eisenhower headquarters. Senator Lodge, Governor Adams of New Hampshire, and others handled floor tactics far better than the bungling Taft lieutenants. If Taft could have been his own floor leader, he might have done better—but the historian can multiply the *ifs* that seem to explain his defeat. The nomination of Taft would have violated the doctrine of availability that most Republican conventions have respected. The successful candidates seldom come from the conservative right.

Nixon Nominated for Vice-President

The vice-presidential choice of the Eisenhower high command was Senator Richard M. Nixon of California. The selection recognized the youth movement in the party—he was thirty-nine—and acknowledged the importance of the Pacific Coast. It was designed also to point up the Communism-in-government issue, because Nixon, as a member of the House Un-American Activities Committee, had played a major part in the Alger Hiss case. In other respects the nomination was highly unorthodox for the Republicans. It denied the Taft minority a customary consolation prize and departed from the usual practice of choosing among important state governors or Senate veterans. Nixon was a junior senator as obscure

as the Truman of 1944 and far more inexperienced; but he was a fluent
speaker who appeared to advantage on television, and his attractive wife
was not the least of his campaigning assets.

The Stevenson Draft

President Truman's decision not to run again, announced in early
April but made long before, opened the way for a free-for-all battle for
the Democratic nomination. Though the civil rights issue was present,
there was not the sharpness of alignment and consequent bitterness of the
Republican struggle. The Democrats, chronically inharmonious, expected
a fracas over candidates or platform planks or both.

Senator Estes Kefauver of Tennessee was the most persevering of the
active candidates and the leader in pledged delegates. The lanky Tennessean had become a national figure by heading a special Senate committee
to investigate crime, whose televised proceedings made him a popular
hero; but he had incurred some enmities by exposing the tie-in of certain
local politicians with gangsters and gamblers. Also, his early announcement of his candidacy without consulting party leaders, at a time when
Truman was still expected to run, did him no good with organization
men, and his New Deal and Fair Deal record kept southern conservatives
away. Lacking money and organization, he conducted an informal but
extensive street-corner and hand-shaking campaign, assisted by his prepossessing wife, and won a number of surprising primary successes. His
reforming record, his coonskin-cap emblem, his opposition to boss rule,
and his vague liberalism attracted young voters, moral reformers, antior-
ganization people, small-town Democrats, and some liberals. Opponents
charged that his primary victories were won over weak candidates or
organization unpledged slates.

A more openly anti-Truman candidate was Senator Richard Russell, a
highly respected Georgia conservative who was backed by state-rights
southern Democrats and Dixiecrats. He rallied southerners who wanted to
force concessions from the northern liberal majority.

Among favorite sons were W. Averell Harriman of New York, Senator
Robert S. Kerr of Oklahoma, and Vice-President Alben W. Barkley. Harriman, millionaire son of E. H. Harriman of railroad fame, was a Roose-
velt-Truman loyalist who had served capably in several administrative
posts, had strong labor backing, but was inexperienced in politics, with
New York his only large bloc of votes. Senator Kerr, a wealthy oil man,
was an administration supporter in most respects, but northern liberals
were cold toward him, and a setback at Kefauver's hands in Nebraska left
him with only scattered support outside Oklahoma. A late entrant was the
beloved "Veep," Alben Barkley, who was informed that the Truman

administration was ready to take him, as none of the other possibilities fitted the situation. He could easily have been nominated had he been ten years younger, but labor leaders turned him down flatly because of his age, seventy-four.

The most suitable candidate from availability angles was Governor Adlai E. Stevenson of Illinois. His public career included service in responsible posts with the Navy and State departments before Colonel Jacob M. Arvey, shrewd Chicago party head, spotted him as a fine prospect to recapture the state house from the Republicans. He had won by a landslide in 1948, running ahead of Truman in Illinois. His record as governor, working with a Republican legislature, added to his reputation. Also in his favor were his middle-western roots, a grandfather who had been vice-president with Cleveland, and brilliant public speeches studded with apt quotations and clever quips. His Ivy League education (Princeton was his alma mater) recommended him to "high and middle brows," if not to the commonalty. His recent divorce and a deposition he had once signed attesting to Alger Hiss's good character were not regarded as serious drawbacks.

But Stevenson refused to run. He insisted that a second term as governor was his only ambition. A strong movement in the Truman administration and in important state organizations to line up delegates for him was stalled. A group of Illinois admirers, including members of the University of Chicago faculty, refused to be discouraged and set up Stevenson headquarters to keep the door open for a draft. As the national convention was about to open, Mayor David L. Lawrence of Pittsburgh and other influential state leaders threw their support to the Draft Stevenson movement. It gained momentum hourly and the governor, apparently torn by conflicting emotions, could not stop it.

The convention opened two weeks after the Republican conclave in the same International Amphitheater, with 1,230 delegates present. Governor Paul A. Dever of Massachusetts was temporary chairman and keynoter, and veteran Sam Rayburn, Speaker of the House, succeeded him in the chair. At the opening session a "loyalty" pledge was put through by a northern liberal bloc requiring all delegates to agree to use all honorable means to get the nominees of the convention on the state ballots as Democrats. In view of the misuse of the electoral system by the Dixiecrats in 1948, this mild proposal seemed to be quite in order.

Southern opposition to a specific pledge flared up, however, with Senator Byrd of Virginia, Governor Byrnes of South Carolina, and Governor Kennon of Louisiana representing the die-hards, who would not sign the pledge. Finally, on the fourth day, the convention voted, 615 to 529, to seat the Virginia delegates without the pledge. Assurance was given that Virginia laws covered the matter. Then South Carolina and Louisiana were also seated, without a roll call. The vote on the Virginia case

showed that the southern contingent had the backing of important northern machine leaders against a Harriman-Kefauver liberal bloc. Harmony
had triumphed over party discipline.

Rather surprisingly, the platform caused no difficulty in the convention. The troublesome civil rights statement of 1948 was virtually
repeated in demands for federal legislation to secure equal rights for all
with regard to employment, security of persons, and political life. It was
not opposed except by Mississippi and Georgia, which were recorded as
voting against the platform as a whole. The Republican plank, with its
specific mention of antilynching and anti-poll-tax legislation and an end
of segregation in the District of Columbia, possibly made the Democratic
position appear milder to the southern wing. In the civil rights section
was a statement favoring an end of Senate filibusters, long a weapon of
the southern minority.

Other planks defended the Truman foreign policy of resisting Communist aggression through collective security; commended congressional
exposures, under Democratic leadership, of dishonesty and disloyalty in
the public service; favored tax reduction, but only when defense requirements would permit it; upheld the Truman loyalty program for government officials; promised the farmer 90 percent of parity; and, for labor,
favored the repeal of the Taft-Hartley Act.

The Democrats were generally as immune to political spellbinding as
the Republicans, but they did demonstrate warmly for two party veterans, Vice-President Barkley and Mrs. Franklin D. Roosevelt. One other
speaker, Adlai E. Stevenson, in his brief address of welcome as governor
of Illinois, was highly effective and gave a strong impetus to the draft
movement he had disavowed.

Hours of nominating speeches for eleven men, and the battle over the
loyalty pledge, delayed the balloting until Friday afternoon. The first
ballot gave Kefauver 340 votes, Stevenson 273, Russell 268, Harriman
123½, Kerr 65, Barkley 48½, and 8 others scattering votes. On the second
ballot Stevenson went up to 324½ and Kefauver to 362½ as the favorite
sons began to drop out. The third ballot produced a general shift to
Stevenson. He had 617½ votes, Kefauver 275½, Russell 261, and Barkley 67½. The Stevenson draft had succeeded.

The nominee appeared before the convention, was introduced by President Truman, who had arrived from Washington, and delivered a
moving acceptance speech whose exalted, idealistic tone and expressive
phraseology made it a classic of convention oratory. Quite in contrast was
the down-to-earth fighting speech of Truman that ended the session.
Unfortunately for the Democrats, most Americans had gone to bed and
did not hear the two speeches that presented the party's case most effectively.

Next day, the convention nominated Stevenson's choice for vice-president, Senator John J. Sparkman. The big, curly-haired likable Alabaman, fifty-two years old, was a liberal, though opposed to civil rights legislation, had fought the Dixiecrats, and had compiled a good record in his sixteen years in the House and Senate. He had also been a delegate to the United Nations General Assembly. Southern conservatives were cold toward both nominees but at least gave no consideration to the idea of separate Dixiecrat candidates, as in 1948.

TV Shows Convention Weaknesses

Both conventions came in for a good deal of criticism from watchers at TV sets. The noisy inattention of delegates, the artificial demonstrations (the Republicans even had paid performers), the banal oratory, the parliamentary tangles and public quarreling, the mysterious deals and shiftings of votes behind the camera's eye, the "show-off" delegates who demanded polls of their delegations just to give themselves a brief television appearance, the hectic carnival atmosphere—all were disillusioning to citizens who, before the television era, had thought of a convention as a kind of deliberative assembly. Radio had revealed unlovely aspects, but the camera was devastating. Thoughtful observers wondered about substitutes such as a national primary that would let the voters nominate. The skeptical pointed to the enormously expensive sales campaigns necessary to win votes, which might make the nominee the one with the slickest publicity men. At least the convention system had produced two excellent candidates in 1952, and by and large it had not worked badly. If it had rejected front runners in favor of a Pierce or a Harding, it had also produced a Lincoln and a Wilson, both availabilities. Where the public voice was clear, it had responded. Grant, Cleveland, the Roosevelts, and Hoover were popular choices, whatever their merits as chief executives.

The Eisenhower Sweep

In the Republican camp Arthur Summerfield, who had swung unpledged Michigan to Eisenhower at Chicago, became national chairman and campaign manager. Governor Sherman Adams of New Hampshire was personal adviser to the candidate. A Citizens Committee for Eisenhower, which had worked for his nomination, continued its separate organization and aimed its propaganda at independents and Democrats. Stevenson chose Stephen A. Mitchell, a Chicago lawyer whose experience was more legal than political, but who brought new blood into the organization, and Wilson W. Wyatt of Kentucky, a founder of the liberal Americans for Democratic Action (ADA), to handle his campaign, with Mitchell as national chairman. Both had had experience in Washington positions. Sinclair Weeks handled finances for the Republicans; Beardsley Ruml for the Democrats.

The big Republican problem was Taft's attitude. The boos that had greeted Eisenhower when he called at Taft headquarters just after the nomination indicated the feelings of the Taft supporters. Taft himself formally endorsed the nominee, then left for his summer home in Quebec. Apparently he was prepared to sit out the campaign, and his devoted following might do likewise. They regarded Eisenhower as the tool of the "Dewey people" and another "me too" candidate. Not since the Taft-Roosevelt feud in 1912 had there been such fratricidal strife in the party. Eisenhower moved to heal the breach by inviting Taft to his home on Morningside Heights. They conferred on September 12, and a manifesto written by Taft was accepted with only slight changes by the candidate and made public. It committed him to the orthodox (to Taft) position on all major points, except for some "differences of degree" on foreign policy, and promised equality of treatment for Taft supporters as to offices.

This "surrender," as Democratic critics termed it, brought the Ohio senator into the fold; his lieutenants went to work, and party unity seemed to be assured. Eisenhower appeared with Senators Jenner in Indiana and McCarthy in Wisconsin, though Jenner had called his old mentor and friend, General George C. Marshall, "a front for traitors" and "a living lie," and McCarthy had been equally harsh. Possibly, Eisenhower was thinking that he would need support from the Taft wing, so powerful in Congress, if he won in November. In any case, Republican nominees for office received pats on the back wherever the head of the ticket appeared.

Stevenson's troubles lay southward. There the conservatives were unhappy over the civil rights issue, and Texas, Louisiana, and Florida had a special grievance—Truman's vetoes of bills giving title of offshore lands to the states. The candidate refused to back away from his platform. Referring to civil rights, he told a Richmond (Va.) audience: "I should justly earn your contempt if I talked one way in the South and another way elsewhere." Later, in Texas, he upheld federal control of offshore lands and damned himself with the oil interests and with states-rights people generally.

These issues and the widespread dislike of southern conservatives for the Truman administration caused bolting to Eisenhower that was like the Hoovercrat revolt against Alfred E. Smith in 1928. Governors Byrnes of South Carolina, Kennon of Louisiana, and Shivers of Texas led the rebels, while Senator Byrd of Virginia criticized Stevenson without announcing for Eisenhower. Most members of Congress were loyal, but many gave the ticket lukewarm support. Several important newspapers led by the *Atlanta Journal* came out for Eisenhower. The loyalty pledge of the Democratic national convention was observed everywhere, and

Stevenson electors ran as Democrats. To avoid the Republican imprint, Eisenhower Democrats offered independent electoral tickets in South Carolina and Mississippi. Eisenhower campaigned vigorously in the South and drew large crowds. And sentimental southerners did not forget that he was born in Texas.

Using train and plane, the two rivals displayed their bald heads all over the continent. Important addresses in key cities were televised. This meant a different speech for each occasion, and a corps of skilled phrase-makers supplied much of the ammunition. This was particularly necessary in Eisenhower's case. Not well informed on domestic questions, nor blessed with the gift of eloquence, and inexperienced before the television camera, he had much to learn about campaign spellbinding. But his technique improved under coaching, and his audiences liked him for his sincerity, his humanness, his informal presence of folksy ways. They were not too concerned about what his advisers put into his set speeches. In his whistle-stop appearances, when he talked in familiar, if hackneyed, terms about his middle-of-the-road philosophy with Mamie waving at the cheering throngs, he was at his best. He was not a good partisan, he had no grudges, he chose to attack the "administration" rather than Truman, and his Communism, Korea, and corruption lacked personal devils. Yet, while he had trouble acting like a strong party man, he belonged in the Republican Party. Fundamentally, he was a conservative.

Stevenson was a surprising discovery to most Americans. This not very impressive man with a receding hairline and a slightly paunchy middle immediately moved into the front rank of American political orators of all time. He had a good voice, but his speeches read even better than they sounded. He had a gift for the telling phrase, a probing wit, a keen mentality, and a challenging, if troubled, idealism that sometimes emerged in passages of moving eloquence. The intellectuals that had enlisted with FDR in the depression years, but had found themselves pushed aside by the "cronies" under Truman, thronged into the Stevenson camp, for they saw him as one of their own kind. But these "eggheads" were not all gain. In the climate of anti-intellectualism engendered by fears of Communist infiltration and McCarthy accusations, many voters confused loyalty with conformity and suspected men who thought too much. The Wisconsin senator went on the air to smear Stevenson and his personal staff, and Senator Nixon echoed McCarthy that Stevenson had never expressed one word of indignation at Alger Hiss's treachery. Leftists were not to be trusted.

While Ike was a world figure, the Democratic candidate was virtually unknown when nominated. Even at the campaign's end, he was still, to many voters, an uncomfortable type of party leader. He was almost too clever, too witty, too abstruse. Ike's platitudes and homilies, they understood and accepted. More important, the supreme commander of World War II seemed to be better equipped to end the stalemated Korean War.

His master stroke of the campaign, suggested by a shrewd journalist, was the eleventh-hour announcement that, if elected, he would go to Korea in person. Stevenson, carrying the weight of Truman's Korea burdens, could only reply that Moscow, not Seoul, held the key to peace.

The most dramatic development of the campaign involved Nixon, the Republican choice for vice-president. In late September, the *New York Post* featured a story saying that, as senator, he had been subsidized by a secret fund set up by California millionaires. Nixon, then campaigning in the West, admitted that the fund had existed, but asserted that it had been used for purely political expenses and involved him in no obligations to his benefactors. The fund treasurer opened its books, which revealed expenditures of about $18,000 in a year and a half for such expenses as trips to California, printing and mimeographing, and radio and television appearances. The dubious ethics of a public career financed by men of wealth, the size of the fund, and the concealment of its existence seemed to provide the Democrats with an answer to the Republican reiteration of "mink coats" and "deep freezers," symbols of exposures in Washington. Republican newspapers, in alarm, debated whether Nixon should be dropped from the ticket; Eisenhower and his advisers were equally perturbed, but final action was held up until the California senator had offered his defense on television.

That defense saved his public career. Skillfully shifting from the fund issue, where he was vulnerable, to a defense of his reputation for honesty and integrity, he related the history of his personal finances from youth on. It was the story of the honest, poor boy's rise to fame through his own efforts with no ill-gotten gains to smooth his path. His wife (who was with him), her "respectable Republican cloth coat" (not mink), and their children's dog, Checkers, were brought into his affecting story. He invited his listeners to send their opinions to the Republican National Committee, which would decide his case. The result was a deluge of approving messages, and he went East to be greeted by Eisenhower as a man of courage and honor who had been subjected to "a very unfair and vicious attack." "You're my boy," said Ike. Democratic critics called Nixon's performance "ham acting" and "a financial striptease," but he had emerged as a popular hero.

The Republicans kept pounding away at their trinity of Democratic failures: blunders in foreign policy, the "mess" in Washington, the Communist danger within. Other issues were peripheral, but all fitted the slogan, "It's time for a change." As the party of the outs, they could promise much and specify little.

The hard-pressed Democrats had to defend and condone—an admission that all was not well. And so they turned to a weapon that had worked well in the past, and proclaimed that good times would end if the Republicans won. Prosperity and the social gains of the New Deal were in danger. "Don't let them take it away" and "You never had it so good" were their war cries. This was effective enough to cause the Republicans to promise that nothing would be taken away; things would only be made better. For instance, Eisenhower told the Minnesota farmers that they were entitled to 100 percent of parity instead of the Democratic 90 percent, and in New England he promised full employment and an extension of social security.

Public opinion polls indicated an Eisenhower victory, as the trend everywhere was strongly in his favor; but the percentage of undecided was still large enough to hold the balance in many states, and pollsters, after having burned their fingers in 1948, were duly cautious. That Eisenhower seemed to be much stronger than his party was a safe conclusion.

They were too cautious this time. It was an Eisenhower, if not a Republican, landslide. With a total of 442 electoral votes, he had the entire North and West; Virginia, Tennessee, Florida, and Texas in the South; and Maryland and Missouri in the border area. Stevenson, with only 89 electoral votes, carried the rest of the South and Kentucky and West Virginia—9 states in all. Eisenhower had surpassed Truman in 1948 and Roosevelt in 1944 and was 2 votes short of Hoover's total of electors in 1928. He had repeated Hoover's victories in the South, except for North Carolina. His popular vote was 33,936,137 (55.1 percent) to Stevenson's 27,314,649 (44.4 percent). The record total vote was 61,551,118. In contrast to 1948, the minor parties were unimportant.*

The country had voted overwhelmingly for Eisenhower but hesitatingly for his party. His coattails did not carry into office the usual proportion of congressional and local candidates. In the House were 221 Republicans, 213 Democrats, and 1 independent; in the Senate, 48 Republicans, 47 Democrats, and Wayne Morse, Oregon Republican who had bolted and was now an independent. His vote enabled the Republicans to organize the upper house. The defeat of three extreme isolationist senators, and the fact that McCarthy of Wisconsin, Jenner of Indiana, Bricker of Ohio, and Malone of Nevada ran far behind Eisenhower indicated that many independents and Democrats had liked Ike but rejected his party.

Eisenhower's victory was a vote of confidence in the man himself but also in his party's somewhat fictionized picture of him, which assured troubled Americans that he had the answers to all the nation's problems. His appeal was like Harding's return to normalcy. Korean bloodshed, tax burdens, inflation, subversives, corruption—all would yield to the skill of the soldier statesman, and happier days would return.

---

* The older third-party votes were as follows: Vincent Hallinan, Progressive, 140,416; Stuart Hamblen, Prohibition, 73,413; Eric Hass, Socialist Labor (Industrial Government in some states), 30,250; Darlington Hoopes, Socialist, 20,065. Other splinter parties had smaller totals.

XVI

Ike Again

Washington thronged with Republican men and women of distinction when their Homburg-hatted leader—top hats and tail coats were banned —was inaugurated. His idealistic and inspirational address revealed little about policies, but his cabinet choices told more—"eight millionaires and a plumber" was a sardonic characterization. George M. Humphrey, secretary of the treasury, and Charles E. Wilson, secretary of defense, were outstanding examples of the president's reliance upon the business world for administrative talent and guidance. Most of the new appointees had had slight experience in politics, and Secretary Wilson's celebrated remark—"What's good for General Motors is good for the country"— seemed to illustrate their political naïveté. More orthodox were the selections of Herbert Brownell, Jr., of the Dewey inner circle to be attorney general and Arthur Summerfield, national chairman, to be postmaster general. The new secretary of state, John Foster Dulles, long the party's expert on foreign affairs, was a logical appointment.

The president set up an efficient executive staff headed by former Governor Sherman Adams of New Hampshire as presidential assistant. This taciturn Yankee was presently tabbed as one of the most influential figures in the administration. James C. Hagerty, veteran newspaperman, handled press relations. Vice-President Nixon was included in the cabinet group and was especially useful as a party harmonizer and as a good-will ambassador to other lands.

Eisenhower and Congress

Eisenhower's conception of his office followed the pattern of most Republican presidents—cooperation with Congress and a careful regard for its prerogatives. Dynamic leadership was out; teamwork was stressed. This was good political strategy as well, for the suspicious Taft wing, dominating congressional committees, needed to be mollified. An Eisenhower program was still in the formative stage.

This situation and the president's military experience explain his heavy reliance upon staff advisers and administrators. Dulles in foreign affairs, Humphrey in treasury matters, Benson in agriculture, McKay in conservation, and others not only administered but in large measure developed policy. Naturally enough, they—and not their chief—caught the brickbats. His extensive delegation of authority evoked from unfriendly sources a comparison with a constitutional monarch who reigned but did not govern.

The high level of public esteem for Ike owed something at first to editorial friendliness. In sharp contrast with their acid treatment of Truman, news weeklies of large circulation seemed to have rediscovered some long-unused adjectives for syrupy descriptions of the doings of Ike and Mamie. The editorial comments and the columnists of the 80 percent friendly press were more restrained, but even isolationist misgivings over policies usually absolved the president from any blame. And, a few years later, even the criticism of his many hours spent playing golf was gentle.

At his press conferences, though there were moments of constraint and tension at first, Eisenhower soon handled himself with skill and poise. After all, he was hardly a novice in dealing with newspapermen. A notable innovation was the occasional admission of television and newsreel cameramen, though all film was screened by Secretary Hagerty before its release. The president's television technique for nationwide telecasts was made more folksy and relaxed under the direction of actor Robert Montgomery, who became a White House staff member.

Taft, miffed because he had not been consulted about cabinet appointments but determined to have the new administration succeed, assumed the post of Senate leader. Eisenhower's skill as a conciliator and Taft's influence with the Republican right wing operated to keep the majority reasonably harmonious in the first session of Congress. Whether the Eisenhower-Taft alliance could have held up under the stresses and strains of the McCarthy controversies will never be known. Taft died, a cancer victim, on July 31, 1953. His personal selection, William F. Knowland of California, became majority leader. Knowland was not an ideal choice for administration men, but Democratic votes were usually available to make up for Republican defections.

McCarthyism and the Loyalty Question

Many pages could be filled with the doings of Senator McCarthy. His charges of Communism and disloyalty led to a witch hunt, with the resultant guilt by association, blacklists, loyalty oaths, and secret informers.

His investigations of disloyalty in the government, starting with the

State Department, reflected on the vigilance of the Eisenhower administration as well as its predecessors and ultimately brought him into a head-on conflict with Secretary of the Army Robert T. Stevens, who charged that McCarthy and his chief counsel, Roy Cohn, had sought favored treatment for Cohn's assistant, G. David Schine, recently inducted into the army. The nation watched on television screens the Senate investigation of the charges and countercharges. Later, a select committee headed by Senator Arthur Watkins of Utah investigated McCarthy's methods and conduct, and the result was a censure resolution passed by the Senate by a vote of 67 (44 Democrats, 22 Republicans, and one Independent) to 22 (all Republicans). Knowland, majority leader, voted against censure. With the loss of his chairmanship in the new Democratic Senate, McCarthy disappeared from the headlines. The press relegated his intermittent sniping to the inside pages. He died in 1957, completely discredited.

Campaign pledges were carried out by a bill returning the tidelands oil reserves to the states and by some modest tax reductions; but the budget could not be balanced until 1955–1956, and foreign-aid requirements continued high. The most notable administrative achievement was the ending of hostilities in Korea. In Indochina, where the president refused to intervene with armed forces, France yielded the northern provinces to the Communists. Taft Republicans had rejoiced over the "unleashing" of Chiang Kai-shek on Formosa and the subsequent warning by Dulles of American "massive retaliation" against aggressors. But these Republicans presently had to support the administration in following what was virtually a continuation of the Truman-Acheson foreign policy. Isolationists and conservatives had to swallow the defeat of a proposed constitutional amendment, offered by Senator Bricker of Ohio, to restrict the treaty-making powers of the president. Eisenhower was disappointing the extremists, but his popularity was undiminished.

The approaching midterm elections of 1954 forced Republicans of all viewpoints to fall in line behind the president. Maine elected a Democratic governor in September; a mild business recession affected employment in some industrial centers; signs of dissatisfaction with Secretary of Agriculture Benson's farm policy appeared in the western farm belt; and certain local situations seemed to favor the Democrats. To counteract this Democratic swing, the cries of Communism and corruption were revived, and Vice-President Nixon, campaigning in the doubtful states, arraigned the Democratic Party for harboring Communists and subversives. Whether he called the Democratic Party the party of treason was a matter of controversy later, but thereafter he was political enemy number one for loyal Democrats.

Even Eisenhower was drawn into active, last-minute campaigning with peace and prosperity his themes, but the Democrats captured the Senate, 49 to 47, and the House of Representatives, 232 to 203. Seven close states, including New York and Pennsylvania, elected Democratic governors. The voters had slapped down the Republican Party, if not the president.

The Preliminaries of 1956

The aftermath was anything but the "cold war" Eisenhower had predicted if the Democrats controlled Congress. Committee chairmanships went largely to southern conservatives who agreed with his position on most domestic matters. Nearly all the Democrats stood with him on foreign policy where his own party sometimes wavered. His preference for the soft answer over the big stick, and his past annoyance—expressed in private—at the Republican right wing, made it easy for him to work with Senator Lyndon Johnson of Texas, now majority leader, Senator Walter George of Georgia, foreign-affairs chairman, Speaker Rayburn, and others.

The results were creditable: foreign aid on a somewhat reduced scale, a fifty-billion-dollar highway construction program, a liberalization of social security benefits, a soil-bank plan to reduce farm surpluses. Federal aid for school construction lost in the House of Representatives when an antisegregation amendment, added by a Republican-liberal Democratic coalition, caused southern Democrats to join Republicans in opposing the bill. The administration won a victory in the Senate when a bipartisan combination defeated a proposal for a government-financed dam in Hell's Canyon on the Oregon-Idaho border. The president vetoed a bill to exempt natural-gas producers from federal regulation, passed by another bipartisan alliance, when unsavory lobbying activities were exposed.

A Senate investigation discredited and killed the administration's Dixon-Yates contract, a bungling attempt to subsidize a private power company at the expense of the Tennessee Valley Authority. Other investigations produced a few cases of "conflict of interest" by holders of important federal offices—who apparently had synchronized their public and private interests to assist the latter—and an instance of influence-peddling by a former campaign manager of Vice-President Nixon. On the whole, Eisenhower fared well at the hands of the Democratic Congress.

The president's popularity zoomed to new heights after the Big Four summit conference in Geneva in July 1955, which had lessened the tensions of the Cold War. Then Fate intervened. While on a Colorado vacation in September, Eisenhower suffered a heart attack. It was soon evident that he would recover, but his steady improvement still left in doubt his future physical fitness. If he retired, a bitter intraparty conflict would break out and Republican chances for victory might be wrecked. The problem was solved finally in March when, after a favorable report by medical specialists, he announced that he would run again, although he would have to restrict his activities to the primary duties of his office. Republicans all but danced in the streets on the night of his acceptance telecast.

Then, on June 8, came a second blow. The president suffered an attack of ileitis and an emergency operation was necessary. His recovery was fairly rapid, however, and he soon resumed his duties. But the health issue and the importance of Vice-President Nixon were already grist for the Democratic campaign mill.

The situation had its humorous aspects. It was 1944 in reverse. The Republicans now had the indispensable man, and the Democrats were shaking their heads about his uncertain health and his approaching sixty-sixth birthday.

Meanwhile, an unexpected battle for the Democratic nomination—conceded earlier to Adlai Stevenson—began when Senator Kefauver announced that he would contest important primaries. Favorite sons, smelling the possibility of a deadlock, displayed signs of receptivity, with Averell Harriman, elected governor of New York in 1954, the most receptive. A further complication was an upsurge of race antagonism in the deep South over the implementation of the Supreme Court's pronouncement against segregation in the public schools. State sovereignty, next to "Americanism" the last refuge of intolerance, was hauled out, and southern Democratic politicians harked back to John C. Calhoun, its patron saint, to justify their yielding to white-supremacy extremists. In the North, urban Democratic tacticians, long aware of the voting weight of minority groups, took strong antisegregation stands. Governor Harriman spoke their language. Stevenson favored moderation in reaching a solution, and party leaders friendly to him sought to avert a southern bolt. Kefauver refused to sign a manifesto of southern senators against desegregation.

The early primaries did not clear the Democratic picture. Kefauver, past master of the art of personal solicitation, carried New Hampshire and Minnesota. The Minnesota result shocked the Stevenson forces. Their favorite had campaigned in person with Senator Humphrey's backing. Yet the indefatigable Tennessean, by promising more farm relief, shaking more hands, and drawing Republican votes into the Democratic primary (so the Stevenson men charged), had scored an upset victory.

But Minnesota was Kefauver's zenith. New Jersey rejected him for Governor Meyner's slate, and Stevenson, copying his rival's tactics, won in the Florida, California, and Oregon primaries. In states using the convention system the organizations named delegates hostile to Kefauver. On August 1 he acknowledged defeat by withdrawing in favor of Stevenson, though he had bagged 165 delegates.

Worried Stevenson partisans and some more objective commentators sharply criticized the primary system for putting a premium on sales skills and irrelevant personality traits at the expense of statesmanship and national fitness. The shades of the old standpatters of the Progressive Era must have listened with sardonic amusement; but those scarred battlers for the direct primary, Theodore Roosevelt and Bryan, would not have been amused at these revisionist liberals.

Democratic Repeat Performance, 1956

Both parties held their 1956 conventions unusually late. Only the Civil War Democratic convention of 1864 had been later. Air transport, radio, and television had made short, intensive campaigns possible, and early nominations unnecessary and even unwise. A late August convention could come closer to anticipating and expressing the voters' November moods than a June one.

On August 13 Democratic delegates, casting 1,372 votes, assembled in the air-conditioned International Amphitheater at Chicago. The keynote speech by young Governor Frank Clement of Tennessee was a crowd-pleasing performance of alliterative gibes and perfervid denunciations and pleas that ranged from Bryanic heights to the levels of a backwoods camp meeting. Stern-faced Sam Rayburn, House Speaker, took command as permanent chairman on the second day with a more sober attack.

The general expectation that it would be a dull week had already been upset by the early arrival of former President Truman and his announcement on Saturday afternoon that Governor Harriman had his support for the presidential nomination. The wealthy New York governor had become an active candidate some weeks earlier, with Carmine De Sapio, astute head of Tammany, as his strategist. His strong civil rights stand had antagonized the South, but he had corralled some delegates in the mountain states and had Governor Raymond Gary of Oklahoma as his manager. The Truman blessing put new life into his campaign, and Harriman backers proclaimed that Stevenson was stopped.

Most of the favorite-son contingent now became active. Those with pledged delegates included Governors Frank J. Lausche of Ohio, Albert B. ("Happy") Chandler of Kentucky, and G. Mennen ("Soapy") Williams of Michigan, Senators Lyndon Johnson of Texas and Stuart Symington of Missouri, and Representative John McCormack of Massachusetts.

The smoothly running Stevenson organization, headed by a skilled Philadelphia professional, James A. Finnegan, worked to counteract Truman's announcement. Stevenson, feeling, he said ruefully, like a prize Angus bull on exhibit, visited delegation after delegation. Mrs. Franklin D. Roosevelt staunchly supported him with her customary reasoned and temperate arguments, and Truman did not help Harriman by blasting Stevenson as a conservative and a defeatist who lacked fighting qualities and who would carry no more states than in 1952. In a convention talk, Mrs. Roosevelt indirectly struck at the former president by calling for a young, forward-looking leadership and a turning-away from old attitudes and old issues.

Stevenson's lines held firm, and Governors Williams of Michigan and Meyner of New Jersey added their delegations to his total. Most of the candidates had their names presented to give nominators and seconders some platform publicity and to let the demonstrators have some fun, but the battle was over. When the roll call on Thursday reached Pennsylvania, Governor Leader jubilantly announced that its vote was putting Stevenson over the top. The final count gave him 905½ to Harriman's 210, with 7 others dividing the rest of the 1,372 votes.

Then followed a surprising pronouncement from the winner. Coming to the convention platform, he stated that he was leaving the choice of a running mate to the delegates. Important leaders and some of his closest advisers were against such a step. The result was too unpredictable. But it proved to be both shrewd politics and popular. It relieved the candidate of a disagreeable responsibility; it was a demonstration in democracy; and it gave Democrats a chance to taunt the Republicans with the cut-and-dried character of the approaching San Francisco choice of Nixon.

The night of Thursday, August 16, produced some of the wildest politicking in convention annals. A group of promising young bloods, including Senators Hubert Humphrey of Minnesota (a candidate before the convention met), John Kennedy of Massachusetts, Kefauver and Albert Gore of Tennessee, and Mayor Robert Wagner of New York, went the rounds of the delegations pleading for support. On the first ballot on Friday afternoon Kefauver had 483½, Kennedy 304, Gore 178, Wagner 162½, Humphrey 134½. Kefauver, opposed by his own section and by most of the organization leaders elsewhere, had powerful farmer and labor support in the middle and farther West. To stop him, most of the South and the East concentrated on Kennedy, who went into the lead as the second ballot moved along. But last-minute changes from Humphrey and Gore to Kefauver put the lanky Tennessean across. As finally recorded the vote was 755½ to 589. Kennedy then moved that the nomination be made unanimous.

The most surprising feature of the sharp contest had been the large vote given young Kennedy, an Irish Catholic, by southern states. In part it was anti-Kefauver, but it did suggest that the religious barrier to national preferment might not be as insurmountable to a personable, Harvard-educated scion of a wealthy family as it had been to that ex-clerk in a fish market and Tammany politico, Alfred E. Smith.

The platform, adopted before the nominations, did not produce the expected civil rights melee. Representative John McCormack, heading the platform committee, worked tirelessly to preserve harmony. The civil-rights statement in the final draft displeased some southerners who kept silent and some liberals who presented a minority report. A thirty-minute debate, with Truman induced to speak for the majority version, ended in a voice vote upholding it. Chairman Rayburn's gavel cut off a demand for a roll call. Neither extreme had much stomach for an all-out struggle. The losers were talking for home consumption, and the southerners did not want to bolt.

The civil rights plank promised to continue efforts to eradicate discriminations of all kinds. It recognized the importance of recent decisions of the Supreme Court on segregation and accepted them as the law of the land, but rejected "all proposals for the use of force to interfere with the orderly determination of these matters by the courts." There was no pledge to implement desegregation.

The rest of the 12,000-word platform attacked, deplored, and viewed with alarm the Eisenhower policies. It charged that the administration had injured America's standing with other nations, fraternized with the Communists, increased the risk of war, and weakened national defense. It had failed to provide adequately for farmers, small business, low-income workers, and the elderly. The long farm plank offered 90 percent price supports on basic crops as opposed to the Benson flexible plan, and suggested a number of measures to handle the problem of surpluses. Labor was promised the repeal of the Taft-Hartley Act and a minimum wage of $1.25 an hour; and state right-to-work laws were opposed. Tax reduction for people with small incomes and a $200 increase in income-tax exemption, a balanced budget, better protection and conservation of natural resources, and government plants for the production of atomic power were other major stipulations.

Republican Repeat Performance, 1956

Vice-President Nixon announced late in April that he would seek a renomination. He had refused the president's offer of a cabinet post as an alternative, and support in the party seemed to assure him an uncontested nomination. Four weeks before the national convention was to meet, Harold Stassen, now disarmament adviser to the president, announced at a news conference that Nixon's name on the ticket would reduce the Eisenhower vote some 6 percent—he had done some polling—and that Governor Christian A. Herter of Massachusetts would make a stronger candidate. This startling pronouncement was made with the knowledge, but not the approval, of the president, who assumed a hands-off attitude. Soon afterward it was reported that Herter had agreed to place Nixon in nomination.

Stassen insisted that Herter could be drafted, and took a month's leave of absence from his office to head an Eisenhower-Herter movement. Pledges of support for Nixon and denunciations of Stassen by party leaders, big and little, and the hostility of the Republican press soon made it evident that his cause had slight support. If any prominent Republicans sympathized with him, they did not dare to reveal it, for he was being branded a traitor to his party.

The Republican national convention met in San Francisco's Cow Palace, August 20–23. Delegates and visitors were there to enjoy themselves, for all the business of the convention was prearranged and, except for the Stassen flurry, there was not merely harmony but unanimity. The television watchers, consequently, found little to interest them. Governor Arthur B. Langlie of Washington gave the keynote address, a sober pointing-with-pride presentation—"We have come a long way in a short time." Senator Knowland, temporary chairman, and former Speaker Martin, permanent chairman, hammered harder at the Democrats, but the angry vehemence of 1952 was missing. General MacArthur and Senator McCarthy were conspicuously absent. Dewey, booed in his seat four years ago, now had a speaking role and was warmly received, even by old enemies. One veteran reappeared—for the seventh time. Herbert Hoover, though still warning against dangers to personal liberty, was more optimistic and mellower than in the past and drew an impressive ten-minute tribute.

Seventeen candidates for Senate and House from close states, fourteen women speakers—carefully rehearsed and timed beforehand—and paid entertainers tried to hold the attention of the delegates when headliners were not performing. Organized squads of Young Republicans, imported from all parts of the country, provided numbers and snake dances whenever needed, both inside and outside the convention. California hospitality took care of the evenings, as there were no night sessions. Governor Goodwin Knight's "champagne supper" for eleven thousand invited "guests" amazed even veteran journalists.

The Stassen insurrection against Nixon provided materials for news stories and television interviews, but was kept alive only by the remote possibility that Eisenhower might yet proclaim a "free-for-all" on the vice-presidential choice. Without endorsing Nixon, he had expressed himself as "delighted" if the convention should renominate him. Governor Knight of California was reportedly opposed to the vice-president; Governor Theodore McKeldin of Maryland and one or two others were mentioned as possible candidates; and Nixon himself declared for an open convention and canvassed the various state delegations. But the temper of the delegates was shown by threats that Stassen would be denied unanimous consent to address the convention, since he was not a delegate, and by reports that a walk-out might occur if he appeared. He was even booed by Young Republicans during a television interview. President Eisenhower, who arrived Tuesday night, refused to change his position, and next morning announced in a televised press conference that Stassen had decided to support Nixon and would even second his nomination.

Stassen's capitulation made the nominating session a formality. Representative Charles A. Halleck of Indiana nominated Eisenhower, and Governor Herter presented Nixon's name. Eight seconding speakers followed Halleck, and six, Herter. A Nebraska delegate tried to nominate "Joe Smith" for the vice-presidency, but the chairman had the sergeants-at-arms escort him from the convention. He insisted later that his fictitious character was "a symbol of a wide-open convention," but Joe Smith got no votes. This was the only bit of unplanned business during the entire convention, and the press at least welcomed it.

At the final session on Thursday, decorous unanimity turned into a tumultuous welcome for the nominees, with parading delegates jamming the aisles and a barrage of Ike and Dick balloons let loose overhead. In his acceptance speech, Eisenhower called the Republican Party the party of the future, "of long-range principle, not short-term expediency," and he used the broad policies of his administration to prove his case. The tone of the address was idealistic, middle of the road, optimistic, as he lifted examples and quotations from one hundred years of Republican Party history. His ideas were in accord with those of a recent book, A *Republican Looks at His Party*, by Arthur Larson, undersecretary of labor, who had upheld the thesis of Republican progressivism, now called "new Republicanism."

The platform, presented by Senator Prescott Bush of Connecticut, chairman of the resolutions committee, had been adopted before the nominations by a unanimous vote. It was even longer than the Democratic declaration, but not unlike it in many of its positive commitments. On the touchy farm problem, the Republican plank upheld the administration's "versatile flexible program" and promised continued efforts to help farmers get full parity. The Democrats had offered rigid price supports at 90 percent of parity. On civil rights the Republicans went a little further than their opponents in accepting the Supreme Court decision for desegregation in the schools and favoring "all deliberate speed" in carrying it out, but opposing the use of force. The Republican platform also declared for tax reductions (the budget permitting); development of natural resources through partnership agreements between the federal government and lesser agencies; revision and improvement of the Taft-Hartley Act; a strong national defense that already had "the strongest striking force in the world"; and a federal aid program for schools.

The foreign policy plank credited the administration with reducing the threat of global war and checking the advance of Communism. It favored collective security, a strong United Nations, aid for underdeveloped countries, and other features of the Eisenhower-Dulles program. It made no concessions to isolationist sentiment. The president's acceptance speech was even stronger. He called it "madness" to suppose that the United States could be "an island of tranquillity" in a "sea of wretchedness and frustration." He even held out the hope of a peaceful coexistence with a more conciliatory Communist world, a far cry from the plank of 1952 denouncing the "immoral policy of containment."

Minor parties—some seventeen with eleven separate tickets, according to the *New York Times*—struggled for places on the ballot; but only one caused more than a ripple of interest. A States Rights gathering nominated T. Coleman Andrews, formerly President Eisenhower's commissioner of internal revenue and a sharp critic of the income tax. Former Republican Representative Thomas H. Werdel of California was his running mate. A Constitution Party and a For America Party also backed them. This ticket represented a protest movement against both major parties by extreme conservatives, isolationists, segregationists, and state-rights reactionaries. There was a remote possibility that it might draw enough votes in one or two southern states to hold the balance of power. The older third parties had their candidates at the starting gate as usual but, as usual, they were left at the post.

Ike Versus Issues

Stevenson appointed James A. Finnegan, his preconvention strategist, as his campaign manager, with Paul Butler continuing as chairman of the national committee. A separate organization, the Volunteers for Stevenson-Kefauver, was designed to operate outside the party fence. It tapped the enthusiasm and energy of the younger voters.

In early September the Democratic nominees attended a series of regional meetings with party leaders and state and local candidates to coordinate the different levels of the campaign. To offset the personal popularity of Eisenhower, Stevenson needed to activate party loyalties and to make common cause with strong local vote-getters—coattails in reverse, it was dubbed. Nine eastern and middle western states had elected Democratic governors since 1952. Their aid and the voting pull of popular candidates for the Senate might swing close states. Kefauver was to center his efforts in the western farm belt, where he had never lost a primary, and where the rural voters liked his homespun personality. After joining with Stevenson in the television opening of the campaign in Harrisburg, Pennsylvania, he embarked on his canvass of the common man.

The Democratic campaign was given a sudden lift on September 10 when traditionally Republican Maine reelected its popular Democratic governor Edmund S. Muskie, and for the first time in twenty-two years sent a Democrat to Congress from one of its three districts. Maine had been an uncertain barometer in past presidential elections, but the size of the Democratic victory there could not be overlooked in the crystal balls of the forecasters.

Stevenson set out to show himself to as many voters and to shake as many hands as possible. He directed his talks at ordinary folk, ever suspicious of highbrow candidates with flashing rapiers. Consequently, he was less witty, more down-to-earth than in 1952. Major addresses were televised. From friendly quarters came occasional expressions of disappointment that he was not projecting his speeches well, that his perfectionist concern with the text did not include its delivery, which sometimes left the impression that he was still pondering over his sentences. His technique improved toward the end, but his appeal was rational, not emotional. Yet he had attracted a devoted personal following centering in the Volunteers for Stevenson, who too often had to take over registration drives, circulation of campaign literature, telephone canvassing, and other tasks when party organizations were dragging their feet or pushing only local candidates.

The Republican campaign, directed by Leonard W. Hall, national chairman since 1953, was planned to start late, use Nixon for heavy barnstorming, and call upon Eisenhower only for a token trip or two to demonstrate his physical fitness. But the Maine outcome, the early burst of Democratic energy, disaffection in the Republican farm belt, and pleas for the use of his coattails by hard-pressed senatorial candidates—several of them his personal selections—drew the president into making some half a dozen forays that reached nearly all of the key states. But for the Near East crisis, he would have spent most of the final week on the trail. He drew larger crowds than Stevenson and helped mightily to restore party morale.

The Republican appeal added peace and prosperity to "We Like Ike." The administration had ended the Korean War and had stabilized prosperity without war and inflation. "America is happier than it was four years ago," said Eisenhower again and again, and crowd responses to his smiling face and confident voice made his discussion of issues almost a waste of time.

The Democrats answered that the prosperity was inherited, that Stalin's death had made possible the Korean truce, that Democrats in Congress had done more for Ike than his own party. Stevenson tried to draw his opponent into debates on specific policies but had only limited success. His problem was to find vote-getting issues and to break through Nixon, Dulles, Benson, and the rest of the White House cordon to battle with the chief himself. Foreign policy, farm problems, national defense, conservation, aid for public schools, and the broader questions of Eisenhower's past conception of his office and his fitness for future leadership, with Vice-President Nixon's role a major consideration, all were legitimate subjects for party debate, but the Democratic candidate could not stir a complacent electorate. Attacks on the Dulles foreign policy were shrugged off so long as the nation was at peace. Farmers were dissatisfied but, outside certain western drought areas, not distressed, and the Democratic offer of 90 percent parity was viewed with mixed feelings, even by the considerable number who disliked Secretary Benson's flexible price supports and his soil conservation plan.

Stevenson threw national defense into the campaign hopper by suggesting the possibility of an end to the draft system, and later by proposing that the United States offer to join with Russia in stopping hydrogen bomb tests. Both propositions met with Republican charges that they would weaken national defense, and Eisenhower's stand carried special weight here, though the proposed ban on bomb tests did provoke discussion and disagreement among scientists as to the health hazards involved in repeated testing.

"Giveaway" charges leveled at the administration's partnership policy toward power projects had some effect in the Pacific Northwest and entered into the defeat of former Secretary of the Interior Douglas McKay by Senator Wayne Morse for the Senate seat from Oregon. The fact that in Congress a number of Democrats had voted with Republicans on school-aid and natural-gas regulation bills made it difficult for Stevenson to use these issues, about which few of his listeners were well informed or felt much concern, in any case.

The Democratic candidate put the greatest emphasis on the failure of Eisenhower to provide strong leadership. The president, he charged, "has never had the inclination and now lacks the energy for full-time work at the world's toughest job." A man whose age and state of health were serious voter considerations became a more doubtful risk, Democrats argued, when the Republican vice-presidential choice was evaluated. Kefauver was expected to carry more than his weight; Nixon less than his. No Republican name called forth such roars of boos at Democratic rallies. The "hatchet man" tactics of past campaigns and his popularity with right-wing Republicans made "this man of many masks" (Stevenson's characterization) the one personal devil all Democrats could assail.

The vice-president's answer was to conduct a campaign to sell a "new Nixon." His speeches dealt with the accomplishments of the administration—"the best four years of our lives"—and the commanding stature of the president. Skillfully intermingling statistics with praise and pleas, he answered Democratic charges by comparing the records of Eisenhower and Truman, and the merits of Ike and Adlai. The slashing partisanship of 1952 and 1954 was missing, and personal attacks upon him were not answered in kind. While he disappointed the McCarthy following by ignoring the Communist issue, the new Nixon filled more effectively the role of the second in command. His strenuous barnstorming—42,000 miles —was a model of efficient management. He consulted with local leaders, eulogized local candidates, fitted his remarks to his audiences, and was especially effective in appealing to women and young voters. At his side was Mrs. Pat Nixon with an appeal of her own. Yet, to the end of the campaign, Democrats saw only the horns of the old Nixon.

One issue was not emphasized on the national level—segregation in the schools. Eisenhower insisted that it made no difference whether or not he endorsed the Supreme Court decision, that the question must be handled on a state and local basis, that his record in the army and as president spoke for itself. Stevenson upheld the Supreme Court but agreed with his party's platform in rejecting the use of force to interfere with the orderly determination of such matters by the courts. Senator Eastland of Mississippi, an active segregationist and chairman of the Senate Judiciary Committee, was an embarrassment to northern Democrats, for Republicans charged that he would block all civil-rights legislation with the support of other southern Democrats. Congressman Adam Clayton Powell, Jr., of New York, a black Democratic leader, after an interview with the president, announced that he was supporting him. Several black newspapers and a number of prominent professional people were reported as turning to the Republicans.

Organized labor—now the united AFL–CIO—through its executive council voted to endorse Stevenson, although eight of the twenty-two members were against any endorsements. Walter Reuther, head of the United Automobile Workers, led the Stevenson forces and was the most active labor leader in the campaign, both for the national ticket and for other candidates. In states where labor endorsed senatorial or gubernatorial candidates, as in Michigan and the Pacific Northwest, doorbell ringing by union workers increased Democratic registration and ensured a heavy vote.

Secretary of Labor James P. Mitchell, popular in labor circles, worked strenuously to convince the rank and file that the administration was friendly to labor and that southern Democrats would, if Congress were Democratic, block prolabor and social welfare measures. The peace-prosperity theme was used in urging workingpeople to discard their old distrust of the Republican Party.

With no burning issues to stir a complacent electorate, Stevenson and Kefauver could not overlook the old battle cry that the Republicans favored big business, the Democrats were for the little people. "It is time to take the government away from General Motors and give it back to Joe Smith," declared Stevenson. Eisenhower defended his appointees from the business world as men who had demonstrated administrative fitness. His party, he said, supported social welfare measures but would do for the people only what they could not well do for themselves; the Democrats would guide and direct from Washington.

In the final two weeks of this lethargic contest American voters were shaken out of their complacency by the news of a bloody revolt against Communism in Hungary, which required Russian tanks to suppress, and an Israeli invasion of Egypt, followed immediately by Anglo-French military intervention at the Suez Canal. The American government supported the United Nations in condemning aggression in both areas, and this course did not draw direct partisan fire. But Stevenson, who had been attacking the Dulles "brinkmanship" policy for its failure to checkmate Communism, its lack of direction, its rose-tinted view of the world's problems, now saw in these eruptions "the total bankruptcy of the administration's foreign policy," "The NATO alliance is crumbling," he charged. "The Middle East is in shambles." Communism had benefited, he said, and the United States had been cut off from its old friends.

Eisenhower, in the one speech he made after the Suez crisis, discussed only the broad principles of American policies. He said that he was undisturbed by "the strident voices of those who seem to be seeking to turn world events to political profit"—his only reference to his critic. The election was too near for these explosions abroad to have much effect on the voters. Their minds were already made up.

Eisenhower Reelected

The first returns on the night of November 6 pointed to an Eisenhower victory that soon became an avalanche surpassed only by the Roosevelt sweep of 1936. The president polled 457 electoral votes and 35,585,245 popular votes to Stevenson's 73 and 26,030,172.* One electoral vote went to Judge Walter B. Jones of Alabama from an Alabama elector who violated his party pledge.

Of the Eisenhower states of 1952, only Missouri shifted to Stevenson; but Kentucky, West Virginia, and Louisiana left the Democratic column, which consisted of only North Carolina, South Carolina, Georgia, Alabama, Mississippi, Arkansas, and Missouri. The explanation was simple. The nation voted its confidence in an experienced leader whose administration had a peace-and-prosperity record, whose middle-of-the-road policies fitted the mood of the American people, and whose services, despite his age, seemed indispensable with external dangers mounting. Generally, except in the western farm belt and California, his margins were larger

* Minor parties polled 409,955 votes, three-fourths of the total going to various state-rights tickets.

than in 1952. His best showings were in the urban East, where foreign problems mattered most, and in the South, where apparently a shift of Negro voters swelled his totals.

Nevertheless, the nation elected a Democratic Congress, the Senate 49 to 47, the House 234 to 201. Why Eisenhower's coattails pulled so badly was hard to understand in view of his pleas and his party's well-filled coffers. It was conjectured that party lines had come to mean little, that voters were picking candidates on their merits or personalities. One might more logically argue that Democrats had come to outnumber Republicans, that they tended to vote for party candidates for Congress and state offices, but that large numbers liked Ike and voted for him in spite of his party.

Viewed in its immediate aftermath, the election, then, was actually a vote for a bipartisan administration—a perplexing verdict for believers in party or parliamentary government. The voters wanted peace and prosperity continued, and this was their solution. They trusted Eisenhower to preserve the one, the Democrats to safeguard the other. In 1956 this seemed to make sense.

Congress became more Democratic as a result of the midterm elections of 1958. A sharp business recession, farmer disapproval of Secretary of Agriculture Benson's policies, and Republican sponsorship of antiunion, right-to-work laws in several states were factors in what was a near-debacle. Two Republicans withstood the Democratic sweep. Liberal, personable Nelson Rockefeller was elected governor of New York, and outspoken Senator Barry Goldwater, right-wing Republican, was reelected from Arizona.

The civil rights issue was moving to the center of the stage. Negro organizations began to use economic boycotts, sit-in demonstrations, and other passive resistance tactics with some success to end discrimination in public transportation facilities and business places. Two civil rights acts of Congress did not greatly alter the voting situation in the South. President Eisenhower used federal troops in 1957 in Little Rock, Arkansas, to enforce school desegregation when Governor Orval E. Faubus attempted to block Negro enrollment in a public high school. The question of school desegregation continued as the 1960 election approached.

XVII

The Kennedys Take Over

THE PRESIDENTIAL SWEEPSTAKES on the Democratic track had four strong contenders, with entries expected from the usual number of favorite sons. Strangely enough, all four were members of the Senate. Democratic governors, with New York now Republican, were overshadowed by senatorial aspirants in a period of grave national problems.

Majority leader Lyndon B. Johnson of Texas had been as successful in managing his badly divided, sectionally minded following as any of his predecessors and, if congressional support could have nominated, would have won handily. But he could not escape the deadly embrace of the conservative segregationist South, even though civil rights legislation had had his strong backing. Nor was his Texas upbringing an asset. Even with Speaker Sam Rayburn's support, Johnson's candidacy seemed to present a typical Texas image with its oil politicos, ten-gallon hats, and beautiful girls chanting "All the Way with LBJ." Johnson's formal entry came late, after the primaries had been held. But he was the strongest southern Democratic candidate since antebellum days and in a deadlocked convention might draw heavy second-choice support.

Hubert Humphrey, for twelve years the voice of farmer-labor Minnesota, suited the liberals in his votes and speeches, but was a little too left-of-center and too much the representative of his section to appeal to the large-state leaders. Humphrey was an able debater, and his rapid-fire fluency appeared to advantage on the stump. Hampered by lack of funds, he still had to make a strong showing in the primaries to shorten the long-shot odds against him. Probably he was more nearly Stevenson's heir than any of his rivals, and had hopes that a liberal coalition might look in his direction if the balloting was prolonged.

Stuart Symington of Missouri had left a successful business career during the war to take high administrative office, then had won election to the Senate, where he became a leading authority on national defense. His general record was satisfactory to almost every segment of the party outside the South, but his rather colorless personality lacked voter appeal, and his reputation was confined chiefly to Washington and Missouri. He was a good compromise solution. He had Truman's endorsement.

John F. Kennedy, reelected to the Senate from Massachusetts in 1958 by a landslide, had more assets and heavier liabilities than any of his rivals. Son of Joseph P. Kennedy, Roosevelt's isolationist ambassador to England before World War II, he had on the credit side a keen mind, family wealth, good looks, a Harvard education, a record of heroism as a naval officer in the war, authorship of a best-seller biography, *Profiles in Courage* (1957), and a very attractive young wife and small daughter. During his Massachusetts battles he had drawn to him a young and very able group of organizers headed by his brother Robert. Also, the devoted Kennedy family was a host in itself. The senator's mother (daughter of John F. Fitzgerald, once a Boston mayor and congressman), his two brothers and three sisters, and the in-law contingent were active wherever their services could be used. The elder Kennedy preferred to remain in the background where his millions and presumably conservative views would not embarrass his son. The candidate's wife, Jacqueline Bouvier Kennedy, also was not on political display. A second child expected in the fall was reason enough.

But a heavy liability, which had been an asset in his rise in Massachusetts politics, was Kennedy's Roman Catholic religion. Even his coreligionists among party leaders were not convinced that a Catholic, even if nominated, could be elected. Against Kennedy also was his comparative youth—he was approaching forty-three—his lack of administrative experience, and a not particularly outstanding record in Congress, although it was acceptable to labor and liberal groups. There was also some question as to whether he had sufficiently recovered from a back injury and operations to correct it to undertake the burdens of campaigning. A story was even circulated that he was a victim of Addison's disease.

Kennedy necessarily had to take the primary route to show that he had the qualifications of a winner. In a few instances favorite sons were accepted as Kennedy stand-ins. Only Humphrey chose to contest with him.

Early Primaries

New Hampshire's primary came first. Kennedy had no opposition, but was complimented by a large vote. Wisconsin, in Humphrey's territory but with a large Catholic population, voted next. The result was indecisive. Kennedy had six of the ten districts, and led on the statewide vote, but it was charged that Catholic Republicans had crossed over to vote in the Democratic primary for him. West Virginia was a better test of his strength. It lay on the edge of the Bible Belt, where anti-Catholic prejudice was strong. Kennedy met the issue head-on and won by a wide margin. Superior organization and use of television, and the necessary funds for both, played an important part in selling the Harvard candidate. Humphrey's withdrawal followed his defeat. The remaining primaries, largely uncontested except for Senator Wayne Morse's candidacy in Oregon and Maryland, gave the Kennedy cause a momentum that weakened the neutrality of the uncommitted large states.

If either Adlai Stevenson or Estes Kefauver had waited until 1960 for his second run, Kennedy would have found the primary road a difficult one. Stevenson was still not entirely out of the picture. His devoted following talked of a Stevenson-Kennedy ticket as the ideal solution. He was out of the country for several weeks during the preconvention struggle and kept out of the battle for delegates. On his return he refused to endorse any candidate, and a movement to draft him showed signs of life. It had a good deal of support in California, but it was fragmentary elsewhere, although Gallup polls rated him second only to Kennedy as a popular choice.

The tide was running strongly for Kennedy when the delegates assembled in the new Sports Arena in Los Angeles on July 11. All the candidates were present and were expected to visit and display their talents to state caucuses, much like bathing-beauty contestants. Large-state leaders from New York, Illinois, and Pennsylvania, however, committed their states to Kennedy before the first session. Governor Edmund G. Brown of California could not overcome strong Stevenson support, and his delegation was badly divided. The Kennedy board of strategy had a superb organization with helpful information compiled on every delegate. Robert Kennedy was his brother's manager, but he had a veritable army of operatives.

The first national convention in Los Angeles history departed from tradition by beginning its sessions in late afternoon to suit the convenience of eastern viewers. At 7:15 P.M., eastern time, Chairman Paul Butler rapped for order and introduced Archbishop Francis Cardinal McIntyre, who gave the invocation. Thereafter the convention went the noisy, inattentive way of so many of its predecessors. Youthful-looking Senator Frank Church of Idaho sounded the keynote with a recital of the derelictions of the Republican "tranquillizing" administration. Genial Governor LeRoy Collins of Florida took over as permanent chairman next day and had his difficulties. Speaker Sam Rayburn had preferred to lead the Lyndon Johnson supporters instead of presiding.

Two speakers held the attention of the convention and the TV listeners. Senator Eugene McCarthy of Minnesota, in nominating Adlai Stevenson, made a brilliant and impassioned appeal for the idol of the liberal wing. Mrs. Eleanor Roosevelt was accorded a great ovation on her convention appearance and was listened to with the respect due her attainments. The rest of the oratory was largely wasted. Delegates and outsiders milled in the aisles, and television interviews added to the confusion on the floor.

Stevenson was the local crowd favorite. An endless chain of Stevenson paraders marched outside the convention hall, and his loyal following ruled the galleries. Their hero was almost mobbed by his admirers on the second day when he entered the hall and attempted to reach a seat with his delegation. Next day his supporters, after his name was presented for the nomination, again staged a wild demonstration, but the paraders in the aisles included few delegates, and much of the noise came from upstairs. By various maneuvers, his local retainers had acquired a disproportionate share of admission tickets, not the first time gallery-packing had occurred. But this sound and fury did not signify votes.

The platform as presented by Chairman Chester Bowles of Connecticut had been long in preparation. Preliminary work by the Advisory Council to the Democratic National Committee, appointed in 1956, was followed by hearings for interested groups in different parts of the country. The convention viewed a film showing how this was done. In the platform committee, the civil rights issue had produced a sharp division between the liberal majority and a southern minority. Outvoted 66 to 24 in the committee, the minority carried the fight to the floor of the convention, but were defeated by a voice vote after a rather mild debate.

The civil rights plank was a declaration for "equal access for all Americans to all areas of community life, including voting booths, schoolrooms, jobs, housing, and public facilities." It called for federal action to ensure the right to vote and favored a federal Fair Employment Practices Commission to end job discrimination. The South was asked to achieve "first step compliance" with school desegregation by 1963. Black Congressman Adam Clayton Powell of New York approved the plank, but angry southern spokesmen said that it would lose the party most of the South.

The "Rights of Man" sections called for a broad program of public-welfare measures to bring about full employment, decent living for the farmer through price supports of 90 percent of parity, an expanded federal housing program, and medical care for the aged based on the social security system. The Eisenhower administration was charged with failure to promote the growth of the national economy and with an exaggerated concern over balancing the budget.

On foreign policy the Democrats promised more vigorous action along all lines, coupled with a diversified national defense program sufficient in quantity and quality to deter aggressions, both limited and general.

Nominating speeches were scheduled for the third day. Two favorite sons, Governor Herschell C. Loveless of Iowa and Governor George Docking of Kansas, yielded to Kennedy persuasion, but Governor Meyner of New Jersey held out. Nine candidates were put in nomination. After the usual demonstrations, supposed to be limited to ten minutes but running far over, the balloting began. When Wyoming was reached, Kennedy needed 11 votes for a majority. That state then provided 15. The official roll call showed Kennedy had 806, Johnson 409, Symington 86,

Stevenson 79½, others 140½. Missouri's Governor James Blair moved that Kennedy be nominated by acclamation, and this was done.

Failure of a first-ballot nomination might have been serious for Kennedy. Several states, voting under the unit rule,were held by thin margins. A few defections might have stalled the streamroller.

The big surprise of the convention came next day when Kennedy announced that Lyndon Johnson was his choice for running mate. Negotiations in the night had done the work. Liberals of the Americans for Democratic Action (ADA) protested that Johnson was too conservative and would cost the party labor and black votes. Many middle westerners were disappointed. They had expected a Protestant from the farm belt to balance the ticket. Symington would have suited both groups.

But the Kennedys were realists and saw that Johnson could do more than any other man to hold the wavering South in line. Hard-headed northern party leaders also saw the light. Southern die-hards from the lower South, angry over the civil rights plank, were upset at Johnson's acceptance. Why the latter chose to give up his vote for a gavel—which he had said he would never do—occasioned much comment and conjecture. Apparently the honor associated with the second highest office, where he might still exercise influence without the heavy burdens of floor leadership, was more appealing than he had realized earlier. And most commentators seemed to have forgotten that no candidate with a real chance for first place would admit beforehand that he would settle for second.

The opposition could find no one willing to come out against Kennedy's choice. After a nominating speech by Governor David Lawrence of Pennsylvania and enough seconding speeches to present a picture of unanimity, Johnson was nominated by acclamation, although a good many noes were ignored by the chairman.

The Friday acceptance ceremonies, held in the Los Angeles Coliseum, overflowed with harmony and good will. Kennedy reached a high note of idealism when he called upon Americans to conquer the "New Frontier" of the 1960s, "with its unknown opportunities and perils . . . It sums up not what I intend to offer to the American people but what I intend to ask of them."

Nixon in Charge

In spite of the Democratic sweep of 1958, Republicans remained hopeful about 1960. A presidential election has different conditioning factors, as both Truman in 1948 and Eisenhower in 1956 had shown, following party midterm reverses. The country still liked Ike, if not Ike's party, and the potency of his victory magic might save the White House for his heir apparent, although both houses of Congress would almost certainly be Democratic. Then, too, there was a fair prospect that the Democratic convention would concoct such a bitter brew out of religious differences, liberal-conservative feuding, desegregation, personal ambitions, and sectional differences that the party would defeat itself.

The one bright spot in the Republican picture in 1958, the victory of Nelson A. Rockefeller as governor of New York, had created an unexpected problem for Nixon. Here was a possible rival for the nomination. The Rockefeller family had long since lived down the robber-baron reputation of its Standard Oil progenitor and was respected for its leadership in the business world and its philanthropic interests. The New York governor had served in various capacities under three presidents, was especially concerned about international problems, and had left Washington in 1956 both because he was unhappy over the direction of administration policies, as was indicated by his later public pronouncements, and because he was not making headway in politics. He had surprised the New York party regulars by taking the gubernatorial nomination away from former National Chairman Leonard Hall, and then defeating Governor Harriman by an impressive margin. He had much to recommend him —an engaging personality, a handsome profile, a familiar name, a grasp of public affairs, financial independence, and demonstrated organizing ability.

Rockefeller added to his reputation by his early accomplishments as governor. He was clearly a man with a future in national politics. Presently he set up an organization to sound out party sentiment and measure his chances as a presidential aspirant. He also made trips to different parts of the country to see for himself. The results were not encouraging. People were interested in meeting him, but the delegates were another matter. The resurgent Taft regulars could not stomach his internationalist outlook and his domestic liberalism, and the Eisenhower men were satisfied with Nixon. To enter the primaries would place the challenger in the role of critic of the administration, and win few delegates. And so Rockefeller announced, late in 1959, that he would not be a candidate, without, however, endorsing Nixon. This oversight occasioned a good deal of comment. Was the door left ajar for a draft?

The vice-president, with Leonard Hall directing his forces, might have relished a battle for the nomination. It would have meant an easy victory with plenty of favorable publicity. With the Rockefeller threat removed, however, the proper strategy was to favor the New Yorker for second place. This would ensure harmony and a balanced ticket. But the lesser post had no appeal for the governor. He not only declined to be considered, but also countered, early in June, a time of growing international tensions, with an amazing statement. It criticized the party leadership and the "leading candidate" for not offering a definite program, in view of the serious problems confronting the nation, and proposed, under nine headings, courses of action that covered every major aspect of national policy.

The immediate effect of this insurgent outburst was a belated draft-Rockefeller movement. It stirred up a flurry of letters, telegrams, and columnist comments, but not much more. For the national convention to ignore his program was another matter, however, particularly if he chose to fight.

Charles H. Percy, a Chicago businessman of middle-of-the-road views, had been working for months as chairman of a committee to devise a forward-looking program, and he was accorded the honor of heading the Republican convention's platform committee. It began operations a week ahead of the national convention, had a White House draft to guide it, and worked out a set of statements that tried to embrace enough of the Rockefeller position to prevent a fight.

The governor was not satisfied and said so publicly. Nixon then took the initiative. He arranged for a secret meeting in New York where the two men ironed out their differences. He honestly did not believe they were very far apart. He had tempered his views in the interest of party harmony and loyalty to Eisenhower, and may have welcomed the opportunity to clarify his position. But the result seemed to be a surrender, on his part, on basic points, particularly civil rights and national defense. When the members of the platform committee, which was predominantly conservative, learned of this cavalier treatment of their labored handiwork, they vented their indignation in cries of "dictatorship" and "Munich surrender," and threatened to ignore the terms of the Nixon-Rockefeller compact. But the vice-president, arriving in Chicago on Monday, by using both diplomacy and pressure, won a majority of the committee to his position on the all-important civil rights plank and secured a national defense statement that was acceptable to both Rockefeller and Eisenhower. This averted a bitter convention battle that might have left its mark in November.

The Republican Convention

The twenty-seventh Republican convention opened in the Chicago International Amphitheater on Monday, July 25, with National Chairman Thruston Morton, wielding the gavel. Proceedings went strictly according to script. Mindful of the roving television eye, the managers saw to it that delegates behaved and listened, and camp followers did not clutter up the aisles. With its decisions preordained, the convention became a series of pep rallies with the pep ebbing out, as repetitious and generally dull speakers used up their allotted time.

At the Monday evening session ex-President Hoover humorously made his customary farewell speech, and Senator Goldwater, a convention favorite, was warmly received. Representative Walter Judd of Minnesota, a veteran of the lecture platform, made the keynote speech. It was a rabble-rousing recital of past Democratic misdeeds of foreign policy with the audience roaring approval at each stab. Representative Charles Halleck of Indiana took over as permanent chairman on the second day, which was highlighted by President Eisenhower's appearance. He was given a great ovation, and responded with a review and defense of his administration.

The convention performed its important functions on Wednesday. The platform was presented with a film accompaniment, as in the case of the Democrats. It was adopted unanimously.

The controversial civil rights plank was a little more general than the Democratic statement, omitting any mention of a fair employment practices commission, but was satisfactory to the Rockefeller liberals and angered the helpless southerners. The platform walked a tightrope on defense. It claimed that America was the world's strongest military power, but added that expanded production and new defense efforts might be needed. In dealing with domestic problems, the party conceded that the pace of economic growth must be quickened, but insisted that the private sector of the economy must be chiefly responsible. The farm plank made general promises without commitments as to price-support levels.

The central theme of the Republican document was the danger of Communist imperialism and the need for responsible and mature leadership to meet it. The Eisenhower administration had provided such leadership, and Nixon would continue it. The vice-presidential candidate was Henry Cabot Lodge of Massachusetts.

The Campaign of the Great TV Debates

Senator Henry Jackson of Washington succeeded Paul Butler as Democratic national chairman, but the young Kennedy organization, much expanded, planned and directed the strategy. Lawrence F. O'Brien, chief Kennedy organizer in Massachusetts and in the primary states, became director of organization for the national committee. Byron ("Whizzer") White of Colorado, a past football all-star, looked after the National Citizens for Kennedy-Johnson, designed to operate outside the party lines. Closest to the candidate was his manager and brother, Robert F. Kennedy. Pierre Salinger, press secretary, Kenneth P. O'Donnell, in charge of scheduling, Theodore C. Sorensen, policy adviser and brain-trust director, and Louis Harris, chief pollster, were other key figures. A squad of Harvard professors headed by Archibald F. Cox supplied materials for speeches, and made suggestions on policies.

The candidate, delayed by the fruitless summer session of Congress, took to the hustings on September 2 and opened the campaign formally in Detroit on Labor Day, September 5. Thereafter his jet plane carried him on a carefully planned but exhausting campaign that overlooked no section of the nation, although it did concentrate to a degree on the large key states of the East and Middle West.

Nixon had announced in his acceptance speech that he would begin his campaign at once, and that he would go into every one of the fifty states. (Alaska had become a state on January 3, 1959; Hawaii, on August 21, 1959.) His organization was also headed by a United States senator as national chairman, Thruston B. Morton of Kentucky, a staunch Eisenhower supporter. Former Chairman Leonard Hall, who had managed Nixon's preconvention campaign, and Robert Finch, a Los Angeles lawyer, played major roles in directing the Nixon strategy. Charles S. Rhyne headed the Volunteers for Nixon-Lodge. The national committee created a special advertising agency, "Campaign Associates," with Carroll Newton and Edward A. Rogers in charge, to handle publicity. A brain trust of economic and governmental specialists included two Harvard professors. The vice-president believed that a campaign should build up gradually to reach a peak just before the election, and that too rigid planning was unwise, as it left no room for maneuver when circumstances might require it.

The climactic event of the campaign was a series of four television debates arranged by the three great national networks. The results were no Lincoln-Douglas classics. The rivals battled for points and displayed their skill in fast exchanges and sharp returns, with occasional misses. Performance overshadowed content.

Kennedy drew first blood, although he had been given the underdog rating. Various explanations were offered for Nixon's poor initial showing before the relentless TV camera—bad lighting, bad makeup (it was even charged that a Democrat had done the job), campaign weariness, the disconcerting self-possession of his supposedly immature rival, or some other less tangible factor. Whatever the reason, his past mastery of television seemed to have departed at the outset, and he appeared haggard, ill-at-ease, perspiring with nervousness, and on the defensive. Kennedy, more photogenic, projected to the viewers the image of a coolly confident, highly articulate, quick-witted antagonist who measured up to the requirements of national leadership. The immaturity charge lost its momentum.

Nixon was more like himself in the later debates and scored effectively, especially in the area of foreign relations, but the effect of the first encounter could not be undone. People forgot the arguments and remembered what they saw. This may have been the turning point of the campaign. After the first debate the Kennedy forces were buoyed up by favorable polls and the mounting size and enthusiasm of his crowds. Ten of the eleven southern governors attending a conference fell in line and sent a telegram of congratulations.

On the campaign trail the two candidates, with much repetition, developed the major issues. Kennedy favored expanded federal action to deal with social and economic problems and to strengthen the American economy. Nixon held that federal power should be used only to stimulate private enterprise and to deal with situations where local solutions had failed.

On foreign relations Kennedy assailed the administration for following a policy of drift and stagnation that was not checking the inroads of Communism. Nixon defined the policy as one of peace without surrender of principle. On the question of the defense of the Chinese offshore islands of Quemoy and Matsu, charges and countercharges seemed to show that both candidates were occupying practically the same position. As to Cuba, Nixon charged that Kennedy was "dangerously irresponsible" in demanding more vigorous measures against Castro. Kennedy had called him "trigger happy" as to Quemoy and Matsu.

Religion and Race

The religious issue was brought into the headlines when a hundred and fifty Protestant ministers and laymen held a secret meeting at Washington, called by the Reverend Norman Vincent Peale, and listened to speeches on the dangers of Vatican control under a Catholic president. A manifesto of similar tenor was issued. Kennedy answered these "Citizens for Religious Freedom" in a notable speech before the Greater Houston Ministerial Association. He declared in favor of the absolute separation of church and state, and "against unconstitutional aid to parochial schools," and pledged himself to make decisions "without regard to outside religious pressures or dictates." Dr. Peale and his cohorts called Kennedy's Houston stand "complete, unequivocal, and reassuring," and the Kennedy managers sent taped recordings of the Houston performance to all parts of the country. The upper air of the campaign was cleared for more vital issues, but there were lower levels where the miasma of ancient prejudices could not be dispelled.

While Kennedy was confronted by the religious problem, Nixon ran afoul of the race question. The strong civil rights plank of the Republican platform, largely his work, not only angered southern racists and conservatives, but was not used effectively to draw Negro support in the big northern states. An incident involving the South's outstanding black leader, the Reverend Martin Luther King, Jr., gave Kennedy an opportunity that Nixon missed. Arrested for participating in a "sit-in" attempt in an Atlanta restaurant, King was sentenced in late October to serve a prison term at hard labor. Kennedy, advised of the situation by watchful members of his staff, telephoned Mrs. King to offer his sympathy and support, and next day his influence operated to help secure King's release on bail. His quick action, contrasted with Nixon's silence, accelerated a black swing to Kennedy, which may have accounted for Democratic victories in five or six states.

Johnson and Eisenhower Campaign

In the South, however, the major factor in combatting Republican appeal was the campaign activity of Lyndon Johnson. He whistle-stopped his way across the old Confederacy on the LBJ Victory Special, "the grandson of a Confederate soldier," who talked the language of his listeners and who knew how to stir up the lagging loyalties of the party regulars who would get out the vote. His most effective work—and Speaker Rayburn assisted here—was done in Texas, twice carried by Eisenhower.

The struggle was a bitter one. Late in the campaign the vice-presidential candidate and Mrs. Johnson, entering a Dallas hotel for a public meeting, were booed, jostled, and shoved around by a group of well-dressed Nixon supporters. This treatment of a distinguished native son exceeded in political stupidity the acts of some Michigan irresponsibles who hurled eggs and tomatoes at the Nixon entourage, and a Milwaukee woman who threw a glass of whiskey into Kennedy's face. But only the Dallas episode backfired seriously in terms of votes.

Only in the final week did President Eisenhower take to the stump, although an earlier nonpolitical tour was reminiscent of some of Franklin D. Roosevelt's subterfuges. The Nixon strategy was to build up the campaign to a grand finale, with Eisenhower the great drawing card the last week. In metropolitan New York, accompanied by Nixon, and in Pittsburgh and Cleveland, the president extolled the merits of the experienced Republican candidates who could be depended upon to keep the peace and prevent inflation. He called Kennedy "this young genius" who lacked the knowledge, wisdom, and experience necessary for a president.

Earlier in the campaign Nixon had sought to dispel any impression that he was an apron-strings candidate. He wanted to project the image of a leader who would stand broadly for the basic policies of the administration, but who was prepared to offer new programs where needed. But now, with the election a toss-up, the voters needed to be reminded that they still liked Ike, and that Nixon was Ike's choice. The president was warmly greeted by his usual large and enthusiastic crowds, but some hindsight Republican critics thought that Nixon waited too long to use him, and wasted his help in states that did not prove to be close.

Kennedy Elected President

Early returns on November 8 pointed toward a Kennedy sweep of the coastal East by large majorities. In the lower South he seemed to be holding much of the normal Democratic strength, although Virginia, Kentucky, and Tennessee were evidently repeating the defection of 1956, and unpledged electors were ahead in Mississippi and Alabama. But early talk of a Kennedy landslide subsided when the Middle West reported. Ohio and Wisconsin soon were conceded to Nixon—Kennedy's biggest disappointments—and the western agricultural states were almost solidly Republican. The election turned into one of the closest in American history. In four states—Illinois, Michigan, Minnesota, and California—early Kennedy leads were being whittled away by a heavy Republican nonurban vote. Nixon needed all four to win an electoral majority; Kennedy needed two. Mississippi's eight unpledged electors and Alabama's six (Kennedy had the remaining five) could play a decisive role if neither candidate had a majority.

Before noon on Wednesday, the four doubtful states fell into the Kennedy column, and Nixon formally conceded his defeat. Later, a surprisingly large number of absentee ballots in California, counted after the election, shifted his home state to Nixon. Little Hawaii's 3 votes were not finally determined for Kennedy until the electoral college was meeting. This made his total 303 electoral votes to Nixon's 219. Senator Byrd was the choice of the 8 unpledged electors of Mississippi and the 6 of Alabama, and also of an Oklahoma Republican who defected from Nixon.

Republican charges of fraud in Texas and Illinois lacked sufficient evidence to warrant the prolonged court battles that would ensue if the official count were questioned. Kennedy's margin in Illinois was 8,858 votes; in Texas 46,233.

By the tabulation of the clerk of the House of Representatives, Kennedy had 119,450 more popular votes than Nixon in a total of 68,836,385, a difference of one-tenth of 1 percent. Other tabulations differ slightly from this. The mixed result in Alabama is the chief complicating factor. This was the closest voter verdict since 1880. Minor parties and unpledged electors accounted for enough popular votes to put both major party candidates below 50 percent of the total.*

* Congressional Quarterly, *Presidential Elections Since 1789*, gives the following totals: Kennedy, 34,221,344; Nixon, 34,106,671; Faubus, National States Rights, 209,314; Mississippi unpledged, 116,248; Haas, Socialist Labor, 47,522; Decker, Prohibition, 44,087; Dobbs, Socialist Workers, 40,166; others, lesser numbers.

Both houses of Congress were Democratic as expected, the Senate 64 to 36, the House 263 to 174. The Republicans had gained two Senators and twenty-one representatives, and elections of state governors put fifteen Democrats and twelve Republicans in office, a net gain of one Republican.

Kennedy had swept the East, except for upper New England (Maine, New Hampshire, Vermont), divided the Middle West with Nixon, captured the lower South, except Florida and the unpledged electors of Mississippi and Alabama, lost the upper South (Virginia, Tennessee, and Kentucky), and carried only Nevada and New Mexico in the Great West north and west of Texas. Outside the South, it was largely urban America against small-town and rural America.

The victor's religion won back defecting Eisenhower Catholic Democrats but cost the candidate heavily in the rural Protestant areas, although the peace-prosperity appeal operated in favor of Eisenhower's heir in the old isolationist sections. In any case, the nation had elected the first Roman Catholic to the presidency. Kennedy was also, at forty-three, the youngest man elected president.

Campaign finances had become the most serious problem in party management. The rising costs of transportation, advertising, registration drives, polling, and other indispensables of an intensive struggle for votes made the campaign of 1960 the most expensive in history. On the national level the major parties spent over $25,000,000 as compared with a total of $17,200,000 in 1956. The Democrats, if labor disbursements are included, spent slightly more than the Republicans nationally, although the former ended up with a huge deficit. Victory gave its customary stimulus to post-election fund raising and saved the party's credit. If the expenditures at state and local levels are added, the grand total has been estimated at $175,000,000. To meet such outlays, fund-raising dinners, large contributors, and state quotas, which passed the burden on to local organizations, were the chief sources, but these were in danger of being wrung dry by Election Day. A partial solution pointed toward some form of government subsidy.

The newspapers and the magazines of opinion, as in the past, displayed a heavy Republican editorial preponderance, but narrow partisanship in the form of slanted news stories and misleading headlines seemed to be less marked. The press in the many one-paper or one-ownership cities in the main recognized its responsibility to give equal space to and objective presentation of campaign activities of both parties. The working journalists who followed the campaign trail were charged by the Nixon staff with a Kennedy preference that, it was alleged, infiltrated their news stories. Certainly, the Kennedy entourage included a more sympathetic journalistic retinue, and the Democratic candidate achieved a rapport with press representatives that Nixon did not.

But contributing to the decline of newspaper editorial influence was the wide use of television. It provided candidates with direct contacts with the voters, who could see and hear them at close hand, and judge accordingly, if often irrationally. Kennedy demonstrated his maturity and increased his public stature by his television performances, particularly in the great debates. He believed that they made victory possible. Most political experts agreed with him.

Kennedy's "New Frontier"

President Kennedy's "New Frontier," made some limited advances, but the bipartisan bloc of Republicans and southern Democrats operated much as it had in the Truman years, so far as domestic issues were concerned. He secured the creation of a Peace Corps of American volunteers for humanitarian and cultural work in the more backward nations and an Alliance for Progress to aid Latin American nations. Both were popular at home and abroad. His inaugural address on January 20, 1961, included the now-famous line, "Ask not what your country can do for you—ask what you can do for your country."

The "Bay of Pigs" fiasco, an attempted invasion of Cuba by anti-Castro exiles in April 1961, which had American encouragement but insufficient American aid, gave the Republicans a promising issue for future use. But the edge was dulled by the president's success in getting Khrushchev to yield on the issue of constructing Russian missile bases in Cuba, in October 1962. Kennedy also supported and encouraged the space program. On July 20, 1969, Neil A. Armstrong became the first man to walk on the moon.

A strong conservative movement began to make considerable headway in the Republican Party. Among the more extreme groups was the John Birch Society, founded by Robert H. W. Welch, Jr., a retired candy manufacturer, who called President Eisenhower a "dedicated, conscious agent of the Communist conspiracy." Operating in secret and well financed, it viewed Washington as a center of subversion and attacked the Supreme Court as communistic because of its civil rights decisions, its banning of official religious exercises in the public schools, and its decision in *Baker v. Carr* requiring redistricting by state legislatures where apportionment of seats disregarded population. While many moderates were critical of the Court, the Birch solution—"Impeach Chief Justice Earl Warren"—was copied only by rightist groups flocking to get into the promising financial waters of extremism.

In the midterm elections the Republicans lost four Senate seats and added only four to their House minority, but they captured the governorships from the Democrats in Michigan, Ohio, and Pennsylvania, and Governor Rockefeller was reelected in New York. These gains were partially offset by Nixon's defeat by Governor Edmund Brown in California. Of the newcomers, George Romney of Michigan, former head of American Motors, and William Scranton of Pennsylvania attracted attention as possibilities for 1964. Governor Rockefeller, an early favorite, now raised doubts about his availability by marrying a divorcée after a divorce from his first wife.

The most striking development in Republican ranks was a Goldwater boom. Frank and forthright in speech and actions, this son of a Jewish father and Protestant mother had become the voice of the booming Southwest with his simple conservative philosophy that found expression in his *The Conscience of A Conservative*. He opposed the whole fabric of the welfare state, questioned the final authority of the Supreme Court, would limit the scope of civil rights legislation, and held to a strongly nationalistic position on foreign policy, favoring an end of diplomatic relations with Iron Curtain countries and a hard line toward Castro in Cuba. A "Draft Goldwater" movement headed by F. Clifton White of New York operated under cover for several months before coming out into the open in early 1963. The reluctant Arizona senator finally accepted the fact that he was a candidate and made a Phoenix friend, Denison Kitchell, his manager later in the year.

The Democrats were troubled by rising tensions over race relations in the South. The use of troops was required at the University of Mississippi to put down a riotous outbreak over the admission of a black student. Attorney General Robert Kennedy bore the brunt of criticism for this and other school desegregation actions. Governors George Wallace of Alabama, Ross Barnett of Mississippi, and other segregationist leaders planned to preempt the Democratic emblem for unpledged electoral tickets, wherever possible. Their aim was to capture the balance of power in the electoral college and throw the election to the House of Representatives.

President Kennedy secured Senate approval for a treaty with the Soviet Union banning atmospheric nuclear tests and gave administration approval to the sale of large quantities of surplus wheat to that nation. A tax-cut proposal was stalled by Senator Byrd, chairman of the Finance Committee.

On the business front Kennedy had come under fire for his policies, but a boom was getting under way in late 1963, no new crisis seemed to be impending with Iron Curtain countries, and the prospect was fair for the Kennedy ship to unfurl all its sails for a peace-and-prosperity campaign in 1964.

But the ship was never to sail. On November 22, 1963, while traveling through Dallas, Kennedy was shot and killed, and the grief and horror of the nation obliterated party lines. Even the voices of the extreme Kennedy haters were silenced, and their propaganda, ready for the coming campaign, became a liability. Vice-President Lyndon Johnson became the thirty-sixth president of the United States.

XVIII

LBJ All the Way

Lyndon Baines Johnson came to the presidency with the best preparation of any vice-president suddenly elevated to the highest office. While not a member of the Kennedy inner circle, he had participated in the deliberations of the cabinet and the National Security Council and had played an active part in other top-level matters, including the exploration of space. He had gone abroad as a good-will salesman for his country, and his range of greetings encompassed rulers and camel drivers.

The tall Texan, possessed of superabundant energy, self-assurance, a rather sharp temper, and an instinct for politics, lacked Kennedy's intellectual interests and gift of speech, but he was a skilled tactician in the art of the possible who operated best through personal contacts, and he had an unsurpassed knowledge of the people and methods of Capitol Hill. He had outgrown his Texas territorialism and was strongly committed to civil rights legislation and other major Kennedy measures.

That he would be nominated at the 1964 Democratic national convention was taken for granted, presumably with a liberal from the East or Middle West as his running mate. But to win in November he needed to convince the urban Kennedy strongholds that he had no southern sectional spots on his national toga.

The president, operating with a practiced hand in the legislative field he had ploughed so often, secured the passage of the long-delayed tax-reduction measure and a stronger civil rights bill than the original Kennedy measure. A bipartisan combination backed the civil rights measure with Senate Republican leader Everett Dirksen leading the conservatives of the midlands to its support after securing some clarifying amendments. Senator Goldwater was one of six Senate Republicans who voted against it. He called certain provisions unconstitutional and feared their enforcement would produce "a police state" and "an informer psychology." The Senate passed the bill on June 19. Goldwater was already well in the lead for the Republican presidential nomination.

In the early spring the contest for the Republican prize had seemed invitingly open. The New Hampshire primary of March 10 produced a surprise result. A well-organized write-in campaign for Henry Cabot Lodge, ambassador to Vietnam, put him ahead of Goldwater, Rockefeller,

Nixon (also a write-in choice), Senator Margaret Chase Smith of Maine, and Harold Stassen.

Down to the California primary the Republican voters confused the experts with their own confusions. Candidates avoided direct primary battles where the results appeared doubtful, voters used write-ins frequently, and favorite-son figureheads enabled some states to postpone commitments. In the convention states of the South and West Goldwater zealots were capturing the delegates. Rockefeller won a surprising victory in the Oregon primary over Lodge, which practically eliminated the latter. Goldwater wisely had abandoned Oregon to his rivals. But contrary to pollster predictions he carried California over Rockefeller by a 68,350 margin in a total vote of 2,172,456. This meant 86 delegates. Later conventions, which included Texas, added enough, by his supporters' claims, to give him the 655 votes needed for the nomination.

Republican moderates, in alarm, looked to Eisenhower to encourage a stop-Goldwater movement, as the former president had made statements about the need for a candidate in the mainstream of Republican thinking. But, when no help came from Eisenhower, Governor William Scranton of Pennsylvania announced his intention to run and set about belatedly to win the uncommitted and the loosely committed delegates to his support. The prepossessing forty-six-year-old governor, who smiled easily and spoke fluently and with serious conviction, argued that Goldwater's votes and utterances were out of line with past Republican platforms. Could the party, he asked, "stand with one foot in the twentieth century and one in the nineteenth?"

Rockefeller, Romney, and Lodge were ready to help, and Lodge joined Scranton on a western delegate hunt, but the results were not encouraging.

The convention opened in San Francisco's Cow Palace on July 19 with National Chairman William Miller presiding. Governor Mark Hatfield of Oregon, in his keynote speech, emphasized the humanitarian heritage of the party. When he castigated extremists and lumped together the John Birch Society, the Ku Klux Klan, and the Communist Party, there were ill-concealed murmurs of disapproval. Next day when Eisenhower spoke on the same general theme, an incidental reference to "sensation-seeking columnists and commentators" produced a roar of approval and an eruption of fist-shaking directed at the occupants of television booths and press seats. This showed the temper of the majority, convinced of the bias of eastern news media.

The platform committee, headed by Representative Melvin Laird of Wisconsin, had met the week before the convention opened to hear speakers for all manner of causes. The finished product did not suit the liberals. Senator Hugh Scott of Pennsylvania, Scranton's manager, offered three amendments: a repudiation of extremists, with the John Birch

Society mentioned by name; a reassertion of presidential control over nuclear weapons (not giving commanding officers in the field an option as to nuclear tactical weapons, as Goldwater had suggested); and a stronger statement for enforcement of the civil rights law. All were voted down, as were similar amendments offered by Governor Romney. But the most astonishing incident of the convention was the treatment of Rockefeller when he tried to speak for the first proposal. From the galleries came boos and hisses and cries of "We Want Barry," and Chairman Thruston Morton had great difficulty getting order for the grim-faced governor to speak for his allotted four minutes.

The platform on key points was a Goldwater textbook. Its central themes were the dangers to liberty at home from an expanding federal power, and the need for a dynamic strategy against Communism to secure victory for freedom "every place on earth." Democratic failures and weaknesses in both areas were cited at length. The touchy civil rights question was disposed of with a promise of full implementation of the Civil Rights Act of 1964 and continued opposition to discrimination, with the qualification that the elimination of such discrimination is "a matter of heart, conscience, and education, as well as of equal rights under law." Endorsement was given to constitutional amendments to permit religious exercises in public places and to enable states having bicameral legislatures to apportion one house on a basis other than population.

At the Wednesday evening session, nominating speeches provided eight candidates. The customary demonstrations followed, with most of the sound and fury for Goldwater, nominated by Senator Dirksen. The one ballot gave Goldwater 883 votes; Scranton, 214; Rockefeller, 114; Romney, 41; Mrs. Margaret Chase Smith, 27; Walter Judd of Minnesota, 22; Hiram Fong of Hawaii, 5; and Lodge, who had withdrawn, 2. Scranton moved that the nomination be made unanimous.

The ticket was completed with the nomination of Congressman and National Chairman William Miller of New York for vice-president. Miller was a conservative, a Roman Catholic, had slight strength in his home state, and was better known to party professionals than to the rank and file of party voters. But he did seem to give balance to the ticket.

In his acceptance speech Goldwater offered no olive branch to the defeated. He reiterated his conservative creed and stirred his listeners with his challenging statement: "Extremism in defense of liberty is no vice . . . moderation in pursuit of justice is no virtue." The counterrevolution had been successful, and the "Eastern Establishment" had been toppled in the dust, even stamped upon.

The Goldwater forces took control of the Republican National Committee immediately after the convention. Dean Burch, a thirty-six-year-old Phoenix attorney who for several years had been a member of the senator's Washington staff, became national chairman. Denison Kitchel, a

Harvard-educated lawyer, was Goldwater's personal manager. A long-time friend, he had taken over direction of the preconvention campaign but preferred to work in the background. The southern Goldwater forces were represented by John Grenier of Alabama, who ranked next to Burch in authority. Ralph Cordiner, former chairman of the board of General Electric, handled finances.

Old professionals, such as former national chairman Leonard Hall of New York and Ohio state chairman Ray C. Bliss, were ignored as much as used for advisory purposes. The committee organization was staffed by the "Arizona Mafia" in all important positions. A new crowd was running the show, and the preliminary planning was done efficiently, on paper.

Johnson Plans the Democratic Convention

The Democratic national convention met in Atlantic City on August 24 with everything planned in advance by President Johnson, although he withheld the name of his running mate until the time came for nominations. Governor Wallace of Alabama had upset preconvention harmony by entering the primaries in Wisconsin, Indiana, and Maryland against favorite-son stand-ins for Johnson. He won no delegates but polled a considerable vote with his racist appeal, getting 43 percent in Maryland, where white resentment against black militancy was especially strong.

A revised formula for apportionment of delegates provided for 2,316 convention votes as against 1,521 in 1960 and the 1,308 voting delegates to the 1964 Republican convention. In all, 5,260 officially accredited Democrats came to Atlantic City. Of these, 2,944 were delegates, 108 were the voting members of the national committee, and 2,208 were alternates.

Senator John Pastore of Rhode Island offered a slashing keynote address, sprinkled with jibes at Goldwater's irresponsible utterances, and presided as temporary chairman. He was succeeded in the chair next day by House Speaker John McCormack.

The credentials committee was faced with the problem of two Mississippi delegations, a regularly elected one and a contesting "Freedom" group. The convention adopted a solution that gave seats to the regulars on the condition that the delegates take a pledge to support the ticket, and allotted two seats at large to the Freedom claimants. Only three signed the loyalty pledge, and the Freedom group rejected the compromise. The Alabama delegates were also asked to take a similar pledge, but only eleven complied and were seated.

The lengthy platform, presented by Representative Carl Albert of Oklahoma, promised "unflagging devotion to our commitments to freedom from Berlin to South Vietnam," the further isolation of Fidel Castro's

Cuba, and a continued resolve, under tested leadership, to use every resource to find the road to peace.

On the domestic front it offered a broad federal program of social and economic welfare measures covering education, Medicare, civil rights, the war on poverty, farm policies, urban improvement, and conservation. Labor was promised repeal of the Taft-Hartley Act. The Ku Klux Klan, the Communist Party, and the John Birch Society were condemned as extremist organizations. Thirty-eight citations from the platform of 1960 were followed by the accomplishments of the Kennedy-Johnson administration in each case.

The nominating session was a formality. President Johnson surprised everyone by coming to the convention, accompanied by his family, to announce that Senator Humphrey would be his running mate, which was no great surprise in itself. Senator Eugene McCarthy, also of Minnesota, had been regarded as the only other possible choice, with Robert Kennedy eliminated earlier by Johnson's politic decision not to take anyone from the cabinet. Kennedy was taken care of by an invitation from a New York group to run for the Senate from that state. Humphrey, a middlewestern liberal, had tempered his early crusading zeal into a more realistic willingness to work for the possible, had demonstrated his skill as party whip in the Senate, was a popular figure outside the lower South, and had no peer as a rapid-fire, extemporaneous speaker. Both Johnson and Humphrey were nominated by acclamation.

At the closing session on Thursday, tributes were paid to three deceased party notables. John F. Kennedy was eulogized by his brother Robert, who was given a moving thirteen-minute ovation; Mrs. Eleanor Roosevelt by Adlai Stevenson; and Sam Rayburn by James Farley. Acceptance speeches by Humphrey and Johnson followed. The former shook the convention out of its Kennedy nostalgia with a stirring recital of Goldwater's negative Senate votes until his listeners began to chant with him "—but not Senator Goldwater." Johnson offered no flaming battle cries but pictured the nation on a course of peace and prosperity moving toward the "Great Society." "Let us be on our way," he ended.

The Atlantic City gathering had been a party jamboree, with a good time had by all, in spite of complaints about the resort city's not very modern host-city facilities. The delegates had come merely to ratify, and the performance satisfied its director.

The Consensus Campaign

Before beginning his campaign, Goldwater conferred with Republican notables, including governors and gubernatorial candidates, in Hershey, Pennsylvania. He tried to restore unity by clarifying his views on major issues to show that he was repudiating extremism of both the left and the right. Most of those present expressed approval of his explanations.

But the cleavage was too deep to be repaired in this fashion. Disaffection developed on a scale unequaled since the Bull Moose split of 1912. Among candidates who refused to endorse the Goldwater-Miller ticket were Senator Keating of New York and Governor Romney of Michigan, while several others, including Senator Hugh Scott of Pennsylvania, Robert Taft, candidate for the Senate from Ohio, and Charles H. Percy, running for governor in Illinois, conducted virtually independent campaigns. Senators Case of New Jersey, Kuchel of California, and Javits of New York, not up for reelection, withheld endorsement. Governor Rockefeller gave a nominal support to the ticket. Of the better-known figures only Nixon and Scranton went on the campaign trail.

In the South, Governor Wallace dropped the idea of an independent candidacy but refrained from any endorsement to avoid embarrassing Goldwater, he said. He supported his unpledged electoral ticket. But in South Carolina Senator Strom Thurmond, a segregationist and a conservative, joined the Republican Party.

Prominent Republican business and financial leaders and several Eisenhower officeholders, including four former cabinet members, took the bolters' path. The larger metropolitan pro-Republican and independent newspapers and periodicals were almost a unit in support of Johnson. In terms of circulation, the press was heavily anti-Goldwater, an unprecedented situation for a Republican candidate. Members of the working press in the Goldwater entourage were sometimes greeted with boos and insulting remarks. The Republican candidate, feeling that he had been the victim of misinterpretations of off-the-cuff remarks in the past, dispensed with formal press conferences and presented his case in prepared speeches and television appearances.

In one respect, the war of paperbacks, the Goldwater attackers far outdistanced the Johnson defenders in verbiage and venom. Right-wing organizations circulated thousands of copies of this hate literature, whose authors footnoted one another to prove that the nation was in the clutches of a conspiracy of subversion, with the particular devils varying according to the speciality of the author.

Citizens' organizations appeared outside the regular party fences, aimed at bolters and independents. Citizens for Goldwater-Miller and National Citizens for Johnson and Humphrey led the procession, but auxiliaries and subdivisions for various professions and skills multiplied until the Republicans were accredited with thirty, the Democrats with twenty-eight, according to press reports. Here the advantage lay heavily with the Democrats, for the masses of Republican bolters could find congenial company in citizens' committees for Johnson, while Democratic bolters were lonesome outcasts, outside the South.

Goldwater opened his campaign formally on September 3 in Prescott, Arizona, the starting point for his two senatorial campaigns. He attributed to the administration "the way of the regimented society," "the way of mobs in the streets," appeasement in foreign affairs, unilateral disarmament in the face of militant Communism, and a low tone of morality in the public service. He emphasized his own devotion to peace through strength. These themes he returned to repeatedly in later speeches, with the need for morality in public life getting more and more attention toward the close of his campaign.

The slogan of the Republican campaign, "In Your Heart You Know He's Right," appeared in every kind of publicity put forth by the Goldwater supporters. It was easy to parody, and its interminable repetition possibly was a mistake.

The Democrats made sure that Goldwater's utterances before he became a candidate would return to plague him. He was called trigger happy because of his statement that the field commander might have the option of deciding when to use tactical atomic weapons, and the horrors of nuclear war were pictured in paid television propaganda. He was charged with hostility to social security because of a remark, before the New Hampshire primary, that it should be made voluntary, and he made matters worse by attacking Medicare. A television picture of a social security card torn in two was an effective Democratic rejoinder. His vote against the Civil Rights Act of 1964 blotted out the memory of his support of the earlier acts. His campaign declarations against both forced segregation and forced integration appealed only to the South.

The issue of morality in government became Goldwater's strongest weapon. Two cases, both close to Johnson, came to light. Bobby Baker, Senator majority secretary and once a protégé of Johnson, had been forced to resign the preceding year while under investigation for possible conflicts of interest. The Rules Committee reported in July 1964, that he was guilty of "gross improprieties" but left the question of law violations for the Justice Department to handle. Republicans charged that the report was a whitewash, that prominent Democrats were involved, and demanded that the Baker case be reopened. Unanswered questions about various Bobby Baker deals provided Republicans with excellent campaign ammunition.

Late in the campaign Walter Jenkins, long a confidential assistant to Johnson, was convicted on a morals charge. He was at once dismissed and placed in a hospital. The effects would have been more damaging but for startling news from abroad: Khrushchev had been deposed, and Red China had detonated a nuclear bomb. The Jenkins affair was overshadowed by these developments, although not forgotten.

The Baker and Jenkins cases became Republican evidence of "a cloud over the White House" and "a mess in Washington." Immorality and loose standards at the top were trickling down to infect the nation, Goldwater asserted. But he rejected as racist a documentary film entitled "The Choice," which was designed to depict moral rot and violence in the streets. He refused to permit its use in the campaign.

The Democratic campaign management was headed by Chairman John Bailey, a professional who depended on professionals, but Johnson did his own planning; tactics and itineraries were changed on short notice. His personal control rested on groups of overlapping staff specialists— speech writers, television publicity men, campaign planners, directors of voter registration, citizens' committees, and minorities, and a flock of others. Several key members of the 1960 Kennedy team held important posts, notably Lawrence O'Brien and Kenneth O'Donnell.

The president began his campaign in Cadillac Square in Detroit on Labor Day. His theme then, and later, was national unity on a program of prosperity, justice, and peace. He set up the "Great Society" as his goal, with unemployment and poverty eliminated and equal opportunities for all. In the final weeks of the campaign he was on the stump almost as much as his rival and far excelled him in handshaking, crowd mingling, and folksy speeches. Although buoyed up by the favorable reports of the polls, he wanted to win by a landslide and set out to cover every section of the country. Critics dismissed his extemporaneous remarks largely as homilies and hokum, but he knew how to please the huge crowds and did not let some heckling, most evident in his own South, disturb his happy front. Both Mrs. Johnson and Senator Humphrey had encountered some hostile treatment in tours of the race-conscious southern states.

Humphrey's long record as a battler for liberal causes and his membership in the Americans for Democratic Action labeled him as a Socialist in Republican propaganda and as a Communist in extreme rightist nomenclature. Miller, termed the hatchet man and the bantam gut fighter by hostile sources, confined his stumping chiefly to the smaller cities. Unlike the polyloquent Humphrey, he settled down to one basic speech that he could fit to different audiences with minor changes.

Smear tactics were used with little restraint on both sides, with hate more in evidence in extreme Republican propaganda and fear in Democratic. Bruce L. Felknor, executive director of the Fair Campaign Practices Committee, said that it was "the most vicious and bitter campaign I've ever seen, or for that matter, heard tell of."

Republican efforts to arrange some type of televised debate by the two major party candidates ran into snags in Congress and in the White House. The Senate on August 18 killed a proposal to suspend the section of the Communications Act that prevented such confrontations. Senator Dirksen and most of the Republicans were in the minority. The National Broadcasting Company offered to arrange for joint appearances of the candidates in a series of news interview programs, but President Johnson declined to participate. Cries of "chicken" from the Republicans were ignored.

Before his nomination, Goldwater had refused to debate with Rockefeller and Scranton but now was ready to meet Johnson. Observers above the partisan smoke questioned whether it was in the national interest for an incumbent president to become involved in a forensic duel while handling delicate matters of foreign policy on which he could not speak freely. Johnson, at least, believed it was not in his own interest.

Minor parties played insignificant roles. The veteran Prohibition, Socialist Labor, and Socialist Workers parties made their quadrennial appearances, with E. Harold Munn, Sr., Eric Hass, and Clinton DeBerry as their respective candidates. Less well known were some six or seven other candidacies, mostly of recent vintage. Three on the extreme right regarded Goldwater as too liberal. Of the ten or more minor candidates (some self-nominated), six were on the ballots in a total of twenty-two states, according to a *New York Times* tabulation.

Johnson and Humphrey Elected

The popular verdict on November 3 was more decisive than the Harding and Roosevelt landslides. Johnson received 43,126,584 popular votes to Goldwater's 27,177,838; in percentages 61 to 38.5.* The electoral votes were 486 to 52. Goldwater's electoral votes came from Arizona and five southern states—South Carolina, Georgia, Alabama, Mississippi, and Louisiana. The Senate was Democratic, 67 to 33; the House of Representatives, 295 to 140. In the governors' races the Republicans won only 8 of 25 contests. Romney's success in Michigan kept him in the picture for 1968.

To defeat an incumbent riding a prosperity-peace horse has been proved an impossible task in the past, but the race would have been closer if a less vulnerable candidate had been named. An "echo" would certainly have run better than the "choice." At least the mortality percentages for lesser offices would have been reduced. The Goldwater record and bad strategy, which gambled too much on the white backlash, were the major causes of the debacle.

Goldwater's victories in the deep South added seven Republican members to the House of Representatives. These were elected as segregationists and only complicated matters for the party in the North. It was an anomalous situation for the party of Lincoln to have received nearly all of

* Minor parties and independent tickets polled 336,682 votes. Of these, the Alabama unpledged electors had 210,732 votes.

its electoral votes from the former Confederacy. Goldwater did not carry a state that had voted for Lincoln, Theodore Roosevelt, Hoover, or Eisenhower, except Arizona in the last two cases and Louisiana in Eisenhower's second election.

The debacle produced an outburst of angry recriminations in Republican ranks. Goldwater loyalists blamed the defeat on the failure of the moderates to give the ticket united support and contended that their idol's conservative philosophy had been approved by twenty-seven million voters. Opponents countered that the majority of these were loyal Republican regulars who would vote for any party candidate, and that the swing to the right had driven away the moderates and the independents who had been so responsible for past Republican successes. The restoration of some degree of unity was the Republican goal and problem for the immediate future.

Both parties' expenditures set new records. On the national level, total spending for the campaign was nearly $35,000,000, divided among a large number of committees of both parties. The Republican total was over $17,000,000, the Democratic, $12,000,000; but the Democrats benefited also from the independent spending of labor and other Democratic-oriented groups. The 1964 campaign was unusual in the increased number of large givers to the Democratic campaign, notably in the case of the President's Club, which consisted of some 4,000 donors of $1,000 or more to Johnson's election. In the Republican camp, money came from more small contributors than in the past, largely as a result of direct mail and television solicitation. Goldwater's special appeal to middle-class business and professional people and the zeal of his workers, mostly amateurs, further explain this broadened financial base. Actors Ronald Reagan and Raymond Massey were especially effective at television solicitation.

The grand total of all election expenditures, national, state, and local, from preconvention to final accounting, has been estimated at $200,000,000.* This exceeded by $25,000,000 the former record set in 1960.

The election of 1964 was marked by an improved method of reporting the returns, which was used again in 1968. A centralized system, the National Election Service, set up by the three national television networks and the two major press associations, provided quicker service at lower cost than the old competitive methods. Thousands of workers at the precinct level reported returns to state centers for tabulation. As these reports were analyzed, reasonably safe predictions could be made as to trends and outcomes. A more sophisticated tool for rapid prediction and analysis of election outcomes was Vote Profile Analysis, set up by the Columbia Broadcasting System and two other sponsors. It was used in 1962, and in primaries and elections in 1964 with apparent success. However, this early forecasting of final results aroused criticism in several quarters. Voters in areas where the polls were still open, it was charged, were thus being told that the battle was over and their participation would have no effect. Preelection polls also came in for unfavorable comments for affecting rather than reflecting voting trends.

The Aftermath of 1964

President Johnson, assured of the support of a strongly liberal Congress, set about to reap the fruits of his great victory. In the two sessions of the Eighty-ninth Congress, platform promises in the more important fields were carried out by the enactment of a far-reaching program of legislation, notably with regard to Medicare for the elderly, aid to education, federal supervision of voting rights, urban problems, air and water pollution, automobile safety, the war on poverty, and the Economic Opportunity Act of 1964. The Civil Rights Act of 1964 prohibited discrimination in voting, public education, and employment. It also established the Equal Employment Opportunities Commission (EEOC).

The most serious problem for the administration was in Vietnam, where the bombing of the Communist North brought only limited military gains and seemed to promise a further escalation of the war. American involvement in Vietnam had started in 1961 with the sending of military advisers to South Vietnam. But the involvement had been escalated and, by the end of 1965, about 184,000 American troops were there. The North Vietnamese were being supplied by Mainland China and Russia with arms. Opposition to the Johnson policy (he had authorized the bombing of North Vietnam) found vent in public antiwar demonstrations and in Senate criticisms, notably by Chairman William Fulbright of the Foreign Relations Committee and by Wayne Morse of Oregon, both of whom won some degree of support from a number of their colleagues. The terms "hawks" and "doves" came into the political vocabulary as applied to supporters and opponents of Vietnam escalation. The president was relying too heavily on two cabinet "hawks," Secretary of State Dean Rusk and Secretary of Defense Robert McNamara, according to his "dovish" critics. Republicans, with a few exceptions, were "hawkish," calling for even more vigorous measures against the Communist aggressors.

On the economic front, heavy military expenditures, the costs of the war on poverty, the threat of inflation, and the prospect of tax increases disturbed business and middle-class friends of the administration. Labor

* See Herbert E. Alexander, "Financing the Parties and Campaigns," in Milton C. Cummings, Jr., ed., *The National Election of 1964* (Washington, D.C. 1966), pp. 158–198.

pressures for wage increases added to fears that the prosperity machine was grinding to a halt.

Black militancy, caused in part by the limited practical gains in the civil rights struggle, led to outbreaks of violence in the black ghettos of Los Angeles, Atlanta, Cleveland, and several other cities in 1965–66. The rise of a "Black Power" leadership in certain black protest groups and a white backlash reaction seemed to threaten an increase in racial tensions, especially where open housing and school busing as a desegregation tactic were issues.

These various discontents commingled to create a national mood of insecurity and dissatisfaction with things as they were and affected the midterm elections of 1966. The old political axiom that unhappy voters take it out on the party in power operated in favor of the Republican "outs." They reduced the Democratic majorities in Congress by forty-seven seats in the House of Representatives and three in the Senate, and won eight additional governorships to bring their total to twenty-five, which included five of the seven largest states.

Improving Republican prospects foreshadowed a sharp struggle for the presidential prize at the convention of 1968. The early listing of possibilities included George Romney, returned to Michigan's governorship by a landslide; Charles Percy of Illinois, elected to the Senate over a veteran liberal Paul Douglas; Ronald Reagan of California, former movie favorite, who had defeated Governor Edmund G. Brown in the latter's try for a third term; James A. Rhodes of Ohio, reelected governor by a record margin; and Richard M. Nixon, who built up good will by campaigning in 1966 wherever Republican candidates could use his services. Governor Rockefeller of New York ruled himself out of the contest, but his impressive victory for a third term in New York could not be overlooked. Only Reagan wore a conservative collar, although Nixon had made himself acceptable to the right wing. Retiring Governor Scranton of Pennsylvania declared himself no longer available for public office.

In the Democratic ranks, President Johnson seemed assured of a renomination, even though his escalation of the American military commitment in Vietnam had antagonized liberal groups who had supported his domestic policies. News media criticisms that he was withholding information on important matters from the public and creating a communications gap further depressed his poll popularity. The much-publicized rift between the president and Senator Robert Kennedy seemed to be largely personal, but shades of difference over policies might sharpen as tensions increased. Kennedy's aim seemed directed toward a nomination in 1972.

In Alabama, George Wallace, whose wife Lurleen had succeeded him as governor in 1966, was planning an independent candidacy for the presidency if the old party nominations did not conform to his state sovereignty views. This threatened to confuse further the party situation in the deep South, where the Republicans had captured two governorships in 1966 and almost won a third in Georgia—where the legislature voted in the Democratic contender, a racist, in a contested outcome. The once Democratic South was becoming incorrigibly wayward.

XIX

Nixon and Agnew

THE REFORMING TIDE that followed President Johnson's consensus victory of 1964 ebbed in the Congress elected in 1966 but was still strong enough to bring about a continuance of the Great Society program, a civil rights bill for open housing and better protection of voter rights,* and some other regulatory measures less political in character. To check inflationary pressures and strengthen the dollar internationally, in 1968 Congress reluctantly levied a 10 percent surtax on incomes but attached requirements for a heavy reduction in federal spending.

The most widespread racial violence in the nation's history scarred the American image in 1967. Federal troops were required to quell the disorders in Detroit, but Newark and many other cities were afflicted only in lesser degree. The president appointed a special advisory commission on civil disorders which reported on March 2, 1968. It called for drastic measures to be taken in the areas of employment, education, welfare, and housing. With a national election impending, neither Congress nor the president was inclined to press for action. Rioting in the wake of the assassination of the Reverend Martin Luther King, Jr., on April 4, 1968, in Memphis, and a six-week encampment of poor people, mostly blacks, in "Resurrection City, U.S.A.," Washington, D.C., did not help the cause of racial reconciliation.

Meanwhile the growing opposition to the Vietnam War and the draft boiled up in demonstrations on campuses, at induction centers, and wherever proadministration speakers were scheduled to appear. A national gathering of various antiwar and left-wing organizations in Washington in October 1967, required special marshals and military units to protect the Pentagon from the more activist demonstrators.

---

* The Supreme Court on June 17, 1968, expanded the act's provisions by applying the Civil Rights Act of 1866 to bar all racial discrimination in the sale and rental of property.

"Concerned Democrats" Offer Eugene McCarthy

But the various peace groups were too splintered and politically impotent to be considered a threat to the renomination of President Johnson until Allard K. Lowenstein, a former president of the National Student Association and a liberal whose restless energies drove him away from university teaching positions, began to organize the dissenters. Using student groups and his connections with the Americans for Democratic Action, he launched a "Dump Johnson" movement with an evangelical fervor that took him wherever a peace dove cooed. His "Concerned Democrats" group attracted support, but his search for a candidate was fruitless until he used his persuasive eloquence on Senator Eugene McCarthy of Minnesota.

In late November McCarthy announced that he would contest certain Democratic primaries with President Johnson or whoever ran as stand-in for him. He would run as an antiwar candidate, although critics conjectured that other motives were involved. The tall, sharp-witted, soft-speaking senator, philosophical and reflective in temperament rather than self-assertive, more popular outside the upper house than in it, took upon himself the role of crusader in the cause of peace with little hope of being nominated but to demonstrate through the primary route the strength of the peace marchers. Such seedling groups as the Dissident Democrats and the National Conference of Concerned Democrats endorsed him, and a flock of antiwar groups soon established McCarthy-for-President clubs, but money and organization on any considerable scale were lacking. Unfriendly critics suggested that McCarthy might be a stalking-horse for Robert Kennedy, but the two had not been particularly close in the past and Kennedy gave no indication of approving this surprise candidacy.

The course of events helped McCarthy's cause. Secretary of Defense Robert McNamara resigned and was succeeded by Clark Clifford, one-time Truman assistant and a trusted advisor of Johnson, who was reputedly more inclined than McNamara toward a hard-line policy on Vietnam. Before he took office, the Viet Cong offensive during the Lunar New Year celebration on January 31 altered the military situation, increased American casualties, and made the war an even more divisive political issue.

McCarthy, with limited funds and a makeshift organization, went into New Hampshire to oppose the regular party organization that was backing Johnson with a write-in program. The long-shot contender, whose calmly reasoned speeches did not dramatize his cause, found eager listeners in the liberal students of eastern schools—idealistic, antidraft, and unhappy with the world of their parents. Busloads of these students poured into New Hampshire in the closing days of the campaign to lick envelopes, ring doorbells, and try to sell their candidate by personal persuasion. Beards, shaggy locks, and too abbreviated miniskirts were ruled out for the door-to-door solicitors of votes. The hippie image would damage the candidate with staid Yankees. McCarthy was developing the "egghead appeal" of Adlai Stevenson.

The result was a surprising McCarthy vote. He had 41.9 percent of the Democratic preference vote to 49.4 for Johnson, but captured twenty of the state's twenty-four delegates. More important, he had badly damaged the president's standing with politicians and voters generally.

Robert Kennedy Enters the Race

The New Hampshire vote brought Robert Kennedy into the race. Explaining that the party was already badly divided and that Johnson's policies had met the nation's crises with "too little and too late," he announced his candidacy on March 16 in the Senate Caucus Room, where his brother had taken the same step in 1960. Kennedy's late start had kept him from entering the early primaries, but he indicated his readiness to help McCarthy in Wisconsin, Pennsylvania, and Massachusetts, although he made it clear he intended to run against him in later tests. McCarthy rejected the offer. In New Hampshire he could have used Kennedy's help. Now he no longer needed it.

McCarthy's expected victory in Wisconsin against a disorganized Johnson following was suddenly deprived of its importance by an astonishing development. Addressing the nation in a television broadcast on Sunday night, March 31, President Johnson announced that American bombing raids on North Vietnam would be ended except for defense purposes in certain contingencies. This unexpected shift of policy, which pointed toward negotiations with Ho Chi Minh, North Vietnam's political leader, was overshadowed by his concluding sentences in which he announced that he would not seek and would not accept a nomination for another term. The reason he gave was "the divisiveness among us all tonight." With America's future under challenge at home and the world's hopes for peace in the balance, he did not want the presidency involved in partisan divisions.

Johnson's abdication coup produced a revolution in American politics. He had deprived his critics of their chief issue and of their personal devil. The chant of anti-Vietnam marchers—"Hey, hey, LBJ, how many kids have you killed today?"—ceased to be heard, and the number of antiwar demonstrations abated. In the score sheets of pollsters, the president's popularity zoomed upward. Kennedy and McCarthy had to revamp their strategies, and party regulars and others who had been lukewarm toward Johnson but not attracted to the dove-leftist orientation of his opponents now rediscovered his merits and looked around for a proadministration candidate.

Humphrey Announces Candidacy

Vice-president Hubert Humphrey was the immediate and almost the only choice. His experience in national affairs, his domestic liberalism, his loyalty to the president, especially on Vietnam, his strength with labor, and his reputation as a campaign exhorter were all in his favor. Paradoxically, in the South this veteran champion of civil rights was developing strength with conservatives who had no use for Kennedy and who could not stomach McCarthy's peace stand. The vice-president delayed announcing his candidacy, kept out of the primaries, and let state organizations and favorite sons try to block the Kennedy-McCarthy drives. Finally, on April 27, when his organization and financing had been set up, he hoisted his standard at Washington and pledged himself to a campaign of moderation and restraint with party unity his goal. Senators Walter F. Mondale of Minnesota and Fred Harris of Oklahoma were his joint managers.

As predicted, McCarthy carried Wisconsin over Johnson, 56 percent to 35 percent, two days after the latter had announced his withdrawal as a candidate. An army of middle-western collegians provided enthusiasm and doorbell ringing, a following that was better organized than the administration forces. But the gloss of New Hampshire was missing. He had defeated a noncandidate.

Kennedy and McCarthy
Vie for Delegates

Although their appeals on major issues were not substantially different, Kennedy and McCarthy battled for delegates in Indiana, Nebraska, Oregon, South Dakota, and California. The assassination of the Reverend Martin Luther King, Jr., and the rioting that followed made civil rights problems even more pressing. Kennedy's record was better in this area, and his name meant more to ghetto dwellers and other underdogs. He had more experienced aides, funds for all purposes, and the prestigious Kennedy clan in his corner. Only Oregon, without ethnic blocs and serious urban problems, went for McCarthy, who drew more upper-middle-class support. This was the first defeat for a Kennedy in a primary since John F. had set out to run for office in Massachusetts.

This setback made the California primary a make-or-break test for Kennedy. Both candidates had only a week after Oregon for intensive stumping but did appear together on a television panel, which revealed no clear differences on any important issues.

By midnight of June 4, the nation's most populous state registered a safe but not overwhelming margin for Kennedy, 46 percent, as opposed to 42 percent for McCarthy and 12 percent for an uncommitted group. That same evening, South Dakota gave Kennedy 50 percent of its total, with Humphrey and McCarthy dividing the rest.

But what started out as a night of victory turned into a night of anguish. An assassin's bullet cut down a second Kennedy on June 5 in the kitchen of the Ambassador Hotel in Los Angeles.

Kennedy's leaderless forces continued to offer slates of delegates who would uphold his principles in the remaining states. They would not accept McCarthy, and Humphrey's Vietnam stand repelled them, although the Kennedy field marshal, Lawrence O'Brien, moved into the vice-president's camp and took over direction of his strategy. Senator George McGovern of South Dakota offered a solution by a belated announcement of his candidacy just two weeks before the date of the convention. Antiwar and a liberal on domestic policies, he drew in a considerable number of Kennedy political orphans. But Humphrey was apparently too far in the lead in delegate count to be affected by this late candidacy.

Republican Possibilities

Among the Republican possibilities, Governor George Romney was off to an early start by an announcement of his candidacy on November 18, 1967. A western tour and some other public appearances seemed to reveal a haziness on major issues that was made worse by some inept extemporaneous utterances. In answer to a question in a television interview about his shift of views on Vietnam, Romney stated that he had been "brainwashed" by administration experts at the time of his earlier stand. Some other off-the-cuff answers to reporters' questions further damaged his public image.

Romney's apparent decline was accompanied by a rise in the poll popularity of two noncandidates, Governor Ronald Reagan of California and Governor Rockefeller of New York, now in his third term. Reagan, attractive in appearance and skilled in audience appeal, was the conservative choice to wear Goldwater's mantle, but insisted he was only California's favorite son. Rockefeller, committed to Romney and faced with the hostility of the Goldwater alumni, resisted the pressure of liberals and independents to become a candidate. Senator Charles Percy of Illinois remained in the Polk-Pierce category.

Romney made a trip around the world to gain insight into foreign policy and entered the New Hampshire primary to contend against Richard Nixon, who declared his candidacy on February 1, 1968. Both Romney and Nixon campaigned for· the Granite State's delegates but the former's balloon had so shrunken that he suddenly announced his withdrawal on February 28, less than two weeks before Election Day. Nixon secured the state's 8 delegates by default, polling 78 percent of the Republican preference vote to 11 percent for Rockefeller, for whom a belated write-in campaign had been started after Romney dropped out. The more liberal Republicans increased the pressure on the New York governor, and he weakened enough to say that he would not refuse the national convention's call if its voice were clear. This was ten days after New Hampshire voted.

But the shifting political winds of this unpredictable April soon blew Rockefeller's noncandidacy from its moorings after President Johnson's withdrawal. Senator Thruston Morton of Kentucky and William Miller, Goldwater's running mate in 1964, began to operate a draft-Rockefeller movement. Governor Reagan was showing signs of extending his favorite-son role to include California's neighbors which could cut into Nixon's western support. In several other states, such as Ohio, favorite sons were holding out to help create a deadlock. With Nixon vague and vulnerable on Vietnam and ghetto problems, Rockefeller saw the opening widening for a liberal opponent. On April 30, he announced that he would run. It was now too late to enter the remaining primaries.

The New York governor had to sell himself through personal appeal and large-scale organized efforts as the one Republican candidate who could capture the Democratic liberals and independents so necessary for electoral success. Too many of the delegates were already chosen and committed, which made it harder to shake Nixon's hold. Rockefeller offered a fresh approach, a "New Politics," stressing his handling of urban problems in New York and outlining a four-point program on Vietnam in contrast with the cautious Nixon who, after a sweeping victory over Reagan in Oregon, ceased to campaign actively.

Robert Kennedy's death had a significant impact on the Republican situation. Rockefeller, using his talents as a crowd pleaser, spoke of the similarity of his program to the deceased senator's, and the "Rocky" badges and youngsters clamoring for autographs suggested that if he were not capturing some of the Kennedy youth contingent, at least he was drawing a GOP adolescent legion who could provide enthusiasm if

not votes. Whether the crowds that surrounded him, and his heavy spending for television and newspaper advertising, could produce much of a
delegate shift was doubtful, but opinion polls kept him optimistic, and he
campaigned up to the date of the national convention.

Nixon's Second Chance

In choosing a southern meeting place for the Republican national convention, the national committee seemed to break with tradition, but
Miami Beach had far greater kinship with the affluent North than with
the old Confederate South. Several considerations explain the choice, but
the beach city's island location, which insulated it from neighboring
Miami with its ghetto problems, ensured the convention against the pressures from outside demonstrators that might have occurred if Chicago's
bid had been accepted. But the local security authorities took no chances.
A six-foot chain-link fence surrounded the convention hall, and police
were stationed at all key points. Delegates, newspeople, and spectators
had to provide proper credentials at every turn.

Some members of the Poor People's Campaign staged brief demonstrations in the convention area, and a group attended the Tuesday session on guest tickets, but delegates were hardly aware of their presence or
of the violence that erupted in the Miami ghetto on two nights of the sessions.

The twenty-ninth Republican national convention began its deliberations on Monday, August 5, with 1,333 accredited delegates present and
National Chairman Ray C. Bliss presiding. Introduction formalities,
organization matters, the usual platform exposures of miscellaneous minor
celebrities and candidates, and speeches brimming with confidence occupied the two sessions. The first evening's oratorical festival headlined
former President Eisenhower, who was heard via a brief inspirational
message recorded at Walter Reed Hospital, where he had been confined
by a heart attack; Senator Edward Brooke of Massachusetts, temporary
chairman; Barry Goldwater; and Governor Daniel Evans of Washington,
who gave the keynote address. All the main speakers adhered to the
theme of restoring national unity with new leadership and new programs.
Not one touched on the current prejudices and hates or anything else
likely to inflame the emotions of the listeners.

On the second day, after accepting committee reports and listening to
Thomas E. Dewey and Representative Gerald R. Ford of Michigan, permanent chairman, attack the Johnson administration, the delegates were
presented with the platform. The show was then taken over by Senator
Everett Dirksen, chairman of the platform committee, whose unruly gray
hair, rumbling voice, dark-rimmed glasses, and old-fashioned oratory had

given him status as a television personality in addition to his minority leadership in the Senate. His denunciation of rioting and crime and his references to the unsafe streets of Washington and Cleveland captured his audience as the liberal pronouncements of the preceding night had not.

The moderately long (11,500 words) platform was presented in summarized form by several speakers, each dealing with one section. Dirksen took over again at the end. A week of hearings before subcommittees and the full committee had produced a platform whose chief planks had been worked out in a form acceptable enough to prevent floor fights. Urban problems and Vietnam were the original apples of discord but, as the party out of power, the Republicans could attack, generalize, and evade as the administration party could not. Differences were easier to resolve.

A preamble viewed with alarm the dire state of the nation, called for new leadership, and set forth the party's aims and pledges. A special section headed "Crisis of the Cities" began with a promise to "transform the blighted areas into centers of opportunity and progress, culture and talent." Then followed a list of broad proposals with emphasis upon federal support of state and local programs and "a greater involvement of vast private enterprise resources." Measures to alleviate and remove the frustrations that contribute to riots were advocated along with the support of "decisive action to quell civil disorders."

A special section of the platform was devoted to crime. Improved law enforcement was to be promoted in a number of ways, but the enactment of gun control legislation was to be a state responsibility with only such federal laws as might be necessary to "better enable the states to meet their responsibilities" recommended.

Welfare and poverty programs were to be overhauled, tax credits were proposed for employers who would provide job training, and local ownership of business in depressed areas would be encouraged by state and community development corporations and other aids. Youth was given a special section which included a recommendation to the states to consider giving eighteen-year-olds the right to vote, and promises to liberalize the draft system with a volunteer military force a future possibility. Education was covered in a detailed list of proposals, with federal assistance in the form of grants and loans to states and individuals a leading feature. In general, the document was liberal and forward-looking on domestic affairs and had fair words, if not many specific proposals, for taking care of every important element of American life.

On Vietnam the platform committee had been pulled between the hawkish views of Reagan and the dovish inclinations of Nixon and Rockefeller. A carefully worded compromise proved surprisingly acceptable, with the doves having the better of the solution. The final version criticized administration policies as political, military, and diplomatic failures and called for new leadership and a strategy concentrating on the security of the Vietnamese population and the development of a greater sense of nationhood along with "a progressive de-Americanization of the war." A fair and equitable settlement was promised—"Neither peace at any price nor a camouflaged surrender of legitimate United States or allied interests"—and a willingness to pursue peace negotiations "as long as they offer any reasonable prospect for a just peace." Neither a bombing halt nor possible further escalation of military activity was mentioned.

Other aspects of foreign relations and national defense were covered in generalities and ambiguities on the positive side, although Israel was promised "countervailing help" to offset the imbalance created by Soviet military build-up in the Middle East. The strong anti-Communist tone of the 1964 platform was absent from the 1968 party pronouncement.

The platform was adopted without opposition, although a North Carolina delegate was prevented by a dead microphone from offering as an amendment a stronger plank on Vietnam.

Nixon, last of the candidates to appear on the scene, arrived on Monday evening to find his carefully planned organization functioning smoothly. Rockefeller and Reagan, who announced his candidacy Monday afternoon, had been presenting their cases to state delegations and key individuals, but Nixon held open house in his Hilton Plaza headquarters while his hundreds of workers looked after his interests from branch centers in various hotels. A communications network coordinated activities. All indications pointed toward his nomination if his lines held firmly.

At the nominating session on Wednesday, August 7, twelve candidates were put in nomination, with speeches and demonstration ceremonies consuming more than seven hours. Two favorite sons, Governor Walter J. Hickel of Alaska and Senator Strom Thurmond of South Carolina, heard their merits recited, then withdrew in favor of Nixon. The balloting, completed at 1:52 A.M., gave Nixon 692 votes, Nelson Rockefeller 277, Reagan 182, Rhodes 55, Romney 50, Senator Clifford P. Case of New Jersey 22, Senator Frank Carlson of Kansas 20, Governor Winthrop Rockefeller of Arkansas 18, Senator Hiram L. Fong of Hawaii 14, Harold E. Stassen 2, Mayor John V. Lindsay of New York 1. Wisconsin's 30 votes had given Nixon the 667 votes necessary for the nomination. Changes of votes added to his total, but Governor Reagan's motion to make the nomination unanimous seemed to have been overlooked by Chairman Ford.

Agnew for Vice-President

After many hours of consultation with party bigwigs and selected lesser lights, Nixon chose Governor Spiro Agnew of Maryland as his running mate. He arrived at this solution by a process of eliminating names of the too-liberal and too-conservative possibilities, such as Mayor Lindsay and Senator Hatfield of Oregon on the left and Reagan and Senator Tower of Texas on the right. He had promised Senator Thurmond, his southern spokesman, that he would not name a man objectionable to the South, which virtually ruled out a northern choice. Nixon would have preferred one of two close friends—either Lieutenant Governor Robert Finch of California or Rogers Morton, a congressman from Maryland—but both refused to be considered.

Agnew had had a satisfactory civil rights record as governor until the Baltimore riots when he angered black leaders with his criticisms of their attitudes and his defense of strong measures to put down rioting. Of Greek ancestry (his father's name had been Anagnostopoulous), the tall, broad-shouldered governor had a direct, forceful manner of speech and promised to be an effective campaigner. Although he had originally favored Rockefeller, he had switched to Nixon and had made the nominating speech for him.

When the delegates reassembled at the final session on Thursday night, liberals objecting to the southward slant of the choice tried to stir up a revolt. However, Rockefeller refused to help, Lindsay refused to run, and the remnant of dissidents ended up voting for Governor Romney, who was nominated by a Nevada delegate. He received 186 votes to Agnew's 1,119, with 28 scattered or not voting. The vote for Agnew was then made unanimous.

Vice-presidential candidates many times have been lifted out of a contemporary anonymity to provide sectional or factional balance to tickets. The Theodore Roosevelts and the Lyndon Johnsons are far outnumbered by the Fillmores, the Hobarts, and many others who may not have lacked merit but who certainly were short in political stature. Governor Spiro Agnew was one of these running-mate dark horses. But Nixon himself had been an unknown quantity to most of the voters in 1952.

Nixon's acceptance speech was one of his best. Most of it was an old story to reporters who had followed him on the campaign trail, but to national television audiences it revealed the new Nixon whose vigor in denunciation was balanced by a forward-looking idealism and warm personal touches, and whose skillful appeal to "the forgotten Americans, the nonshouters, the nondemonstrators" seemed to strike the right chord for the campaign ahead.

Tumult and Strife
with the Democrats in Chicago

President Johnson and Mayor Daley were given the credit for the Democratic national committee's choice of Chicago as the site of the party's 1968 convention. This was on October 9, 1967, but already Black

Power and anti-Vietnam extremists were talking of making the city the scene of mass demonstrations aimed at disrupting the convention and preventing the the renomination of Johnson. Mayor Daley's assurances that security would prevail helped counteract the arguments for Miami Beach, already the Republican choice.

The mayor lived up to his promises by turning International Amphitheater into a fortress protected by 7 feet of barbed wire, an army of security guards, and electronic credential scanners at checkpoints. The Chicago police force of nearly 12,000 was put on 12-hour shifts, and 5,600 national guardsmen and 7,500 federal troops were being kept in reserve for riot duty. President Johnson's withdrawal as a candidate had changed the situation, but there was still the possibility that he might visit the convention. In any case, antiadministration demonstrations that might lead to rioting were to be expected.

Members of the National Mobilization Committee to End the War and the Youth International Party (the "Yippies"), groups of McCarthy's collegians (who came against his wishes), and various New Leftist militants made up the army of protesters who assembled at Chicago expecting to vent their frustrations and disenchantments in mass demonstrations. They were refused permission to parade and were dispersed when they tried to camp overnight in Lincoln Park. Although disappointed at the small total of visiting dissidents, the leaders nevertheless were determined to provoke confrontations with the police. Even though the fear of an outbreak was one reason for the presence of federal troops, the city's black ghetto gave almost no support. In the end, the security forces seemed to have outnumbered the demonstrators.

The thirty-fifth Democratic national convention, a body of 3,099 delegates casting 2,622 votes, opened its proceedings on Monday evening, August 26. It engaged in acrimonious debates interspersed with frequent roll calls for four days and ended its work on Thursday in an atmosphere of angry recriminations. Senator Daniel K. Inouye of Hawaii was temporary chairman, Representative Carl Albert of Oklahoma, permanent chairman. The latter presided during the most tumultuous periods.

The first two sessions were largely taken up with the reports of the credentials and rules committees. The former had been confronted with seventeen contests from fifteen states. Racial imbalance was the issue involved in the challenges in several southern states. In each case, the committee's recommendations, presented by its chairman, Governor Richard J. Hughes of New Jersey, were accepted, but several required roll calls. The Georgia decision was to seat both claimants and divide the vote equally, a solution rejected by Governor Lester G. Maddox who earlier had announced his candidacy for president. In the case of Mississippi an insurgent "loyal" delegation was seated. The regular Alabama group was accepted after a party loyalty declaration had been required of each delegate.

The convention voted to abolish the venerable unit rule, obsolete in most states, and to forbid the use of a unit rule in any stage of the delegate selection process in the future. The national committee was also instructed to make sure that all Democrats in a state should have meaningful and timely opportunities to participate in the selection of delegates.

The platform was presented by Representative Hale Boggs of Louisiana at the Tuesday session. A week of hearings in Washington and Chicago before four panels, a report by a Democratic congressional platform hearing committee, and, reportedly, some strong suggestions from the White House produced a reasonable consensus on all matters except Vietnam. Consideration of a minority report on this issue was postponed to the next day.

The majority report generally upheld the administration policy on the Vietnam War. It favored a total bombing halt only when this would not endanger the lives of troops in the field but promised negotiations with Hanoi for an immediate end of hostilities and the withdrawal of foreign forces. The minority plank represented a consensus of all shades of "dovishness." It called for an unconditional end to all bombing, negotiations for a mutual withdrawal of United States and North Vietnamese troops, and the encouragement of negotiations by the South Vietnamese with the National Liberation Front (the Viet Cong) with a view toward the creation of a broadly representative government for South Vietnam.

The debate, with each side allotted an hour to present its case, was conducted on an unusually high intellectual level for a convention floor battle. More than thirty speakers shared the rostrum.* The minority report lost by a vote of 1,041¼ to 1,567¾. The platform was then adopted by a voice vote.

Its eighteen thousand words reaffirmed the party's position on most foreign and domestic questions and reiterated its object "to march at the head of events," although "we candidly recognize that the cost of trying the untried, of ploughing new ground, is bound to be occasional error." It took pride in the ninety months of recession-free prosperity under Demo-

* Among the better-known speakers were the following: For the majority report—Senators Edmund S. Muskie (Me.), Gale W. McGee (Wyo.), and Frank Moss (Utah); Representative Wayne Hays (O.); Governor Warren E. Hearnes of Missouri, Wilson W. Wyatt of Kentucky; and Representative Boggs, chairman of the platform committee. For the minority report—Senators Wayne Morse (Ore.), Vance Hartke (Ind.), Albert Gore (Tenn.), Joseph Tydings (Md.), and Claiborne Pell (R.I.); Representatives John Conyers (Mich.), Henry Reuss (Wis.), and Phillip Burton (Calif.), who had charge of the minority speakers; Senatorial candidates Paul O'Dwyer of New York and John J. Gilligan of Ohio; Kenneth O'Donnell of Massachusetts; Pierre Salinger of California; and Governor Phillip Hoff of Vermont.

cratic administrations. Accomplishments in such fields as education, health, civil rights, and housing were catalogued and contrasted with the negative attitude of the Republicans toward reform.

The Democrats went beyond the Republicans in declaring for a constitutional amendment lowering the voting age to eighteen. The Peace Corps and other youth programs were praised and their expansion promised. Soviet aggression against Czechoslovakia was condemned, and American contributions to the solid achievements of the free world praised with due credit to Democratic policies. A strong and balanced defense establishment and a strengthening of the ties of the North Atlantic Community were pledged, along with praise for the limited Nuclear Test Ban Treaty, the Nonproliferation Treaty, and the treaty barring the orbiting of weapons of mass destruction.

Continued progress in the removal of trade barriers was advocated, along with provisions to remedy unfair and destructive import competition. Other advanced nations were expected to share in foreign-aid development programs in greater degree. The United States was pledged to continue to accept world responsibilities but would not try to mold the world in its own image.

At the nominating session on Wednesday evening, five candidates were put in nomination—McCarthy, Humphrey, McGovern, Governor Dan Moore of North Carolina, and the Reverend Channing Phillips, a black humanitarian leader from Washington, D.C. Governor Maddox of Georgia had ceased to be a candidate and had gone home. A movement to draft Senator Edward Kennedy aborted when Mayor Daley committed Illinois to Humphrey and Kennedy sent word to the drafters to desist.

Meanwhile, leftist dissidents who had been engaging in skirmishes with the Chicago police for three days in Lincoln and Grant parks attempted to mobilize in front of the Conrad Hilton hotel for a march on the convention hall. Exacerbated by the dissidents' tactics of planned provocation and their refusal to disperse, the police charged upon the jeering demonstrators and proceeded to club indiscriminately whoever happened to be caught in their onslaught net, whether demonstrators, male or female, reporters, photographers, or more-or-less-innocent bystanders.

In the amphitheater angry anti-Humphrey delegates, appalled by the televised pictures of police violence, made Mayor Daley, in a front seat, the particular object of their denunciations and jeers. Senator Abraham Ribicoff of Connecticut used his nominating speech for McGovern to deliver a direct attack upon the mayor for his "Gestapo tactics." Other hostile speakers played upon the same theme, and a Wisconsin delegate tried to interrupt the roll call to move an adjournment to another city.

The balloting produced no surprises. It gave Humphrey 1,760¼ votes, McCarthy 601, McGovern 146½, Phillips 67½, Moore 17½, Kennedy 12¾, Paul Bryant 1½, James H. Gray ½, George Wallace ½, with 14 abstentions. A voice vote made the nomination unanimous, as the chairman ignored a scattering of boos. The galleries, reportedly packed with Mayor Daley's retainers, yelled their approval.

The Thursday session began with a tribute to Robert Kennedy, consisting of a taped speech by Edward Kennedy from Cape Cod and a film eulogy. Delegates sang the "Battle Hymn of the Republic," and some of the angry minority attempted to continue repeating the chorus to delay convention proceedings. A tribute to the Reverend Martin Luther King, Jr., ended the song filibuster.

Senator Fred Harris of Oklahoma, runner-up on the Humphrey list for the second office, presented Senator Edmund S. Muskie of Maine as the nominee's vice-presidential choice. Wisconsin put in nomination Julian Bond of Georgia as a gesture of dissent, but Bond withdrew, since he was only twenty-eight years old, and could not constitutionally qualify. Muskie received 1,922½ votes, Bond 48½, several others 26¾ in all, with 199¾ not voting or not recorded. The nomination was then made unanimous.

The tall, rugged-faced Maine senator was not a surprise choice. Nine years on Capitol Hill after two terms as governor of his state had established his reputation as a working senator, an authority on urban problems, and a liberal with an independent spirit and little taste for power-grabbing and self-aggrandizement. A Roman Catholic and son of a Polish immigrant, (Marciszewski had been shortened to Muskie) he overbalanced Republican Agnew's voting pull in Democratic books, for Polish voters outnumbered Greek by a considerable margin. A Phi Beta Kappa key established his rapport with the intelligentsia.

Humphrey Works for Conciliation

Humphrey's acceptance speech, a masterpiece of his skill at conciliation, expressed regret at the tragic events of the week but warned that violence breeds violence, and assured his listeners that the policies of tomorrow need not be limited by the policies of yesterday. A standing ovation unmarred by boos followed his concluding appeal for unity. President Johnson, with much of the blame for the party's troubles put at his door, celebrated his birthday in Texas, and watched the convention proceedings on television.

Humphrey announced that his campaign manager and the new national chairman would be veteran professional organizer Lawrence F. O'Brien, who had served both John F. and Robert Kennedy, had been postmaster general under Lyndon Johnson, and had joined Humphrey's camp as national campaign coordinator after Robert Kennedy's death. Senator McGovern, candidate for reelection from South Dakota, appeared on the platform with Humphrey, but McCarthy remained at his head-quarters. Later, in a valedictory in Grant Park he advised his followers to work for peace candidates but refused to endorse the national ticket.

Charges that the convention had been rigged and the minority sup-pressed reflected the bitterness of the defeated rather than the actual situ-ation. Mayor Daley's too rigid security measures, some gallery-packing, and the handling of some matters of convention procedure had angered the minority but did not affect the major decisions. They had been made on the floor of the convention after open debate and sometimes acrimo-nious exchanges, with the whole world watching on television, as the street dissidents chanted in front of television cameras. If the game had been played unfairly, the rigging had been done back in the states where the old rules had been followed in electing the delegates. McCarthy admitted later that he could not have been nominated at Chicago even if his sup-porters had not been given the Daley treatment. Charges of majority rig-ging are an old story in convention history.

A Choice of Evils

Nixon opened his campaign in Chicago on September 4 with a ticker-tape-and-confetti motorcade witnessed by several hundred thousand cheering curbside admirers, followed by a televised question-and-answer session with a local panel, which was beamed at a regional audience. Visits to San Francisco, Pittsburgh, and Houston followed. The can-didate was breaking ground for an intensive campaign to capture the large swing states necessary for victory.

Nixon's efficient preconvention organization carried over into the cam-paign, although it was necessarily expanded, and some personnel shifts were made. John N. Mitchell, a law partner, continued as his manager. Mitchell's wide experience in the financial field of state and municipal bonds had given him contacts that made up for the handicap of a late entry into politics. A carefully charted division of labor and a staff largely of younger men not associated with the 1960 struggle relieved the candi-date of the heavy burdens of planning and decision-making except at the top levels. Electronic aids and gadgets of every type made the communi-cations setup a marvel of speed and efficiency.

Working with the newer men were such old friends and associates of the Eisenhower days as Maurice Stans, heading the Republican finance committee; Charles S. Rhyne, a law-school friend, in charge of the United Citizens for Nixon-Agnew; Herbert S. Klein, a San Diego editor, who became director of communications; and Robert Finch, lieutenant gover-nor of California, an old friend and closest to the candidate personally.

Former Governor William Scranton of Pennsylvania was sent on a scouting trip to Europe and served as a roving foreign-affairs adviser. National Chairman Ray Bliss was outside the Nixon orbit and dealt with state and local politicos and their candidates.

Dropping the plane-hopping and whistle-stopping methods of 1960, which exhausted the candidate physically and mentally, the new Nixon limited the number of major addresses, had one basic speech for ordinary party jubilees, followed a carefully timed schedule, and used all the resources of television and radio to present his case. In answering questions from selected panels or telephoned in by interested listeners, he sought to match Humphrey's skill in extemporaneous speech without the latter's volubility. In his appearances in motorcades and at open meetings he was bothered very little by hostile demonstrators and hecklers who found better game elsewhere. Only near the end of the campaign did he resort to some old-fashioned barnstorming and stumping, mostly in Ohio and Pennsylvania.

The new Nixon offered the country a new leadership and a new approach. Assailing administration policies and Humphrey as a responsible formulator of policy, he summed up his campaign appeal in an oft-repeated key statement: "I say the man who helped us get into trouble is not the man to get us out." He broke with the traditional Republican concept of the presidency, to which Eisenhower had adhered, by taking an activist view of the office whose occupant must provide leadership above all else. He called for an "open administration"—a thrust at the credibility gap charged against Johnson.

On Vietnam Nixon was carefully noncommittal. He explained that he did not want to say anything to undercut the Paris negotiations with North Vietnam or to reveal his hand as to the policy he might follow as president. He held the administration responsible for the war, but he did not pinpoint its mistakes. The Soviet invasion of Czechoslovakia, he felt, justified a postponement of ratification of the Nuclear Nonproliferation Treaty. He would strengthen national defense to eliminate the "security gap" that Johnson-McNamara policies had permitted to develop.

On domestic issues, the Republican candidate called for reduced federal spending, a balanced budget, and other measures that might be found necessary to combat inflation and strengthen the dollar. He sent a letter to two thousand leaders in the business of handling securities in which he denounced the Democrats for heavy-handed regulatory schemes and promised an independent, comprehensive study of the entire role played by financial institutions in the economy. Nixon denied Humphrey's charge that he was opposed to social security and Medicare and promised to make them work better for the people they were supposed to help.

On the problems of the ghetto Nixon held to the platform pledge to encourage the private sector of the economy through tax incentives and other aids to create employment and to develop "black capitalism." Little effort was made to win black votes. Few blacks came to Nixon meetings; neither Nixon nor Agnew campaigned in person in the urban ghettos; and Agnew was reported to have commented, "When you've seen one [ghetto], you've seen them all." There is evidence that late in the campaign a little-publicized effort was made by spending money and sending out field workers to build up Nixon as a friend of blacks, but it came too late to get results or to disturb his rapport with the Thurmond South.

Nixon, like Wallace, who accused him of thunder-stealing, got the most mileage out of the law-and-order issue. He warned of the ominous increase in crimes of violence, deplored the failure of the administration —and Attorney General Ramsey Clark in particular—to use federal power to curb rioting and lawlessness, and promised the "forgotten people"—the law-abiding middle-class citizens—that the streets would be made safe for them and their children. In his southern forays the new Nixon did not repudiate desegregation but spoke out against the use of federal grants to force compliance on school districts and, while favoring open housing, implied that it might be handled better at state and local levels.

Vice-President Humphrey, after a brief Minnesota vacation, came to Washington to address a B'nai B'rith convention on Sunday, September 8. Then on Monday he began in Philadelphia his first campaign trek, which took him across the large industrial states. With much of the South abandoned to Wallace, the Democrats had to reinvigorate the loyalties of city ethnic groups, propitiate antiwar defectors, and work with organized labor leaders to offset the pull of the Alabama governor on the blue-collar workers of the North.

Humphrey's campaign encountered heavy weather from the beginning. Peace extremists and other antiadministration dissidents organized demonstrations to disrupt his meetings with hecklings, antiwar chants, and walkouts. When Senator Edward Kennedy appeared with Humphrey at a political rally in his home city of Boston, even he was shouted down. With the organization still being structured, financing unsettled, and local disaffection a drag on party energies, the Democrats seemed to be facing a November disaster. But Chairman O'Brien presently got his house in order and made some changes in publicity arrangements. With campaign consultant Joseph Napolitan as director of advertising, the Democrats put on a belated but effective television blitz that hurled spot commercials at the enemy, presented Humphrey to advantage in a documentary, and showed him at his extemporaneous best in selected film clips. Financing improved with the Democratic candidate's rise in poll percentages but remained a problem to the end.

At first Humphrey tried to reach too many people in too short a time. He could not keep to his planned schedules. Sometimes he overtalked to the point of blurring rather than clarifying his stands and, when he was not too ebullient, was too vehement and too denunciatory. Presently hoarseness, frayed nerves, pressure from his advisers, and evidence of growing party unity helped to tame down somewhat this battler for a seemingly lost cause in his attempt to emulate Truman's feat of 1948.

President Johnson at first took an aloof and almost disparaging attitude toward his vice-president, as, for example, when he openly contradicted Humphrey's overoptimistic prediction that a beginning of troop withdrawal from Vietnam might come in late 1968 or early 1969. But on October 10 he gave a fifteen-minute endorsement of Humphrey intermixed with slams at Republican "reaction and inaction" and Wallace's "empty rhetoric and violent appeals to emotion." On later occasions he spoke out wholeheartedly for the candidate and appeared with him before a capacity crowd in the Houston Astrodome at a final rally. However, he did his party's cause the most good when he announced a bombing halt in Vietnam just before the election.

Humphrey's early campaign speeches followed the pattern of his liberal past. He pointed to the years of prosperity under Democratic rule but said he was looking forward to a new day of equal rights for all, and promised a national attack on the problems of poverty, health, and education. Nixon he called a social reactionary. The lukewarm responses of his audiences and the widespread concern over rioting and increases in crimes of violence compelled him to shift his emphasis to the law-and-order issue, which he coupled with justice for all. Toward the campaign's close he was promising federal funds and other aids to strengthen and improve local law-enforcement agencies, legislation to deal with guerrilla bands and vigilantes, and a firearms registration law. He accused Nixon and Wallace of stirring up fears and emotions without offering programs and of ignoring the need to combat poverty, despair, and alienation. He also denied that court decisions were a factor in the crime increase.

Labor's leadership backed Humphrey solidly and pressured the rank and file to resist the Wallace lure. The Alabama governor's record was combed for evidences of antilabor views and acts, which were then cited in pamphlets circulated by the thousands by the AFL–CIO's Committee on Political Education.

Humphrey's stand on Vietnam bombing was his and the party's most difficult problem. In a nationwide televised address on foreign policy given in Salt Lake City on September 30, the candidate teetered in the balance by promising to end the bombing while at the same time saying that he "would place key importance on evidence—direct or indirect, by deed or word—of Communist willingness to restore the demilitarized zone between North and South Vietnam." Otherwise, bombing might be resumed.

On October 8, before an editors' group, Humphrey invited the Soviet

Union to take the responsibility for seeing that Hanoi did not show bad faith once the bombing had been stopped. This implied that he was now committed to an unconditional bombing halt. But not until President Johnson did declare an unconditional bombing halt just before the election did the candidate get completely out of the Vietnam tangle.

Senator McCarthy had left Chicago without endorsing Humphrey and remained inactive until he returned from a trip to Europe. Then he began to campaign for senatorial peace candidates and, although he gave Muskie a verbal pat on the back, he still insisted that certain conditions he had laid down before he would support his party's candidates had not been met. But the pressure for party unity was pulling most of the McCarthy and McGovern dissidents into the path of orthodoxy, particularly those who were themselves running for office. McCarthy finally fell in line with a half-hearted endorsement of the national ticket a week before the election but confirmed it more warmly on a Humphrey telethon on election eve.

The major candidates for vice-president, comparatively unknown outside their own states, developed contrasting images. As Maryland's governor, Agnew had affronted black civil rights leaders, and his blunt law-and-order campaign speeches did not mollify them. His inexperience in national politics led him to make loose statements that had to be explained away, such as using the belittling terms "Jap" and "Polack" for Japanese and Polish citizens. But his forthrightness possibly helped Nixon counteract the Wallace pull.

Muskie was more of an asset to Humphrey. He answered hecklers with calmness and restraint, praised the McCarthy youth for their involvement in politics, and was especially effective with Polish audiences. His height and craggy features were in the Lincoln mold and added to his crowd appeal.

Wallace and the American Independent Party

George Wallace announced on February 8 that he would run for president as the candidate of the American Independent Party. Not until shortly before the election did he find a running mate, General Curtis E. LeMay, former Air Force chief of staff. His appeal was to racist Democrats in the deep South, where many Democratic candidates and local organizations supported him or preserved a careful neutrality.

Outside the South various rightist groups helped, but it was his appeal to the dissatisfied that threatened to make serious inroads into old party strength. He offered an antifederal government, pro-state rights, and a law-and-order package with racism inside the wrapper. He derided or assailed "pointed heads" (intellectuals), beatniks, the Supreme Court, bureaucrats, school busing, "national liberal parties," pollsters, and national news media. On Vietnam, he would end the war quickly by negotiation, but if that failed, would let the Joint Chiefs of Staff take over.

Other Minor Parties

Dissatisfaction on the left did not jell into a party for lack of a national candidate. When McCarthy refused to let his name be used, some of his following decided to organize a New Democratic Coalition to back local peace candidates and work to get control of Democratic state organizations for future battles, while sitting out the presidential election. Other groups of dissatisfied leftists called themselves the New Party but solved the candidate problem by accepting black splinter-party nominations or voting for McCarthy without his consent.

A Peace and Freedom Party, at a national convention in August, nominated extremist Black Power author Eldridge Cleaver of California as its presidential candidate. A more moderate faction backed Dick Gregory, well-known entertainer, who ran as a Freedom and Peace and New Party choice in five states, mostly in the East. Cleaver, a Black Panther leader in California, drew most of his support in that state.

The older minor parties, the Prohibition, Socialist Labor, and Socialist Workers, also offered candidates as usual, and a woman, Mrs. Charlene Mitchell, ran as a Communist candidate in Minnesota and Washington; she was the first Communist presidential candidate since 1940. Some overlapping of endorsements by splinter parties and some ballot write-in candidates added to the complexity of tabulating minor-party votes.

Unlike the anti-Goldwater line-up of 1964, the press was largely pro-Republican in 1968, as it had been in the Roosevelt–Truman years. The Republican Goldwater defectors returned to their old faith. The Scripps-Howard newspaper chain represented the most significant shift from its 1964 policy when it declared for Nixon. The more liberal independent papers inclined toward Humphrey, with the *New York Times* his outstanding supporter. Most striking was the lack of enthusiasm for either of the major-party candidates and the almost universal hostility toward Wallace. But newspaper editorial endorsements carried little weight compared with the direct appeal of candidates through television.

The closing session of the Ninetieth Congress had campaign repercussions. A virtual filibuster prevented action on President Johnson's nomination of Justice Abe Fortas to succeed Chief Justice Earl Warren, who had offered to resign. Conservative dislike of the Warren Court and Republican arguments, supported by Nixon, that a lame-duck president should leave such an important vacancy to be filled by his successor seemed to account for the rejection by nonaction on Fortas.

The Senate also refused to act on a House measure to suspend the provision of the Communications Act that required equal treatment of all candidates by the television networks. This would have permitted the three candidates to debate before a nationwide audience, like the Kennedy-Nixon confrontation of 1960. It was Senator Dirksen who prevented action on the proposal. Nixon felt that he had nothing to gain in a triangular free-for-all and did not relish getting involved in a law-and-order melee with Wallace which would sharpen the line between them.

Republicans answered Humphrey's charge that Nixon was afraid of a duplication of the Kennedy-Nixon affair of 1960 by pointing to Johnson's failure to take on Goldwater four years earlier and Humphrey's refusal to lock horns with McCarthy during the recent Democratic primary battles. The Democratic candidate offered to share with his rivals an hour of Sunday evening prime time, but Nixon ignored the invitation, although Wallace was willing. Humphrey then used the hour, on October 20, for a program of his own. In his later speeches, he referred to Nixon as "Richard the Chicken-Hearted." All three candidates made final television appearances on election eve, Humphrey and Nixon in live question-and-answer sessions, Wallace with a taped speech.

A Hairline Decision

Last-minute poll predictions of a close election were borne out by early returns on November 5. Humphrey was running surprisingly well in the East and was in a close battle for the Middle West. Nixon was sweeping the upper South and most of the trans-Mississippi West. Not until shortly before noon on Wednesday, when three large doubtful states, California, Ohio, and Illinois, were accredited to Nixon, was it certain that he had won.

Nixon carried Tennessee, Kentucky, Virginia, the Carolinas, and Florida in the South, the West except for Texas, Washington, and Hawaii, and the Middle West except for Michigan and Minnesota. In the East, New Hampshire, Vermont, New Jersey, and Delaware were the only Republican states. The rest of that section plus West Virginia, Maryland, and the District of Columbia constituted a contiguous Humphrey electoral bloc. Humphrey, Muskie, and Nixon carried their home states; Agnew lost his. Wallace had only the 1964 Goldwater South—Georgia, Alabama, Mississippi, and Louisiana, with Arkansas instead of South Carolina.

Nixon received 301 electoral votes, Humphrey 191, and Wallace 46.

One North Carolina Nixon elector defected to Wallace. The final tabulation of the popular vote gave Nixon 31,785,148 (43.4 percent), Humphrey 31,274,503 (42.7 percent), Wallace 9,901,151 (13.5 percent).* The American Independent candidate had received the largest vote ever cast for a third party choice, and only Theodore Roosevelt in 1912 and La Follette in 1924 had greater percentages of the popular vote.

The closeness of the contest after the landslide predictions of early autumn caught political pundits and commentators by surprise. The late shiftings, as shown by the final polls, had given them no time to attempt new diagnoses. Most of the post-mortems offered several explanations for the hairline outcome: the exertions of labor leaders to keep blue-collar admirers of Wallace in the Democratic fold; the courageous battle Humphrey had waged against apparently overwhelming odds; the failure of Nixon to debate with Humphrey; Agnew's slips; the unexpected popular appeal of Muskie; and President Johnson's last minute announcement of a bombing halt which may have helped bring dove holdouts into line for Humphrey. It is also to be remembered that the fires of party insurgency tend to abate with the approach of November, the more so if the alternatives are unattractive. And the decrepit old Roosevelt coalition of interest groups had more vitality than the experts suspected.

If Nixon's strategy did not secure the mandate he wanted, at least it had paid off in giving him an electoral majority. The nomination of Agnew and the support of Strom Thurmond had saved the Carolinas and the upper South from Wallace. Nixon's exploiting of the law-and-order theme, his avoidance of a Vietnam commitment, and his emphasis on administration failings, domestic and foreign, and the need for a change kept the party unified and worked well enough outside the East.

In the congressional races, the voters seemed to have resolved their perplexities by voting for familiar names. Incumbents were generally successful, regardless of party, and Democratic majorities held up. The Republicans netted only four more seats in the House of Representatives and five in the Senate. The new line-up in the House was 243 Democrats and 192 Republicans; in the Senate, 58 and 42. These results did not reflect as much of a swing to the right as the presidential vote seemed to indicate. In the state elections the Republicans did somewhat better. With victories in thirteen of twenty-one governorship contests, they now had control of the statehouses in thirty-one states, although Agnew's resignation returned Maryland to the Democrats.

In the South the spread of the Republican party and the intransigent

---

* Minor party candidates received the following votes: Henning Blomen, Socialist Labor, 52,591; Fred Halstead, Socialist Worker, 41,390; Dick Gregory, New Party and Freedom and Peace, 47,097; Eldridge Cleaver, Peace and Freedom, 8,736; E. Harold Munn, Sr., Prohibition, 14,915. Although not a candidate, Eugene McCarthy received 25,552 votes in five states.

racism of Wallace's American Independent Party had created the incon-
gruity of a three-party system in national elections and a two-party line-
up at the lower levels. Many Democratic candidates for state and local
offices endorsed Wallace or came to terms in some fashion with his supporters to save themselves. If he and his following continued to dominate
the old cotton South, it seemed fated to remain a racist enclave with its
own type of politics.

From all quarters came a demand for an end to the old electoral
system that, for a few hours on election night, held over the country the
danger of a constitutional crisis and an interregnum that could possibly
end with a subversion of the popular will. The nation might not be so fortunate next time.

President and Mrs. Johnson did their part to make the transfer of
authority and responsibility to the new administration one of the smooth-
est on record for a party change. With the books closed on the Johnson
years, commentating journalists, donning the garb of Clio, the Muse of
history, and impatient historians, in their concern for posterity and profit,
were offering their ratings of the proud, controversial Texan. The most
objective felt that Johnson had foundered on Vietnam; although he had
been remarkably successful in the field of domestic legislation, he had
contributed to his difficulties with the press and public by a deviousness
and lack of candor (the "credibility gap"); and excessive personal vanity
and a display of quirks of temperament and temper had further flawed
his presidential image.

Not to be minimized is the hard fact that from the moment of his
accession to the presidency, Johnson had had to contend with a Kennedy
myth and a Kennedy cult, too ready to downgrade his performance. Yet,
in the company of the activist-reforming presidents, he might well rate a
place in the front row.

XX

Nixon's Landslide

RICHARD MILHOUS NIXON had pledged to end the bitter Vietnam War honorably, but despite his determined efforts the conflict went on. Another 13,000 Americans died in Indochina by January 1972—bringing total casualties to 45,639 since 1961. Opposition to the war raged at home, creating personal tensions and weakening respect for government. The tragic killings by National Guardsmen at Kent State University on May 4, 1970 during peace demonstrations emphasized how the unpopular war had bitterly divided the American people. The extent of antiwar sentiment was demonstrated when some 200,000 people converged on Washington in May 1971 to voice their dissatisfaction with Vietnam policy.

Issues Facing the Candidates

In the summer of 1971 public-opinion surveys showed that two parallel desires dominated the national mood—a determination to get out of Vietnam and a resolve to take care of domestic problems. The latter included widespread use of drugs, permissiveness, welfare fraud, unemployment, women's rights, and environmental protection. In political terms this discontent with existing policies and leadership jeopardized Nixon's reelection. He had won a three-cornered race in 1968 with only 43 percent of the popular vote, and in the spring of 1971 the president trailed Senator Edmund Muskie of Maine in a Harris survey—47 to 39 percent, with George Wallace receiving 11 percent. Nixon and his aides recognized the political peril. The president wrote later that "it seemed possible that I might not even be nominated for reelection in 1972."

Nixon's prospects soon began to improve. Skillfully, the White House used the advantages of incumbency to improve the president's image and to ameliorate dissatisfaction. Detente, a strategic arms limitation accord with the Soviets, and summit trips to Moscow and Peking all established the president's reputation in foreign relations.

On the domestic front Nixon showed no hesitation in using deficit spending to stimulate the economy while he experimented with wage-

and-price controls to restrain inflation. To protect his vital southern political base Nixon vigorously opposed busing school children, appointed four
conservative justices to the Supreme Court, and announced quotas on textile imports. Nixon also wooed the construction unions and replaced the
hated draft with a volunteer army, another move that lessened antiwar
resistance. Despite these gains, the president did not consolidate his political position, and as the election year opened his performance rating was
only 49 percent in public opinion polls.

Democratic Contenders

It is almost always difficult to defeat an incumbent, but many Democrats thought that Nixon could be beaten if the opposition coalesced
around a strong challenger. There were three individuals with enough
stature and public recognition to undertake the challenge—Hubert Humphrey, Edward Kennedy, and Edmund Muskie, all members of the
Senate.

Although the durable and affable Humphrey remained available for
another presidential run, his support for the unpopular war still rankled
antiwar liberals. Humphrey's strength rested on his appeal to organized
groups—blacks, ethnics, and labor—and his strategy hinged on his suitabil-
ity as a compromise should the front runners falter.

Kennedy, the youngest of the Massachusetts clan, was the sentimental
favorite among Democrats, for he had the charm and charisma of his
deceased brothers and unparalleled name-identification as well. As late as
December 1971, the polls indicated that he led both Muskie and Humphrey among Democrats. Still, there was an overriding reason for the
young Massachusetts senator to avoid the 1972 presidential contest. Ugly
rumors surrounding an incident at Chappaquiddick in Massachusetts in
July 1969, when Kennedy's automobile ran off a bridge, killing a young
woman passenger, raised unanswered questions about the young legislator's emotional maturity and judgment. In January 1971, Kennedy moved
to quiet the scandalmongers. He announced he would not be a candidate
—that way removing himself from the presidential sweepstakes unless a
deadlocked convention handed him a nomination.

The door to a presidential bid seemed open for Muskie, the craggy-
faced New Englander of Polish ancestry, who was often compared to
Abraham Lincoln. Muskie had impressed the electorate in 1968 as Humphrey's running mate, and he actively solicited endorsements from party
leaders and the support of all elements in the Democratic Party—including antiwar liberals. As the obvious front runner, Muskie sought to lock
up the nomination before the primaries with backing from fellow members of Congress.

Muskie's candidacy collapsed in the first phase of the Democratic nominating contest. Several factors contributed to this unexpected result. For one thing, Muskie lacked the enthusiastic support of organized labor, which preferred Humphrey or Senator Henry M. Jackson of Washington. The AFL–CIO declined to endorse Muskie's candidacy at the campaign's onset. Also, as a television campaigner Muskie left much to be desired. His lawyerlike speaking style, somewhat ponderous and imprecise, had a dulling effect on reporters, and his attempt to woo left-of-center Democrats with antiwar comments aroused questions among organized labor and conservative factions.

Primary Election System Dominates

Of great significance for Muskie and the other Democratic candidates were alterations in the rules for selecting convention delegates and electing a party standard-bearer. The 1968 convention had authorized a sweeping review of procedures—and a commission chaired by Senator George McGovern wrote new rules for the next national convention. These forbade the unit rule, which had obliged all delegates from a single state to vote as a unit. New guidelines required selection of delegates in the convention year and opened the process to the participation of blacks, women, and young people. The Twenty-sixth Amendment, ratified in June 1971, had lowered the voting age to eighteen.

No longer would organized labor, big-city bosses, and party functionaries dominate national conventions. In the place of such delegates with a continuing stake in the party would come issue-oriented and candidate-directed activists. Because the guidelines required delegates running in state primaries to indicate their presidential preference on the ballot, there was less opportunity for the state parties to send uncommitted delegates to national conventions. Fearing that the activists would use these new rules to take over party caucuses, the party professionals encouraged state legislatures to establish new presidential primaries.

Dominance of the primary-election system distinguished 1972 from previous presidential years. In 1968 there had been only 17 primaries, and 42 percent of the Democratic delegates came from primary states. Now they produced the majority of delegates. Sixty-three percent were elected in the twenty-three primary states—and a proliferation of primaries made the nominating process grueling for a front runner who dare not err.

There was another consequence unknown to the candidates as 1972 opened. The proliferation of primaries weakened party organizations and strengthened the influence of issue-oriented candidates and television in the selection process. While caucuses were considered dull and uninteresting, primaries had news value—pitting candidates against each other and the unpredictable elements. The assassination of Senator Robert Kennedy in 1968 demonstrated that television networks could not ignore the competitive primaries—for news was where the candidates pressed human flesh. As a consequence, the McGovern Commission had inaugurated one of the most sweeping changes in the presidential selection process since the 1820s when the congressional caucus system disintegrated and the national conventions emerged in the 1830s.

Hubert Humphrey had captured the 1968 nomination without entering a single primary. But only McGovern seemed to recognize clearly that the party nominee in 1972 must go the difficult primary route if he expected a first-ballot nomination.

A number of ambitious Democrats tested the waters and considered seeking the party's nomination. Senators Humphrey and Jackson expected Muskie would run well in New Hampshire, and they both decided against that early test. Also, there were several other senators with White House aspirations—Fred Harris from Oklahoma, Harold Hughes of Iowa, William Proxmire of Wisconsin, and both Indiana senators, Birch Bayh and Vance Hartke. Two House members, Shirley Chisholm, a black, and Wilbur Mills, the influential Ways and Means Committee chairman, looked for an opportunity to advance politically. So did two mayors—Sam Yorty of Los Angeles and John Lindsay of New York. From the South there were two other candidates, the fiery Alabama Governor George C. Wallace and former North Carolina Governor Terry Sanford, who fancied himself as an alternative to Wallace.

The Philosophy of McGovern

But the candidate to watch was McGovern, a dark horse who, like Wallace, had a protest constituency. The South Dakotan had become a vigorous critic of the Vietnam War, and he sought to harness this issue to his drive for the presidency. In January 1971, a full year before the first primary, McGovern announced his candidacy in a televised speech and outlined the twin campaign themes—withdrawing every American soldier from Vietnam and shifting budgetary resources away from defense spending in order to rebuild this country. He labeled the Vietnam involvement a "dreadful mistake" and asserted: "There is now no way to end it and to free our prisoners except to announce a definite, early date for the withdrawal of every American soldier. I make that pledge without reservation." McGovern also deviated from traditional practice in another way— he promised to "speak the truth" and to reveal his financial arrangements to the public.

The earnest South Dakota Democrat was not the type of candidate a convention of party regulars would select in any brokered convention. He was not a party insider, a charismatic campaigner, or a candidate with a large electoral base. A historian turned politician, McGovern mirrored the idealism of a professional academic, the populism and isolationism associated with the Great Plains, and his own deep religious convictions, the product of a strict Wesleyan Methodist upbringing. A moral tone and the social gospel infused his stump speeches, but McGovern was not a second Bryan. His speaking style was dry and somewhat monotonous. If McGovern also lacked the personal charisma of a Kennedy, he had a tough, pragmatic approach to politics—and sometimes this side of his personality shocked committed idealists drawn to his crusade.

Early in 1972 McGovern was a long shot. In a January Gallup poll of Democrats, he gained only 3 percent support, running far behind front runner Muskie with 32 percent, Kennedy with 27 percent, and Humphrey with 17 percent. Yet McGovern was determined, had a strategy, and was building a nationwide organization. As he wrote later, his campaign strategy rested first on co-opting the left, enlisting antiwar activists who backed Eugene McCarthy and Robert Kennedy four years earlier. He would develop a strong grass-roots organization, using antiwar money raised through direct-mail techniques, to contest the primaries, gradually beating more conservative Democrats until the nomination was his. Then McGovern intended to reach out to party regulars, to the organized groups who opposed him but who were vital to win a national election. At that point, McGovern was certain it would be easy to defeat Richard Nixon "by appealing to the decency and common sense of the American people."

The Primaries

The national media covered the New Hampshire primary, expecting the Granite State to go for its neighbor from Maine, Edmund Muskie but, as it turned out, New Hampshire began Muskie's collapse. Four years earlier McCarthy won over Lyndon Johnson in the same primary with an unexpectedly strong showing; now McGovern would repeat this performance, stunning the confident Muskie forces with 37 percent of the vote and holding Muskie to only 46 percent. In a literal sense, Muskie had won —he had collected more votes—but television commentators interpreted the results differently. McGovern gained an important moral victory because he performed better than expected. The New Hampshire test had also called into question Muskie's general qualifications for office. After a newspaper published an unflattering account of his wife, Muskie broke down in a tearful defense, and this episode, which television carried nationally, raised questions about the Maine senator's ability to absorb criticism and maintain his emotional stability.

A week later in Florida Muskie's front-running candidacy suffered further damage, and the field of candidates narrowed somewhat. Alabama Governor Wallace, whose third-party challenge helped clinch Nixon's election in 1968, played the spoiler again. His issues dominated the primary—school-busing, taxing the rich, and cracking down on crime. Muskie, eager not to offend his liberal backers in the North, attempted to avoid a clear-cut position on the emotional issue of busing school children for racial purposes, and this harmed his candidacy in Florida. Then, when Wallace won 42 percent of the popular vote and 75 of 81 convention delegates, Muskie had the temerity to denounce Wallace as a "demagogue of the worst kind." This statement destroyed Muskie's standing among many southerners.

From a fourth-place finish in Florida, the faltering Muskie struggled on into the crucial Wisconsin ballot on April 4. In the Badger State McGovern's carefully developed grass-roots organization made the difference, and he won a significant victory over Wallace, Humphrey, and Muskie, who again finished fourth. Finally, Muskie's candidacy came to an end in late April when Humphrey triumphed in Pennsylvania, while McGovern won in Massachusetts. Belatedly the Maine Senator awoke to his campaign mistakes. He had erred in running in each of the first eight primaries, while his principal opponents selected contests suitable to themselves. For instance, McGovern's effort to capture the left hinged on doing well, at first in New Hampshire, and then winning in Wisconsin and Massachusetts, two states with strong antiwar constituencies. Similarly, Wallace began with his firm southern base, while Humphrey relied on his backing from labor, blacks, and Jews to capture Pennsylvania. But Muskie, the candidate who collected endorsements and spread himself thin, had failed.

After the Keystone State there were only three major candidates left to grapple for the nomination at Miami Beach. There was McGovern positioned on the left, Humphrey in the center, and George Wallace appealing to his own unique blue-collar constituency in the South and industrial North, which was frustrated with heavy taxation and court-ordered busing.

McGovern Under Attack by Democrats and Republicans

At this point McGovern's honeymoon ended. The national media and rival Democrats began focusing closely on what he advocated, probing his views and ideas. In Nebraska Humphrey charged that McGovern's stands on abortion, marijuana, and amnesty for Vietnam deserters were too liberal. In the June 6 California primary, Humphrey's last chance to derail the McGovern campaign express, the Minnesotan stepped up his vigorous attacks. He lashed at McGovern's controversial plan to cut defense spending substantially and at another proposal to give every American a one-thousand-dollar grant as part of welfare reform.

The impact of these sharp criticisms on a national television audience was catastrophic for the McGovern candidacy. While he did hold on to win California by 5 points, and under California rules captured all of the state's 271 convention delegates, the public began to perceive the South Dakotan as an extremist—as a Barry Goldwater of the Democratic Party's left. McGovern himself deeply resented his old friend Humphrey's vicious campaign tactics. "The fears, anxieties, and wounds opened in those debates were sweet music to the Nixon strategists," he later claimed.

Another development also contributed to McGovern's loss of public standing. On May 15, 1972, a social misfit, Arthur Bremer, critically wounded Governor Wallace at a Maryland campaign appearance. The injuries resulted in paralysis. This apparently removed the danger of Wallace's waging a vigorous independent third-party campaign in 1972, as he had done in 1968, which might have weakened Nixon enough in the South to elect McGovern in November.

Meanwhile, President Nixon had taken action to bomb Hanoi and mine Haiphong Harbor, and a few days later he traveled to Moscow for a summit meeting with Soviet leaders. These events improved the president's public approval and weakened his opponents. A Harris survey in early May had shown Nixon leading McGovern 48 to 41 percent and leading Humphrey 50 to 42 percent, but a month later the president had gained a convincing 53 to 37 percent lead over McGovern. Undoubtedly, Humphrey's criticisms, which had emphasized McGovern's liberal positions on marijuana, abortion, and amnesty, helped alienate blue-collar workers and shattered the hope that the latter might inherit Wallace's protest vote in northern industrial states. The war issue also was an important factor in McGovern's decline.

Nixon boldly harnessed the Vietnam issue, using military force against North Vietnam while McGovern imprudently branded this "the most dangerous act of the entire war." He accused Nixon of a "flirtation with World War III," but the average man was more impressed with the results. Then in Charleston, South Carolina, the South Dakota senator made a statement that would haunt him until November. He told an audience that, as president, "I would go to Hanoi and beg if I thought that would release the boys one day earlier. . . ." Republicans promptly leaped on this statement, and Vice-President Spiro Agnew branded the liberal Democrat as the "darling of the advocates of American retreat and defeat."

The California Challenge

When the five-month delegate-selection process ended in June, McGovern had a commanding lead on paper—1,378.9 committed delegate votes. He needed only 130.1 more to capture the nomination on the first ballot. But the Humphrey forces and other anti-McGovern Democrats were not disposed to give up the fight, believing that in the credentials committee they might chip away at this strength. A series of complicated parliamentary maneuvers over the composition of state delegations would determine whether McGovern obtained the nomination or not—and the key was the California challenge. McGovern's opponents, who incidentally lost the popular vote in California, challenged his right to take all 271 delegates because this winner-take-all primary contradicted the spirit of party reforms.

However, McGovern's followers, who had authored the rules changes in question, refused to budge, believing a united California delegation was crucial to a first-ballot victory. McGovern even went so far publicly as to tell *Life* magazine that he would "repudiate the whole process" and support a third-party ticket if convention maneuvers denied him the nomination. Then in a controversial ruling, party chairman Lawrence O'Brien determined that 120 McGovern delegates not challenged could vote on the disputed California delegates. This parliamentary decision effectively enabled McGovern to reestablish his claim for the entire state delegation on the convention floor. This complicated maneuver was the key to what happened to the convention nomination.

Still, the brutal credentials struggle had taken a heavy toll. For one thing, it prolonged party division. Also, the parliamentary maneuvers compelled McGovern himself to engage in an intensive delegate-holding operation for five weeks that might have been used to select carefully a vice-presidential nominee or to conciliate other factions of the Democratic Party. McGovern also believed that had Senator Edmund Muskie endorsed his candidacy after California, the party might have avoided additional acrimony and enhanced its own prospects for a successful campaign against Nixon in November.

The Democratic Convention

The thirty-sixth national convention, which opened in Miami Beach on July 10 with O'Brien presiding as permanent chairman, hardly resembled the tumultuous session four years earlier in Chicago. Not only had the rules for delegate selection changed, but so had the delegates themselves as the Democratic Party opened itself to new participants. In 1968, only 2.6 percent of the delegates were under 30; 5.5 percent were black; and 15 percent were women. But in 1972, 23 percent were under age 30, 15 percent were black, and 38 percent were women. There were other important differences. The 1972 convention containd fewer delegates with previous convention experience. Only 13 percent of the delegates were labor union members. Only fifty-eight Democratic members of Congress attended. In the majority this time were issue-oriented liberal enthusiasts —more than half the delegates called themselves liberal or very liberal— although only a third of those who called themselves Democrats in the general population accepted the liberal designation. Actress Shirley Mac-Laine captured the spirit of Miami Beach best when she described her California delegation as looking like "a couple of high schools, a grape boycott, a Black Panther rally, and four or five politicians who walked in the wrong door."

On July 11 Florida Governor Reubin Askew delivered the keynote address and called on Democrats to join a "coalition of protest" that would promote change in America. He predicted that this coalition could unite Americans and make a difference "but only if it holds together." The party's internal divisions, to which Askew had alluded, quickly surfaced in the debate over a party platform. The document, which was approved after a number of challenges, was liberal in tone, reflecting the sentiments of McGovern's supporters. It was vague on federal measures to curb inflation, except for cuts in defense spending. Instead, the platform contained some controversial planks, unacceptable to Governor Wallace and more conservative Democrats. It called for massive increases in welfare spending "to ensure each family an income substantially more than the poverty level, ensuring standards of decency and health." In favoring busing of school students, the document took another controversial position that might have been injurious to the party in a close contest. The platform said "transportation of students" was "another tool to accomplish desegregation." And, although some delegates demanded a more forthright statement in behalf of gay rights, the platform simply said "Americans should be free to make their own choices of lifestyles and private habits without being subject to discrimination or prosecution."

Democrats also accepted planks proposing a ban on sale of handguns and abolition of capital punishment, as well as reiterating the party's longstanding commitment to a universal national health-insurance program, reforms to plug tax loopholes, and a government-sponsored full-employment program. Undoubtedly the plank closest to candidate McGovern's heart was the statement on Vietnam. It said: "We pledge, as the first order of business, an immediate and complete withdrawal of all

U.S. forces in Indochina." Also, the platform included a pledge to declare an amnesty for those who refused to serve in the military services when United States troops and prisoners returned from Indochina.

Five names were put into nomination on July 12—George C. Wallace, Terry Sanford, George McGovern, Shirley Chisholm, and Henry M. Jackson—the last nominated by Governor Jimmy Carter of Georgia. In nominating McGovern, Senator Abraham Ribicoff said he was a "winner," contrary to other predictions. He emphasized that an immediate end to United States involvement in Vietnam would be the major issue of a McGovern presidential campaign. But organized labor, and other establishment Democrats such as Mayor Daley of Chicago, had not succumbed to the McGovern magic. Labor distributed printed materials to delegates critical of McGovern's record. Daley was denied a seat in the convention. Although Humphrey was the sentimental favorite of most Democrats across the nation, a preconvention poll indicated McGovern had enough votes to capture the nomination. On the first ballot he collected 1,715.35 votes—1,509 were needed—to 534 for Jackson and 385.7 for Wallace. Chisholm gained 151.95 and Sanford 77.5. The remaining delegate votes were cast for candidates not officially nominated.

Eagleton for Vice-President

Preoccupied with winning the nomination, the party's nominee had given little personal attention to the selection of a vice-presidential running mate. McGovern still believed that in the end Massachusetts Senator Edward Kennedy would accept his invitation. But Kennedy declined for personal reasons, and McGovern then approached both Senators Walter Mondale of Minnesota and Gaylord Nelson of Wisconsin before finally turning to Thomas Eagleton, an urban Catholic from the border state of Missouri, who had good ties with organized labor and the Muskie campaign.

On the surface it was a good match—for Eagleton had strong backing from factions of the Democratic Party where McGovern was weak. McGovern would have preferred Kennedy or even his Senate friend Abraham Ribicoff of Connecticut, but they both took themselves out of consideration. Forced to make a swift decision about a running mate he hardly knew, the presidential nominee selected Eagleton, and this fateful decision would soon shatter what remained of the ticket's prospect for success against Nixon.

On the convention floor Eagleton won the necessary majority, but not with unanimous backing. The combative delegates nominated seven other candidates, and altogether thirty-nine persons received votes on the roll call—including Archie Bunker, the television character; CBS newscaster

Roger Mudd; and Martha Mitchell, wife of the former attorney general who now directed Nixon's reelection drive. The unruly convention delayed McGovern's acceptance speech, which was finally delivered about 3:00 A.M., long after the prime-time television audience had gone to bed. The nominee later said this incredibly bad timing cost him an opportunity, perhaps the last possible opportunity, to create favorable acceptance of his candidacy. But the South Dakotan's own advisers must bear the blame for this slip-up. They did not request that O'Brien postpone the acceptance speech and extend the convention a day so McGovern could appear on prime time.

In his acceptance the nominee reiterated his familiar campaign themes. He had no secret plan for peace in Indochina. Instead, he pledged publicly to halt the bombing on Inauguration Day. Within ninety days, he promised, "every American soldier and every American prisoner will be out of the jungle and out of their cells and back home in America where they belong." Furthermore, a McGovern administration would "turn away from excessive preoccupation overseas to rebuilding our own nation." To his credit, the senator remained consistent throughout his campaign—he proposed to end an unpopular war and to redirect government priorities inward. To some it was the siren call of a new isolationism, but in the climate of 1972 this appeal had potential impact on a war-weary electorate.

In balance the Democratic convention further injured McGovern's election prospects. On television some fifty million people across America saw the disputatious McGovernites espouse busing, abortion, and amnesty —and inevitably the actions of some zealous delegates were associated with the party nominee. Congressman James O'Hara, who chaired the rules committee, said later: "I think we lost the election at Miami. . . . The American people made an association between McGovern and gay lib, and welfare rights and pot-smoking and black militants, and women's lib, and wise college kids." Public-opinion surveys confirmed that conclusion. Ordinarily the nominee's standing in the polls improves during a convention—at least temporarily. This did not happen to McGovern. Miami Beach was a public relations disaster. Instead of boosting McGovern, Nixon benefited.

McGovern's misfortunes had not ended. For one thing organized labor was still dissatisfied, and on July 19 the powerful AFL–CIO Executive Council voted to remain neutral—refusing to endorse the Democratic presidential candidate, as was the usual practice. Labor leader George Meany reiterated that McGovern was not "good material," and he said the labor decision represented a "showdown with the new politics," made necessary because a "small elite of suburban types and students took over the apparatus of the Democratic Party." An episode involving the North Vietnamese also corroded the nominee's image. McGovern had encouraged Pierre Salinger, formerly President John Kennedy's press secretary, to contact Hanoi's representatives in Paris to determine discreetly if a few prisoners of war could be released as a symbolic gesture of North Vietnam's readiness to end the war. Later, when a news account indicated that Salinger had told the North Vietnamese they would be better off negotiating with Nixon than waiting for McGovern to take office, McGovern denied the story, a position that cast doubt on the senator's credibility. This flap, however, was small in comparison to the Eagleton affair.

The Eagleton Crisis

Soon after the convention McGovern's aides received an anonymous tip that the vice-presidential nominee had been hospitalized for mental illness on three different occasions and had received electric-shock treatments at least twice. This information, also leaked to the press, had potentially devastating implications. It appeared that McGovern had selected a running mate with serious emotional problems, who, if elected, would be only a heartbeat from the presidency itself. The rumors were soon confirmed. When he was invited to join the national ticket, Eagleton had allowed personal ambition to overcome sound judgment, and he did not mention this health problem to the presidential nominee.

Then, McGovern compounded the mistake. Although realizing the significance of Eagleton's health problem, McGovern reaffirmed his choice of a running mate. He told reporters he was backing Eagleton "1,000 percent." Only then did the consequences of this decision become apparent. Major campaign contributors from around the country shut off the flow of donations unless Eagleton was removed, and editorial writers—who helped shape mass opinion—had a common reaction: Eagleton's health problems raised serious questions about his capability to serve in the White House.

Trapped in an awkward dilemma of his own making—his campaign facing a financial disaster and probable defeat in November—McGovern persuaded Eagleton to resign in the interest of party harmony, not for health reasons. In first defending Eagleton and then dismissing him, McGovern antagonized many Americans, especially idealistic youth supporters, who took at face value the campaign pledge of openness and candor. The St. Louis Globe Democrat asserted that McGovern's handling of the matter "laid bare a lack of public honesty and political guts; it showed him as a blatant opportunist, who would dump his own choice for running mate in the interests of bald expediency." And, McGovern himself conceded later that the episode "convicted me of incompetence, vacillation, dishonesty, and cold calculation."

Never before had a vice-presidential nominee withdrawn from a national ticket after the party convention adjourned. Now McGovern desperately searched for another running mate—and approached a variety of party leaders—including Florida Governor Askew, Senator Kennedy, Humphrey, Muskie, Mike Mansfield, and finally Sargent Shriver, the dynamic former Peace Corps official and Kennedy in-law, who accepted. Shriver later quipped he was McGovern's "seventh choice." On August 8 the Democratic National Committee met in Washington to nominate Shriver, a man who had never before run for elective office. He received 2,936 votes—nearly unanimous—although Missouri delegates still cast their votes for Eagleton.

Nixon's Campaign Strategy

While Democratic political fortunes slowly disintegrated, as the national ticket careened from one misfortune to another, Richard Nixon's prospects brightened dramatically. His precedent-setting trip to the People's Republic of China in February and to Moscow in May were enormous public relations successes which his domestic critics could not match. Gradually the incumbent pulled ahead in opinion surveys. In both foreign and domestic affairs the administration took major initiatives, using the inherent powers of the presidency for maximum political advantage.

Until the Democrats actually tapped McGovern, Nixon had assumed he would face either Edmund Muskie, Edward Kennedy, or Hubert Humphrey in the autumn election—and each of these senators in his own way was a formidable opponent. The Nixon camp made exhaustive preparations. Knowing that voters with Republican affiliations were a distinct minority—about 25 percent of the electorate, while 44 percent considered themselves Democrats—the White House sought to project the image of President Nixon running for reelection. To enlist the backing of independent and even disenchanted Democrats, they established the independent Committee to Reelect the President (CREEP) separate from the Republican National Committee. Nixon's former law partner and attorney general, John Mitchell, resigned from the administration in February 1972 to coordinate the reelection campaign, and Commerce Secretary Maurice Stans stepped down from government to collect a reelection war chest.

Expecting another close contest against a well-known, adequately funded opponent, the Nixon staff devised a complex and sophisticated strategy to maximize their advantages. It was decided the president himself would remain in the White House as long as possible, attending to affairs of state and gaining free publicity, while cabinet officials and other surrogates toured the country responding to criticisms and describing the Nixon record. Since the new campaign law restricted television spending

—and the Nixon campaign had been accused of employing television to "sell the president" in 1968, they devised an alternative strategy. (The Federal Campaign Act, passed in February 1972, restricted the amount a candidate might spend on broadcasting, newspapers, and automated telephone systems.)

This time the president's backers would rely heavily on direct-mail techniques, sophisticated public-opinion surveys, and telephone banks to identify potential supporters, communicate with them, and mobilize pro-Nixon voters on Election Day. There was a single purpose behind this elaborate effort—creating a vast Nixon majority on Election Day, but not also a Republican majority in Congress. From the opinion surveys Nixon's strategists were able to position their candidate effectively on the issues of concern to average voters. The electorate was generally dissatisfied but, they determined, the president could successfully identify his programs with the quest for change and, thus, focus public dissatisfaction on Congress and the federal bureaucracy, not on the White House. Recognizing, too, that many voters perceived Nixon as a cold and evasive personality, they sought to portray him as a shy professional, tough but competent. The approach was sophisticated and single-minded; it would advance Richard Nixon without regard for the fortunes of other Republican candidates.

For a while, it appeared Republican dissidents would offer an effective challenge in the primaries as Democratic dissenters such as Eugene McCarthy had done to President Johnson four years earlier. Paul ("Pete") N. McCloskey, Jr., a California congressman, sought to wage an anti-Vietnam War challenge from the Republican left, and on the other side of the spectrum conservative John Ashbrook, from Ohio, also entered the early primaries as he sought to reverse the perceived "leftward drift" of Nixon's policies—particularly greater deficit spending, cuts in military preparedness, and abandonment of Nationalist China.

But these challenges made little headway. McCloskey did gain extensive attention in the national media. Having underestimated the McCarthy phenomenon in 1968, it was natural for television to exaggerate the challenge in 1972. In New Hampshire, the election bellwether for both parties, Nixon easily rolled up 68 percent of the Republican vote and in Florida he commanded 87 percent. After these initial triumphs it was obvious that neither McCloskey nor Ashbrook would be a major force at the Republican convention. Nor did either of the president's principal party rivals—New York Governor Nelson Rockefeller or California Governor Ronald Reagan—make any move to unseat the incumbent. However, had the lesser-known aspirants dented Nixon in the early primaries, Rockefeller and Reagan might have jumped into the ring.

Initially Nixon had wanted to hold the nominating convention in San Diego, near his California home, but circumstances forced a belated change in preparations. There was concern that antiwar demonstrators would converge on San Diego and complicate security problems. Furthermore, the national press carried reports that the International Telephone and Telegraph Corporation (ITT) had pledged to underwrite a large portion of the convention's costs in return for a settlement of an antitrust suit against the communications giant. In May the national committee voted to switch the site to Miami Beach, making the Florida city only the fourth ever to host both major political conventions in a single election year.

The Republican Convention

The thirtieth national convention, which opened on August 21, was a marked contrast to the Democratic conclave held in the same auditorium six weeks earlier. The Republican sessions moved punctually under the direction of Ronald Reagan, the temporary chairman, and Gerald R. Ford, the permanent chairman. Principal speeches and nominations took place during prime television viewing hours. On the first evening there were three short keynote addresses, presented by Richard Lugar, the mayor of Indianapolis; Edward W. Brooke, the black senator from Massachusetts; and Mrs. Anne Armstrong, a national party official from Texas. These projected the principal campaign theme—one inviting Democrats and independent voters to join the Republican ranks at a time when the larger party was in disarray.

In a twenty-five thousand-word platform, which was quickly approved with only a minor change, the Republicans sought to win over Democrats disenchanted with the McGovern selection. The other party, Republicans claimed, "had been seized by a radical clique which scorns our nation's past and would blight our future." The statement of party intentions offered a different set of prescriptions than had the Democratic Party. Republicans blamed Congress for irresponsible deficit spending, expressed irrevocable opposition to busing school children for purposes of achieving racial balance, opposed the legalization of marijuana, pledged to safeguard the right to own and use firearms, and offered a "salute" to the "statesmanship of the labor-union movement." The last compliment was inserted to appease organized labor, which with few exceptions, still distrusted George McGovern.

One of Nixon's rivals in Republican politics placed the president's name in nomination. In performing this important duty, Governor Nelson Rockefeller of New York, asserted: "We need this man of action, this man of accomplishment, this man of experience, this man of courage. We need this man of faith in America." The Nixon forces had the convention well in hand.

Representative McCloskey had only one delegate vote, insufficient under rules of the convention even to have his name put in nomination. As a consequence, there was no opportunity for Republican liberals to voice dissatisfaction with the administration's Vietnam policies. On August 22, as everyone predicted, Republicans renominated Richard Nixon on the first ballot by a vote of 1,347 to 1 for McCloskey. Delegates also renominated Nixon's choice for vice-president, Spiro T. Agnew.

In his acceptance speech the president containued the appeal for a "new majority" that would sustain the progress of the past four years and the "progress we have made in building a new structure of peace in the world." He rejected the notion of dividing Americans into quotas as the Democrats had done. "The way to end discrimination against some is not to begin discrimination against others." He said the choice in the 1972 election was not "between radical change and no change"; rather it was "between change that works and change that won't work." He exhorted Democrats, Republicans, and independents to join "a new American majority bound together by our common ideals," not a movement "on the basis of the party label." Like Lyndon Johnson in 1964, Nixon invited all who shared his philosophy and ideals to join with him politically, and in the climate of 1972 the appeal seemed persuasive.

The Eagleton episode overshadowed other matters, which were only dimly understood in 1972, such as the break-in at Democratic National Committee headquarters in the Watergate building in Washington, D.C., by a small group of burglars who were linked to CREEP. This sordid episode occurred in June, and charges of political corruption and cover-up appeared in the papers and became part of the election campaign. But, political corruption had little impact on voters, who tended to think cynically that wrongdoing and politics were indivisible. As a McGovern campaign aide remarked afterwards: "Most people took the view that there was nothing exceptional about the Watergate incident except that the perpetrators were caught."

Nixon Wins

Some 78 million Americans voted, and 60.69 percent cast their ballots for Nixon and Agnew. The Republicans won in 49 states, amassing 521 electoral votes on paper, while McGovern and Shriver gained only Massachusetts and the District of Columbia, with a total of 17 electoral votes. Final figures gave Nixon 47,170,179; McGovern received 29,171,791. For the president it was a popular mandate comparable to the one Franklin D. Roosevelt had in his 1936 landslide and that Lyndon Johnson had in 1964. Nixon won, but his electoral vote total declined slightly when a Virginia elector voted for the Libertarian candidate.

It was not a good year for minor candidates, except for John G. Schmitz, the American Independent Party candidate, who came in third with 1,090,673 votes. Among the others: Dr. Benjamin Spock obtained 78,751 votes; Linda Jenness, the Socialist Workers, with 37,423. Also, Socialist Labor candidate Louis Fisher obtained 53,811 votes; Gus Hall of the Communist Party had 25,343; and Earle H. Munn, the Prohibition Party nominee, won 12,818.

Significance of the Election

The Nixon landslide produced several important results. For the first time the solid South voted solidly for a Republican presidential nominee. Also, the president got 60 percent of the Catholic vote and 61 percent of the blue-collar vote as laboring people deserted the Democratic Party to vote against McGovern. Interestingly, Nixon did surprisingly well among 18-to-20-year-olds who were eligible to vote for the first time, because ratification of the Twenty-sixth Amendment to the Constitution had lowered the voting age. After Eagleton was removed, enthusiasm for the Democratic ticket dropped sharply on college campuses.

But two traditionally Democratic constituencies remained loyal to McGovern—Jews gave him 63 percent of their vote, and blacks voted 87 percent for the South Dakotan. It was a stunning defeat for the "New Politics." McGovern became the first presidential candidate since Adlai Stevenson in 1956 to lose his home state.

Yet, for Democrats in general the presidential disaster had a limited spillover effect. They actually gained one governorship and two Senate seats, while in the House races Republicans picked up only twelve seats, far short of the forty-one needed to obtain control and reverse eighteen years of Democratic rule. As a result, the president became the first chief executive ever to begin two terms with an opposition Congress each time.

What was the lasting significance of the 1972 landslide? Although some commentators seized on the results to find a dramatic turning point, as Democrats crossed over to back Nixon in record numbers, no fundamental realignment occurred. Rather, far more than many national elections, this was truly an issue-oriented campaign. The president and his opponent disagreed fundamentally on how to conclude the war in Vietnam, how to manage defense and economic issues, and how to resolve emotional social questions—busing school children, amnesty, income redistribution, and drugs. Voters were dissatisfied, and economic troubles as well as charges of political corruption bothered them. Foreign affairs was the dominant issue area, and here Nixon's experience and achievements overwhelmed his untried challenger. The president had displayed keen ability in negotiations with the Soviets and Chinese as well as a determination to end the Indochina war on terms favorable to the United States. The voters may have been confused—and some were dissatisfied with Nixon's policies—but the negative McGovern image more than offset these concerns. McGovern seemed moralistic, self-righteous, and excessively critical of the nation's tragedy in Southeast Asia.

Ironically, although McGovern outspent Nixon on television advertising, this deluge probably harmed rather than helped, for it drove home the negative image voters had already fashioned of George McGovern. The two parties spent about an equal amount in the primaries and general elections of 1972, but the Republicans, who did not have a serious primary struggle, outspent the Democrats in the general election by a ratio of 2 to 1. From 1912 to 1956, the cost per vote ranged from around 20 cents to about 31 cents, but in 1972 the cost soared. More than $103 million were spent in the general election, and each vote cost about $1.36. Because the McGovern campaign skillfully raised funds through direct-mail solicitations and other techniques to obtain money from 600,000 contributors, McGovern ran the only Democratic presidential campaign since Franklin Roosevelt that did not leave a budget deficit.

Nixon Resigns

In retrospect, Richard Nixon's real enemy in 1972 was not his opponent, because McGovern failed to wage a credible campaign and establish a broad-based popular following. His toughest adversary was the press. Although only 5.3 percent of the nation's newspapers backed McGovern's candidacy—and some 71 percent endorsed Nixon—the national media, especially the *New York Times,* the *Washington Post,* and the television networks, were hostile to Nixon. In emphasizing Watergate, political corruption, and sabotage they kept alive the issues that would eventually bring the president's resignation on August 8, 1974.

Watergate is a long, involved, and sordid affair, which revealed that Richard Nixon's worst enemy was, in the final analysis, himself. As the president later conceded in his memoirs, he had sought to postpone and divert criticism of the bungled burglary so as to enhance his reelection prospects against the ineffectual McGovern. In the process Nixon obstructed justice, destroyed his credibility with the electorate, and finally left office in disgrace.

XXI

An Outsider's Victory

CYNICISM AND ALIENATION were widespread as Americans prepared to celebrate the nation's bicentennial and elect a president in 1976. In public opinion surveys ordinary citizens spoke their minds, voicing deep pessimism about the country's future, distrust for professional politicians, dissatisfaction with established institutions, and an overwhelming desire for honest and effective national leadership.

Emphasis Now on Domestic Problems

The last four years had been difficult ones. Although the long Vietnam War had ended and prisoners had returned, the peace accords soon disintegrated, exposing in stark relief America's first defeat in war. With the conclusion of this bitter chapter, public priorities changed. Since 1940 mass opinion had regarded foreign affairs and defense as the leading problem area facing the nation—but no longer. In January 1976, 70 percent named economic needs and problems, while only 5 percent listed foreign affairs and 3 percent mentioned energy. As in the 1930s Americans were putting domestic bread-and-butter issues first and choosing to disregard foreign dangers—such as the relentless build-up of Soviet military power and the spread of that nation's influence into the Middle East and Africa. At home there were difficult economic problems. The major one was inflation, partly the result of huge budgetary deficits and soaring petroleum prices. Inflation reached the highest level since the Korean War, economic growth slowed, and unemployment climbed to a 30-year peak—averaging 8.5 percent in 1975.

Scandals in Washington further eroded public confidence in the presidency and Congress. In October 1973, Vice-President Spiro Agnew resigned after pleading guilty to income-tax evasion. Under provisions of the Twenty-fifth Amendment, President Richard Nixon nominated House Republican leader Gerald Ford to replace Agnew, and Congress confirmed this selection. Meanwhile, other members of the Nixon administration faced prosecution for charges connected with the June 1972 break-in of Democratic national headquarters in the Watergate building. Attorney General John Mitchell and the president's chief assistants, H. R. Haldeman and John Erlichman, were both convicted in 1975. However, nothing was as damaging to public confidence in elected officials as the events that in August 1974 forced Nixon from office—the first chief executive ever to resign.

His successor, the candid and athletic Ford, projected an image of personal integrity and responsibility, but he promptly encountered political problems that would damage his effectiveness. Ford granted the former president "a full, free, and absolute pardon" so as to avoid emotional court proceedings, but this decision seriously damaged his own public-approval ratings. Public disgust with the Republicans showed in the 1974 midterm elections when Democrats picked up five governorships, three Senate seats, and forty-three House seats. Now Ford had to cope with a Congress in which the opposite political party had a veto-proof majority. The deadlock in government continued, and although Ford recovered some popular approval, his rating in January 1976 was only 39 percent. The media served to emphasize Ford's shortcomings and to harm his effectiveness by reporting occasional verbal lapses and physical stumbling. The public saw pictures of Ford tripping as he descended from *Air Force One*, falling down on skis, or hitting his head on a helicopter—all of which reinforced the negative comment attributed to former President Johnson that Ford could not walk and chew gum at the same time. What emerged from such reporting was the image of President Ford as a bumbler.

Changes in Primaries and in Financing Campaigns

In 1974, the Federal Elections Act, established public financing for presidential campaigns. This tended to encourage a proliferation of individual candidacies for party nominations because the federal government would provide candidates with up to $5.5 million on a matching basis. Each applicant for federal aid had to demonstrate broad national support by raising at least $100,000, with $5,000 coming from each of 20 states. Because no individual contribution could exceed $250 to qualify for matching funds, the presidential candidates could not rely on traditional fund-raising efforts or on large contributions. Also, both Democrats and Republicans would receive public money to conduct national conventions, and each party nominee would receive $21.8 million from the United States Treasury for the final campaign phase.

There were several disadvantages to this experiment in public financing. For one thing, the new law was complicated, and the requirements for obtaining small contributions to qualify for federal assistance proved difficult for many candidates. Also, the law effectively limited the amount of money spent on presidential campaigns, forcing candidates to concentrate money on television advertising at the expense of bumper stickers, signs, and campaign headquarters which boosted public participation in the campaign process. Finally, no one expected the disruption and uncertainty caused when the Supreme Court struck down provisions of the federal statute in January 1976, and Congress had to restructure the Federal Elections Commission so that it could disburse public funds to candidates requesting public money.

There were other developments inviting a proliferation of individual candidacies. The Democratic Party had approved new rules that forbade winner-take-all primaries, such as the disputed 1972 California contest, and now all candidates who received at least 15 percent of the popular vote would obtain a share of the state delegation. The party also sought to end open primaries, which allowed independents and even Republicans to influence the Democratic Party's selection. Other new rules required that all convention delegates must announce their presidential preference before the primary.

These changes had several significant implications. It appeared early in 1976 that no single candidate would emerge from the various state primaries, based on a proportional distribution of delegates, with enough support to win the party's nomination on the first convention ballot. As a consequence, Democrats would probably have to select their nominee through the traditional brokering process. But, since the new rules discouraged uncommitted slates of delegates, and this eroded the impact of traditional power centers such as organized labor, urban bosses, and elected officials, it appeared that newcomers—especially issue-oriented activists and candidate-oriented delegates who had no established stake in advancing the party's long-term interest—would have the controlling voice.

Under pressure from the electronic media to open the political process and from party activists to abandon party caucuses, more state legislatures scheduled primaries. In 1976, 29 states and the District of Columbia would use this procedure to choose convention delegates—and 73 percent of the delegates would be selected or bound by primary results. In 1968, only 38 percent were bound this way, but in 1972, 61 percent were.

The Increased Influence of Television

Reliance on direct primaries shifted candidate selection even further away from party officials and established leaders, who often were in the best position to evaluate a candidate's experience and abilities, to the media moguls who communicated audiovisual images about candidates to television viewers. Only a few presidential aspirants fully appreciated the revolutionary impact of television on the selection process and understood how to use the technology for personal advantage. In front of television cameras even the most experienced politicians could blunder, as Edmund Muskie had done in 1972, and look bad. Attractive new faces would emerge suddenly from virtual obscurity to acquire nationwide recognition and support; television created instant celebrities. In bypassing the traditional parties as vehicles to recruit and campaign for officeseekers, television came to dominate the selection process. On one level electronic communications made the general public more sensitive to images and issues than ever before, although the attentive public still relied heavily on newspaper and magazine analysis to fashion attitudes and opinions. And, on another, television made the political process more volatile. An inept remark or a tasteless gesture could cripple a candidacy, while a calm, attractive, and articulate individual could utilize television to become an instant celebrity.

The new technology—and its enormous cost and complexity—had several other implications for 1976. Television, computer technology for direct mailing and polling, and telephone banks were costly—and with spending severely limited, professional campaign consultants advised candidates to cut hoopla in favor of mass-advertising techniques. Finally, while ward walkers and campaign workers remained important in large cities to identify voters and turn out supporters on Election Day, strategic campaign decisions increasingly were made by a new middle-class, educated elite—professional campaign managers and consultants with no lasting personal allegiance to the candidate himself. Patrick Caddell, the youthful pollster for McGovern and then Carter, and Robert Teeter and John Deardourff, who served President Ford, were representatives of the new campaign elite who emerged on the scene.

Democrats Look for a Candidate

Ford's weak popular standing, dissatisfaction with incumbents, economic troubles, and the legacy of Watergate all seemed to benefit a Democratic presidential challenger. But which Democrat would carry the party standard? A Gallup survey in December 1975, indicated that Senator Hubert Humphrey remained the first choice among members of his party. Thirty percent favored the Minnesotan; 20 percent preferred Alabama Governor George C. Wallace; 10 percent, Senator Henry Jackson; and 5 percent, Senator Birch Bayh. Although Senator Edward Kennedy, last of the Kennedy brothers, had taken himself out of consideration, both Humphrey and Senator Edmund Muskie of Maine were available if the convention deadlocked. Neither wanted again to submit to a physically exhausting and emotionally draining series of primary campaigns, but each was still eager to serve as president. Humphrey and Muskie, who were experienced campaigners and publicly known figures, decided to wait for the front runners to fall before making their own moves.

By the end of 1975, a number of Democrats were considering presidential candidacies, and many had congressional credentials, for service in the Senate was now the established training ground for the White House. Senator Henry M. "Scoop" Jackson, the talented and experienced legislator from Washington, sought the nomination again, and he had vigorous backing from influential Jewish leaders, organized labor, and the defense establishment. Senator Walter Mondale, Humphrey's colleague from Minnesota, also tested the waters and then announced he would not seek the prize.

There were other Senate hopefuls—Lloyd Bentsen from Texas, Birch Bayh of Indiana, and Frank Church from Idaho. In addition, there were former Senator Fred Harris of Oklahoma, a self-styled Populist, and Congressman Morris Udall of Arizona, who hoped to inherit the McGovern support among Democratic liberals. Along with Kennedy in-law Sargent Shriver, the 1972 vice-presidential candidate, several governors hoped to move up—George C. Wallace of Alabama, Milton Shapp of Pennsylvania, and former Governors Terry Sanford of North Carolina and Jimmy Carter of Georgia.

The Philosophy of Jimmy Carter

A dark horse, Carter soon replaced Humphrey as the front runner. Carter offered voters a fresh face and different credentials. He was an Annapolis graduate who had served briefly with nuclear-submarine builder Admiral Hyman Rickover, and then returned to Georgia to tend the family peanut-growing business, run for the legislature, and eventually serve one term as governor, during which he reorganized state agencies. Although Carter lacked experience at the high levels of national government, he correctly diagnosed the national mood and organized a sophisticated campaign to win the White House. Convinced the public wanted an outsider, "not one associated with a long series of mistakes made at the White House and on Capitol Hill," Carter turned his lack of experience in Washington into his asset. He also recognized that the public was more interested in personal qualities—honesty, competence, and trustworthiness—than in complicated position papers, and he sought to appeal to this desire for change rooted in America's own traditions. A devout Southern Baptist whose sister was an evangelist, Carter pledged: "I'll never tell a lie. I'll never make a misleading statement." His approach was moralistic and traditional. In a low, quiet voice he would express his

desire for "a government as good and honest and decent and compassion-
ate and filled with love as are the American people."

Carter's approach might have grated on the sensitivities of experienced
politicians, but he was no marshmallow. Beneath the southern charm and
ethical appeal was a steely determination. "I don't intend to lose," he said.
There was also an element of southern Populism, as Carter railed against
"three-martini lunches," tax loopholes, and privileges of the rich, and
invited his primary supporters to visit him in the White House later—a
move reminiscent of Andrew Jackson.

Carter's Campaign Strategy

Intelligent, ambitious, and determined to win, Carter and his small
band of Georgia advisers, none of whom had extensive experience in
national politics, devised a strategy for success. It rested on his declaring
his candidacy in December 1974, and then spending nearly two years
campaigning. Without executive responsibilities after leaving office,
Carter could travel extensively—and did—in 1975 to forty-six states, establishing personal contacts with supporters, appearing on local television
programs, and cultivating the nation's most powerful political reporters
and editors to gain frequent mention as a presidential candidate.

Although the peanut-farmer-for-president campaign depended heavily
on the aggressive preprimary campaign for media visibility, its success
rested on winning several quick victories in caucuses and early primaries.
Rejecting the common wisdom that a brokered convention would decide,
Carter set out to win, knowing that party leaders would not choose him
unless he had the delegate votes in hand. His campaign strategy was
to foster excitement nationally with a strong showing in the January 1976
precinct caucuses in Iowa, then campaign intensively in New Hampshire
and use a strong showing in the Granite State to prove that a southerner
could win in the North. This claim would enhance his prospects in the
Florida primary against Alabama Governor Wallace, whom Carter had to
defeat in order to establish himself nationally as a southern alternative
to the perennial symbol of regional discontent.

Carter's bold plan succeeded. He captured attention on national television with a 2-to-1 victory over Bayh in the Iowa caucuses. Political analysts marveled at Carter's broad-based support. It included both small
towns and urban areas, both blue- and white-collar workers, both blacks
and whites.

When Jackson opted to avoid the New Hampshire free-for-all, Carter
promptly established his own position as the centrist Democrat. Bayh,
Harris, and Udall each battled for liberal support. On Election Day Carter's approach was vindicated when he won 23,373 votes (28 percent of

the Democratic primary vote), and it was sufficient to lead the field. The Georgian promptly interpreted this result as evidence that "a progressive southerner can win in the North." And the television networks dutifully proclaimed Carter the winner.

This interpretation had far-reaching consequences, as Carter's advisers fully understood. Because New Hampshire was the first primary, it received the most attention, despite the small vote, and one study indicates that 30 percent of all network news coverage accorded the early primaries focused on the Granite State. As a result, Carter immediately appeared on the covers of two major news weeklies—*Time* and *Newsweek* —and soon he was perceived as the candidate most likely to win future primaries and the nomination. Ironically, Senator Jackson won a far larger victory the next week in Massachusetts, where he accumulated 164,393 votes. Carter finished a poor fourth. But this result captured little media attention, for national television had moved its cameras southward to follow the Florida primary and the interesting match between Carter and Wallace.

Carter mounted a vigorous campaign against his southern rival—pointing out to Florida voters that it was time to stop sending a message of discontent to Washington and, instead, send a president. Wallace played into Carter's hands. Not only did he repeat shopworn campaign themes —denouncing forced busing, welfare cheaters, and federal bureaucrats— but he also forecast victory and attacked Carter by name. The last undoubtedly strengthened Carter's standing among blacks, who detested Wallace. Organized labor, anxious to torpedo a Wallace candidacy in the South before the fiery Alabamian carried his protest themes to the industrial North, also helped Carter. These tactics succeeded, and Carter won the crucial round—taking 35 percent of the Democratic vote to 31 percent for Wallace.

In defeating Wallace in Florida, and again in Illinois and North Carolina, Carter demolished the brokered-convention strategy. It became clear that Wallace would not be a power at the national convention. Instead, a former governor of Georgia was now the leading candidate. He had proved he was a southerner who could win in the North as well as the South—obtaining votes from liberals and conservatives, blacks and whites, and voters from different income strata.

What had happened to the fiery Wallace—a major figure in Democratic politics since the early 1960s? In part, the South had changed more quickly than the Alabama governor, and voters looked for a new face. More important, however, was the health issue. Although Franklin Roosevelt had run successfully for president four times while paralyzed, he had not done so under the glare of television lights. Wallace, bitterly disappointed, grumbled that voters only saw spokes on his wheelchair. "The only thing wrong with me is that I can't walk," he said. "But, you don't vote for an acrobat." Voters took a different view. One postelection survey in Florida showed that some three out of five people who voted for Wallace in the 1972 primary did not do so in 1976 because of his health.

After Florida, only three strong candidates remained in the primaries —Carter, Jackson, and Udall. During April Carter would bruise and batter this opposition. Udall desperately needed a win in the April 6 Wisconsin primary, but this Arizona Mormon had difficulty forging a successful liberal coalition of urban residents, blacks, and labor. In part there was no longer a moral crusade against war to ignite liberals, and in part Udall had poor relations with organized labor. Also, critical to the outcome was a shortage of funds for television and direct-mail activities, after the Supreme Court ordered Congress to restructure the elections commission. With these handicaps Udall lost Wisconsin by only 7,500 votes—a thin 1 percent margin.

Later in April Carter shattered the "anybody-but-Carter" movement in Pennsylvania, where some Democratic officials, organized labor and Philadelphia Mayor Frank Rizzo backed Senator Jackson, hoping that way to keep open an opportunity for old friend Hubert Humphrey. Carter stunned the bosses and powerbrokers, winning a 37 to 25 percent plurality over the plodding Jackson. Once more the Georgian adroitly used television advertising to gather grass-roots backing from a broad constituency—blue-collar and white-collar workers, Protestants, Catholics, young and old, blacks and whites. Significantly, Carter had finally won in a northern industrial state over labor and the party functionaries.

In pursuing his exhausting run-everywhere strategy, Carter made serious mistakes. Increasingly, television news picked up and magnified these errors. Comments about "ethnic purity" created a brief flap, and his "fuzzy" positions on issues caused problems in Wisconsin. But fundamentally Carter was overexposed—and in the final primaries two new challengers, Senator Frank Church, the boyish-looking foreign-affairs specialist, and popular California Governor Jerry Brown created temporary enthusiasm. Church won in Nebraska, Idaho, Oregon, and Montana, while Brown triumphed in Maryland and California.

But these much-publicized victories obscured an underlying reality—Carter had too much momentum to be stopped. While Brown and Church had some successes, Carter continued to win primaries—especially in the South—and accumulate delegate votes. Carter won more than half the primaries in May and June, maintaining his percentage of the popular vote near 40 percent, and by May and June public opinion polls indicated he was the preferred party nominee.

The end came on June 8 when Carter won the Ohio primary, and Humphrey, who had indicated he might still jump into the race if Carter fared poorly in the Buckeye State, acknowledged the obvious—Carter had a "commanding lead" and was "virtually certain" to be the party's nominee. Senators Edward Kennedy and George McGovern offered similar assessments. Only the youthful California governor and Udall held back, refusing to jump on the fast-moving Carter bandwagon.

With the nomination virtually in hand, Carter had time to rest, plan additional strategy, and conciliate Democratic factions who opposed his candidacy. Also he could give attention to the careful selection of a vice-presidential running mate. He devised a lengthy screening process, in which the principal candidates were questioned about their health, finances, and personal lives. After giving close attention to Maine Senator Muskie, Ohio's John Glenn, and several others, Carter eventually tapped Minnesota's Walter Mondale, an intelligent, experienced senator with a liberal voting record. Although the choice of Mondale gave regional and ideological balance to the Democratic ticket, the Georgian was impressed with Mondale's interest and deemed him personally compatible, an important consideration if the vice-presidential nominee were to wield real influence in a Carter administration. Also, in selecting a highly regarded member of the Senate, the outsider had moved to conciliate the Washington establishment and secure the talents of an experienced legislator who might ease relations with Congress.

The Democratic Convention

The thirty-seventh Democratic national convention opened July 12 in New York's Madison Square Garden. Party Chairman Robert Strauss had devoted the last three-and-a-half years to making sure that this convention, unlike the ones in 1968 and 1972, would function smoothly, and not end either as a riot or a fiasco, which would jeopardize the party's chances in November. Strauss had even made elaborate preparations to break a deadlock after two ballots and form a unity ticket. This convention, unlike the one that met in New York in 1924, would not go 103 ballots. Harmony prevailed, also, because the Carter forces were in firm control of the crucial credentials and platform committees. This time, in the interest of party unity, no delegate challenges went before the full convention, and there was no floor fight on aspects of the platform. Recent lessons were all too fresh for the 3,008 delegates and their leaders. This time accommodation would prevail over doctrinal differences.

The platform contained few surprises—and papered over serious differences. Democrats wanted to reduce unemployment to 3 percent within four years, pledged tax reform "to ease the burden for the poor and increase it for the rich," urged simplification of the welfare system and passage of a comprehensive national health-insurance program financed by a payroll tax and general revenues, and endorsed legislation to keep oil companies from holding interests in competing forms of energy. The platform also favored busing for desegregation but only as a "judicial tool of last resort," opposed a constitutional amendment to prohibit abortions, and rejected both planks to decriminalize marijuana and endorse homosexual rights.

While urging more firmness in negotiations with Communist countries, the party document recommended a $5–$7 billion cut in the defense budget and parity with the Soviet Union on strategic weapons. With few exceptions, the manifesto reflected the party nominee's position, and these stances were selected to harmonize differences, except in one crucial area—economic policy. Here the choice between Democrats and Republicans was crystal clear. Democrats would assign greater priority to combating unemployment than to controlling inflation. Interestingly, the document barely mentioned some of the conflicts that had divided party and country over the last decade—the Vietnam War, alternative lifestyles, civil disorder, and the flow of illegal immigrants.

New party leadership was in evidence at the convention. Congresswoman Lindy Boggs chaired the sessions. Former astronaut John Glenn, now a senator from Ohio, and Barbara Jordan, a black congresswoman from Texas, presented keynote addresses on the first night. Glenn called for new leaders to "set a different tone for this nation," and Jordan stirred delegates when she emphasized, "There is something different and special about this opening night. . . . The past notwithstanding, a Barbara Jordan is before you tonight. This is one additional bit of evidence that the American Dream need not forever be deferred." She was the first black and the first woman to present a keynote address, and it was a moment that the delegates and millions of television viewers would remember.

Jimmy Carter and Walter Mondale also symbolized new political leadership. Carter was to be the first southerner since the Civil War to gain a major party nomination, and this meant the divisions caused by Civil War and racial strife had finally healed. Mondale, who also came from a small town, was the first Korean War veteran to appear on a national ticket.

To nominate Carter, the convention heard New Jersey Representative Peter Rodino, an Italian Catholic who had achieved fame during the Nixon impeachment hearings, and he emphasized the importance of Carter's accession. "As he brought a united South back into the Democratic Party, he will bring a united Democratic Party back into the leadership of America and a united America back to a position of respect and esteem in the eyes of the world." Another Georgian, Congressman Andrew Young, a black, seconded Carter's nomination, saying, "I'm ready to lay down the burden of race, and Jimmy Carter comes from a part of the country that, whether you know it or not, has done just that."

There were three other nominations—Udall, Brown, and antiabortion candidate Ellen McCormack—but Carter won easily on the first ballot as had been predicted. He obtained 2,238.5 votes of a 3,008 total; Udall gained 329.5; Brown had 300.5; McCormack 22; and others not formally nominated received 117.5.

Hubert Humphrey climbed to the rostrum to nominate his old aide Mondale, and the former vice-president praised the Carter-Mondale ticket for offering the country a "new generation of leadership." It "represents the final reunification of North and South . . . from the Canadian border to the Rio Grande, from the Golden Gate to the Potomac." Three other names also went to the convention—a black activist, an opponent of busing, and a draft resister—but Mondale won easily, receiving 2,817 votes.

Shortly before 11:00 P.M. on Thursday, July 15, Jimmy Carter entered Madison Square Garden to present his acceptance speech, one that would reach out to divergent factions of the party, enlist them in the Carter campaign, and project Carter's themes to millions of television viewers. His first words were "My name is Jimmy Carter, and I'm running for president." The nominee, who had used this introduction throughout the arduous campaign, quickly moved to his key themes of healing the nation's torment with new ideas and new leadership. His address, presented softly and unemotionally, expressed a variety of points for Democrats of different ideological persuasions. In a conservative vein, he lashed out at wasteful federal bureaucracy, called for balancing the budget, and urged "minimal intrusion of government in our free economic system." In a more liberal manner, he endorsed national health insurance, branded the current tax system a "disgrace to the human race," and pledged efforts to end discrimination according to sex and race. Other sentences offered thinly veiled criticisms of his Republican predecessors. "I see no reason why big-shot crooks should go free and the poor ones go to jail." And he lashed out at President Ford's troubles with a Democratic Congress, saying, "we need a Democratic president and a Congress to work in harmony for a change, with mutual respect for a change, in the open for a change." Most of all, while Carter promised to govern with "vigor and vision and aggressive leadership," he offered competent administration. "We can have an American government that has turned away from scandal and corruption and official cynicisms and is once again as decent and competent as our people."

It was a memorable spectacle—a presidential nominee from the Deep South appealing in his inimitable moralistic style to a party in which ethnics, blacks, Catholics, and urban machine politics played such an active role. This time the Democrats had nominated a bright, ambitious peanut farmer from Plains, Georgia, and this Southern Baptist had selected another small-town boy, Walter Mondale, the son of a Methodist minister from tiny Ceylon, Minnesota, as his running mate. As the convention came to a close, they joined with the delegates, black and white, in singing "We Shall Overcome," the song made famous by the civil rights movement. The scene emphasized how the currents of change had reshaped American thoughts, values, and attitudes over the last fifteen years.

The Republican Primaries

Among Republicans the bicentennial year was to see the most intensive battle for the party's nomination since 1920. After Nixon had nominated Gerald Ford to succeed the disgraced Agnew, the legislator had told a congressional committee he would not seek election in 1976 in the event he became president. However, circumstances changed, and so did Ford's decision. By November 1974, the new president was saying he probably would seek the White House in 1976. Like many others who entered the presidency, Ford had found the job exciting, and he wanted to continue so as to implement the Vietnam accords and prosecute the war against inflation at home. There were other calculations as well. In order to discourage other Republican aspirants from jumping into campaign waters, to work effectively with a heavily Democratic Congress, and to maintain the respect of foreign governments, Ford deemed it important to establish publicly that he was no lame duck.

Behind these maneuvers loomed the spectre of a clash with former California Governor Ronald Reagan, a onetime movie actor and a former Democrat who had now become the darling of Republican conservatives. Reagan, who was sixty-five, two years older than Ford, had inherited the ideologically intense following of Barry Goldwater but was an outsider, much like Jimmy Carter. He had never served in Congress or in a Republican administration, and was not the preferred choice of those Republicans who had served in government. To Reagan's professional campaign managers—including the youthful John Sears—this was an asset to be exploited at a time when voters had turned against professional politicians and the Washington establishment. They recognized too that Ford lacked a national constituency, had never run a national campaign, and could not escape the Watergate issue and dissatisfaction with the economy, which need not handicap a Reagan candidacy.

Most of all Reagan's staff realized that the widespread use of television, which was the former governor's ideal medium for reaching and influencing voters, and the implementation of new federal campaign laws, which reduced the advantage of incumbency in obtaining campaign funds, could facilitate a Reagan challenge. In November 1975 Reagan announced for the presidency, indicating he was not running against Ford or the Democrats. "We were running against evil incarnate as embodied in the buddy system in Washington."

Strategists for both Reagan and Ford believed in a political domino theory—as New Hampshire went, so would go the nation. This first heavily televised primary, they understood, would give the victor an enormous boost in momentum—perhaps 15 to 18 percentage points—in the Florida primary two weeks later. Since both candidates were hampered by insufficient funds to wage thirty primary campaigns, a victory in the Granite State could be decisive in determining the outcome of the Republican nomination. Both sides understood that if Ford lost, the president's chances would be severely damaged, and he probably could not win in Kansas City. The Californian wanted to prove his candidacy had appeal outside the sun belt, and in New Hampshire, where Reagan enjoyed the backing of Governor Meldrim Thomson and the only newspaper with statewide circulation, he had several important advantages.

The former movie star captured more television attention in New Hampshire than did Ford, but it was not always advantageous. In a Chicago speech Reagan had called for turning over to the states $90 billion in federal programs—involving welfare, education, housing, food stamps, Medicaid, and community and regional development. But the president's aides quickly pointed out that such a transfer would compel New Hampshire to pass income and sales taxes, something that did not appeal to the state's thrifty residents.

During the heavily publicized contest, both Reagan and Ford were hampered by inadequate funds. The challenger devoted twenty-one days to the Granite State, but the president could afford only two trips because of the vast cost involved in transporting a presidential entourage. Ironically, Ford's second campaign trip depended on the phone company's rebating deposits—a vivid indication of the campaign's financing problems.

Reagan strategists expected to win a primary with low voter turnout, because the Californian's fervent backers would come to the polls in numbers even under the most adverse weather conditions. But, Tuesday, February 24, was a warm, sunny, winter day—quite unusual for the state—and voters swarmed to the polls in large numbers, giving Ford a narrow 1,600-vote victory. A jubilant president described the outcome as a "great springboard" to a first-ballot victory in Kansas City. Interestingly, he had won only 49 percent of the Republican vote; Reagan received 48 percent, a higher percentage than either Eugene McCarthy in 1968 or George McGovern in 1972. Yet although the national media had proclaimed McCarthy and McGovern victors, because of their surprisingly strong showing, this did not occur in the Reagan-Ford match. The reason is that Reagan's highly organized campaign had anticipated a clear victory—perhaps by 5 percentage points. When they failed to achieve the expected, the press played the story as a Reagan defeat and a Ford victory. Ford had demonstrated, the media claimed, that he could appeal to voters outside of his Grand Rapids, Michigan, home while Reagan failed to establish a viable candidacy in the North. By only 1,600 votes Ford secured media credibility as a viable candidate, but Reagan exhibited serious weaknesses against the lightly regarded Ford.

Until the Granite State vote, Reagan had been leading in Florida, but his margin soon vanished. In subsequent weeks Ford's new-found momentum produced primary victories not only in the Everglade State but also in Massachusetts and Illinois. It seemed for a while that Reagan might be forced to withdraw, but late in March the tide turned again. Overly confident, after early triumphs, the Ford camp canceled a proposed presidential trip and last-minute television advertising in North Carolina, but Reagan launched a vicious television blitz. It featured a thirty-minute program claiming that Ford and Secretary of State Henry Kissinger had dangerously weakened American defenses and proposed turning over the Panama Canal to a tinhorn leftist dictator. Reagan used demagoguery successfully to turn the Panama Canal into a vital campaign issue with his emotional assertion: "We built it, we paid for it, it's ours, and we are going to keep it!"

The stunning upset, which caught even Reagan's supporters by surprise, revived his sputtering campaign and punctured the myth of an incumbent president's invincibility. Although Reagan's advisers had blundered in not devising a broadly gauged alternative strategy after New Hampshire, which included campaigning for delegates in New Jersey, Ohio, Maryland, and West Virginia, they had several advantages to exploit. For one thing the coming primaries were in southern and western states, for the most part, where Reagan's support was firm, and the Republican Party, unlike the Democratic, still retained winner-take-all primaries, which could benefit Reagan in big states such as California and Texas.

Reagan's attack on Ford's foreign policy continued in Texas, and on May 1, the president lost all ninety-six delegates—the worst primary defeat ever experienced by an incumbent. Over the next ten days, Ford lost four more primaries—in Georgia, Alabama, Indiana, and Nebraska— and the crossover of independents and Wallace Democrats contributed to the Reagan momentum. Quickly Reagan moved from a serious disadvantage in April to a lead in early May in the delegate quest. Pressed as no incumbent ever had been in primaries, Ford invested his prestige in a make-or-break Michigan primary on May 18. If his home state turned against the embattled president, it was generally conceded Ford could not capture the nomination. While Reagan openly appealed for former

Wallace supporters to cross over, Ford's followers urged independents and Democrats to vote for Ford out of local pride. This factor, which would also benefit Carter in the South during the general election, as well as the president's last-minute whistle-stop campaign trip and extensive reliance on television, turned the tables. His mandate was 326,000 votes, or a percentage distribution of 65 to 34 percent.

The primaries proved indecisive. Both Ford and Reagan had more than 40 percent of the delegates, which had historically started convention bandwagons, but not this time. A final 400 delegates, to be chosen in state caucuses or who were elected as uncommitted delegates in primary states, would determine whether Ford or Reagan gained the coveted 1,130 delegate votes for a first-ballot victory. In this intensive phase Ford had a major advantage. He could, and did, invite delegates to the White House for personal discussions.

Sears, fearing the incumbency would gradually prevail, conceived a series of bold maneuvers to shake up the process—and these began with Reagan's announcement that he had selected a liberal Republican, Senator Richard Schweiker of Pennsylvania, as a vice-presidential running mate. In demonstrating his flexibility and desire for party harmony, Reagan hoped to pick up uncommitted delegates in the East, but the tactic backfired, causing the thirty-vote Mississippi bloc to question Reagan's commitment to conservative principles. Still the battle for the nomination was not won before Republicans traveled to Kansas City in August.

While the primaries and preconvention maneuvers had not settled the nomination, the preliminary combat left its mark on the party and the Ford campaign. Reagan's assault had exposed Ford's weaknesses as a campaigner for the entire country to see and compelled the president to modify his campaign organization and strategy. In exposing Ford's shortcomings, the vigorous contest eroded the president's image and deprived him of vital time that might better have been allocated for broadening the small Republican base of support and preparing to meet the Carter challenge in November. The threat from the right handicapped Ford's efforts to construct a middle-of-the-road national constituency.

The Republican Convention

The thirty-first Republican convention opened August 16 in Kemper Arena. Senator Robert Dole of Kansas was temporary chairman, and House Minority Leader John J. Rhodes became permanent chairman. Quickly the Reagan managers devised a procedural test of strength over whether convention rules should be revised to require each candidate for the presidential nomination to designate his vice-presidential choice before the presidential balloting began. In essence, the Reagan forces hoped to force Ford to name his running mate and in the process alienate some delegate support that Reagan might then inherit. It was a desperate ploy —but one that failed when the much-lobbied Mississippi delegation decided to cast all their votes against the rule revision. This technical issue was the critical battle, and Reagan's support gradually ebbed away.

Two days later Ford won the nomination, receiving 1,187 votes, or 57 more than necessary. Ronald Reagan obtained 1,070. Governor William Milliken of Michigan put the president's name in nomination; he praised Ford for having "brought strength in a time of crisis, order in a time of chaos." Senator Paul Laxalt of Nevada nominated Reagan, calling the former California executive the "man who can whip the irresponsible Congress into line." "I would dearly love to see Ronald Reagan debate Jimmy Carter," Laxalt quipped. "After one round of debating with Ronald Reagan, he would have to go back to shucking peanuts."

Eager to unify a divided party, Ford consulted with the defeated rival, who took himself out of vice-presidential consideration, and announced an old congressional friend, Senator Robert Dole as his running mate. The Kansan, a wounded World War II veteran, had a reputation as a sharp-tongued partisan fighter who might use his talent to good advantage against Carter. Also, his conservative political philosophy was acceptable to Reagan's followers. Thus Dole was compatible with both factions of the divided party, and it seemed his candidacy would strengthen the Republican ticket's appeal in the farm states.

Having obtained the nomination and selected a suitable running mate, Ford turned to his third convention objective—delivering an effective acceptance speech to a national television audience that would help cut into Carter's thirty-point lead in the polls. The president and his advisers knew this occasion to address millions of potential voters was perhaps the best opportunity to counter serious image problems—and they carefully rehearsed. Ford was up to the occasion and did present an effective defense of his policies as well as a sharp attack on Jimmy Carter and the Democratic Congress. The speech contained several oblique references to the Georgian. Ford pledged to "build on performance, not promises; experience, not expediency; real progress instead of mysterious plans to be revealed in some dim and distant future."

Then the president surprised many listeners by inserting a paragraph in his prepared text. He challenged Carter to a "face-to-face debate on the campaign's real issues." This carefully planned gambit was intended to discourage voters from reaching a premature decision, to reveal Ford's own knowledge of foreign affairs and expose Carter's lack of experience, and to obtain additional free television time to address the national electorate. It was a daring, perhaps an essential, ploy. For in volunteering to debate, Ford boldly defied the common political wisdom that incumbents not share a debating platform with challengers. In this instance, the conventional approach seemed inappropriate, for Carter held a substantial lead. A series of debates might enable Ford to offset the early Carter advantage.

Ford and Carter Campaign

Because the new elections law severely limited the combined spending of Carter and Ford to $43.6 million—less than half of what both parties spent in 1972—strategic planning and the adroit allocation of campaign funds had become critical. Both sides decided to dispense with hoopla items—buttons, banners, bumper stickers, and local campaign headquarters—except where absolutely necessary, and instead earmark funds for candidate travel and intensive television advertising in about 8 swing states. The Ford campaign had the more difficult problem, overcoming a 20-point opinion gap in 73 days from the political base of a minority party while spending the same amount of money as the more popular challenger.

Media consultant John Deardourff and pollster Robert Teeter, the principal professional managers to Ford, bluntly outlined the difficult situation. A majority of the American public did not perceive Ford as a strong, decisive leader and some did not even consider him smart enough to be president. No candidate, they said, had ever faced such formidable odds.

The Rose Garden strategy, as it was known, was devised to cope with this predicament. It called for keeping Ford in the White House, performing presidential duties in the most visible manner, until late in the campaign. This approach would take full advantage of the incumbency and shelter Ford, who was an inexperienced campaigner prone to using strident and partisan rhetoric, while Jimmy Carter roamed the country encountering one unexpected situation after another. Meanwhile, Ford would rely on sophisticated television advertising to project strengths—especially that people perceived him as an honest, family man trying sincerely to do his best for the country in difficult times. Also, the Republican campaign would employ negative advertising to portray subtly Carter's weaknesses—he was an unknown, inexperienced candidate who was fuzzy on significant issues and used religion for political purposes. In essence Ford strategists decided to turn the campaign focus away from hard, complex issues—such as solutions to unemployment and inflation—to concentrate instead on the images of presidential candidates, an aspect neglected in the lopsided 1972 race.

There was no margin for mistake this time. Ford's advisers believed that with about two more fumbles they could lock themselves into a hopeless McGovern-type situation. The critical element in this grand strategy was a series of public debates. In taking the initiative to challenge Carter, Ford would act dramatically to combat the competence issue, and the promise of debates would encourage the country, and especially the media, to withhold judgment. The commitment to future debates would also keep the hypercritical national media from "eating Ford alive" as he remained in the White House performing official duties, they thought.

Strategists for both candidates knew the elction would hinge on eight swing states with large blocs of electoral votes—specifically, California, New York, Pennsylvania, Texas, Ohio, Michigan, New Jersey, and Illinois. For Ford to win he would need six of these, plus the rural states west of the Mississippi that traditionally voted Republican. Ford had almost no margin for error, since Carter was expected to capture the solid South. To ensure his victory, he needed only to divide the critical eight swing states.

Carter's battle plan rested firmly on his advantage with underlying issues. The public was dissatisfied with eight years of Republican rule, Watergate, and economic problems. Yet, for a different set of reasons the Carter camp wanted to debate. They believed the intelligent Georgian could demonstrate convincingly that he had presidential stature, while under the rugged crossfire of questioning, Ford would confirm the public suspicion that he was an unintelligent bumbler.

The spectre of Eugene McCarthy haunted the Democratic nominee. Claiming that the "Democratic platform looks like the Republican platform of 1952," McCarthy sought to place his name on the ballot and offer voters an independent candidacy. He proposed to reduce the work year from 50 to 48 weeks in order to create jobs, to cut military spending $20–$30 billion, and to centralize government agencies. Democrats feared that McCarthy, although he was ineligible for federal election funds, could hold the balance of power, as a spoiler, perhaps gaining 10 percent of the national vote and depriving Carter of liberal support in critical swing states of the East and Midwest.

Carter opened his campaign not in Detroit's Cadillac Square, as Democrats did traditionally, but in Warm Springs, Georgia, where he invoked the memory of the last governor to serve as president, Franklin D. Roosevelt. During September, however, a series of pseudoissues damaged Carter's public standing. He differed with Catholic bishops on a constitutional amendment to restrict abortions, argued with the White House over a trivial indiscretion involving FBI Director Clarence Kelley, and misstated his own position on tax reform.

Perhaps the most harmful episode was another tempest in a teapot— Carter's interview with *Playboy* magazine. In this freewheeling discussion of his religious views, Carter indicated he had "looked on a lot of women with lust" and had "committed adultery in my heart many times." For those who heard only sensational excerpts, the interview raised serious questions of judgment. As one Kansas newspaper grumbled: "Discussing one's religion in offensive terms to a nudie-magazine editor as part of one's presidential campaign does not seem dignified." Opinion surveys showed that the episode damaged Carter's standing with nonworking women, in particular.

Although the president remained insulated from similar media and public pressures, a series of highly publicized episodes raised questions about Ford's own integrity and morality, as well as the character of his administration. He acknowledged accepting free golf holidays and plane flights from corporate friends while serving in Congress. Ford had to deny allegations from former Nixon aide John Dean that he had attempted to squelch an early congressional investigation of Watergate. Finally, the Watergate special prosecutor began investigating charges that the incumbent had misused congressional campaign contributions and, although he was eventually cleared, the media continued to rehash allegations that served to reinforce in public minds the negativism of the whole Watergate interlude. Finally Agriculture Secretary Earl Butz was forced to resign after using obscene language in a private conversation to describe blacks.

The Television Debates

For both candidates the televised debates afforded a unique opportunity to refocus the campaign and speak directly to the American public, not through the media's distillation of campaign issues and images. In contrast to the 1960 debates, both candidates sought not so much to gain quick debating points but to project broad images to the general public—competence, integrity, and experience.

In the first encounter, held in the old Walnut Street Theater in Philadelphia on September 23, Ford quickly established his presidential demeanor in the vital first minutes, while Carter seemed nervous and uncertain. This encounter revealed distinct differences on basic economic issues. Carter emphasized the creation of government-service jobs to mop up unemployment, while Ford stressed stimulating the private sector with tax incentives to create productive employment. Under the pressure of television debate, these differences tended to blur for casual viewers—and what was more important was the public perception of who won and lost. The Gallup poll indicated Ford had benefited more. Before the event Carter led Ford by 18 percent, but afterward his lead dropped to only 8 percentage points.

The first debate was not fatal for Carter, but the second on October 6 may have been for Ford. He made a serious blunder in an area where the president supposedly had experience and knowledge—foreign affairs. There was "no Soviet domination of Eastern Europe and there never will be under a Ford administration," he said. What the president meant was that the United States did not accept Soviet domination of this region, but his verbal error reinforced his negative image as an inept bumbler. With only three weeks left until Election Day, the president's comeback momentum halted—and two weeks would pass before he began to recover. More than any single event, the second debate helped torpedo Ford's election chances, for it alienated ethnic voters of East European descent and reinforced an unfavorable image of the president.

There were no similar surprises in the final debate on October 22 from Williamsburg, Virginia. Both candidates steered cautiously. Asked what sacrifices they would require of the citizenry in these difficult times, Ford emphasized that an "adequate military capability" would require a "few billion dollars" more in defense spending. Carter, however, asserted "the sacrifices would be much less" in his administration.

The vice-presidential nominees also debated on national television on October 15. Dole used needlepoint barbs to establish his points, while Mondale relied more on idealism and clarity of expression to influence the television viewers. Inexperienced in the use of television, Dole erred in employing blunt statements and harsh accusations, such as his claim that 1.7 million Americans had been killed and wounded "in the Democrat wars in this century." Such assertions pleased Republican partisans, but did little to win independent voters whom the Republicans desperately needed. The consensus judgment was that Mondale, in balance, helped Carter more than Dole benefited Ford—but that was predictable. Carter had carefully selected his running mate to complement the ticket, whereas Ford needed to heal internal party wounds before leaving the Kansas City convention.

As the exhausting contest came to a close, what had threatened to become a Carter landslide in September became a cliff-hanger in November. Skillfully using the incumbency for maximum advantage, Ford had slowly erased Carter's lead—largely through the brilliant use of television advertising to raise public doubt about Carter's inexperience and the dangers of placing national leadership in untried hands. Deardourff and his colleagues skillfully employed individual-in-the-streets ads to establish their point. Perhaps the best known was an interview with an Atlanta woman who said: "My friends here in Georgia don't understand when I tell them I'm going to vote for President Ford. It would be nice to have a president from Georgia—but not Carter." Later Carter conceded that Ford's major thrust against him was "fear—fear of change, fear of the future." The challenger never found how to deal successfully with Ford's principal advantage—incumbency. He said: "Every time I made a mistake, it was news." But Ford's news was that he "came out into the Rose Garden and signed a bill and he was in charge of things, very authoritative, sure of himself—no problems, no squabbles, no mistakes." Coping with the incumbent president's inherent advantages, Carter said, was a "crippling thing"—something we "didn't know how to deal with."

But Carter had advantages of his own, including his unique opportunity to wave the rebel flag and appeal to regional sentiment. Carter's advertising emphasized that a vote for the Georgian would force the rest of the nation to stop treating the South as a whipping boy. Also, the economic news did not benefit Ford. Unemployment was reported at 7.8 percent, and the economy seemed to be slowing down and not generating jobs as rapidly as before. In addition, the United States Supreme Court gave Carter some last-minute aid when it rejected a request from independent candidate Eugene McCarthy to set aside a New York court order keeping him off the New York presidential ballot. Had McCarthy's name been on the ballot, Democrats feared that he might take votes from Carter and tilt the outcome to Ford. Later results indicated that had McCarthy won less than 5 percent of the total vote there, Ford might have won the election.

Finally, Ford may have lost some support after a black clergyman, the Reverend Clennon King, attempted to gain membership in Carter's church in Plains, Georgia, because suspicions circulated that this was a Republican trick designed to influence the election's outcome.

Carter Is Elected

On November 2, Carter became the first nominee from the Deep South to win since before the Civil War, and the first successful candidate with a background as governor since Franklin D. Roosevelt. In a sense Carter's election marked a return to two earlier patterns—when the South provided national leadership and the statehouse served as a presidential training academy. Ford was the first incumbent to lose a bid for reelection since Herbert Hoover lost during the Great Depression.

The Carter strategy had succeeded. He won 23 states and the District of Columbia with 297 electoral votes—27 more than required for a majority. Ford received 241 electoral votes, although one Seattle elector actually voted for Reagan because he preferred the Californian's stand on abortion. Carter captured 4 of the 8 key swing states—Pennsylvania, Ohio, New York, and Texas. Final results showed Carter with 40,830,763 popular votes and Ford with 39,147,793. Independent candidate Eugene McCarthy got 756,691 votes, and his candidacy may have cost Carter victories in Iowa, Maine, Oklahoma and Oregon. His nonappearance on the New York ballot, in a state with a strong liberal community, may also have been decisive. Once again the pollsters had predicted the outcome correctly, anticipating a narrow Carter victory.°

A record number of Americans voted—nearly 82 million, some 4 million more than in 1972—but voter participation continued to decline. Only 54 percent of those over 18 went to the polls, a decrease from 55.4 percent in 1972 and a record 62.8 percent in 1960. What happened was that 27 percent of the people over 18 voted for Carter in 1976; 26 percent selected President Ford; and 47 percent stayed away from the polls altogether.

Traditionally, a presidential candidate delivered a coattails benefit to members of his own party, but this was not so noticeable in 1976. Democrats gained only one governorship, and there was no net change in the composition of Congress. Ticket-splitting continued, and partisanship declined with independent voters determining the outcome of many races. In the eighteen states that Carter won, where there was a Senate or gubernatorial contest, he ran ahead of the state candidates in only five instances. A plausible case can be made that the Democratic presidential candidate benefited from a reverse coattails effect in some cases. Senate candidate Howard Metzenbaum defeated Robert Taft, Jr., in Ohio by 118,000 votes—a plurality more than 10 times Carter's margin over Gerald Ford.

The election revealed several other interesting patterns. Carter won the South decisively, carrying states that had not voted Democratic in presidential elections for twenty years. In the process Carter demolished the Republican "southern strategy" that had elected Nixon twice. He also revived the old Franklin Roosevelt coalition of Dixie and the industrial North, which had also benefited Harry Truman and John F. Kennedy, but with a significant difference. Southern blacks took no significant part in the Roosevelt coalition, but now in the South Carter benefited from a record black turnout—obtaining 93 to 95 percent of black votes—and the decision of many white southerners to vote for Jimmy Carter because he came from a region that had not elected one of its own for more than a century. Interestingly, Carter had a Populist appeal in his own home region—gathering support from poor whites and poor blacks, but losing urban areas such as Birmingham, greater Charleston, and greater Richmond.

Undoubtedly, a $2 million voter-registration drive enhanced the Democratic vote in Ohio, Texas, and Pennsylvania, where organized labor helped register more blacks, Chicanos, and Puerto Ricans, almost certain

---

° Minor-party candidates received the following votes: Roger MacBride, Libertarian, 173,011; Lester G. Maddox, American Independent, 170,531; Thomas Anderson, American, 160,773; Peter Camejo, Socialist Worker, 91,314; Gus Hall, Communist, 58,992; Margaret Wright, People's, 49,024; Lyndon H. LaRouche, U.S. Labor, 40,043; Benjamin C. Bubar, Prohibition, 15,934; Jules Levin, Socialist Labor, 9,616; Frank P. Zeidler, Socialist, 6,038.

to vote Democratic. Overall labor spent an estimated $11 million mobilizing voters for Carter—and this activity helped offset the advantage of Ford's incumbency. Also, Carter successfully conciliated the old urban Democratic machines. Organized labor and urban bosses such as Mayor Richard Daley of Chicago and Mayor Frank Rizzo of Philadelphia helped accumulate majorities for Carter that had been denied George McGovern, the ideological outsider unable to appease traditional power centers.

Interestingly, Ford scored better with Catholic voters than any Republican in modern times, and the incumbent president carried the female vote by a margin of 51 to 48. But had only men voted, Carter would have increased his margin. Male voters favored Carter 53 to 45. Altogether a switch of only some 10,000 votes in Ohio and Hawaii would have swung the electoral victory from Carter to Ford.

Opinion surveys indicate that issues did not determine the election's outcome. Personal characteristics and style were the decisive factors. For the first time in more than a generation, foreign policy did not loom large in the minds of voters. Although a majority of voters thought the Democrats would do a better job in reducing unemployment and managing the economy, this issue had less impact on the outcome than some advisers expected. The principal issue was one of trust, integrity, and leadership. Ford's aides had attempted to emphasize how the incumbent had restored confidence in the presidency, and they tried to keep alive public doubts about Carter's reliability. For in pledging never to lie and to honor his campaign commitments, Carter ran as an untypical politician. Carter also had problems with the hard-bitten national media, which found his moral self-righteousness irritating and looked eagerly for contradictions in words and deeds. Inevitably, inconsistencies emerged as Carter abandoned his outsider image from the primaries to co-opt Democratic functionaries for the autumn campaign.

If the campaign shifted away from substantive issues to magnify ephemeral events, the long campaign marathon did at least expose the candidates—especially the challenger—to dynamic testing and probing from the media. It showed how each could function and survive under unremitting pressure. Some campaign consultants would assert this was the most valid test of all. Since issues change and officeholders must choose among a complex set of policy options, it is perhaps too much to expect an election to establish policy commitments for the future.

In what direction would the new president lead the country? It was not clear, for in the campaign the Democratic candidate often seemed vague. Like Richard Nixon in 1968, he skillfully avoided specific analysis of complex policy issues, projecting instead his own idealism, leadership, and competence to satisfy voters. Lacking either an overwhelming electoral mandate or close allies in Congress to implement his programs, Carter at first continued to campaign, skillfully projecting the image of a

Populist reformer in order to build public support for his legislative initiatives.

On inauguration day the president and his family broke with tradition and walked down Pennsylvania Avenue to the White House. He subsequently gave "fireside chats" in the Franklin D. Roosevelt tradition, attended town meetings across the country, and took other steps to open the presidency to the press and public. He canceled limousine service for White House staff members and even sold the presidential yacht. Behind these gestures was a measure of careful political calculation. Carter's advisers believed too many good people had been beaten "because they tried to substitute substance for style," and they urged the new leader to utilize symbols to strengthen his influence.

Selected Bibliography

The following suggestions for further reading or reference are intended to give the reader a fair sampling of the vast literature of past American politics. Space limitations rule out the extensive fields of biography, memoirs, and journals, and permit only a selection of the many books dealing with the more restricted areas of party history, regional or topical in approach.

I. General Accounts of Nominations, Elections, and Parties, and Reference Works.

BAIN, RICHARD C. AND PARRIS, JUDITH H. *Convention Decisions and Voting Records.* Washington: Brookings Institution, 1973.

BINKLEY, WILFRED E. *American Political Parties: Their Natural History.* New York: Knopf, 1947.

BURNHAM, W. DEAN. *Presidential Ballots, 1836–1892.* Baltimore: Johns Hopkins University Press, 1955.

BURNS, JAMES MAC GREGOR. *The Deadlock of Democracy: Four-Party Politics in America.* Englewood Cliffs, N.J.: Prentice-Hall, 1963.

CHAMBERS, WILLIAM N. *Political Parties in a New Nation: The American Experience, 1776–1809.* New York: Oxford University Press, 1963.

CHASE, JAMES S. *Emergence of the Presidential Nominating Convention, 1789–1832.* Urbana: University of Illinois Press, 1973.

Congressional Quarterly. *Presidential Elections Since 1789.* 2nd ed., Washington: Congressional Quarterly, Inc., 1979.

CUNNINGHAM, NOBLE E., JR. *The Jeffersonian Republicans: The Formation of Party Organization, 1789–1801.* Chapel Hill: University of North Carolina Press, 1958.

——— *The Jeffersonian Republicans in Power: Party Operations, 1801–1809.* Chapel Hill: University of North Carolina Press, 1967.

DAVID, PAUL T., GOLDMAN, RALPH M. AND BAIN, RICHARD C. *The Politics of National Party Conventions.* Washington: Brookings Institution, 1960.

DAVIS, JAMES W. *Presidential Primaries: Road to the White House.* New York: Crowell, 1967.

DIVINE, ROBERT A. *Foreign Policy and U.S. Presidential Elections, 1940–1948.* New York: New Viewpoints, 1974.

——— *Foreign Policy and U.S. Presidential Elections, 1952–1960.* New York: New Viewpoints, 1974.

EATON, HERBERT. *Presidential Timber: A History of Nominating Conventions, 1868–1960.* New York: Free Press of Glencoe, 1964.

HATCH, LOUIS C. A History of the Vice-Presidency of the United States. Rev. and Ed. Earl L. Shoup. Reprint of 1934 ed., Westport, Conn.: Greenwood Press, 1970.

HEARD, ALEXANDER. The Costs of Democracy. Chapel Hill: University of North Carolina Press, 1960.

HESS, STEPHEN. The Presidential Campaign. Rev. ed., Washington: Brookings Institution, 1978.

HOFSTADTER, RICHARD. The Age of Reform from Bryan to F.D.R. New York: Knopf, 1955.

KEECH, WILLIAM R. AND MATTHEWS, DONALD R. The Party's Choice. Washington: Brookings Institution, 1976.

KEY, V. O. Southern Politics in State and Nation. New York: Knopf, 1949.

KIRKPATRICK, JEANE. The Presidential Elite: Men and Women in National Politics. New York: Russell Sage Foundation, 1976.

LORANT, STEFAN. The Presidency: A Pictorial History of Presidential Elections from Washington to Truman. New York: Macmillan, 1951.

MC CORMICK, RICHARD P. The Second American Party System. Chapel Hill: University of North Carolina Press, 1966.

MAYER, GEORGE H. The Republican Party, 1854–1964. New York: Oxford University Press, 1964.

MAZMANIAN, DANIEL A. Third Parties in Presidential Elections. Washington: Brookings Institution, 1974.

MOOS, MALCOLM. The Republicans: A History of Their Party. New York: Random House, 1956.

MORGAN, H. WAYNE. From Hayes to McKinley: National Party Politics, 1877–1896. Syracuse, N.Y.: Syracuse University Press, 1968.

NASH, HOWARD P. Third Parties in American Politics. Washington: Public Affairs Press, 1959.

PARRIS, JUDITH. The Convention Problem: Issues in Reform of Presidential Nominating Procedures. Washington: Brookings Institution, 1972.

——— AND SAYRE, WALLACE STANLEY. Voting for President: The Electoral College and the American Political System. Washington: Brookings Institution, 1970.

PETERSEN, SVEND. A Statistical History of the American Presidential Elections. New York: Ungar, 1968.

POMPER, GERALD. Nominating the President: The Politics of Convention Choice. Evanston, Ill.: Northwestern University Press, 1963.

ROBINSON, EDGAR E. The Presidential Vote, 1896–1932. Stanford: Stanford University Press. 1934.

——— They Voted for Roosevelt. Stanford: Stanford University Press, 1947.

RUNYON, JOHN H. AND OTHERS. Source Book of American Presidential Campaign and Election Statistics, 1948–1968. New York: Ungar, 1971.

SCAMMON, RICHARD, compiler. America at the Polls (covers 1920–1964). Pittsburgh: University of Pittsburgh Press, 1965.

SCHLESINGER, ARTHUR M., JR., ed. History of U.S. Political Parties. New York: Chelsea House, 1973.

———, ISRAEL, FRED L. AND HANSEN, WILLIAM P., eds. History of American Presidential Elections, 1789–1968. New York: Chelsea House, 1971.

STANWOOD, EDWARD. *A History of the Presidency.* 2 vols., Boston: Houghton Mifflin, 1916.

WILLIAMSON, CHILTON. *American Suffrage from Property to Democracy, 1760–1860.* Princeton: Princeton University Press, 1960.

WILMERDING, LUCIUS, JR. *The Electoral College.* New Brunswick, N.J.: Rutgers University Press, 1958.

YOUNG, DONALD. *American Roulette: The History and Dilemma of the Vice Presidency.* New York: Holt, Rinehart and Winston, 1965.

II. Histories of Some Significant Elections

BAGBY, WESLEY M. *The Road to Normalcy: The Presidential Campaign and Election of 1920.* Baltimore: Johns Hopkins University Press, 1962.

CLANCY, HERBERT J. *The Presidential Election of 1880.* Chicago: Loyola University Press, 1958.

CRENSHAW, OLLINGER. *The Slave States in the Presidential Election of 1860.* Baltimore: Johns Hopkins University Press, 1945.

CUMMINGS, MILTON C., JR., ed. *The National Election of 1964.* Washington: Brookings Institution, 1966.

DAVID, PAUL T., ed. *The Presidential Election and Transition of 1960–1961.* Washington: Brookings Institution, 1961.

DURDEN, ROBERT F. *The Climax of Populism: The Election of 1896.* Lexington: University of Kentucky Press, 1965.

FITE, E. D. *The Presidential Campaign of 1860.* New York: Macmillan, 1911.

GAMMON, SAMUEL R., JR. *The Presidential Campaign of 1832.* Baltimore: Johns Hopkins University Press, 1922.

GLAD, PAUL W. *McKinley, Bryan and the People.* Philadelphia: Lippincott, 1964.

GUNDERSON, ROBERT G. *The Log-Cabin Campaign.* Lexington: University of Kentucky Press, 1957.

HAWORTH, P. L. The *Hayes-Tilden Disputed Presidential Election of 1876.* Cleveland: Burrows, 1906.

JONES, STANLEY L. *The Presidential Election of 1896.* Madison: University of Wisconsin Press, 1964.

KNOLES, GEORGE H. *The Presidential Campaign and Election of 1892.* Stanford: Stanword University Press, 1942.

LUTHIN, REINHARD. *The First Lincoln Campaign.* Cambridge: Harvard University Press, 1944.

MAY, ERNEST R. AND FRASER, JANET. *Campaign '72: The Managers Speak.* Cambridge: Harvard University Press, 1973.

MOORE, EDMUND A. *A Catholic Runs for President: The Campaign of 1928.* New York: Ronald Press, 1956.

MOORE, JONATHAN AND FRASER, JANET. *Campaign for President: The Managers Look at '76.* Cambridge, Mass.: Ballinger Publishing Company, 1977.

MURRAY, ROBERT K. *The 103rd Ballot: Democrats and the Disaster in Madison Square Garden.* New York: Harper and Row, 1976.

NICHOLS, ROY F. *The Democratic Machine, 1850–1854.* New York: Columbia University Press, 1923.

POLAKOFF, KEITH IAN. *The Politics of Inertia: The Election of 1876 and the End of Reconstruction.* Baton Rouge: Louisiana State University Press, 1973.

POMPER, GERALD AND OTHERS. *The Election of 1976: Reports and Interpretations.* New York: McKay, 1977.

RAYBACK, JOSEPH G. *Free Soil: The Election of 1848.* Lexington: University of Kentucky Press, 1970.

REMINI, ROBERT V. *The Election of Andrew Jackson.* Philadelphia: Lippincott, 1963.

ROSS, IRWIN. *The Loneliest Campaign: The Truman Victory of 1948.* New York: New American Library, 1968.

THOMAS, H. C. *The Return of the Democratic Party to Power in 1884.* New York: Columbia University Press, 1919.

THOMSON, CHARLES A. H. AND SHATTUCK, FRANCIS M. *The 1956 Presidential Campaign.* Washington: Brookings Institution, 1960.

WARREN, SIDNEY. *Battle for the Presidency.* Philadelphia: Lippincott, 1968.

WESTON, FLORENCE. *The Presidential Election of 1828.* Washington: Ruddick, 1938.

WHITE, THEODORE H. *The Making of the President, 1960.* New York: Atheneum, 1961.

—————— *The Making of the President, 1964.* New York: Atheneum, 1965.

—————— *The Making of the President, 1968.* New York: Atheneum, 1969.

—————— *The Making of the President, 1972.* New York: Atheneum, 1973.

WITCOVER, JULES. *Marathon: The Pursuit of the Presidency, 1972–1976.* New York: Viking Press, 1977.

ZORNOW, WILLIAM F. *Lincoln and the Party Divided.* Norman: University of Oklahoma Press, 1954.

Index